DID MOLLY PITCHER SAY THAT?

The Men and Women Who Made American History

DID
MOLLY PITCHER
SAY THAT?

The Men and Women Who Made
American History

by Ira Glackens

WRITERS & READERS PUBLISHING
in association with
TENTH AVENUE EDITIONS
New York City

Cover and Title Page Illustration: Molly Pitcher.
Reproduced from the Collections of
the Library of Congress.

Frontispiece: George Washington by Gilbert Stuart,
rescued from destruction by Dolley Madison.
Official photograph, the White House Collection.

Produced for **WRITERS & READERS PUBLISHING, INC.** by
Tenth Avenue Editions, Inc.
625 Broadway, New York, New York 10012.
Editor-in-Chief: Clive Giboire
Managing Editor: Rose Hass
Editorial Assistants: Sandra Hardy & Peter Wagner

Manufactured in the United States of America
ISBN 0-86316-0972 (cloth)
0-86316-0948 (paper)

ACKNOWLEDGEMENTS

I wish to thank Professor James C. Holland of the History Department of Shepherd College, Shepherdstown, West Virginia, for going patiently over my manuscript, detecting mistakes, and instructing me in such obtuse subjects as mercantilism. We did not see eye to eye on some points, but Professor Holland is a liberal-minded savant and said, "It is your book." Mistakes that remain are mine or those of my authorities.

Without the access allowed me to the rich collection of American history and biography in the Ruth Scarborough Library at Shepherd College, I could not have succeeded in this project.

I am deeply grateful to Mr. Clement Conger, the former Curator of the White House, and to Mr. William Allman of the White House curatorial office, who generously responded to my request for photographs of Gilbert Stuart's portrait of Washington (the one Dolley Madison rescued from the British) and George P.A. Healy's splendid "Seated Lincoln," with permission to reproduce them here; they greatly enhance the work. I am also grateful to Mr. Leroy Bellamy of the Prints and Photographs Division of the Library of Congress for his indefatigable search for some of the most interesting and amusing illustrations that brighten this book. Thomas S. Kelch's accurate and vivid maps are gratefully acknowledged.

Ira Glackens
August 29, 1988

PREFACE

History is full of names. The people attached to the names, we know little about. As for being actual human beings, with flesh and blood and human emotions, this is taken on faith. The actions that made them famous are likely to get mixed up. It is confusing. Let's see...

Columbus discovered America—or was it the Vikings? The Pilgrim Fathers are called Plymouth Rocks for stepping on a rock of that name. Benjamin Franklin is called 'the wisest American' for flying a kite in a thunderstorm.

The Bostonians refused to pay a tax on a shipment of poor grade tea sent over from England, and dumped it overboard. This was the Boston Tea Party, and the English were infuriated for not being invited. It caused the Revolution.

George Washington became the Father of his Country after cutting down a cherry tree and standing up in a rowboat. Lincoln freed the slaves, and wrote the Gettysburg Address while traveling to Gettysburg on the back of an envelope. (How's that again?) General Grant won the Civil War in spite of the fact that his uniform was buttoned up wrong.

American history was negligently treated, like Grant's uniform, in my school. We had Ancient History (Greece and Rome, not Egypt) and a simple-minded history of England of which I remember Boadicea, the Venerable Beede and the Field of the Cloth of Gold. I was taken abroad to live before we came to American history, which was squeezed into the curriculum just before graduation.

When, later, I began to take an interest in the history of my native land, I set out to discover what stood behind all the names and how history was invented. I soon found that the names stood for flesh-and-blood people, and all men. Historians (men) have consistently brushed women off with a few words, if they are mentioned at all, and yet women had a hand in shaping some of the decisive events in our history, and were not secretive about it.

I learned of woman suffrage at my mother's knee, long before such a thing existed. As a small boy, aged ten or eleven, I wore a large yellow badge on my overcoat with

VOTES FOR WOMEN on it in bold type, and I was stared at on New York City's Fifth Avenue bus by elderly ladies, sometimes with disapproval, as I journeyed to and from school on East 66th Street and home in Washington Square. I had asked for the badge and wore it defiantly.

I have long believed that women can be very stupid—just as stupid as men—but cannot see why they should be discriminated against for this. Did men fear women would beat them at their own game—become even stupider than *they* were? Impossible! History proves it.

I.G.
Shepherdstown, West Virginia, 1988

CONTENTS

Part One

FROM THE GREAT DISCOVERY
TO GROWING PAINS

1 IN THE BEGINNING THERE WAS THE POPE

"In fourteen hundred and ninety-two Columbus sailed the ocean blue," was a line of poesy that was once known to all American school children. The portentous day was August 3. Columbus's ship, the *Santa Maria,* was accompanied by two other caravels, the *Pinta* and the *Niña.* Queen Isabella of Spain financed the expedition, and was said to have pawned her jewels for the purpose.

On October 12 (after a voyage of seventy days and a crew that had begun to threaten mutiny) land was sighted by a sailor on the *Pinta.* Columbus's log, recently subjected to the relentless scrutiny of a computer, seems to indicate that this land was a tiny uninhabited island, and Columbus sailed on to the next island, which was larger and inhabited. He named it San Salvador (not to be confused with the Central American republic of El Salvador nor its capital San Salvador). Now one of the Bahamas, it is one of the seven hundred or so islands comprising a crown colony of Britain until 1973. These islands are now an independent nation called the Commonwealth of the Bahamas. (One wonders what Ferdinand and Isabella would have thought of that!)

San Salvador was inhabited by a gentle people who some authorities say were Arawaks, and other authorities say were Lucayos. Columbus thought these people were Indians. He was quite wrong, but the name stuck. Whatever the origin of these gentle and unwarlike people, they were soon exterminated for not being Christians. Columbus claimed the place for Spain.

It was a great disappointment to find that there was no gold lying about on San Salvador and the sailors wanted to go home. There weren't even any spices— but there was tobacco on some of the islands subsequently discovered. Nobody had any idea that they had stumbled upon a New World.

Back in Spain, Columbus reported to the King and Queen, who confirmed him in the titles and privileges he had specified before setting out, including the stupendous one of "Admiral of the Ocean Seas." Columbus did not suffer from modesty.

Columbus made three more voyages to what turned out to be two vast continents connected by an isthmus, but he never set foot on any part of the mainland. Back in Spain, his sovereigns were puzzled and did not know what to do with all these islands.

Pope Alexander VI, however, did. He gave the islands outright to Spain, though Ferdinand and Isabella ('the Catholic Kings') probably thought that Spain owned them already. The only catch to this rich papal gift was the fact that His Holiness did not own these islands, this New World. But that is how European monarchs looked upon America for the next 284 years—as something to give away.

To keep everyone happy, the Pope simultaneously gave Africa and India to Portugal.

These lavish gestures are unparalleled in history.

By one of history's little ironies this vast New World was not named for Columbus but for another Italian navigator, Amerigo Vespucci, whose explorations began in 1499 and were confined to the coast of South America. The name "America" first appeared on a map in 1507, but it was not Amerigo who named it.

It was the English kings who really got busy handing out pieces of North America to their friends and acquaintances. These pieces were called "grants," and sometimes a king took a slice out of one of his grants, already granted, and gave it to someone else. (How wonderful to be a king in those days.)

Ignoring the Pope, these kings based their claims to the continent of North America on John Cabot, a Venetian in the employ of Henry VII who sailed along the coast in 1497, not knowing what it was.

The giveaway program did not begin in earnest, however, until 1606 when a company of London merchants extracted a grant from James I with the right to start a colony in Virginia—a vast indefinite tract of wilderness named for the Virgin Queen. In the spring of 1607 three ships sailed into a bay (later called the Chesapeake) and up a river (later called the James). They landed in a low, swampy, malarial place, their provisions exhausted after a five months' voyage. But instead of cultivating the land the newcomers busied themselves looking for gold and the passage to China (surely just around the corner).

Fifteen men died on the voyage and were fed to the sharks. Among the survivors were laborers, as well as the adventurous younger sons of aristocrats, far too highborn to do any work. There were no women or children on the passenger list.

When the sealed orders from the London Company were opened, one of those designated to be on the Council was a certain John Smith. He was chained to a beam in the hold at the time for inciting to mutiny. So they had to unshackle him, but they would not let him sit in council.

John Smith was a born leader, and as time went on proved it. He decreed that those who wouldn't work wouldn't eat. This put a little gumption into the highborn younger sons. But between the Indians, friendly or hostile as the spirit moved them, the malaria from which the settlers must have suffered, and the ignorance of the newcomers in coping with this alien environment, the colony did not prosper. When, in January 1608, ships with supplies arrived, all but 38 of the colonists were dead. In the following August, five hundred new emigrants appeared with supplies, including about ninety hefty English servant girls. Within a week every one of them was a wife, and the descendants of these buxom wenches are among the First Families of Virginia (F.F.V.'s for short), ostensibly the *crème de la crème* of American society.

The winter of 1609-1610 was starving time. The colonists were reduced to eating roots, weeds, and rats, even a dead Indian. But when it was discovered that one of their number had cooked and eaten his wife, his fellows felt that such *gourmandise* was going too far, and he was condemned to death on a full stomach. By March there was very little to eat. In May a relief ship arrived, to be met by living skeletons, 60 of them feebly holding out their hands for food. All the rest were dead, lying in their cabins; no one had strength enough to dig graves. The captain of the ship mercifully put the survivors on board and headed for home. The English adventure in the New World seemed to have come to an end.

Before the ship had reached the mouth of the river she encountered three vessels. They were the fleet of Lord De La Warr, the newly appointed governor of this Virginia wilderness. When he discovered the state of affairs he said they must turn back. He had 150 men with him and a large supply of food. But the settlers continued to suffer from the hostile Indians. The great chief of those parts, Powhatan, did not on the whole care for the palefaces.

He had a little daughter, however, called Pocahontas ("the Playful One"), who did. When she was eight or ten she amused the settlers by turning cartwheels around the stockade stark naked. She must have been a delightful little creature.

One of the settlers, John Rolfe, although a gentleman, was more enterprising than the others and began experimenting with tobacco. He discovered a means of curing it so that it would not choke the smoker to death. When John Rolfe married Pocahontas, a truce was established with the Indians, so that, at least in part, it was a political marriage.

The story of Pocahontas saving John Smith by flinging herself upon him when he was about to be bludgeoned to death on orders from her father, was first told by Smith himself many years later. If it was fiction, John Smith missed his vocation, for it is one of the best known stories in American history.

John Rolfe took Pocahontas and their infant son to England where she was received in ruff and plug hat, as a princess at the Court of St. James'. She acted with dignity.

A year later Pocahontas died. Her son was educated in England, and eventually brought to America by his father. Among his descendants was the second Mrs. Woodrow Wilson, said to have been the secret President of the United States when her husband was incapacitated.

2   THOSE GRIM PILGRIMS

Some Americans, particularly New Englanders, think that the history of the United States began with the "Landing of the Pilgrim Fathers." This occurred in November 1620, thirteen years after the Jamestown settlement, in a section of the country that later became the state of Massachusetts. These "Pilgrim Fathers" were of a most puritanical cast; they conceived of God as a cruel, inhuman monster to whom all pleasure, kindness, and human warmth, were anathema. The Pilgrims' accent was on *grim*. Called Separatists for leaving the Established Church, they found religious freedom on a brief sojourn in Holland, but were not allowed to join the guilds there. They returned to England and set out for America, their last resort, from Plymouth.

Mrs. Hemans, the English lady poet, in her unreliable poem about this landing which American schoolchildren were once obliged to recite, described "the stern and rockbound coast" on which these unlovable people landed. As a matter of fact, it was flat and sandy. Tradition claims that they first set foot on a granite boulder on the beach known as "Plymouth Rock" (for which a fine breed of poultry is named). Some have been heard to mutter that Plymouth Rock should have landed on the Pilgrims. Kinder souls observe that though we hear a lot about the Pilgrim Fathers, almost nothing has been said about the Pilgrim Mothers? They had to endure not only the rigors of the climate, but the Pilgrim Fathers.

The Pilgrims arrived, having been blown off course—they were headed for the mouth of the Hudson River, then part of Virginia—on a hundred-foot-long ship, the *Mayflower*. Escaping the comparative comforts of England, they named the "stern and rockbound coast," with singular originality, Plymouth.

There were 102 passengers on the *Mayflower*. Only one had died at sea, but a child was born to make up the count. Between the two months' voyage and the terrible winter, for which they were in no way prepared, by spring there were but fifty of them left. Fourteen of the eighteen wives had died of exposure, starvation, and the Pilgrim Fathers.

In the spring a kind Indian named Samoset taught the survivors how to plant Indian corn. He brought another Indian, Squanto, homeless and tribeless, who remained with the palefaces when Samoset left, and helped them to get things going.

"New England" designates the part of North America which now comprises the six northeastern states of the Union, and the civilization developed there by the early white inhabitants explains the name. Many of the virtues and characteristics of English ancestors—bravery, determination, nobility in disaster, and others such as insularity, narrow-mindedness and a dislike of good cooking—have been more or less preserved there. New Englanders developed an enviable ability to drive a hard bargain, and necessity being the mother of invention, they became ingenious inventors. In addition they raised frugality to a fine art. The people of New England are the true "Yankees" in the original sense of the word.

While at sea some forty of the Pilgrims signed a compact in which they pledged allegiance to the King, and bound themselves to "obey whatever laws, ordinances, acts, constitutions and offices should be thought most meet and convenient for the general good of the Colony." The *Mayflower Compact* is famous as the first instance of "self-determination," a battlecry which resounds in many parts of the world today.

The Pilgrims' troubles were compounded by the arrival of later ships. The newcomers never brought any food. Among the illusions about America cherished by Europeans was the belief that gold could be had for the picking up, and that food could be plucked (ready roasted) from any adjacent tree.

A young man named William Bradford was elected governor of the Plymouth settlement. He was an efficient manager, but he was strict. Christmas was a work day, functions were conducted without ceremony, and there was no fun to be had, even at weddings and funerals.

The delusion that the Pilgrims were pure is quickly dispelled by a perusal of Bradford's book, *A History of Plimouth Plantation*. His spelling was not of the best, but his reporting was. Every sort of aberration existed at Plymouth, all carefully noted, and some of them would have made suitable bedtime reading for Krafft-Ebing and Freud.

The settlers of Virginia, on the other hand, were there chiefly on business, employees, so to speak, of several combined stock companies subscribed to by optimistic Englishmen back home. They were expected to find gold, and a passage to India. What most of them found was death. But the South they settled was never cursed with the miasma of Puritanism, occasional whiffs of which can still be detected in many parts of New England.

Virginia, with its tobacco, became a plantation society, the plantations being large and self-sufficient, and the towns far apart. Parishes might stretch for fifty miles, and consequently the clergy could not keep so close a watch on their parishioners, and things tended to get a trifle lax. In the little New England towns everyone could, and did, see what everyone else was up to.

The New England "town meeting" (so admired by that astute French observer, Alexis de Tocqueville), where the townspeople governed themselves and voted their own taxes, would have been impracticable in Virginia, and a central House of Burgesses became the representative assembly.

3   FOR BETTER OR WORSE, THE PURITANS

Excelling all whose sweet delight pursuits
In heavenly matters of theology.
—Marlowe, *The Tragical History of Doctor Faustus*, Act 1

SAMPLE PURITAN.

Ten years after the Pilgrims, came the Puritans. There is not much to choose between them; if anything they were worse. The counterfeit presentment reproduced here speaks louder than words.[1]

These people arrived in June instead of November, in eleven ships. They numbered some 900, and they even brought food (for a wonder), along with tools, furniture, artifacts, a charter from Charles I, and a grant of land. The English kings were still being generous.

One John Winthrop and others had formed a corporation in London called the Massachusetts Bay Company, and their intention was to trade with (i.e. cheat) the Indians. While nothing flourished with the Pilgrims, everything seemed to flourish with the adept Puritans. Colonists came pouring in until, by 1643, the population had risen to 16,000, with John Winthrop as Governor. This was the real beginning of New England. It is difficult to resist the impression that the Almighty favored commerce here over religion.

The Puritans, while successful, were even more bigoted than the Pilgrims, if this is possible. Complete acceptance of their faith and tenets, down to the most minute detail, was obligatory in the colony. They were fanatics. The Quakers—mild, peace-loving and abhoring all the sins—were persecuted savagely when a few turned up, whipped and driven into the woods. Eventually several were hanged, including a woman, just for being Quakers. Calvinism had here reached its apogee.

Theology was a lively subject among the Puritans, and occupied much of their time. Anne Hutchinson, who had emigrated from Lincolnshire in 1634 was a great arguer. She took on anyone opposing her views, even God's ministers. She believed in the "Covenant of Grace," which held that Faith alone was necessary for salvation. Feeding the starving, clothing the naked, good works—all were useless for gaining heaven. Faith alone would do the trick.

In 1637 Anne Hutchinson was declared a heretic by John Winthrop and others; she defied them all and was tried in the General Court, found guilty of "traducing the ministers," and banished.

One feels sympathy for poor Mr. Hutchinson who accompanied his wife into exile. She ended up in the colony of New York near Pelham, where she and all but one of her family were massacred by the Indians. The Hutchinson River and the Hutchinson River Parkway, daily traversed by thousands coming to New York, or fleeing from it, commemorate this disputatious lady, near the place where she met her fate in 1643. Her meteoric career in the New World lasted only nine years. She had not learned discretion.

Along with a fervent belief in God, and a mean-spirited God at that, among the theology-ridden Puritans, went a belief in the Devil and witches. From time to time a witch was hanged. But in 1692 an outbreak of witches occurred at Salem

Cotton Mather. Reproduced from the Collections of the Library of Congress. The bushiest wig and the fuzziest brain.

that was so severe as to rank as an epidemic, and put Salem (about forty miles from Plymouth) on the map.

Two little Salem girls had a wonderful time. They went into convulsions whenever they chose; they were able to vomit at will, to the wonderment of onlookers. They saw things no one else saw, including a yellow bird that flitted in and out and brought them dreadful messages from the Devil. A doctor was summoned. His diagnosis was that the girls were bewitched. That began it.

The little tykes agreed with the doctor's diagnosis and named two humble women, Goody Good and Goody Bishop, who kept a tavern. These women were sent to jail in chains, along with the former's five-year-old daughter Dorcas, also named as a witch. The two women were condemned and hanged.

Cotton Mather had a larger and bushier wig than most men, and a fuzzier brain. He was a Congregational clergyman and the author of over 400 works, among which was *Memorable Providences Relating to Witchcraft and Possessions* (1689). This made him an authority, and when the magistrates of Salem appealed to the clergy of Boston about the awful outbreak of witches in their town, he drafted the reply on which the prosecutions were based. He attended the trials, investigated many cases personally, and saw that the accused were *brought to punishment*. He believed in the Devil, diabolical possessions, sea serpents, signs and portents, and that the New World had long been the undisputed realm of Satan before the colonists came to challenge his rule. There was little the reverend man of God didn't believe except facts, and he consequently earned a place in colonial history.

When Governor Phips (who had been on a long sabbatical seeking, and finding, sunken treasure in the Caribbean, and was therefore out of touch with things) returned to his province, he was appalled at what had been going on for four months, ordered those still held in jail released, and dismissed the magistrates who had presided at the trials.

But a voice had already been heard in the wilderness. It was that of the young pastor of a church in Salem, some forty years before the arrival of the witches. His name was Roger Williams, and he was the first, and remains one of the greatest liberal-minded Americans.

He believed that the State had no control over a man's conscience, and that in spite of the Royal Charter the land really belonged to the Indians! For these heresies, especially the second, he was banished from the Colony in 1635.

Roger Williams made his way through the unbroken wilderness in the savage New England winter, succored here and there by hospitable Indians. He reached Narragansett Bay in the spring of 1636 and purchased a tract of land from the Narragansett Indians, started a settlement, and called it Providence.

There were others who could no longer stand the Puritans and they joined

Williams. Soon four small villages were settled. They were collectively called "Rhode Island and Providence Plantation."

Roger Williams was an extraordinary man, for his or any age. Everyone was welcome in Rhode Island, agnostics, Jews, pagans, no matter; everyone could do the work of his choice, no one had to go to church who didn't care to, and there was complete separation of Church and State. The Puritans of the Massachusetts Bay Colony looked down on Rhode Island with scorn. They called it a sewer.

In 1643 a New England Confederation was formed for the purpose of taking defensive measures against the Indians, the French in Canada, and the Dutch, who had settled along the Hudson River. Rhode Island and Providence Plantation was not invited to join.

4   FRENCH, INDIANS AND BEAVER HATS

The French held Canada because they were the first to get there. Jacques Cartier, a Breton sea captain, made three voyages to North America, in 1534, 1535, and 1541, and discovered the St. Lawrence River, though, like all the other explorers, he was seeking a passage to the gold-laden East. Cartier's third voyage was made under the command of the Sieur de Roberval, whose purpose was to found a colony—somewhere or other. But after one winter in those climes he and all his colonizers had had enough and left for France as fast as they could.

Newfoundland belonged to Spain, or at least Pope Alexander said so, but English fishermen had been operating in those waters since 1550 and the Spaniards were too busy exploring the sunny Caribbean and South America to bother much about those frozen regions in the north.

The Grand Banks, the great fishing grounds of the continental shelf, south of Newfoundland, were being fished by Spaniards, Portuguese, Englishmen and Frenchmen by the 1580's, Pope or no Pope.

Then the French and Basque fishermen began a trade in beaver pelts with the Indians. This was bad news for the beaver. France offered a monopoly to anyone who would start a settlement, and for the next two hundred years the unrestricted massacre of animals was the history of Canada.

A French gentlemen, the Sieur de Monts, secured this fur monopoly and sailed with about 125 settlers to found a colony in "Acadia," a region now comprising Canada's Maritime Provinces. Accompanying him as the expedition's cartographer, was Samuel de Champlain, but the Sieur de Monts discovered his monopoly to be impossible to enforce. French fishermen could not be prevented from trading with the Indians and, when his monopoly was cancelled through the machinations of powerful enemies in France, the Sieur de Monts returned home. Champlain remained behind. He was the executive type. He chose the formidable rock of Quebec for his base in 1608, one year after the settlement of Jamestown.

In 1609 he became embroiled in a war between Indian tribes. The Algonquins, the Hurons and the Montagnais were bitter foes of the powerful Iroquois, who lived south of the St. Lawrence. Champlain joined the Algonquins against the Iroquois because the pelts they furnished from more northerly regions were of better quality, and the expedition was successful. But so implacable was the hatred between these tribes that in the end it contributed to the permanent downfall of New France.

On his successful mission against the Iroquois, Champlain discovered a river that he named for his powerful supporter at the French court, Cardinal de Richelieu; but when he came upon a larger and more beautiful body of water, he named it for himself. Lake Champlain was destined to play a strategic role in the history of the United States.

5   THE DUTCH CAN'T TAKE IT

The Dutch West India Company was an excellent corporation, doing a thriving business in spices, slaves and other commodities. It had an impressive board of directors sitting in Amsterdam. These far-seeing men, aware of the burgeoning English activities on continental North America, got the message. Soon England would be gobbling up the whole place. So they decided to colonize the Hudson River Valley and the excellent harbor at its mouth where there was an island the Indians called "Manhatos"—or something similar. It is now known as Manhattan.

They based their claim on the adventures of an Englishman named Henry Hudson who, in their employ, had discovered the Hudson in 1609, and sailed up that majestic river as far as the present city of Albany in his famous little vessel, the *Half Moon*. This naturally gave the Dutch the right to the river, the territory on both sides, the island of Manhattan and the superb harbor there. So, just as England claimed most of North America on the voyage of a Venetian, the Dutch claimed the Hudson Valley on the explorations of an Englishman.

Dutch traders arrived on Manhattan Island in 1623. (There were already a few scattered here and there along the river as far as Albany.) This settlement, consisting at first of a few huts, and located at what is now The Battery at the foot of the island, was named New Amsterdam.

There was a turnover of governors; it was the third, Peter Minuet, who belatedly bought the island of Manhattan from the Indians for 60 guilders, which amounted to $24. He paid in trinkets for one of the most famous land deals in history.

The Dutch had a different system of governing from the English. They gave magnificent estates along the Hudson to rich proprietors or "patroons," who lived in feudal splendor with servants brought from Holland whose status was very like those of serfs—or slaves.

In 1647 Peter Stuyvesant became Governor; he had formerly filled this post in the Dutch West Indies island of Curaçao. He was a crusty, explosive man with a wooden leg, but which leg was the peg one is a question that has never been decisively answered, and this has posed a problem for sculptors commissioned to make statues of him.

Peter Stuyvesant had more bluster than brains. Nevertheless he governed New Amsterdam for seventeen years.

New Amsterdam was from the start a polyglot place, with the Germans, French, Swedes, Spanish, Turks, Jews and Italians who were attracted there for some reason, not to mention the Dutch themselves, and the English who began trickling in from the other colonies, no doubt to escape the Puritans. New Amsterdam was never a puritanical place, and when she became New York the tradition was maintained.

New Amsterdamers were in a constant state of bickering over taxes, land, the authority of the governor, rights to trade; and trouble with the Indians, sometimes brought on by the stupidity of the Dutch, did not improve matters.

This Dutch New Netherland began to worry the English. It lay between their colonies to the north and their colonies to the south, a most inconvenient wedge. Not only did it split their colonies in two, but caused inconveniences in the matter of commerce, and regulations were difficult to enforce.

Charles II mounted the throne of England in 1660, and he had the bright idea of giving New Netherland to his brother the Duke of York (afterwards James II). The Duke is said to have pointed out that New Netherland belonged to the Dutch, and England was at peace with Holland. The King assured his brother that Holland had never owned the land; it belonged to England—all on account of John Cabot in 1497.

The Duke of York's fleet sailed into the harbor of New Amsterdam on September 4, 1664. Peter Stuyvesant was livid—and one can scarcely blame him, especially when he received a demand to surrender the fort at the foot of the island. He had the guns manned and called out every able-bodied citizen. But the inhabitants did not want their town destroyed by the overwhelming fleet in the harbor. When a letter arrived from the Duke's representative saying that if the town surrendered, life and property would be respected, Stuyvesant tore up the letter, half read. The letter was picked off the floor and pieced together. The leading citizens finally prevailed, the fort was surrendered, and Peter Stuyvesant stomped off on his peg leg to his farm, where the church of St. Marks-in-the-Bowery now stands, and where in due course he was buried. New Amsterdam was taken by the English without a shot being fired or a drop of blood spilled.

Besides, most of the inhabitants were glad to be rid of the despotic Dutch regime, and of Peter Stuyvesant.

The British flag now flew uninterrupted from New France (Canada) to the Carolinas (to be explained in the next chapter), but traces of the fifty years of Dutch possession remain, in the architecture of Hudson River towns, and in the names of streets and of old New York families. And we have Rip Van Winkle and his twenty-year sleep as part of our heritage from the Dutch, via Washington Irving.

6   THE FRIENDS WHO WOULDN'T TAKE OFF THEIR HATS

By the time the Cross of St. George was raised over New Amsterdam, in 1664, there were already two more provinces, or "proprietorships," in America, the gift of Stuart kings. Charles I had granted to George Calvert, Baron of Baltimore, a large territory which became Maryland, and, in 1663, not to be outdone by his lamented father, Charles II with a lavish hand presented to eight of his courtiers (some of the cavaliers who had helped him gain his throne) all the land lying between Virginia and the Spanish holdings in Florida. This land became North and South Carolina, the name derived from the Latin for Charles.

These "proprietorships" were organized on a different plan from the earlier grants, but we hurry by this business to save time, pausing only to say that Lord Baltimore discovered that some of his new possessions were already in the hands of the Virginians, and had been for 26 years. This led to various unpleasantnesses that were not entirely ironed out for 267 years.

In the very year that New Amsterdam was seized by the British, the King also gave his brother—should New Netherland prove not large enough—the territory which is now New Jersey. But the Duke handed it away to Lord John Berkeley and Sir George Carteret, a couple of friends of his. (It was given its name because Carteret had been Governor of the Isle of Jersey, a pretty poor reason.)

Eventually Berkeley sold his slice (West Jersey) to one William Penn, a Quaker, and some of the latter's friends; and in 1682 the Carteret heirs sold East Jersey to the Quakers too; so now these people had the whole of it.

The Quakers, or "The Religious Society of Friends" held reasonable beliefs:

the "Inner Light" made the sacraments of the church non-essential; they were opposed to war, and believed that all men are equal. Thus they refused to remove their hats in the presence of anyone—even the King. To remove one's hat to another was a sign of servility; now it is merely politeness. The Quakers were persecuted for their strange belief until the Toleration Act was passed by Parliament in 1689, which saved them much trouble. They could keep their hats on.

William Penn was a high born Englishman, the son of Admiral Sir William Penn. At the age of eighteen he was converted to the Quaker faith, and one can imagine how the Admiral felt about that. Various ruses were tried to lure the young man into more seemly channels, including a trip to Paris, but this did not work. He studied religion there.

When the Admiral died, King Charles owed his estate £16,000 and William suggested that he be granted a pleasant parcel of land in America in payment of the debt. He was displeased with the charter under which the Quakers of New Jersey lived and wanted to set up a colony of his own, west of the Delaware. The King was delighted not to have to pay out £16,000, especially as he did not have such a sum handy, and the deal went through. (The pleasant parcel of land is larger than England and Wales combined.)

The tale is well known of the King looking over the draft of the charter of "Sylvania," which was the name Penn had chosen for his new colony, and writing the word "Penn" in front of it; and of how William objected, saying this would be a piece of vanity. "We will keep it," said His Majesty, "but not on your account, my dear fellow. We will keep it in honor of your noble father."

Here is one of those catch questions the ignorant get caught up on, as everyone who doesn't know better thinks that the Quaker State of Pennsylvania is named for its founder the Quaker Penn, rather than his very un-Quaker father.

Shortly after Penn arrived in his colony, in 1682, he met the chiefs of the Delaware tribe and a famous treaty was signed which promoted long lasting good will between the Indians and the white settlers. The primitive Quaker painter, Edward Hicks, later made many charming versions of this pleasant treaty-signing. But historians, born cynics, have pointed out that the Delawares were a weak tribe and vassals of the powerful Iroquois, who were friendly to the English, and this *may* account for the fifty years of peace that ensued.

Pennsylvania flourished from the start. Penn wrote a pamphlet describing the province in honest terms and offered land at forty shillings for a hundred acres, with a quitrent of one shilling a year. You did not have to be a Quaker to purchase. Many Germans took up the offer, and these are the "Pennsylvania Dutch" of today. The rich could acquire an estate of five hundred acres for one hundred pounds, with an annual quitrent of a shilling for each hundred acres.

William Penn's Treaty with the Indians, engraved from a painting by

But Pennsylvania had no direct access to the sea except by way of the Delaware River, past Maryland. The Quakers abhorred war but they were not averse to gaining their ends by any other means. Penn went to England and persuaded King Charles to cut a swatch out of Maryland and give it to him. The Calvert family were furious, and with good reason. Their charter was violated and Penn returned triumphantly with another piece of land in his pocket: Delaware.

The Penn family now ruled both Pennsylvania and Delaware as Lords Proprietor and did so until the American Revolution. There is nothing like having a friend at Court—especially if he is the King.

7   GENTLEMEN AGREE

Of the three remaining original colonies, the last has a curious history, but we will begin with Connecticut.

The Dutch built a small fort on the Connecticut River in 1633, and at about the same time, the English settlers, trickling in from Massachusetts, established two trading posts in the vicinity (Windsor and Wethersfield). Three years later, Thomas Hooker, a clergyman, led his congregation from Newton (now Cambridge), Massachusetts, and settled near the Dutch fort. A legend states that they saw a beautiful hart ford the river at this point, and named the place Hartford. (It is now the capital of the state.)

Though religion triggered many of the events of American colonial history, Hooker and his people came with the official blessings of the Massachusetts Bay Colony. Their reason was a desire for better land.

After a time the Dutch grew disgruntled at this steady flow of Englishmen pouring in and ruining the scenery, and up and left their fort in 1654. The Englishman was now monarch of all he surveyed, if you don't count the Indians.

The story of New Hampshire is somewhat different, and more royal. The Council for New England received a royal grant of land nonchalantly described as lying between forty and forty-eight degrees north latitude. A glance at the map reveals that this is land stretching from Philadelphia to north of Quebec. The surveyors of those days must have had very inaccurate instruments.

A gentleman favored with the elegant name of Sir Ferdinando Gorges obtained, two years later (1622), the rights to the part of this grant which lay between the Merrimack and Kennebeck rivers. The fact that Sir Ferdinando was a leading member of the Council may have had nothing to do with the matter. The tract of land was called the Province of Maine.

Sir Ferdinando had formed a partnership with Captain John Mason, and by a division in 1629, Mason took the area between the Piscataqua and Merrimack rivers and named it New Hampshire.

8   THE ROYAL NOOSE

—man, proud man,
Drest in a little brief authority . . .
—Measure for Measure, Act II, Scene 2

Life in the colonies soon became stormy. At first the Indians seem to have been treated well. There were worthy attempts to educate them, and to "Christianize" them. But before long the Christianizing took the form of forcing them to sell their lands, and not long after that it took the form of trying to exterminate them. So the Indians attempted to exterminate back.

In New England a sachem named Metacom, but called "King Philip" due to the English inability to pronounce any name not English, inaugurated "King Philip's War." In 1675, Metacom's tribal confederation of Indians, creeping noiselessly through the woods, plundered, burned and destroyed dwellings, barns, humans, and mutilated or killed what livestock they couldn't carry off. "The air was filled with terror-inspiring war whoops and the shrieks of tortured animals and people."[1]

One village after another was annihilated by the aborigines. The same thing occurred in other colonies. It was twenty years before the villages were rebuilt, and forty before the frontiers advanced.

The colonies suffered, too, from the imperial power of kings.

France had become the great international competitor of England, and the French government of Canada was absolutist. It was necessary for Britain (or so she thought) to have in America a stronger, more cohesive colonial government to meet the French commercial threat. So a Revenue Act was passed in 1673, and a body called the Lords of Trade was set up in 1675. To begin with, New Hampshire was made a royal colony in 1679.

Edward Randolph, a special agent for the Lords of Trade, made a study of conditions in New England and found in Massachusetts a complete, shocking disregard of the Acts of Trade (and thus a loss of profit for England), and wicked Massachusetts had its Charter annulled in 1684.

The following May, Randolph wrote Governor Treat of Connecticut that His Majesty (James II) intended to bring all the New England colonies under one government, and "nothing is now remaining on your part but to think of a humble submission and a dutiful resignation of your Charter."

In June, King James commissioned Sir Edmund Andros, Governor of the province of New York, Governor of all New England as well. The noose was tightening. Sir Edmund's overbearing ways, the suppression of charters and colonial assemblies, one by one, and interference with local customs and local rights, caused intense friction everywhere.

Governor Treat and the Council were warned again in December that the Charter of Connecticut must be surrendered. There were letters and petitions to the King, and receiving no answer, Governor Treat put off the surrender of the Charter until the King could be heard from.

So winter, spring and summer passed in apprehension, but in October 1686, word arrived from Sir Edmund that he was coming in person to Hartford to assume the reins of government and possess himself of the Charter. The physical transfer of the Charter would signal the end of the independence Connecticut had long enjoyed.

Sir Edmund arrived from Boston in regal style with a retinue. Governor Treat rounded up the members of the Assembly, and Sir Edmund was welcomed with what pomp and circumstance were available. Poor little Connecticut was facing the demands of a tyrant and the loss of her independence. Nevertheless Sir Edmund was ceremoniously conducted next day to the public meeting house and escorted to the Governor's chair.

Andros ordered the reading of his commission as Governor and the King's order for the annexation of Connecticut. And it was probably at this point that he demanded the surrender of the Charter. The most dramatic incident in the history of Connecticut followed.

Governor Treat "launched into a long and dramatic speech depicting the many privations and dangers experienced in establishing the colony"—which it was now the King's wish to disestablish. The Charter was produced and laid on the table.

It was late October, and as the wrangling and debating went on, darkness fell and candles were brought in.

Then suddenly the candles all blew out! And when they were relighted—the Charter had vanished.

Everyone was terribly apologetic that the candles had blown out like that. And what had become of the Charter? (Zounds!) Everyone submitted of course to Sir Edmund's authority.

Sir Edmund departed in a baffled rage, and King James never got the Charter of Connecticut. Under cover of darkness the precious document had been handed through a window to a fellow named Captain Wadsworth, ready and waiting outside. Captain Wadsworth hid the Charter in the hollow of a nearby giant oak—a tree cherished by the Indians and left standing at their request when the town was laid

The Charter Oak, Hartford, Connecticut.
Brown Thomson & Co. Pub.

out, because when the leaves of the oak were "the size of a mouse's ear" it was time to plant the corn.

The Charter Oak was revered in Connecticut for the role it had played in preserving the liberty of the people, and when it was blown down in a storm in 1856 all the church bells of Hartford tolled and a band played dirges over the fallen patriarch, whose age was estimated to be 1,000 years. In fact, when the news spread it is said that all the church bells of Connecticut tolled for the Charter Oak.

The modern Charter Oak Bridge over the Connecticut River at Hartford, and a granite monument to mark the spot where the patriotic oak grew, preserve its memory.

King James' tyrannical rule became insufferable even in England, and in the "Glorious Revolution" of 1688 James fled (doubtless bearing in mind what had happened to his father Charles I, beheaded by Act of Parliament), and his daughter Mary and her husband William of Orange were invited to sit jointly on the English throne. (James' heir was his infant son, half brother to Mary, but he had the then fatal defect of being a Roman Catholic.)

When news of the revolution in England reached the colonies Sir Edmund Andros was seized in Boston with other hated officials and all were sent to England as prisoners. Connecticut reverted to its Charter, which had been preserved by a tree.

9   FROM EASTER SUNDAY TO JENKINS' EAR

Give every man thine ear.
—*Hamlet*, Act I, Scene 3

Florida is the only state that owes its origin to legend worthy of medieval romance, and the only one on which an authentic Spanish conquistador ever set foot.

Juan Ponce de Leon, Governor of the Spanish island of Puerto Rico, was feeling his age, doubtless having what would now be known as twinges of arthritis. He learned from an old Indian woman that northward lay an island called Bimini on which flowed the Fountain of Youth. Ponce de Leon set out with three vessels to find the island and the fountain, and took along the old woman to guide him.

The land he found, on Easter Sunday 1513 (Flowery Easter) was not, alas, Bimini. The old woman's geography was weak, and this perhaps is why Ponce never found the Fountain of Youth. However, in the ancient town of St. Augustine one can see the reputed fountain. If it is the Fountain of Youth it has lost its powers. Ponce de Leon claimed all the land for Spain.

As will be remembered by the diligent reader, Charles II had granted all land lying between Virginia and the Spanish holdings in Florida to certain favored friends, and it had been named Carolina (the split-up between South and North Carolina came in 1713).

James Edward Oglethorpe was the head of the Royal African Company, the great slave-catching and slave-holding corporation of the day. This was considered a perfectly respectable pursuit. Oglethorpe, nevertheless, was a humanitarian, as humanitarianism went then. He was sympathetic to the plight of debtors and their long prison terms, and conceived the idea of exporting them to America, a lesser evil. With this noble notion he managed to induce George II to carve a slice out of Carolina and grant it to him in 1733. This land was west of the Savannah River.

So Georgia is land that once was Carolina. But this sort of thing never bothered a King!—witness William Penn finagling a slice out of Maryland to make Delaware. It was not the Indians, but British monarchs who were Indian givers.

Oglethorpe's plan touched the hearts of many, and considerable money was raised, including a donation from the Bank of England (the Old Lady of Thread-needle Street was seldom noted for her kind heart). It is doubtful how many debtors were relocated in Georgia, but many persons came, whether debtors or not.

Ponce de León on his Quest for the Fountain of Youth,
1513. Reproduced from the Collections of the Library of
Congress. It seems to have been a No-Go.

There is usually a second explanation for anything that seems unusually altruistic. The Privy Council wanted to create a buffer state between the Spaniards
in Florida and the flourishing colonies of Virginia and Carolina, with their rich
crops of tobacco. What better way to do this than to take a piece out of Carolina,
the unsettled piece to the south, and fill it up with no account folk—people who
didn't matter because they were poor?

Unfortunately the Spaniards in Florida did not get along with their new
neighbors in Georgia, whom they accused of usurping their land. Their great wish
was to annihilate these interlopers. But the Indian nations of the Gulf region, as

well as the Cherokees who inhabited the uplands, had come to dislike the Spaniards, and sided with Oglethorpe. They ceded part of their coastal lands to Georgia, and were ready and willing to join in a war against the Spaniards. The Georgians soon found an excuse to start one.

The English South Sea Company, another slave-trading organization, smuggled more slaves into Florida than the law allowed, which was one ship per annum. They sent a whole fleet of ships with many different cargoes, which were so eagerly bought up by the Spaniards that Spanish trade suffered. Spanish revenue cutters went on a rampage, and one of the smugglers, named Edward Jenkins, was caught and had an ear cropped. Poor one-eared Jenkins was taken to London and displayed in the House of Commons. England instantly declared war on Spain—"The War of Jenkins' Ear" (October 1739).

In no time there was widespread fighting in Florida and various Caribbean islands, in which several thousand volunteers from the colonies engaged. The war spread as far as the strongly fortified port and castle of Cartagena, New Granada (now Colombia), and even to the Pacific coast of Panama which must have meant marching across the fever-laden Isthmus of Panama, for they surely didn't go around the Horn.

In 1744 the War of Jenkins' Ear merged as if by magic into the War of the Austrian Succession, or "King George's War" in which England and Austria saw fit to do battle with France and Prussia over whether or not Maria Theresa had the best claim to the Hapsburg territories, but in 1748 everyone stopped fighting from sheer exhaustion. The Treaty of Aix-la-Chapelle was signed. Maria Theresa won out, more or less, but the Georgia-Florida boundary remained in dispute.

Georgia survived to be the last of the colonies established before the Revolution and that is why there are thirteen stripes on the national emblem, instead of twelve, and why American sailors' bell-bottom trousers were until very recently held up by thirteen buttons.

Jenkins never got his ear back.

10   CONFUSION ON THY BANNERS WAIT!

—Gray, The Bard

The supposedly Utopian New World had been a battleground almost from the first. In the North the British and French clashed continually, beginning as far back as 1613; in the South it was the British and the Florida Spaniards. And when things slowed down, if ever, there were always the Indians to fight. In fact wars proliferated to such an extent that one merged into another, and the military sometimes must have been confused about which war they were fighting.

These wars were collectively called "the French and Indian Wars" but were really aspects of the worldwide struggle for empire. They raged on and off from 1689 to 1763 and were closely connected with simultaneous wars in Europe, most of which were waged over who got what in marriage settlements. The first of these, known in Europe as "the War of the Grand Alliance" and in America as "King William's War"—1689 to 1697—was marked by frontier attacks by the French on English colonies, and by the English on French colonies.

Peace came in 1697, but was short-lived. War Number Two was "Queen Anne's War," a counterpart of the "War of the Spanish Succession." It went on from 1702 to 1713, with many bloody battles in the American colonies. The Peace of Utrecht (1713), considered one of the greatest and most far-reaching settlements of modern history, put an end to French expansion and signaled the rise of the British Empire. In the treaty France handed Newfoundland, Acadia and the Hudson's Bay region to England, and Spain ceded Gibraltar and Minorca to her. During the American Revolution, when England was busy elsewhere, Spain grabbed Minorca back with the help of France, but England retains Gibraltar, a fact over which Spain still understandably seethes.

While all this was going on the busy French were busy elsewhere, too, erecting a far-flung line of missions and trading posts. On Cape Breton Island stood Fort Louisburg, one of the most strongly fortified installations on the continent, to guard the approach to the St. Lawrence (from the English). All along the river feudal lords held "seigneuries." Quebec towered over the river and was the proud embodiment of the French Empire. Farther up the river was Montreal. From there, heading in a northwesterly direction for 500 miles as the crow flies was Sault Ste. Marie; near the junction of Lakes Erie and Huron stood Detroit, a fort and fur-trading post, founded in 1701. Along the Mississippi were four more settlements. On the Wabash, in Illinois country, was the little settlement of Vincennes.

Nor were these all. There were rich plantations on the lower Mississippi with rich overlords, and slaves cultivating rich soil. In Louisiana, at the delta, soon rose New Orleans. East of New Orleans were two towns, Biloxi and Mobile. In all, the string of French settlements of one kind or another, beginning at Fort Louisburg, stretched for roughly 2,000 miles.

Even vast America was not vast enough to hold both the English and the French comfortably. Consequently New Englanders invaded New France and captured that impregnable stronghold on Cape Breton Island—Louisburg. (When the Treaty of Aix-la-Chapelle was signed in 1748, they had to give it back.)

The French needed to control the route between New France and Louisiana and began to erect a chain of fortifications along the Ohio Valley. At about the same time George II granted a tract of 200,000 acres in that direction to the newly formed Ohio Company, composed of Virginia land speculators and Pennsylvania fur traders. They were dead set against any threat to the profitable land across the Alleghenies. The British Government instructed the colonial governors to resist French "encrouchments." The British Government had embarked on a collision course.

Obedient to command, the Governor of Virginia sent a young man of 21 named George Washington to protest to the commanders of these new forts between Lake Erie and the Alleghenies, and thus the Father of his Country makes his first appearance on the stage. His mission was a failure. The French told him politely the land was French.

The Virginians, taking things into their own hands, started to erect a fort at the strategic fork of the Ohio River, where the Allegheny and the Monongahela Rivers join, but they were driven away by the French, who completed the fort and named it Fort Duquesne.

Washington returned with a relief guard from Virginia and clashed with the French in a "brief but bloody skirmish." The Virginians fell back to a hastily constructed stockade called Fort Necessity, but they were overwhelmed and had to surrender on July 4, 1754. The French kindly let them go home.

11   THE FIRST WORLD WAR

He's a zealous fellow, but zeal can't take the place of brains.
—Agatha Christie, *The Murder at the Vicarage*

The action at Fort Duquesne proved that the French intended to stay. They were, in fact, pugnacious about it. This was outrageous. Though Robert La Salle, one of the world's greatest explorers, with his lieutenant Henri de Tonti, built the first boat on the Great Lakes, and with his party descended the Mississippi to its mouth in 1682 (the first white man to do so), and "took possession" of the whole valley (calling it Louisiana for Louis XIV)—had not John Cabot sailed along the Atlantic coast in 1497, thinking it was China or something?

William Pitt, first Earl of Chatham, became popular denouncing government policies, a fertile field in all times. George II was forced to appoint him Secretary of State in 1756, and he found himself the most powerful man in England.

Pitt demanded imperial supremacy over the French, a popular cause, especially with mercantile interests, and with this worthy aim in view he began to reorganize the British regulars in America, strengthen them with colonial troops, and instill a warlike spirit otherwise lacking.

General Edward Braddock had already been dispatched to America in 1755 as commander in chief of the British forces, and in June of that year he set out for Fort Duquesne from Fort Cumberland, Maryland, to wrest it back from the French. He had 1,400 redcoats and a small number of colonial troops. Lieutenant Colonel George Washington went along as a volunteer aide.

Braddock had no experience of Indian fighting. Repeated warnings from the Virginians among his troops were ignored. What did raw colonials know about the proper way to do things? The General rejected all advice, including that of young Lieutenant Colonel Washington. He would not use pack animals to carry supplies, it wasn't *done*. Wagons were the thing—even in a trackless wilderness. A road had to be built; it took 32 days to hack out a rough trail.

With martial music—fife and drum—the redcoats penetrated the Alleghenies, and the music must have sounded lovely there among the hills. It also gave the Indians first hand (or ear) information as to just where the English were, and the strategic moment to strike. The redcoats and the very correct General were within twelve miles of Fort Duquesne when a sudden fire from an unseen foe hidden behind rocks and trees put a halt to the parade. The poor redcoats could not fight an enemy they could not see. Huddled helpless in masses they presented perfect targets.

It was a bloody rout, and wagons, muskets and artillery were abandoned. Of the 1,459 men engaged, 977 were sacrificed to the General's know-how about fighting Indians, and the General had four horses shot from under him, and thus also sacrificed. Finally the General received a mortal wound. Washington lost two horses, but kept his cool and saved the column from annihilation.

Fortunately the Indians stopped to collect scalps and other choice souvenirs, which gave the survivors a chance to get away, rejoin the rear guard, and retreat safely to Fort Cumberland. General Braddock was not among those who fled. He acted with great courage, but dauntless courage is wasted if unaccompanied by brains. The General's grave is near Uniontown, Pennsylvania.

General Braddock's defeat had far reaching consequences. It caused the Indians of the North and West to choose the French as allies; the English frontier was thrown back several hundred miles, exposing the new settlements to murderous Indian raids. Thousands lost all they had and were lucky to escape with their lives.

The Indians seem to have favored the French over the English in all these wars. Perhaps they liked their cooking better.

Perseverance conquers all, and in 1758 Brigadier General John Forbes marched across Pennsylvania and captured Fort Duquesne at last. George Washington was on his staff. The fort was renamed Fort Pitt after the great Prime Minister; the place has grown into a city called Pittsburgh.

Another British military gentleman, General James Wolfe, had been dispatched

Braddock's March. (Note Indian far left.) Collection Prof. James C. Holland.

to America to make history, which he did in the last of the French and Indian Wars. Fortunately for Britain he was dowered with a higher I.Q. than boneheaded Braddock. He wrested the fortress of Louisburg from the French and proceeded to capture Quebec. When frontal attacks failed he staged a sneak attack up-river. Perhaps General Braddock would have found this utterly against the rules.

The Plains of Abraham is the name of a level stretch of land on the heights of Quebec, west of the city, and here General Wolfe surprised and defeated the Marquis de Montcalm on September 13, 1759. Both generals died, affording fine opportunities for impressive and elevated historical paintings, such as "The Death of Wolfe" and "The Death of Montcalm."

The fall of Quebec was a decisive event, and presaged the end of the French Empire in the New World. Montreal fell with scarcely a whimper the next year. The English historian, J. B. Green, observed: "With the triumph of Wolfe on the Plains of Abraham began the history of the United States."

This war was unique because it began simultaneously in places as remote from each other as North America and India, waged by the same old traditional enemies,

Britain and France. In America it was the final episode of those "French and Indian Wars." In India it was waged between the French Governor Dupleix and the British statesman Robert Clive, who collected revenues from the Indian states he subjected. He was the famous victor who wondered at his own moderation in this regard.

The war then neatly blended into the War of the Austrian Succession that had been going on since 1740, waged by Maria Theresa; and soon Frederick the Great had his hand in the pie. We, fortunately, need not go into all this, but the Seven Years War, before it was over, had been waged on four continents—North America, Europe, Africa, and Asia—and involved France, Great Britain, Prussia, Russia, Saxony, Sweden, Spain, and Hanover.

The Seven Years War came to a definite end with the Treaty of Paris (1763). France transferred to Britain, New France (Canada) and all her territories east of the Mississippi, all but two of her colonies in India, and threw in a few of her West Indian islands for makeweight. Spain received New Orleans and the French territories west of that city. And so, except for a few Caribbean islands, and two minuscule islands, St. Pierre and Michelon off the southern coast of Newfoundland, France was out of the picture in the New World. She bided her time; revenge was worth waiting for.

The Seven Years War was the true First World War and it would take seven years to figure it all out.

12   THE POT SIMMERS

I must have all men sellers
And I the only purchaser.
—Massinger, *A New Way to Pay Old Debts*,
Act II, Scene I

Britain, at the conclusion of the Seven Years War, was faced with a staggering debt. It cost money to vanquish the French and become imperial, and some of this debt had been incurred in defending the colonies. It seemed only fair for the colonies to help ease the burden. Heretofore Britain had only reaped a large profit from their trade, though she had freed them from fear of the French. The colonies thought they had done as much as the mother country and had gone into debt too, fighting the Indians and the French. If taxes must be levied, they should be levied by their own legislative bodies. Otherwise, there would be taxation without representation.

But this argument was in vain. Royal Customs, which had been rather lax, must be made more stringent. Old "Acts of Trade and Navigation," smouldering on shelves in Parliamentary archives, were dug out and gone over, and there were found rich lists of items that could be taxed for the benefit of Britain. The Acts were resuscitated.

One item was Madeira, the dessert wine produced in that Portuguese island and which enjoyed great popularity in the colonies. The wine was imported direct from Madeira, payment being made in vast shiploads of barrel staves. This was to stop. Now Madeira must be imported through British shippers at greatly increased cost—and the barrel stave business was done for.

This was but one of many new blows to free trade. All American exports to Europe were now first to be cleared through British ports, where more and more profit was sucked away in taxes, to swell the coffers of Mother Britannia. The more lucrative American commerce became, the larger the slices of it snatched by Britannia. The old girl's avarice was insatiable.

The resuscitation of the Navigation Acts was an attempt to monitor American ships—to ensure that they restricted their activities to the British Empire. The countries of Europe believed that colonies existed solely for the benefit of the homeland, and were supposed to trade exclusively with the mother country—to produce what she needed in the way of raw materials, to consume her wares, and not to compete with her manufacturers. This was part of an elaborate policy called "mercantilism," and as can be noted, it worked in one direction only.

The trouble with this was that prices for all goods were *set in Britain*. Everything—tobacco, cotton, lumber, pig iron—had to be sold to Britain at prices Britain fixed. The buyer has his fortune guaranteed when he can set the price and forbid the seller to sell to anyone else.

There were problems with the West Indies too, some of those islands being French. The West Indies produced the molasses from which the New England distillers distilled their celebrated rum, which everyone drank to excess. Britain had imposed a duty of six-pence a gallon on molasses bought in the French islands (the mouth-watering "Molasses Act" of 1733), but molasses bought in the British islands entered duty free. This would have been fine except that the British islands did not produce enough molasses to keep the New England stills busy, and six-pence-a-gallon duty made the price of French molasses prohibitive, or so the distillers thought.

A vast smuggling trade developed. The naughty colonials enjoyed it. Forged papers to prove a ship was bound for some English port, when her destination was really the French West Indies or the South of France, were taken along as a matter of course. The cargoes of molasses brought back were disguised as British molasses, or concealed under other cargoes, and everybody still had plenty of rum to drink.

In 1765 another blow fell when Parliament decided to impose a direct tax on the colonies. The Stamp Act was passed that year.

George III, grandson of George II, had succeeded to the throne in 1760 at the age of 22. He did his best, for many years, to alienate his American colonies. The passage of the Stamp Act was only one of many provocations, but George continued, with admirable determination, until he succeeded in ridding himself of his colonies entirely. "George, be a King!" his mother, a domineering German lady named Princess Augusta of Saxe-Gotha, had admonished him.

13   BEING A KING

Weiche, Wotan, weiche!
—Wagner, *Das Rheingold*

Under the new Stamp Act all legal documents required a stamp to make them valid. Mortgages, licenses, deeds, wills, bills of lading, even college degrees, required a stamp. Newspapers had to have a stamp in an upper corner, advertisements required one: everything but marriage licenses, which was a sweet thought.

Pandemonium broke loose in America! The heavens fell. The stamp distributors were hanged in effigy; one of them was tarred and feathered. Their houses were torn down. There was mob rule in some cities. Packets of the stamps were burned amid cheers and the beating of drums. People refused to buy the stamps and newspapers appeared with a death's head where the stamp should have been. Americans have always hated taxes, but our ancestors *did* something about them.

Rabble-rousing speeches filled the air. Samuel Adams of Boston was one of the most vociferous—but there were others. Patrick Henry, a young lawyer and a delegate to the Virginia House of Burgesses was a rabble-rouser par excellence, though the burgesses were not rabble. He made an impassioned speech against the Stamp Act: "Caesar had his Brutus, Charles his Cromwell, and George the Third. . . ." "Treason! Treason!" the burgesses shouted, turning pale. When the tumult subsided Patrick Henry continued, "may profit by their example." He had been given the cue for his famous line, "If this be treason, make the most of it." (Patrick Henry's other famous line, known to all Americans, is "Give me liberty or give me death!")

Parliament had not expected any such uproar, though Benjamin Franklin, then in London as a colonial commissioner, warned about the unpopularity of such a tax. The thirteen bickering brats Britain had spawned in the New World were getting to be big boys now. There were problems and rivalry between them, but the Stamp Act united them in a common cause. It proved fatal to Britain's interests.

There were those in Parliament who had warned against the Stamp Tax. General Henry Semour Conway was the first to glimpse "a possibility of fatal consequences" when apparently nobody else did, and voted for repeal. For his stand on this burning issue, several towns in the colonies established in that year (1765) were named Conway in the general's honor.

Just when Britain, flushed and victorious, wanted to consolidate her American holdings, the colonies' need for Mother began to evaporate. They were feeling their oats. It happens in most families.

Associations under the rousing name The Sons of Liberty were formed to organize opposition to the Stamp Act. They met in New York and delegates from nine colonies attended. British goods were boycotted, and Parliament, faced with a loss of trade, repealed the Act in 1766. The Act had lasted less than a year; hardly any of the stamps had been sold.

George Grenville, the Minister who had sponsored the Act, was blamed for all the trouble, and King George, who disliked him anyway (because he was given to lecturing his Sovereign), dismissed him and appointed Lord Rockingham as Prime Minister. Rockingham was a Whig and had been loud in his censure of Grenville, but now that he was in power, he began to expand. The King, who had forebodings about the repeal of the Stamp Act, was greatly pleased when Rockingham's party put through a "Declaratory Act," proclaiming Britain's *inalienable* right to tax the colonies.

What might have prevented future trouble was the King's dismissal of Rockingham and his appointment of William Pitt in his place.

Pitt was a noble man, a lover of liberty, and sympathetic to the colonies' hatred of direct taxation without representation. He feared France, but said, "America must be embraced with the arms of affection." However, he did a fatal thing; he accepted a peerage, became Earl of Chatham, and left the House of Commons for the House of Lords. He was known as "the Great Commoner" no longer; he had abandoned the people for a coronet. His health deteriorated, his gout increased, his temper rose, his language grew foul. Fatally his Chancellor of the Exchequer rose to power, "a statesman who has left nothing but errors to account for his fame."

Charles Townshend had one absorbing interest, to be popular with those who count. Aware of how much the King and the aristocracy resented the repeal of the Stamp Act, he sought other means of taxation. America's rabid hatred of taxation without representation he thought "so much nonsense." A tax was clapped on such goods imported into America as glass, painters' pigments, red and white lead, paper, and tea.

Again a great cry arose in the colonies. British goods were boycotted and again Parliament had to eat their words. The imposts on everything but tea were rescinded. Tea was retained as a symbol of America's subjection, but the tea proved to be a symbol of something else.

14   THE HURRICANE IN THE TOWN-HOUSE

I did something. I spoke for want of power to hold my tongue.
—Jules Verne, *Twenty Thousand Leagues Under the Sea*

Every assault by Britain upon the colonists' liberties roused vociferous defiance, and the defiance kept growing until it erupted into violent action. In a growing list of bungles, Parliament renewed the Writs of Assistance.

The Writs of Assistance were blanket search warrants. They had existed before but had been specific as to what was to be searched for, and where. These new writs were all-embracing. They empowered customs officers, with military protection, to enter or break into any warehouse, store or home. No grounds for suspecting the presence of smuggled goods were required. One writ could cover a whole town. A knock at the door at any hour—and in tramped the customs officers with the police, tore your house apart, riffled through dresser drawers.

James Otis was a young lawyer who had gained distinction serving as advocate general for the Vice Admiralty Court in Boston, but he resigned his commission to oppose the Writs of Assistance as issued by the superior court of Massachusetts. His was a most fiery and denunciatory voice against the Writs, as it had been against the Stamp Act and other violations of colonial rights.

Otis argued before five scarlet-robed judges in the Town House in Boston, and his speech must have been something of a hurricane. It lasted four or five hours. The Writs, he declared, violated the natural rights of Englishmen, and any act of Parliament that violated those rights was void.

John Adams, another young Boston lawyer, a native of the nearby town of Braintree, was a fervent patriot, a man of deep convictions, and destined to play a great role in American history. His dedication to the cause of liberty brought him to the Town House to hear James Otis present his case.

John Adams was bowled over. "With a profusion of legal authorities," he wrote fifty years later, "a prophetic glance of his eye into futurity, a torrent of impetuous eloquence," he (Otis) carried all before him—except the judges. He argued that the power to issue general warrants placed "the liberty of every man at the hands of every petty officer." Otis here spoke the words now familiar to all: "An Englishman's home is his castle." As might be expected, he lost the case.

And Adams concluded, "Then and there the child Independence was born."

Chief Justice Thomas Hutchinson had defended the Writs, and while the authorities waited for word from England, he had his house sacked for his pains.

Though the colonials considered themselves freeborn Englishmen whether they lived in England or in North America, Benjamin Franklin noted that in England

Englishmen referred to their brothers across the sea as "our subjects," as if they themselves were King. Arrogance is catching.

George III had one goal in mind: to pass his empire to his heirs inviolate. He was paranoid about losing an acre of it. He was obstinate, and his fixation allowed no wider view than to fight what he considered to be treason. The authority of the King and Parliament were immutable. His ministers were for the most part politicians who in the struggle for power gave little attention to the colonies; there was no settled policy except the King's—to teach the colonies a lesson and put them in their place. This proved more easily said than done.

With the revival of the Writs good feeling for dear old England quickly evaporated.

A board of customs commissioners was set up in Boston to oversee the collection of duties at all American ports, and these duties were to be used in part to pay the salaries of the royal governors and judges. Thus these officials were freed from any dependence on the colonial assemblies for their support.

Even now Parliament was not content. It suspended the New York assembly for refusing to furnish supplies for the King's troops quartered in the province, thus interfering directly with local governments.

American reaction was like that to the Stamp Act. Our old friend, Samuel Adams, the rabble-rouser, led the revolt. Speeches filled the air, pamphlets showered from the presses. Adams induced the Massachusetts Legislature, of which he was a member, to issue a circular letter to all the towns of the province urging them to unite in protest. The Governor ordered the Legislature to recall the letters and apologize; they refused to do so by a vote of 92 to 17.

The colonials were growing more and more intransigent. The new customs commissioners were so rudely treated in Boston that they panicked and asked that a ship be sent from Halifax to protect them. But more than speeches and pamphlets, it was the new boycott of British goods that hurt the most. Within a year imports had fallen nearly a million pounds.

In the autumn of 1768 a warship and two regiments of soldiers were sent to Boston at the request of the Governor, who was growing nervous. The Legislature refused to supply quarters or food for them. The troops were jeered and called rude names by unruly mobs. They were pelted with sticks, stones, and perhaps rotten eggs.

On March 5, 1770, one of the most famous events in American colonial history took place, its reverberations far exceeding the size of the episode. It was called the "Boston Massacre."

The sentry outside the Customs House was menaced by a jeering crowd of rowdies who called themselves "Liberty Boys." A captain and eight men came to his rescue. The ensuing events are variously reported, but it appears there was some scuffling, insults were flung, brickbats thrown. In an attempt to wrest a musket from a soldier, it went off, and one of the rioters dropped dead. The squad, without orders, then fired into the crowd and four more rowdy Bostonians bit the dust, one of them a black man named Crispus Attucks, who thus gained immortality.

The whole countryside, and then the whole country, was roused by this unfortunate event. It was grist to Sam Adams' rabble-rousing mill. *Innocent Blood Crying to God from the Streets of Boston* was the lurid title of an account of the affair Adams and his cohorts concocted and circulated. It gave the impression that the dead were victims of a deliberate plot instead of a bunch of rowdies bent on making trouble. A successful rabble-rouser must not have a too strict regard for the truth.

And now comes the heartwarming end of the incident, proving that, in spite of the temperature of the times, justice survived undimmed. The soldiers were indicted by the civil authorities, and John Adams, a lawyer, cousin of Samuel Adams, and a bitter foe of Britain, and John Quincy, another patriot, volunteered to defend them, a courageous and noble act.

All were set free but two, who were convicted of manslaughter. In a day or two they also were freed.

But Thomas Hutchinson, who served in the dual capacity of Chief Justice and Lieutenant Governor, ordered the troops from the town, yielding to the thunder and oratory of Sam Adams, who bearded his Excellency in his residence. They went down to the harbor and took refuge in Castle William, on a small island in the bay, no doubt with relief. The customs officials prudently decided to go with them.

15   TEA WITHOUT SUGAR

And what mortal ever heard
Any good of George the Third?
—Walter Savage Landor, "Epigram After Hearing
Thackeray's Lectures on *The Four Georges, 1855*

The excitement of March 1770 died down and three years passed in relative calm. There were only minor troubles over the attempts by British revenue vessels to stop the smuggling. One of these vessels ran aground on a sand pit in Narragansett Bay and was promptly boarded and burned by Rhode Islanders.

The next event was triggered by tea.

The East India Company was in financial straits, and had a large stock of poor grade tea in its London warehouses, seventeen million pounds of the stuff, which could not be cleared until the unpaid back duty was paid.

King George and his Prime Minister, Lord North, had a bright idea. Parliament was induced to come to the Company's relief with the Tea Act. This law permitted the Company to export its product to America without paying the English tax. The Company could thus undersell the American tea merchants. The English supposed that, the tea being cheaper, the colonials would overlook the slight tax *they* had to pay.

But they didn't. If they paid this tax it would be an admission that Britain had a right to tax them. Instead, they took to coffee, chocolate and infusions of various herbs—and smuggled tea from Holland. It was the principle of the thing!

The tea ships were on their way, and leaders in various ports, with strong popular support, began laying plans to prevent the tea from landing. In Philadelphia and New York the captains of the tea vessels were induced to return to England without unloading, but in Boston the patriots, having failed to turn back three ships, took more desperate measures. On the evening of December 16, 1773, three companies made up of fifty men each, thinly disguised as Indians, passed between lines of cheering crowds, boarded the ships, broke open 342 big chests of tea, and threw them overboard.

This was The Boston Tea Party, the most famous tea party ever held. Everyone had a rip-roaring time, unusual at a tea party, and though nobody aboard had tea, the fishes in the harbor drank tea for weeks, and they did not pay the tax either.

The tea was in the water, and the fat was in the fire.

The destruction of the tea outraged the British Government more than almost anything could have done—and this is just what Sam Adams wanted. The Attorney General was asked at a cabinet meeting whether the "late proceedings" in Boston amounted to high treason? If it had not been *tea* perhaps the outrage would not have been so great. "The Boston Tea Party seemed to arouse John Bull far more than having a revenue cutter burnt or soldiers beaten up," and Parliament and public opinion demanded that "Mother England crack down on her naughty brat," though Edmund Burke and other liberal leaders warned against doing so.[1] There was something sacred about tea.

Although a group of Boston merchants offered to pay for the tea, but not the tax, Parliament determined to punish the city, innocent and guilty alike, closed the port of Boston, and moved the custom house to Salem. The closing of the port meant that no ships could enter or leave the harbor, the death of the town, and the starvation of its inhabitants.

Oh Albion! Perfidious you may have been (as Napoleon later claimed), but with that act you were moronic.

The Boston Tea Party, the most famous tea party ever
held. From *The American Revolution, The Picture Source
Book*, by John Grafton, New York: Dover Books, 1975.

Edmund Burke, in the House of Commons, made an impassioned plea, urging
Britain to give up the idea of deriving a revenue from the colonies, and admitting
them to a full share of the freedom enjoyed by their fellow-citizens in Britain. "Magnanimity in politics is not seldom the truest wisdom. A great empire and little minds
go ill together." He was voted down three to one.

"I know what my duty to my country is," said King George, "and threats cannot
prevent me from doing it to the utmost extent"—regardless of consequences. His
duty consisted in making the colonies *submit*: they were traitorously levying a war
against him. No longer disobedient children, the colonists were now outlaws to be
brought to heel and *punished*.

The news of the closing of the port of Boston was received with consternation
and indignation throughout the colonies. The bell in the Unitarian Church at Falmouth (now Portland), Maine was muffled and tolled all day. For this and other

naughty acts, such as refusing to furnish free masts for the King's Navy, a British squadron appeared in the harbor of Falmouth in October, kindly gave the people overnight to remove their sick and infirm, and what chattels they could, fired on the town, burned what was beyond the reach of the cannon, and destroyed three quarters of the houses. This was to teach the inhabitants to be more submissive. It tended, curiously, to have the opposite effect.

Generous quantities of food flowed into the starving town from as far away as South Carolina. Pomfret, Connecticut contributed a flock of sheep, which was driven over the roads. Providence, Rhode Island started building a meeting-house to make work for the carpenters. Virginia sent thousands of barrels of corn, wheat and flour.

Burning towns became a policy with His Majesty's Navy, or perhaps just a habit. The Hudson and the Connecticut Rivers were ideal for the purpose. One could sail up either, enjoying the views (the views of the Catskills from the Hudson are famous), and fire away whenever one pleased. Unprotected towns were burned along the Hudson nearly as far as Albany.

In the Declaration of Independence Jefferson listed among King George's crimes, "He has burnt our towns." Surely that is motive enough for resorting to armed rebellion.

But Parliament, not content with closing the port of Boston and burning towns, enacted three other laws, all to punish Massachusetts, the seat and center of rebellion. Its charter was taken away again and a provincial government substituted, which made the Governor, appointed by the King, virtually a dictator; it permitted officers to be tried for civil offenses in other colonies, and even in England, and it provided for the quartering of troops in people's barns and houses. These laws were known as the "Intolerable Acts."

A fifth act, not aimed particularly at Massachusetts, and known as the Quebec Act, did as much harm to the British cause as any of the others. The Quebec Act extended the province of Quebec southward to the Ohio River, cutting off the western land claims of four states—Massachusetts, Connecticut, Virginia and New York—and surrounding these Protestant colonies with a large territory where the Roman Catholic church and the French custom of absolute rule would prevail. Rumors that the Church of England planned to appoint a bishop for America with the intention of enforcing Anglican authority over all the sects that flourished in the colonies, vied with (surely a foolish) fear that a plot was hatching in London to subject Americans to the tyranny of the Pope. It was too much to be borne.

From New Hampshire to South Carolina the people prepared to take a stand.

There's a divinity doth hedge a king, as everybody knows, but one hedge began to shrivel alarmingly, as in a prolonged drought, revealing the portly form of George

William Frederick, King of Great Britain (and the American colonies) and Elector of Hanover, with all his warts.

Consulting William Makepeace Thackeray's little book, *The Four Georges*, one discovers that George III was the most likable fellow who ever sat on a throne! It must all be in the point of view.

16   THE MOTHER OF PARLIAMENTS

> *Politics we bar;*
> *They are not our bent;*
> *On the whole we are*
> *Not intelligent.*
> chorus: *No, no, no, not intelligent.*
> —W. S. Gilbert, *Princess Ida*, Act I

The First Continental Congress was the result of the "Intolerable Acts." At the proposal of the Massachusetts House of Representatives, approved by other bodies, it convened in Philadelphia in September 1774. Philadelphia was a central point geographically, not only the metropolis of North America but, surprisingly, with its 40,000 inhabitants, the second largest city in the British Empire.

John Adams kept a record of the meeting from which we learn that the members met at a tavern at 10 o'clock on September 5th and walked to the Carpenters' Hall where they "took a view of the rooms." The question being put as to whether they were satisfied, most of them were.

The room might well have pleased the delegates, for the Carpenters' Hall is a beautiful little building, of charming design, erected with loving care by the Carpenters' guild some years before. Still standing today, it may be considered the first Capitol of the United States.

There were delegates from all the colonies except Georgia, men of influence and standing in their communities. They were of differing political complexions; the delegates from Massachusetts—John and Samuel Adams, who had inaugurated the Congress—were matched by the delegates from Virginia—George Washington, Patrick Henry and Richard Henry Lee.

The purpose of this Congress was not to seek independence from Britain, for that was not yet in the popular thinking, but to seek colonial rights, mitigate parliamentary wrath, and restore relations between themselves and the mother country.

But the resolutions included a declaration that no obedience was due the Intolerable Acts (officially called "the Coercive Acts") and a series of retaliatory measures against them were adopted. These were new and more stringent non-importation, non-exportation and non-consumption agreements. It was hoped thus to wring concessions from Parliament. "A Declaration of Rights and Grievances" addressed to "The People of Great Britain" and a petition to the King for Redress were included to appease the moderates.

But pig-headed King George and his toady of a Prime Minister, Lord North, had no intention of giving redress or making concessions.

Most of the delegates knew this, for they added a resolution that unless a redress of grievances be obtained before the 10th of the following May, another Congress be called; and on October 26th the Continental Congress, with due thanks for the hospitality it had received in Philadelphia, "dissolved itself."

The greatest accomplishment of the First Continental Congress was to demonstrate that the colonies could unite and conduct business.

Frederick North, 8th Baron North, called Lord North in the history books, became Prime Minister in 1770 and is an example of an excellent administrator who failed at the crucial moment. He had introduced financial reforms and better regulations for the East India Company, but when it came to colonial affairs it was another story. His reply to The Boston Tea Party was the Intolerable Acts, and the reply to these acts was revolution. King George liked Lord North and Lord North liked to please the King, the Anointed One, come hell or high water. Both came.

North had voted enthusiastically for the Stamp Tax, so devoted was he to "that just right which I shall ever wish the mother country to possess—the right to tax the Americans"—a homemade "just right."

All did not agree with his lordship. Lord Camden said taxation without representation was illegal. Horace Walpole, who spoke little in Parliament, feared that attempts to enforce the Declaratory Act (Rockingham's act about the right to tax the colonies that had so pleased the King), "would risk lighting up rebellion" and that the colonies "would fling themselves into the arms of France or Spain," but the clearer the evidence of this very likelihood grew, the more relentlessly the King, Lord North and Parliament pursued their policies.

The Secretary of War, Lord Barrington, though staunchly in favor of a hard line with the colonies, began to see the light. Clearly Britain could not successfully impose internal taxation; a land war would be ruinous and impossible to win; the land was too vast and a conquered country must be held by large standing armies; the expenses would be endless. Britain's only war aim was to prove supremacy without being able to use it. Wiser words were never wasted on deafer ears.

No ministry ever sent anyone to the colonies to see what was going on, to find facts or to judge the deteriorating situation. The members lolled on their benches in Commons, the Lord Chancellor snoozed on his woolsack and the other lords did what ever their lordships did, their resounding titles and vast estates alone fitting them to govern an empire.

On the following May 10 tremendous things happened.

17   GENERAL GAGE AND THE SILVERSMITH

*They have passed their life in trembling and submission,
and all of a sudden . . . O Lord!*
—Turgenev, *A King Lear of the Steppes*

General Thomas Gage, who had been in America since 1754, was now the King's Governor of Massachusetts, and on the hot seat. He knew the farmers and towns-people all over the province were training as militia. A "Committee of Safety" had been set up by the Provincial Congress, meeting illegally in Concord, and it was headed by John Hancock who had been empowered to call up the militia if occasion warranted. Special groups, within the various militia units, were made up of men who could be counted on to answer a call at a minute's notice, and these came to be known as "minutemen."

General Gage was in an awkward position. His was the unenviable job of en-forcing the Acts of Parliament upon a belligerent people. At every show of force he knew there was a swift massing of this armed militia. But he had to do something. By April 15, 1775 it was known that Gage had detached from each of his regiments grenadier and light infantry companies totalling 700 men and that they were on some sort of maneuvers.

Early April 18 everyone in Boston knew that a raid on Concord was planned for that night. Concord was where the militia had stored gun powder and other military matériel. Gage had another objective too: to capture Sam Adams and John Hancock who were lodging with the Reverend Jonas Clarke at the parsonage at Lexington, close to Concord.

This is where Paul Revere, the most famous figure in the episode, emerges, thanks to Longfellow's poem which recounts his midnight ride to warn the coun-tryside "to be up and to arm." There were other riders—William Davis and Samuel Prescott, who were to go by other routes—but the poet chose to write about Revere, possibly because it was easier to find rhymes for that name.

Paul Revere, a superb silversmith by trade, and likewise a bellfounder, printer and engraver, was above all a fervid patriot. He galloped off to Concord, all along the way banging on doors, shouting and rousing the populace.

"The fate of a nation was riding that night."

His ride saved Sam Adams and John Hancock, who took to the woods. John Hancock was reputed to be the richest man in Boston. He owned a fleet of ships busily engaged in the smuggling business, which was both profitable and patriotic.

Revere started into Concord, but was arrested by British officers who had been sent by Gage to intercept such warnings. He was soon released, but his news had flown on ahead of him.

Paul Revere bringing news of the British troops. From *The American Revolution, The Picture Source Book*, by John Grafton, New York: Dover Books, 1975.

It was past midnight when the British troops approached Lexington. They had glimpsed scurrying figures in the woods, and heard gunfire and the ringing of bells, which was not reassuring. The darkness seemed alive with shadowy figures.

Colonel Francis Smith of the 10th Lincolnshires was in command. He is described as fat and slow-witted. Next in seniority was Major John Pitcairn of the Royal Marines. Though there were no marines on this detail, Pitcairn was well known and respected by the people, whatever their allegiance. Smith, perhaps at the suggestion of the not slow-witted Pitcairn, sent a courier back to Boston asking for reinforcements.

Shortly after sunrise the British troops reached Lexington, where they found some fifty grim, armed men standing on the village green. Pitcairn ordered the "rebels" to disperse. A shot was fired, but by whom is unknown. Pitcairn's report to Gage implies that the shot came from a straggler at the edge of the green, the British troops' order being "on no account to fire or even attempt it without orders." Then there was a volley from the British and eight of the minutemen fell dead. Seeing it was hopeless, the rest withdrew with their dead and wounded. The British troops started on towards Concord.

The men at Concord who had been waiting through the night for news from Lexington, were joined by minutemen from the town of Lincoln. A scout returned with the information that there had been fighting at Lexington, and so the men started towards that town. They had a fife and drum corps before them as they marched to an unknown fate. But a mile out of Concord they caught glimpses of the enemy, in their scarlet uniforms. There were far too many of them, they correctly judged, to be taken on by a hundred men. So they prudently turned, in good order, and with fife and drum before them, marched back to Concord. Romantic pictures of this small brigade are known to all.

The redcoats started after them. At Concord they encountered a larger group, the men having been joined by minutemen from nearby towns, Chelmsford, Carlisle, Acton and Sudbury. They stood, muskets at the ready, by the little bridge over the Concord River.

> *By the rude bridge that arched the flood,*
> *Their flag to April's breeze unfurled,*
> *Here once the embattled farmers stood,*
> *And fired the shot heard round the world.*

(With all due respect to Ralph Waldo Emerson, it seems that the famous shot was fired at Lexington.)

At the bridge the minutemen received a volley, and Captain Isaac Davis of the Acton company was the first to fall. At this the minutemen fanned out, returning

Off to the Battle of Concord. From *The American Revolution, The Picture Source Book*, by John Grafton, New York: Dover Books, 1975.

the fire accurately. Suddenly there was panic among the redcoats, and they broke and fled. (They had been marching all night.) The minutemen did not follow them, and by afternoon the British, having gathered their units together, started toward Lexington in retreat. As they left, the last file turned and fired a farewell volley.

By now the woods were alive with crackling muskets. The British soldiers were not used to this sort of warfare. One marched in orderly fashion, wearing one's bright red coat, stood with one's fellows in a neat row, and at a given signal fired at the enemy, also uniformed and standing in a neat row. War was waged between professionals, the civilian population slipping off to be out of the way. But here were farmers in homespun, in leather jerkins, in rags and patches, and coonskin caps—their work clothes—crouching behind trees, fences, rocks, stumps, picking off the wretched redcoats one by one.

"For a brief moment of history tiny Massachusetts stood alone at arms against an empire that had humbled France and Spain."[1]

Receiving the news of the Battle of Lexington. From *The American Revolution, The Picture Source Book*, **by John Grafton, New York: Dover Books, 1975.**

The relief sent for by Smith or Pitcairn now arrived. It was a large part of the British garrison, but it was of little use. Though there were now about 2,000 troops at Lexington, the retreat was resumed, the poor men hounded and harried by an enemy with whom they could not come to grips. The exhausted redcoats staggered back toward Boston. Two hundred and seventy-three of them had lost their lives. Of the Americans the count was 93. One wonders if the survivors fully realized what they had done—fired on the King's troops!—something almost as wicked as dumping tea into Boston Harbor.

When news of Lexington and Concord reached him, Israel Putnam, aged 58, was plowing his field in Pomfret, Connecticut. He had been in every war available to him since he was a child, and he was not going to miss this one. He left his plow right where it stood in a furrow and without changing his clothes, grabbed his flintlock and started off for the scene of action.

Within 24 hours thousands of farmers were on the road to Boston, carrying their flintlocks, muskets, blunderbusses—any arms they had—dressed in homespun and old caps and tricorns, provisions in sacks and bundles slung over their shoulders, with muddy boots, unshaven, uncouth, and doubtless unwashed. They came not only from Massachusetts, but from New Hampshire, Connecticut, and Rhode Island, a spontaneous uprising as was never seen before. A hundred years of "stupid, greedy bungling"[2] was paying Stepmother Britannia off. Within a few days there were some 16,000 men camped around Boston, and General Gage was besieged in the town, where he probably sat drinking tea with his American wife, whiling away the time in writing an account of the whole unfortunate affair as he awaited reinforcements.

Before his letter reached home, reinforcements arrived with three generals, Howe, Clinton, and Burgoyne. The number of their troops was now about 7,000.

May 10 drew near, the date set for the convening of the Second Continental Congress in Philadelphia.

18   FROM TICONDEROGA TO BUNKER HILL

Lake George is a thirty-mile-long finger lying between the foothills of the Adirondacks of New York and the Green Mountains of Vermont. At its northern end the lake narrows and empties into Lake Champlain, which is 125 miles long and extends into the Province of Quebec. The narrow place between the two lakes was the highway for anyone traveling in either direction: the key to the Hudson Valley to the south and the St. Lawrence to the north. The French, the British, the Americans and the Iroquois and Algonquin tribes all had fought here at various times.

In 1755 the French built a fort at this strategic spot, on the New York side of Lake George, and named it Fort Carillon. General Montcalm defended it against a large British force in 1758, but it took nearly a thousand men to do it.

The next year, however, Lord Jeffrey Amherst seized the fort and it was renamed Ticonderoga, after the nearby village. The British remained in their purloined fort for sixteen years—until the place was suddenly seized by Ethan Allen, a colonial, and his Green Mountain Boys, come over from the Vermont side of the lake. Allen was backed at a distance by Continental troops under Benedict Arnold.

Ethan Allen was a fiery young man of 36 who for years had been disputing the claims of "Yorkers," settlers under New York patents, who were encroaching on New England grants. He had organized the "Green Mountain Boys" to carry on the struggle, and the Governor of New York had put a price on his head. (The Green Mountain Boys were named after the Green Mountains of the territory they were defending, which is now Vermont. A fine reel, bearing their name, is still performed at country dances all over New England, and perhaps elsewhere.)

Capturing Ticonderoga proved easy. It was 3 A.M. and everyone was asleep, including the sentries. Allen thundered on the very door of the fort, and so the story goes, Captain Delaplace, the somewhat elderly man in command of the fort, asked on what authority he should open? Ethan's reply lives immortally because of the splendor of its anticlimax:

"Open in the name of the Great Jehovah and the Continental Congress!"

The surprised Captain opened the portal. He was in his nightshirt and carrying his breeches over his arm. Thus, Fort Ticonderoga fell to the colonials.

Then Allen and his 83 Green Mountain Boys proceeded northward a few miles and wrested Crown Point on Lake Champlain from the British garrison there. Crown Point was the fortification that guarded the approach to Montreal.

Allen sent a collection of captured flags to Philadelphia and they made fine decorations for the hall where the Continental Congress sat.

The Second Continental Congress, made up of the most distinguished men in America, convened in Philadelphia on schedule, on the very day of Ethan Allen's victory. It met this time in the old State House (now Independence Hall). The Honorable Peyton Randolph of Virginia was unanimously elected president of the Congress, and Charles Thomson of Philadelphia, secretary. (Thomson was a native of Londonderry and thus revolutionary by birth.)

The hope of creating unanimity out of so many diverse opinions looked bleak. The stirring events lately occurring in Massachusetts posed weighty problems, and the delegates ranged from conservative to radical. Conservatives like John Dickinson of Maryland, always opposed to independence (Dickinson refused to sign the Declaration of Independence when he had the chance), were pitted against men like Patrick Henry, who said, "Gentlemen, men may cry 'Peace, Peace!' but there is no peace! The war is actually begun! Our brethren are already in the field! Why should we stand idle?"

The conduct of affairs had been snatched from the hands of law-abiding dignitaries by the people themselves. All the delegates could do was to accept this accomplished fact. How to deal with the mother country in the face of this—steer the proper course in resisting her implacable attitude, with the war "actually begun"—was indeed a poser.

Opposite: **The Capture of Ticonderoga. "Open in the name of the Great Jehovah and the Continental Congress!" From** *The American Revolution, The Picture Source Book,* **by John Grafton, New York: Dover Books, 1975.**

John Dickinson persuaded the delegates to send another petition to the King, but nevertheless "A Declaration of the Causes and Necessity of Taking Up Arms," the joint work of himself and Thomas Jefferson, was passed. Colonel George Washington, who had attended all the sessions, towering over the others in his elegant uniform of blue and buff, never saying a word, was raised to the rank of general and appointed chief of all the American forces. The Continental Congress had got the word. Besides, there was no one else. On June 23, Washington set out for Massachusetts to assume command.

On the peninsula of Charlestown, across the River Charles from Boston, there are two hills, Breed's Hill and Bunker Hill. Breed's Hill is 62 feet high, but it is the nearer hill to Boston. Bunker Hill, behind it, is 110 feet high. A few days before Washington left Philadelphia, General Gage and the other generals who had recently come from England to his aid, woke up one fine morning and they found that both of these hills were occupied by the ragtag and bobtail crowd who had been camping in such numbers in the vicinity! And the hills commanded the town. What the four generals had been doing all this time is a question. Perhaps they were playing piquet.

Something had to be done, and just as the General had done something about Lexington and Concord (though it had turned out a debacle), he did something again. On the afternoon of June 17, under the command of General Howe, so lately arrived from overseas, 2,200 British regulars were ferried across the river and started to make a frontal attack on the American breastworks on Breed's Hill.

The motley Americans, ensconced on the hill, were not without leaders. General Artemus Ward was chief commander as head of the Massachusetts troops, and there were General Nathanael Greene of Rhode Island, and grisly General Israel Putnam, Lieutenant Colonel of the 11th Regiment of Connecticut, second in command and—Oh joy!—in another battle.

William Prescott, an officer in charge of erecting the fortifications on Breed's Hill, instructed his men with one short, explicit sentence. "Don't fire until you see the whites of their eyes." Officer Prescott was apparently quoting Prince Charles of Prussia at Jagerndorf, or Frederick the Great at Prague.

All was silence as the redcoats advanced up the hill. They were within fifty yards of the American breastworks when there was a tremendous burst of gunfire—and the advancing line was cut to ribbons. The whites of their eyes had been seen.

The British lines reformed, and two more attacks were made. On the third try the redcoats, what there was left of them, gained the breastworks. The Americans had to give way. They were out of powder, and retreated over the narrow neck of land into Charlestown.

The British found theirs was a Pyrrhic victory. General Howe lost all his staff. His white silk stockings were splashed with blood and had to be sent to the laundry!

One thousand and fifty-four of his men were dead. One eighth of all the British officers killed in the Revolution fell at Breed's Hill.

General Clinton said, "A dear bought victory. Another such would have ruined us." But the fact that untrained colonial troops could stand up to trained British regulars, and wreak such havoc upon them gave a tremendous boost to the spirit of the Americans.

Washington, when the news was brought to him, said simply, "The country is safe."

It threw such a scare into the British that they lay low for nine months.

The second Continental Congress went on sitting in Philadelphia. The delegates were at odds about what all the shooting was for. They announced on July 6: "We have not raised armies with the ambitious design of separating from Great Britain and establishing independent states," though Samuel Adams and Patrick Henry had other views.

Washington assuming command of the Continental Army under the revered Washington Elm, Cambridge, Massachusetts. A famous event that never took place.

Washington reached Cambridge, Massachusetts, two weeks after the Battle of Bunker Hill, to assume command of the Continental Army. But it was a moot point whether Yankees would accept a *Virginian* to command them. And so the General slipped unobtrusively into the encampment, and there is evidence that he attended a bachelor party that night, in which wine was consumed, nuts cracked, and rowdy songs sung.

The often depicted scene of Washington assuming command of the troops under the revered "Washington Elm" at Cambridge is pure fiction. No such ceremony took place.

Instead, the General began as if already installed. It was an accomplished fact before the troops realized it. These troops—easy-going but hard-fighting, of which the General first had a low opinion, calling them "an exceedingly dirty and nasty people," an unflattering remark which unfortunately leaked out to John Adams and other New England worthies—accepted their leader. There was something about the man . . . his martial dignity, his sheer presence. Everyone felt it.

A candid Englishman wrote home, "Not a king in Europe but would look like a *valet de chambre* at his side."

Mrs. John Adams, the bright and observant Abigail, met Washington at this time, and was bowled over. She wrote her husband in Philadelphia, quoting the Queen of Sheba on Solomon, "The half was never told me."

19   COMMON SENSE

He has taken the whiskers off their God.
—Thomas Wolfe, *Look Homeward, Angel*

After the Battle of Bunker Hill there was a pause. The British were stunned. They had lost too many men, and they had all to be transported three thousand miles over the sea, while the colonials were there on the spot. Nothing happened until the New Year. In January 1776, a pamphlet *Common Sense* by Thomas Paine appeared. Tom Paine was a born revolutionary, and an Englishman. He arrived in America in 1774 with letters of introduction from Benjamin Franklin, who was still in London. Paine's pamphlet convinced doubters, and bolstered those already convinced, that the colonies, in some 170 years, had outgrown any need for the mother country. A reconciliation with Britain, if possible, was no guarantee against renewal by Parliament of attacks on colonial liberties. If independent, America could trade with the whole world, do as she pleased, and keep out of Old World brawls. Paine's arguments were unanswerable. "A thirst for absolute power is the natural disease of monarchy." The pamphlet was read by everyone who could read, and those who couldn't had it read to them.

When copies of *Common Sense* reached England, Parliament ordered them burnt by the common hangman (a fate worse than death). Naturally this caused a huge demand. Copies were eagerly sought all over London, where people paid premium prices for a pamphlet they would otherwise never have known existed.

At King George's suggestion, Britain had entered into a contract with the Prince of Hesse and the Duke of Brunswick, heads of two German principalities, to hire mercenaries from them for the purpose of subduing "Britain's rebellious children in America." (The children, as it were, were now 170 years old.) The mercenaries were acquired for a flat fee of £7 apiece, and the Prince and the Duke were each to pocket a tidy little emolument of £11,000 a year as long as the mercenaries were in America. For those who were killed, or wounded beyond use, the Prince and the Duke received compensation—nothing for the men's families. It was nice to be a Prince or a Duke in those days. These poor hired chattels are the "Hessians" of American Revolutionary history, and it is pleasant to learn they were often of little use to King George. They were given to deserting, and thousands of them knew a good thing when they saw it. They never returned to their princely owners who valued them at £7 a piece, but became Americans and stayed in the land of the free.

When Ethan Allen and his Green Mountain Boys took Ticonderoga, they captured what Washington called "a noble train of artillery." The problem was to get it from Ticonderoga to Cambridge, Massachusetts, and this was accomplished by Colonel Henry Knox, on the face of it a most unlikely man to do anything of the sort. Henry Knox kept a little bookshop in Boston and he was on the fat side. But he had read his books on artillery and the use of cannon, and Washington made him Commander of Artillery.

Knox supervised hauling by oxen 59 pieces of ordnance from Ticonderoga to Cambridge, over the snow and ice and 200 miles of largely unbroken wilderness that lay between. It was a prodigious feat. Washington planned to use this noble train of artillery to good purpose. Common sense was working full time.

20   THE GODS INTERVENE

Stay not upon the order of your going,
But go at once.
—Macbeth, Act III, Scene 4

Southwest of Boston is Dorchester Neck, which extends into the harbor. On the night of March 4, 1776, Washington moved 3,000 men onto Dorchester Heights for the purpose of erecting fortifications. Since the ground was frozen too hard for digging, the men brought the material in wagons, thick logs four feet long, and heavy wooden frames, for ramparts. At 3 A.M., their mission accomplished, the 3,000 men retired across the causeway and were replaced by 2,400 fresh soldiers to occupy the fortifications.

General Howe, who had replaced General Gage, was informed during the night that there seemed to be activity on Dorchester Heights, but he believed that nothing could be done about it at the moment, and he would attend to it in the morning.

The dawn's early light revealed to the astonished General just how much had been done during the night. It was like Bunker Hill all over again! Howe had really to do something now, and he decided to indulge in another frontal attack (which had been a disaster before). He embarked a large force by ferries to land on Dorchester Heights to storm the fortifications. This was just what Washington wanted. While so much of Howe's army was engaged on Dorchester Heights Washington planned to enter the city and capture it.

But the gods intervened. The most terrifying storm in the memory of everyone burst upon Boston, and Howe had to call off his troops. Washington couldn't invade the city yet.

At that time there was a belief that any city within range of enemy cannon was untenable. And since it was hopeless to capture the cannon the only thing was to flee. The General was disinclined to face a possible second Bunker Hill and to have his freshly-laundered silk stockings splashed anew. Boston was abandoned in a crescendo of hysteria. The British dumped their cannon in the harbor, spiked their guns, burned the General's carriage so the Americans wouldn't get it, clambered into their ships and sailed away. The Americans entered the city unopposed, and Boston was never again occupied by a foreign power.

Opposite: **General Israel Putnam. Lith. and Pub. by J. Baillie.**

21   THE IRON SON OF '76

Putnam, scored with ancient scars,
The living record of his country's wars.
—Joel Barlow

When news of the evacuation of Boston reached Philadelphia, the delegates at the Continental Congress had not yet agreed about seceding from the Empire. Most of them were in favor, but Maryland and South Carolina were more conservative and did not feel there was sufficient justification for adopting "this ambitious design." New York wavered too. Each state had one vote, and it was felt that on this issue there should be unanimity.

The British, when they abandoned Boston, took with them hundreds of Loyalists, who dreaded their fate if left behind unprotected by the British army; and the whole fleet sailed to Halifax, Nova Scotia.

Washington was sure that when the British fleet returned it would head for New York. He dispatched a number of troops there, in command of General Israel Putnam, charged with the city's defenses. Washington was obliged to go to Philadelphia at the request of Congress for consultations.

Israel Putnam enjoyed Washington's trust, in spite of the fact that he was "a man of the people," with little education, being one of twelve children, and the opposite of Washington in suavity and polished manners. But he was rigidly dependable and his courage was boundless. In his youth he had entered a wolf's den and vanquished the animal in hand-to-hand (as it were) combat. This feat had made him famous.

Later, when on reconnaissance with a picket of 150 men in Connecticut, Putnam was surprised by a corps of 1,500 British dragoons foraging and laying waste farms and villages. Before so great a body of men he ordered his own men to seek safety in a nearby swamp inaccessible to cavalry, and urged his horse down a steep declivity, the side of a precipice, which legend turned into three flights of stairs. The enemy stood in astonishment. A bullet whizzed through his hat, but as he disappeared, if we know old Israel, he saluted the dragoons with one hand and thumbed his nose at them with the other.

General Putnam did not have the dignity of General Washington. Bullets had whizzed about him since he was a boy, and none had ever hit him. He bore a charmed life. He was the one who had driven the sheep over the roads from Pomfret, Connecticut, to Boston when the British closed the port.

An eminent British source states of the old fellow: "His fame in Indian wars, his personal courage, bluff heartiness and good fellowship made him an idol of the rank and file, and he is one of the popular heroes in American history."[1]

22   DECISIONS! DECISIONS!

In Philadelphia Washington told the Congress that the army needed strengthening. He had 19,000 poorly trained troops, and no money at all. But the Continental Congress had no money either, nor any power to tax. It had called on the colonies to raise troops at the outset of the war, and these formed the Continental Army, of which Washington was in command.

There was nothing to do but issue paper money, more and more of it. Not to be outdone by the Congress, the colonies issued their own paper money. It looked pretty, but like the Continental Congress' money it had nothing whatever behind it. An immense inflation naturally followed, and the Continental Congress' money is enshrined to this day in an idiom of American speech to indicate worthlessness: "Not worth a Continental."

Besides financial problems, the Congress had political ones. In view of the fact that war was actually going on, was it not time to abandon all pretense of trying to compromise with Britain, and openly declare independence? And if they did so, would that bring active support from France, Britain's archenemy, still seething over the treaty of 1763 in which she lost New France and a lot more? And as for the populace: they had embraced the "loyal protest" of the colonies, but how would they react to an outright break with Britain? The Congress had to make up its mind.

Richard Henry Lee, one of the Virginia delegation, laid before that body a resolution: The colonies should be free and independent states. This was on June 7. The resolution was given to a committee composed of Benjamin Franklin, John Adams, Thomas Jefferson, Robert R. Livingston and Roger Sherman. They were overwhelmingly in favor of it.

Thomas Jefferson was handed the job of writing the Declaration. Writing was one of Thomas Jefferson's many fortes. So were architecture, science, history, philosophy, astronomy and various other lines, but he could not speak in public. He also lacked a sense of humor; but this was not needed now.

Anthony Trollope, writing in 1862, said of this famous document, "The opening and close of this declaration have in them much that is grand and striking; the greater part of it, however, is given up to enumerating, in paragraph after paragraph, the sins committed by George III against the colonies. Poor George III! There is no one now to say a good word for him; but of all those who have spoken ill of him, this declaration is loudest in its censure." (But, Mr. Trollope, the colonies had more grievances than anyone else!)

There is magic in the lines of the Declaration of Independence, so that such a statement as "all men are created equal" is not at first observed to be ideal rather than real. And the inalienable rights men are declared to possess in that great doc-

"Drafting The Declaration of Independence," engraving
by an unidentified artist after the painting by Chappel.
Reproduced by permission of the National Portrait Gallery, Smithsonian Institution, Washington, D.C.

Congress Voting Independence. **Stipple engraving by Edward Savage. "The Congress of Buckles."**

ument are anything but inalienable. The rights of the weak have been alienated by the strong throughout history.

The Declaration of Independence has deep roots. Closest is the Virginia Declaration of Rights, for which George Mason, a liberal, affluent and influential Virginia planter, must be thanked. The Virginia Declaration of Rights was adopted by the Virginia Convention in Williamsburg June 12, 1776, just twenty days before that famous Fourth of July when the American Declaration of Independence was adopted in Philadelphia. In it Mason stated "All men are by nature equally free and independent and have certain inherent rights, the enjoyment of life and liberty, the means of acquiring and possessing property, the right of trial by jury, the right not to be deprived of liberty except by law of the land or the judgment of one's peers"—and these come directly down from the Magna Carta (1215).

The Declaration of Independence is certainly grand and stirring, and was for many years read aloud at patriotic functions on every Fourth of July, the date it was adopted.

John Hancock, as president of the Congress, was the first to sign, which he did in great big letters, saying, "King George can read that without his spectacles!" "John Hancock" is thus a facetious synonym in America for one's signature when asked to sign documents (e.g., "Kindly put your John Hancock here.").

The Declaration was read to the populace in front of the State House, and the bell in the tower was rung. This huge bell, cast in London in 1752, happened to have around its rim the text from Leviticus XXV:10, "Proclaim liberty throughout all the land unto all the inhabitants thereof." It was remarkably apropos. Benjamin Franklin, as might be expected, made the most sensible remark. "We must all hang together," he said, "or we will all hang separately."

23   THE WISEST AMERICAN

Although one thinks of Benjamin Franklin as the epitome of Philadelphia, he was born in Boston (1706), the son of a tallow-chandler. He left school at ten and was apprenticed to his half-brother, a printer. Dissatisfied, he left for Philadelphia when he was seventeen. He entered the city eating a "great puffy roll," as he tells us in his autobiography—one of the great autobiographies of American literature.

It would take a book merely to list his achievements. Printer, publisher, writer, inventor (of the Franklin stove, bifocal spectacles, lightning rod, and glass harmonica[1]), scientist and discoverer (of the nature of lightning through his famous experiment with a kite and a key in a thunderstorm, and of the Gulf Stream, of which he drew the first map), diplomat *par excellence*, and statesman—he has been called "the wisest American." His sayings in *Poor Richard's Almanac*, which he published for 25 years, are standard proverbs. They praise honesty, prudence, common sense. He also reorganized the post office and made it pay!

Wise, witty and urbane, Franklin was popular with the most brilliant men of France—and the wittiest women. He adroitly charmed the French into declaring war against Britain. One of the greatest of the Founding Fathers, his is a great name in France as well as in America. An engraving made of him in France after

Opposite: **Benjamin Franklin at Versailles. Reproduced from the Collections of the Library of Congress. Ben seems dazzled by the homage, Louis the Sixteenth is astonished and only Marie Antoinette keeps her aplomb.**

the French Revolution bears the inscription, in French and Latin, "He took the lightning from the Heavens and the scepter from tyrants."

Other American commissioners sent to France were not such men of the world. John Adams, from deep in the heart of Puritan New England, was shocked when he reached Paris. Members of the aristocracy, far from being formal as one might suppose, were extraordinarily free and easy in their behavior. Guests came and went from the great houses as they pleased. It was all terribly nonchalant. A respectable lady sits beside Dr. Franklin, an arm around his shoulder, laughing and joking! And Dr. Franklin appears to be enjoying himself! It was never like this in Quaker Philadelphia.

John Adams was annoyed at the British attitude toward him: "fanatic, bigot, perfect Cypher—awkward figure—uncouth dress—no address, no character," was bad enough, but to say he was disgusted with the Parisians made him angry, for he had quickly come round. "I admire the Parisians enormously," he wrote Abigail. "They are the happiest people in the world. . . . If I had your ladyship and our little folks here and no Politics to plague me and a Hundred Thousand Livres a Year Rent I should be the happiest being on earth."

It is well that the Parisians were having such a good time. In ten years many of them were to have their heads chopped off.

24   UNLADYLIKE BEHAVIOR

The daughter of a hundred earls,
You are not one to be desired.
—Tennyson, *Lady Clara Vere de Vere*

Washington, having told Congress the bad news that he needed more troops and money, returned to New York. Some of the British fleet that had fled Boston began turning up in New York's lower bay on July 2, 1776. On the 9th, five days after it was adopted by the Congress, Washington received a copy of the Declaration of Independence, and had it read to his troops. He watched narrowly the reaction of his men. There were cheers!

More British ships were appearing in the bay, but this did not deter the enthusiasm of the civilians. Bonfires were lighted, and crowds rushed to Bowling Green in the center of which stood an equestrian statue of George III made of lead. It was torn down amid whoops and yells, hacked to pieces and sent to Litchfield, Connecticut, where it was melted down into 42,088 bullets for the Continental Army

Tearing down the statue of George III in Bowling Green,
New York. From *The American Revolution, The Picture
Source Book by John Grafton*, New York: Dover Books, 1975.

by the patriotic ladies of the town. British officers began hastily getting out of town,
as did most of the Tory residents.

By July 12 New York harbor was alive with ships, hundreds of men-of-war,
bringing 32,000 men—one third of them, those hired Hessians come to subdue
King George's children, now turned rebels and traitors. When Washington surveyed

this huge armada he was looking at the largest expeditionary force of the 18th Century. The fleet was under the command of Lord Richard Howe, elder brother of General Sir William Howe who had had his silk stockings splattered with blood at Bunker Hill. The men were landed on Staten Island, a fertile track of land fifty miles square in the bay and an ideal place for a British base.

Admiral Lord Howe was an affable gentleman. He said he bore no grudge against the Americans and hoped that the show of such a huge force would convince them that the only sensible thing to do was to lay down their arms and prove that at heart they were still loyal subjects of the King. Lord Howe had a conference with commissioners of the Congress and offered them the alternative of submission and a royal pardon, or to battle against overwhelming odds. The Americans, with their poorly equipped troops, which now numbered about 23,000, and with no navy and no money, without hesitation chose continued war. Britannia was *persona non grata* in the colonies due to that lady's unladylike behavior for over a hundred years.

Admiral Lord Howe, the belted Earl, ensconced himself with his brother the General, on Staten Island, and the cold war continued.

Washington needed information about the plans of the British, and a school-teacher named Nathan Hale, 21 years old, an officer in the Connecticut militia, volunteered for the dangerous mission. His disguise as a schoolmaster, which is what he was, did not save him; he was caught and summarily hanged. His reported last words made his fame: "I regret that I have but one life to give to my country." There is a statue of this national hero in City Hall Park, New York. Not knowing what he looked like, the sculptor, Frederick MacMonnies, depicted him as a hand-some young man with his hands tied behind him. (In World War II a patriotic citizen whose wife joined the WACS said bravely, "I regret that I have but one wife to give to my country.")

The British forces, under General Howe's command, landed near the southern tip of Long Island (Brooklyn Heights), and the Battle of Long Island took place August 27-28, 1776.

It was a terrible rout for the Americans; over a thousand died. Then Wash-ington performed what the British themselves called "a miracle of strategy." This miracle was achieved with the cooperation of a regiment of fishermen from Mar-blehead, Massachusetts, under Colonel John Glover, who ferried 9,500 men, their provisions, equipment, horses and cannon, across the East River to Manhattan, under cover of night and a thick fog.

From then on it was disaster and retreat. Up the island the fortunes of war advanced: the Battle of Harlem, not much more than a skirmish, and the Battle of White Plains, another defeat from which the Americans escaped, moving silently by night.

25   TRAITOR NUMBER ONE

Charles Lee, who now enters the story, is the second nastiest man in the history of the United States.

He was an Englishman, and believed himself to be a military genius, so others thought so too. He had served in the British Army as a major general, but after writing radical pamphlets, and insulting George III to his face, he found it expedient to settle in America, where he had formerly been active in General Braddock's ill-fated expedition against Fort Duquesne. Lee's military reputation earned him a commission in the Continental Army.

He is described as "tall, emaciated, dirty of clothes, voluble, foul-mouthed." He had one redeeming feature—he was devoted to small dogs, of which he had many. Twelve he named after the Apostles, and the other three after the Trinity ("*Sit,* Holy Ghost!"). Each wore a collar with its name in large letters. Their master drank out of the same bowl with them, observing that a dog had never poisoned anyone. He was of that almost extinct breed, a true eccentric, but he was unprincipled. It was galling to be a mere major general under the command of an amateur like Washington, whom he despised.

Forts had been built (actually earthworks) on either side of the Hudson—Fort Washington (where 180th street is now found), and Fort Lee opposite on the New Jersey Palisades, with cannon trained on the river to prevent British vessels passing up stream. A chain of boats with spikes was sunk here, further to hinder British shipping, but ships passed safely over the spikes, and evaded the cannon.

Due to the activities of General Howe, and the movements of his army at Dobb's Ferry and elsewhere, Washington sent 5,000 men across to New Jersey under the command of our stalwart old friend General Israel Putnam, leaving Lee with 7,000 men at North Castle, above Fort Washington. He advised General Greene, in command of both forts, to abandon them as useless. They were now within the British lines.

General Greene should have followed Washington's advice. Fort Washington was taken, with 2,500 prisoners, and renamed Fort Knyphausen in honor of the Hessian general who led the assault.

"This sort of glory, won by German mercenaries against freeborn English subjects has no charms for me," said Edmund Burke in Parliament.

The Revolutionary war was not popular with much of the English public, who saw themselves warring with their own kith and kin; it was Parliament, the King and his ministers who were pursuing the war with grim determination, and no sense.

Washington had waited to see whether Howe would strike northward along the Hudson, or south towards Philadelphia. Howe turned south, and Washington ordered Lee to come with reinforcements.

Lee disregarded Washington's orders and stayed where he was with his 7,000 troops—more than Washington commanded. The opportunity seemed to open up for him to make a brilliant maneuver (with his military genius), put the seemingly beaten Washington in disgrace, and displace him as commander-in-chief of the Continental Army. But on December 13 he found it expedient to follow Washington's orders. He crossed to New Jersey and allowed himself to be captured by a squad of thirty British soldiers in a farmhouse at Basking Ridge. He was taken to New York, and eventually exchanged for a high-ranking officer.

Washington had hoped for new recruits for his army in New Jersey, but few were forthcoming. He had only 5,000 men with short-term enlistments. And General Howe was now after him with a superior force with indefinite enlistments. Howe continued his pursuit, conquering as he went, all across New Jersey. Reaching Trenton, Washington made for the banks of the Delaware. He had sent officers and men ahead, from as far back as New Brunswick, with orders to collect every boat within twenty miles of Trenton. With these the American army crossed the Delaware just as a Hessian brigade entered Trenton with a brass band blaring. And there being no more boats, the Hessians could go no further.

But Philadelphia was lost, and the members of the Continental Congress packed their bags, gathered up their papers, and fled to Baltimore.

26   LOADED DICE

Is it not fine to fling against loaded dice
Yet to win once or twice?
—Elinor Wylie, *Hughie at the Inn*

This was America's darkest hour. Congress had fled. Washington, his staff, including General Greene, and his men were shivering on the banks of the Delaware, badly clothed and badly equipped. Thomas Paine, who was there shivering too, sat down and wrote in *The Crisis*, "These are the times that try men's souls."

The river threatened to freeze over, making it easy for the British to cross in pursuit and destroy the little army. Washington came to a desperate decision. Late on Christmas night, amid sleet, wind and blocks of ice, he led his 2,300 men over the river back to the New Jersey shore.

The painting, *Washington Crossing the Delaware* (or, "Sit Down, You're Rocking the Boat"), painted by Emanuel Leutze, a naturalized American, in Dusseldorf in 1851, is too well known to be reproduced here. This perhaps best known of American patriotic pictures has a decidedly German look and is full of historical inaccuracies.

Next morning at Trenton, which they had so lately fled, the Americans fell upon the Hessians who were sleeping off their Christmas carrousings and had terrible headaches. Nine hundred and eighteen of these myrmidons were captured and their leader killed. It was Washington's first resounding success.

The captured Hessians were exchanged for American prisoners held in prison ships in New York harbor, where conditions were indescribable. Though thus emptied, the ships were soon filled again.

The most notorious of this infamous fleet of prison ships was the *Jersey*, anchored in Wallabout Bay for three and a half years. In ten weeks more than 1,500 men died of smallpox and starvation, and some believe more than 10,000 perished. The British would not let the ill and dying be put ashore, and the dead were buried along the Brooklyn waterfront. In one instance the prisoners were kept for three days without food, and then bread was brought them. It was poisoned, and their sufferings were soon over.

Sir William Howe was having a happy time in New York with his mistress, a Mrs. Loring, while this infamy went on. Of them all it seems as if Gentleman Johnny Burgoyne was the only British general in America with a shred of humanity.

But the Americans were not entirely unbesmirched when it came to the vile treatment of prisoners of war. In Connecticut, west of Hartford, there is an abandoned copper mine (in the town of East Granby), a precipitous descent down ladders and over perpendicular ledges, and here British prisoners were held in darkness under barbarous conditions. The abandoned mine is known as "Newgate Prison," in tender memory of the one in London, and can be visited for a fee.

Lord Cornwallis, second in command under Howe, had packed his bags thinking the war was over, but with the events at Trenton, he had to unpack.

Washington followed up his success by marching on Princeton and defeating three British regiments. Cornwallis withdrew in a panic to the town of New Brunswick, where the British stores were in jeopardy, and Washington moved on to Morristown and went into winter quarters. It seemed, by tacit agreement, that there would be no more war until the weather improved.

27   THAT CHARMING YOUNG FRENCHMAN

The young Marquis de Lafayette had been fired by the remarks of the Duke of Gloucester about the worthiness of the American cause when they met at Metz. Overcoming immense difficulties, he acquired a ship, signed up a dozen of his friends as romantic as he, and sailed from Bordeaux for America in April 1777. They all bore commissions in the American Army, or thought they did, given them by Silas Deane, a diplomatic agent sent to France by the Continental Congress, who had no authority to commission anybody, nor is there any proof that he ever did. It was one of those unfortunate misunderstandings. When Lafayette and his companions reached Philadelphia and called on the Congress late in July, they were coldly received in the street.

Then Lafayette wrote a letter to Congress offering to serve without pay as a volunteer. Congress, amazed at this, took another look at the young Frenchman's credentials, and a letter arrived from Benjamin Franklin saying that the young man "is a young nobleman of great family and great wealth. He is exceedingly beloved and everybody's good wishes attend him." Franklin asked Congress to do something special for him. Congress made Lafayette a major general but decided to thank his friends and send them home expenses paid. They left in a great and understandable huff, but Lafayette retained three of them as aides.

Lafayette met Washington for the first time at a dinner in Philadelphia, and there was an immediate rapport. Lafayette wrote in his memoirs, "the majesty of his countenance and of his figure made it impossible not to recognize him, he was especially distinguished by the affability of his manners and the dignity with which he addressed those about him."

The charming young Frenchman made an immediate strong impression upon Washington. To the childless man he took on the image of a son; Lafayette's father was dead. Cut adrift in a new world to which he had come against the wishes of his family (his father-in-law had tried to have him locked up in the Bastille to prevent his leaving, and he had escaped to Bordeaux in disguise), he found a father. Washington invited him to make his home at his headquarters.

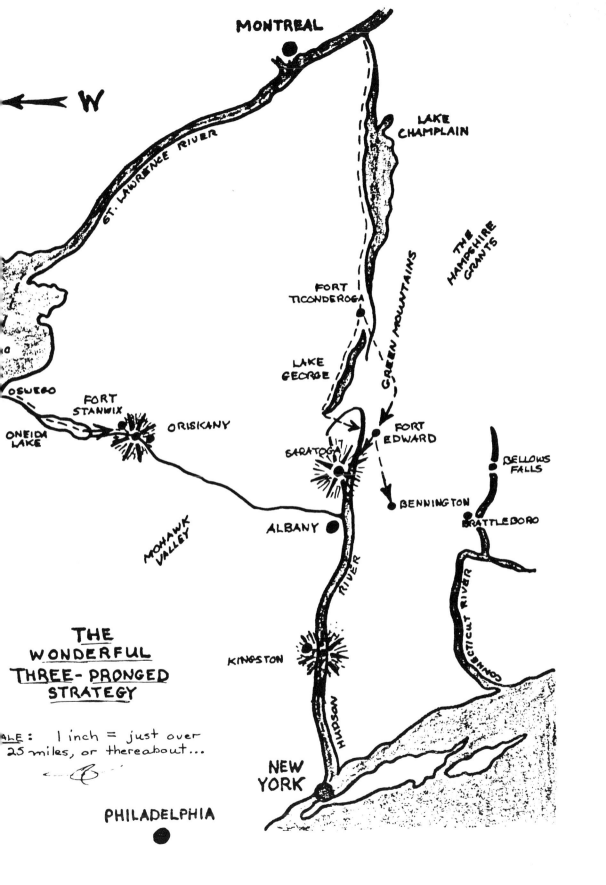

28 PASTURES NEW

To be commenced in stronds afar remote.
—*King Henry the Fourth, Part One*, Act 1, Scene 1

In London nothing was known of conditions in North America. The strategists conceived that terrain to be a continuation of the gentle counties of England, Surrey or Kent for instance, with their rolling hills and civilized landscape. But America was mostly wild virgin forests trod only by Indians.

The war was being directed by the War Minister, Lord George Germain, back in London, 3,000 miles away. A letter might take from a month to five weeks or so to reach its destination. It was a leisurely age; there was no way to speed things up.

But aside from the British dislike of warring in winter, especially an American winter, there were plans hatching in London for a different approach to the problem from the one pursued so far with less than satisfactory results.

The plan was to conquer New York by seizing the forts along the Hudson, thus cutting New England off from the colonies to the south. General Burgoyne, who is believed to have concocted this plan, was to march down from Canada via Lake Champlain and the Hudson Valley with an army of some 9,000 regulars, Hessians, Canadians and Indians, to Albany. This was Part One of the plan.

Lieutenant St. Leger was to come eastward from Lake Ontario through the Mohawk Valley and join Burgoyne in Albany. This was Part Two of the Plan.

Part Three was for General Howe to lead, or send, forces up from New York to join the other two. Thus the country would be rendered limb from limb, and helpless. This is called Strategy, and what is a war without Strategy, no matter how ridiculous?

None of this fine, three-pronged Strategy worked. Nobody got to Albany.

Washington was waiting for new enlistments for the campaign of 1777 and wondering why Howe, comfortably returned to New York, did not come out and put an end to his little army, which now numbered about 4,000. Morristown was only forty miles from New York.

For General Howe, with a force of 27,000 men, and the service of his brother's (the Admiral's) fleet, all assembled in New York, the way to seize the Hudson was to go there; but whether or not Howe was fully apprised of Burgoyne's plan, or what his part in it was to be, has been a matter of dispute ever since. His dearest wish was to take Philadelphia, the seat of the Continental Congress. This would so dismay the country that the war effort would collapse—or so he thought—and laurels and acclaim would be his.

It was said in London that Lord Germain, the War Minister, whose duty it was to coordinate all these plans, dictated a letter to Howe, and then rushed off for some holiday or other, or for grouse-shooting, and his secretary stowed the letter away in a pigeon-hole, and rushed off too. The tiresome American problem was swept under the rug and forgotten.

Howe, however, had some knowledge of the great strategy, for he ordered General Clinton to proceed with forces up the Hudson toward Albany, while he felt free to pursue his dream of capturing Philadelphia. To achieve this dream, instead of marching to the City of Brotherly Love, a distance of ninety miles, which could be covered in three or four days without undue trouble, Howe set sail in a fine flotilla supplied by his brother (the Howe boys enjoyed a close family relationship). The flotilla sailed for Hampton Roads and up Chesapeake Bay, becalmed much of the time. The voyage managed to take five weeks, and when the General did disembark with his troops, at the Head of Elk, he was still fifty miles from Philadelphia. An Englishman has observed of this cruise, "Britannia has rarely ruled the waves in so leisurely a manner.[1] (Forty miles in five weeks! Aesop's tortoise would have done better.)

Colonel Harry St. Leger had moved up the St. Lawrence to Oswego on Lake Ontario and then across country to lay seige to Fort Stanwix in Mohawk country, New York, which he reached on August 7, expecting a great uprising of Loyalists. (The British were forever expecting great uprisings of Loyalists, which somehow never materialized.)

General Nicholas Herkimer, marching to the relief of Stanwix with his militia, was ambushed at Oriskany Creek by Mohawk braves and received a mortal wound, but heroically continued to direct the battle. Benedict Arnold, with a small force, was also on the way to relieve Stanwix. He spread false rumors of a huge continental army approaching, and the Mohawks fled. St. Leger abandoned the siege of the fort, and retired to Canada.

And General Burgoyne, "Gentleman Johnny," struggling southward from Montreal with his heterogeneous army—his hosts of camp followers of both sexes, his mistress (wife of his commissary officer), the wives of other officers (who snubbed the mistress), their pet dogs, and his baggage train many miles long, loaded with dress uniforms, feminine finery, champagne, brandy (no caviar for the General?), provender for some 9,000 people for an indefinite length of time, military supplies and far too many pieces of ordnance—began to bog down in the thickness of the Adirondack forests. (The sobriquet, "Gentleman Johnny," seems to have been invented by Bernard Shaw in his comedy *The Devil's Disciple*, produced in 1897, and now is firmly attached to the hapless general.)

This absurd caravan included, besides the British regulars, the 400 Indians, the Germans ("Hessians"), musicians, cooks, etc. a German baroness (wife of Baron Riedesel, who commanded the Germans), their three little girls in lace drawers and ruffles, lords and ladies, and several members of Parliament come to see the fun

General Herkimer directing the Battle of Oriskany. From
The American Revolution: The Picture Source Book by John
Grafton, New York: Dover Books, 1975.

in their silks and satins, perukes and periwigs and buckled shoes. They rode in
calashes, a kind of two-wheeled cart without springs. Due to the wild terrain, however, they must have often preferred to founder through the North Woods afoot,
stumbling over fallen trees, tripped up by roots, holes and twining vines. This unique
expeditionary force presents us with one of the farces of history.

Burgoyne began losing artillery, and many of his two-wheeled wagons broke
and had to be abandoned. It is said they carried enough for an army of 50,000.
Thirty wagons, it was averred, served to transport Gentleman Johnny's wardrobe
and cellar, and if so, one hopes that none of these was among the casualties.

The grand cavalcade, which started out early in June, finally arrived at Ticonderoga early in July.

General Clinton, supposed to comprise the third prong of the Strategy, had finally pulled himself together and started up the Hudson on October 2, two months after Howe had started for Philadelphia, and three months since Burgoyne left Montreal. When Clinton got as far as Kingston, eighty miles south of Saratoga, he came to the conclusion that he lacked sufficient troops, and started back to New York. Thus Gentleman Johnny was abandoned by two of the "prongs."

Ticonderoga, held by a small garrison under Major Arthur St. Clair, was evacuated in the face of Burgoyne's redcoats, Hessians and Indians on July 6, and St. Clair led his men to Fort Edwards on the Hudson to reinforce the northern army under General Snyder. Ticonderoga was Burgoyne's only victory, earned without any fighting.

But the going was rough. The Indians, finding there was to be no scalping— or any other such fun, the general forbade it—began decamping with all the whisky and blankets they could grab. The New York militia, the Green Mountain Boys, men from all over New England, "swarmed about him like hornets" and had to be driven off.

From Ticonderoga Burgoyne sent a detachment of unmounted German heavy dragoons with Colonel Baum and 300 Canadians and Indians into the New Hampshire grants (later Vermont) where his scouts informed him there were rich stores of foodstuffs, cattle and horses in the town of Bennington. Gentleman Johnny thought that these conquering troops, laden down with all the Bennington plunder, could then march over the mountains of Vermont to Bellow's Falls on the Connecticut River, down river to Brattleboro, and, thence, back cross-country to Albany, collecting more loot as they went along—a rough distance of 200 miles as the crow flies. But the troops were not crows, nor were the horses and cattle they were supposed to seize, without resistance of course. This was to be accomplished in two weeks, or, as Gentleman Johnny and everyone else at the time would have said, a fortnight. Then they would rendezvous and rejoice in Albany.

29   A BASIC FACT IGNORED

Our notice "Trespassers will be prosecuted" is the most venerable formula that we have.
—W. M. Flinders Petrie, *Social Life in Ancient Egypt*

Among many things that Gentleman Johnny Burgoyne did not know were the geography, history and politics of the region he was sending his hapless men to invade, as Horace Walpole caustically observed, "with a hop, step and jump." The inhabitants were an unusually tough mixture of farmers, hunters, backwoodsmen and homesteaders who had defied New York when they had settled on the disputed land grants claimed by New York. They were ready to give short shrift to any invaders of their territory, foreign or domestic; they had organized a state of their own, unrecognized by Congress, which did not wish to affront or alienate the rich and powerful state of New York; they had gone so far as to coin money. Independence was their middle name in extra large type.

It is curious that it never seemed to occur to the British invaders that there might be obstacles in their path in the form of opposition. They entertained the belief, again and again, that Loyalists would rise in great numbers to embrace them with joy, due to their devotion to that divine monarch, appointed by God, George III. It appeared impossible to disabuse them of this curious fallacy.

John Stark was an old soldier. He had seen action on the Plains of Abraham and at Bunker Hill, and was with Washington at Trenton and Princeton, but, becoming disgruntled over the promotions of others, he returned to his farm in New Hampshire. As he would be in command of the New Hampshire militia, the Green Mountain Boys, independent of Congress, he buckled on his sword when called upon, and exclaimed, "We'll beat the bastards today, or Molly Stark will be a widow tonight!"

Gentleman Johnny complained, "Wherever the King's forces point, militia to the number of three or four thousand assemble in a few hours." He was beginning to learn.

Although there were not that many at Bennington, John Stark led his Green Mountain Boys out to meet "the King's forces," and on August 16 killed or captured the whole lot.

The Hessians' overcoats were long, their swords tripped them up, and their clumsy German boots, weighing twelve pounds the pair, were no help. Two hundred and seven were killed, 700 taken prisoner, and only nine escaped. An army of rustics had defeated a much greater force of experienced soldiers.

Congress made it up to John Stark by creating him a brigadier general, and presented him with a splendid uniform, which one hopes fitted.

And though Molly did not become a widow that night, the road that leads from Bennington over the Green Mountains of Vermont, eastward to Brattleboro on the Connecticut River, is today, the Molly Stark Highway.

Burgoyne, despite losing over a thousand men between Bennington and the St. Leger fiasco in the Mohawk Valley, was as jaunty and unperturbed as ever. He crossed the Hudson to the west bank on September 13, bound for the great reunion at Albany. Now in rich farming country where there was plenty of ripening wheat, corn and apples for men and horses, he still found the going tough. Annoyingly, the Americans had felled trees across the roads and destroyed bridges, and his circus procession (lacking only elephants) was able to progress but a mile or two a day. Burgoyne had to carry with him provisions for nearly 10,000 people, and it is a wonder he ever got anywhere. (The logistics of this campaign are mind-boggling.) One hundred and eighty Canadian *bateaux* (flat-bottomed boats) were required, and had to be hauled by horses and oxen over the portages between the two lakes and the Hudson.

The resounding victory at Bennington put new spirit into the patriots, and hundreds of men showed up at the headquarters of General Gates, whom Congress had put in command of the Northern Army. The place was called Bemis Heights or Freeman's Farm, and was south of the town of Saratoga, in the colony or state of New York (depending on which side one favored).

Horatio Gates was an Englishman, a godson of Horace Walpole, and had fought with the British army in the French and Indian wars, after which he bought an estate and settled in Virginia. He seems to have been promoted into positions beyond his capacities.

Burgoyne, arriving at Freeman's Farm, found he could not proceed to Albany due to the provoking fact of Gates and his army barring the way. He then occupied a hill commanding Gates' position; and though Gates outnumbered Burgoyne two to one, he refused to make a move. General Benedict Arnold, back from Fort Stan-wix, begged to "begin the game," and Gates reluctantly consented on September 19. Arnold was joined by General Daniel Morgan, and they both acted with great daring. Morgan's "turkey-call" pierced the din, for he used such an instrument, meant to decoy turkeys with a "gobble-gobble," to rally his famous regiment of crack marksmen ("Morgan's Riflemen") who, perched in trees, picked off the officers identified by their uniforms. General Burgoyne headed a column and also acted with great daring. At sunset the battle was over. The British still held the field, and both sides had lost between 500 and 600 men.

30   THE STRATEGY FIZZLES

Burgoyne's situation grew worse. His communications with Canada were cut by a force of New England militia under John Stark, he was running low on provisions, his foraging parties were menaced, his field hospital full of sick and wounded, the weather was growing nippy, and the men's winter clothing had been left at Ticon-deroga in expectation of a walk-over at Albany.

Among Burgoyne's problems was lack of news from General Howe, who would soon be prancing and pirouetting in the non-Quaker ballrooms of Philadelphia. General Clinton, who on Howe's orders had advanced up the Hudson and reached Kingston, about eighty miles south of Saratoga, had decided to return to New York for reinforcements, as we have seen. Thus Burgoyne was abandoned by both of his colleagues in this wonderful three-pronged Strategy, and left to fight it out alone.

Undaunted, the man attempted to reprieve his losses at the Second Battle of Freeman's Farm on October 7. Arnold, without Gates' permission, threw himself into the battle with reckless abandon. "He acted like a madman," one of his adversaries reported; Arnold had been drinking. The British were driven back. Two of their generals were mortally wounded, one taken prisoner, and Gentleman Johnny got shot through his hat and had his waistcoat torn. The Hessians were a disappointment. Some went to the rear; others surrendered. Burgoyne was thrown back and suffered heavy losses.

For Burgoyne it was a rout. He now had less than 6,000 men, his means of retreat were cut off, and he knew the jig was up. Debonair as ever, he sat amid the roar of cannon and the stench of corpses, drinking champagne with his mistress on his knee. The unpleasant task of burying the dead was sloppily performed, fifteen or twenty bodies being thrust into a common grave, arms and legs sometimes protruding above ground. (Officers were put into a hole by themselves.) The German baroness, Madame Riedesel thought Burgoyne had lost his mind; but he didn't care anymore; he had done his best. He sent a flag of truce to Gates and asked for terms.

A lengthy correspondence with Gates about the terms of surrender took place, for at this period protocol and agenda were of the utmost importance, down to the last niggling detail. On October 16, 1777, the articles were signed.

The next day General Burgoyne and his officers marched, with drums beating and the honors of war, to meet General Gates. Gates "was gravely unobtrusive in plain blue," but Gentleman Johnny was wearing a rich royal uniform of splendid scarlet and "a hat with streaming plumes." (English gentlemen have always known how to dress.) Gentleman Johnny surrendered six generals, 300 other officers, and 5,500 troops.

"The fortunes of war, General Gates, have made me your prisoner." Gates replied, "I shall always be ready to bear testimony that it has not been through any fault of your Excellency." Gates made up for his lack of panache by doing one thing in high style—he refused Burgoyne's proffered sword. He did more. His troops remained within their lines until the British had piled their arms. "Every circumstance was avoided which could give the appearance of triumph." The British sick and wounded were cared for, and the wants of the vanquished officers and men liberally supplied.

General Gates, however, in his report to Congress, made no mention of Arnold and Morgan, to whom the victory was due, and he did not trouble to inform General Washington, his chief, of his victory at all.

He wrote his wife: "Burgoyne and his whole army have laid down their arms. . . . Thanks to the Giver of all victories for this triumphant success." He gloated

The Surrender of Burgoyne by John Trumbull. From the collections of the Architect of the Capitol and the Library of Congress.

a bit over his distinguished prisoners. "Major General Philips, who wrote me that saucy note last year from St. John's, Lord Petersham, Major Akland, son of Sir Thomas, and his lady, daughter of Lord Ilchester, sister to the famous Lady Susan, and about a dozen members of Parliament, Scotch lords, & c. . . . If old England is not by this lesson taught humility, then she is an obstinate old Slut, bent upon her ruin."

Not to leave the gentry abandoned on the banks of the Hudson in their (surely by now) tattered silks and satins, we must record the pleasant fact that these people were housed, fed and entertained by the American gentry whose guests they, willy-nilly, found themselves. They were royally treated, though officially enemies, all the way to New York, where they could seek passage home. Nobody was impolite enough to tell them what jackasses they were, and besides they probably knew it already.

Britain enjoyed a remarkably free press, much of it in the hands of the radical opposition, and after Saratoga there were long continued post mortems. Where should the blame for the debacle be fixed? Was it the fault of Burgoyne, Howe or Lord Germain, the War Minister? *The Morning Post* suggested it was the immense and complex supply train, sufficient for 50,000, that slowed things down.

Finally a satirical correspondent in *The Morning Chronicle* suggested that full blame for Saratoga should fall upon General Arnold and General Gates. He recommended that these men "be taken into custody and ordered to attend at the Bar of the House for contempt."

It seemed to have occurred to no one before that the British armies were being outfought and out-generaled as well, because such a thing was inconceivable.

Sir Edward Shepherd Creasy, in his classic *The Fifteen Decisive Battles of the World from Marathon to Waterloo*, gives a stylish account of Saratoga (the thirteenth battle), and in the succeeding pages it will be made clear why. In the well-equipped American parlor of the mid-19th Century there was likely to hang a handsome steel engraving in a watergold frame, *The Surrender of Burgoyne*, after John Trumbull's painting. (This historical engraving met with but moderate if any demand in England.)

In the meantime General Howe, having finally reached terra firma at the head of Chesapeake Bay, did actually start for Philadelphia. Washington met him with all the troops he could muster and opposed him at the Battle of Brandywine (September 11, 1777) but was defeated; this was followed by another Continental defeat, the Battle of Germantown. The Continental Congress fled Philadelphia.

The British, traditional Europeans, believed that if the capital of a country was captured, the Government collapsed and the will to fight died. But the Continental Congress had only to pack their grips, gather up their papers, and move to some other town, which, presto, became the capital. The capital this time was York, Pennsylvania, about a hundred miles west of Philadelphia.

Other patriots were busy too. They dismounted the great Liberty Bell, weighing 2,080 pounds, from the tower of the Philadelphia State House (now Independence Hall) and hauled this already sacred symbol out of the city by oxen to Allentown, sixty miles to the northwest, where it lay hidden in the basement of the Zion Reformed Church until the British left town.

Howe's entry into Philadelphia was triumphant. The place seemed suddenly full of Loyalists who welcomed the invaders with joy. If Howe was disappointed that the war went on in spite of his capture of the city, he did not say so. A whole delightful winter ensued. The British officers were fêted at balls and banquets; for them it was roses, roses . . . all winter long.

31   TRIAL BY ICE

These boys are boys of ice.
—All's Well that Ends Well, Act II, Scene 3

On December 19 Washington encamped with his troops on a plateau about twenty miles northwest of Philadelphia and its festivities, where the Schuylkill and a stream called Valley Creek join. Here there was a ford across the Schuylkill, and on the creek an old abandoned forge known locally as Valley Forge.

As it would be impossible to spend a winter here in tents, there were immediate orders to build huts of a prescribed pattern, and this the men did—freezing as they were. They felled trees, split them into boards, built chimneys somehow, and slowly a village of drafty, hardly livable huts arose—in spite of the shortage of tools and nails. There was a shortage of food, too, supplies arriving at odd intervals; water had to be hauled from the creek a mile away in buckets; soap was rare, and the

Valley Forge. From *The American Revolution: The Picture Source Book by John Grafton*, New York: Dover Books, 1975.

drafty huts inducive of colds and other ills. Hands were chapped, and feet were frozen. And be it remembered that warm underwear had not then been invented. Warm underwear seems to be one of the basic inventions Benjamin Franklin had failed to invent. A guard stood at his post presenting arms, standing on his hat to keep his feet out of the snow.

The suffering of the men at Valley Forge has entered the consciousness of the American people as no other single episode has, and makes the name of Valley Forge a symbol of the endurance of the American Army in the Revolution.

Foreign officers, of which there were a surprising number at Valley Forge, declared that no troops they had ever known would have "kept the field" under these conditions. "The men simply set their teeth and stayed alive."

The officers made a joke of the rough living when they could, and some gave a little party to which no one was admitted who had a whole pair of breeches.

George Washington was not the cold, aloof marble statue that he has become in the popular mind—perhaps a result of *too many* statues. In 1832 Congress passed an act granting veterans and their widows a pension for six months' service in the Revolutionary War. They were obliged to submit narratives of their service; over 80,000 of these are in the National Archives. In a number of instances there are accounts of personal encounters with General Washington, and in every one of them he emerges a human, warm, fatherly figure. In the dark days of Valley Forge he made direct appeals to the men to continue in service after their enlistments expired, and many did so as a personal favor to their friend, General Washington.

The General shivered in his tent until all his men were housed, and then moved into a small stone building, the Isaac Potts house, close to the junction of the Schuylkill and Valley Creek, and sent for Martha.

Martha Washington has remained a shadowy figure in American history, and undeservedly so. She fulfilled her duties as the wife of the Commanding General at Valley Forge and elsewhere, assiduously visited the sick in their inadequate quarters with warm smiles and kind words, and did what she could to alleviate their sufferings. Her frequent visits to the sick were looked forward to by all, and when she found herself suddenly the First Lady of the Land, she rose to that occasion too.

Martha Washington, née Dandridge, married Daniel Park Custis at eighteen and bore him four children, two of whom died in infancy. When Custis died she was 26 and one of the richest women in Virginia. Washington met her the following year and knew a good thing when he saw one. They were married in January, 1759.

Washington longed for domestic life, of which he was to have so little, and Martha did what she could to supply it. She lacked a great brain, but she was a lady, gracious, dignified, discreet and unassuming; and she could chat about domestic affairs. People liked her.

Soon there were other ladies at Valley Forge: Mrs. Nathanael Greene; the wife of General William Alexander who called himself Lord Stirling (after an unrecognized Scottish earldom); their daughter; and a young friend of the latter who was one of that now extinct species, a "belle." A belle at Valley Forge! And there was that charming young Frenchman, the Marquis de Lafayette, who spoke fluent English with a strong French accent. These people met at each others' quarters or at headquarters (the Isaac Potts house, to which a makeshift addition had been constructed), with the General sometimes present. They drank tea and coffee, but the only entertainment was singing.

Among those who flocked to Valley Forge was Benedict Arnold, whom nobody liked; and that lanky and unlovable Englishman, General Charles Lee, whom we have already met, who detested Washington and admired himself inordinately, and whom we shall have the misfortune to meet again.

32 BEN FRANKLIN AND THE BARON

Benjamin Franklin, busy in Paris winning over Louis XVI and the Comte de Vergennes, the Foreign Minister, was the most popular diplomat any country ever sent to France, due to his charm, his humor, his sauvity, his diplomacy and his shrewdness. He was the man of the hour. The Comte de Vergennes had held off alliance with the United States because of a treaty with Spain. But now he urged Spain to furnish aid to America. Hating England as Spain did, she was ready and willing to do so.

Franklin's diplomatic role in France cannot be overemphasized. Paris was a beehive full of spies and secret agents, one of whom was Franklin's colleague, a traitorous American named Dr. Edward Bancroft. The astute Franklin never suspected him, nor did anyone else, and not until 1866 was it revealed that "the seemingly honorable and patriotic gentleman" was "one of the most able spies of all time." He hailed from Westfield, Massachusetts.

Franklin was thoroughly hoaxed (surely the only time in his life) by Edward Bancroft, but not by Baron Friedrich Wilhelm Ludolf Gerhard Augustin von Steuben, in spite of his dizzying name. The Baron had served in the army of Frederick the Great of Prussia, although in the capacity of Captain (on half pay) and not Lieutenant General as his record proclaimed. But Franklin recognized him as a valuable asset when the Baron waited on him in Paris with a request for help in getting to the new United States to serve in the Continental Army. It is suspected that wily old Ben either connived at or even helped prepare an even more exalted record to impress the Congress. In doing this, "Franklin probably performed his greatest service to the American Army."[1]

Von Steuben, arriving at Valley Forge, was not dismayed at the dreadful conditions he encountered, nor at the ragged, hungry, ill-clad and undisciplined men he began to drill. Speaking a little French, his only foreign tongue, he reorganized the Army. His instructions had to be translated from German to French to English by his French secretary or by several other volunteers, including Lieutenant Colonel Alexander Hamilton.

Americans were not accustomed to snapping to attention at Prussian commands, but the Baron had something about him the men respected. By reorganizing the manual of arms, teaching the difference between right-face, left-face and about face, and how to perform these and other maneuvers, the Baron produced a new American Army on "the bleak plateau of Valley Forge."[2] It was able to face the British regulars at the approaching Battle of Monmouth and subsequent battles; the soldiers had become professionals.

One of history's more incredible facts was the role played in France at this time by Caron de Beaumarchais, who began life as a humble watchmaker. By marrying well twice, and becoming a favorite (for a while) of Louis XVI's three mean old maiden aunts (to whom he gave lessons on the harp), and by the success of his play *Eugenie*, he rose, then fell, and rose again, in the esteem of the fickle public. By his humor, wit and good looks he penetrated the highest circles and was entertained by dukes and counts. Successfully employed by Vergennes to recover incriminating documents in England, he became an ardent adherent of the American cause. His letters to Vergennes and the King were so exuberant and irresistible that they influenced France's final decision to embrace the Americans openly.

His comedies, *The Marriage of Figaro* and *The Barber of Seville*, and his drama *Don Giovanni* still hold the stage, thanks to their musical settings by Mozart and Rossini.

Silas Deane, who was supposed to have handed out commissions to ardent young aristocrats, without authority, was sent to Paris in 1776. A naive Connecticut Yankee without a word of French was thus set adrift and friendless in the most sophisticated city in the world. Nevertheless, he worked with Beaumarchais, who had no word of English, in secretly securing military supplies and other aid for the colonies, and this aid turned the tide at the Battle of Saratoga. In Paris, Beaumarchais was nicknamed "l'Americain," which pleased him.

Chatham, in the House of Lords, seeing an approaching war with France, pleaded for immediate peace with America that Britain might marshal all her forces. He was voted down by a large majority of the lords, who were furious at Burgoyne for his "cowardly surrender to a mob of poltroons."

It was so much easier not to surrender at Saratoga while comfortably ensconced in Whitehall.

By now, even the King and Lord North were ready to make concessions to the Americans, and granted them everything they wanted except independence. But the offer was two years too late.

In 1779 Spain joined in alliance with France against Great Britain, and Holland followed in 1780. Britain now faced, beside her American problems, three more enemies at once.

Washington and his Army stuck it out at Valley Forge, but there were deserters and expired enlistments, until by spring his 8,000 troops had been reduced to less than 6,000. General Howe, who had at least 17,000 well-fed troops in Philadelphia, twenty miles off, did nothing all winter but dance the nights away. It would have been almost too easy to corral Washington's troops at Valley Forge.

Howe's inaction has been the wonder of historians, and several explanations have been advanced. One is that he hoped to let things ride until the Revolution wore itself out. Another is that he was suffering from a delayed neurosis brought on by the carnage at Bunker Hill. Another explanation here humbly offered is that it was too warm and comfortable in Philadelphia, and who would not quail at the thought of quitting it for Valley Forge, of all places? General Howe knew American winters; he had chased Washington across New Jersey at Christmastide in 1776; he had had enough.

Dissatisfaction with Washington began to grow. He had seen nothing but defeat since Trenton and Princeton, and some members of Congress and several generals thought that General Gates, the Hero of Saratoga, should be supreme commander. Gates himself concurred in this belief.

Congress made Gates President of the Board of War, and now Washington was his subordinate. An Irishman named Thomas Conway, whom Congress had made a Brigadier General, was behind the scheme to supplant Washington, who knew all about it and sent Congress some of the slurring articles against himself that had been appearing in the newspapers. Serene and unperturbed, he made no comment.

The Conway Cabal collapsed like the empty thing it was. Congress recovered their wits, dismissed Gates, and sent him back to the Army. Conway wrote an abject letter to Washington and disappeared from history.

33   LOUIS XVI TAKES NOTE

Revenge, that thirsty dropsy of our souls
—Massinger, *A Very Woman*, Act IV, Scene 2

The news of the surrender of Burgoyne at Saratoga (October 17, 1777), was a shock to England. No British army had surrendered in years, and now to a ragtag, bobtail bunch of raw colonials! It was unbearable! But it was not until the following spring that more good news arrived for the "colonials." An alliance with France!

The startling news reached Valley Forge on May 8, 1778, nearly two years after the Declaration of Independence was adopted. For those 22 months the weak, ambitious little coalition of colonies, without a friend, had been facing the most powerful nation in the world. The men, at last thawed out, put on what they could of a celebration.

There were some whose joy was tempered with apprehension. Would France take over and attempt to make an empire in America to replace the one she had lost? Would they be trading one tyrant for another, all hope of independence gone? How far was France planning to go in her revenge on Britain?

France had been wary of forming an alliance with the self-proclaimed new nation, though secretly supplying it with help, until some proof appeared that America was likely to be victorious. Saratoga furnished that proof.

"The time seemed to have arrived for the house of Bourbon to take full revenge for all of its humiliations and losses in previous wars."[1]

Besides an understandable thirst for revenge, a ravishing aroma of money whetted the nostrils of France. Britain had forbade her colonies to trade with her archenemy of course, and a large and growing field for profit was thus out of bounds to the French. France also hesitated to make an alliance with the rebellious colonies of Albion out of anxiety that, once free from the British yoke, they would split up into thirteen little independent republics, bickering among themselves and impossible to do business with? There were such considerations.

34 FESTIVITIES IN PHILADELPHIA

Come, and trip it as you go,
On the light fantastic toe.
—Milton, *L'Allegro*

With the French alliance came immediate changes in the aspect of the war. It had become an international war, and Europe was becoming more and more sympathetic to the American cause. The Comte d'Estaing had already sailed for America with twelve ships of the line (ships large enough to take the first line in battle formation) and a number of regiments.

In the spring General Howe was replaced in Philadelphia by General Sir Henry Clinton. Even in London, they couldn't get over Howe's placid inaction. But before Howe left the City of Brotherly Love, 21 of his officers subscribed £3,312 to give him a grand soirée and fête never seen in that Quaker City before nor since. It was called a "Mishianza" (variously spelled) because it was "made up of a variety of entertainments."

The officers attended in court costume of the time of Henry IV and the ladies came as Turkish maidens. One shop took in £12,000 sterling for silk and other materials for the costumes. At the banquet there were places set for 330. Ships brought tropical fruits from the West Indies for the occasion. Innumerable toasts were drunk to the King and Queen. A procession of barges, richly caparisoned, sailed down the Schuylkill, watched by enthusiastic crowds along the banks.

The leading light in arranging this Arabian Nights entertainment in the Quaker City was a young British major named John André who was aide-de-camp to General Grey and later a deputy adjutant general under General Clinton. André was in his twenties, affable, charming, good looking in a pretty way. He danced, he flirted, he sketched well, he wrote verses, and the young ladies of fashion were much taken with him. Major André had charge of the ladies' headgear for the Mishianza. He said he had been made a "complete milliner." He also painted the scenery. He was a man of many talents as we shall see.

Even Loyalists were shocked at the bad taste displayed at this extravaganza while the country was at war. When the accounts reached England the press expressed indignation at this triumph "given a commander who had almost lost the war."

Sir Henry Clinton did not enjoy his new assignment long. With the news of the approach of a French fleet he had to quit Philadelphia too. The forts along the Delaware were inadequate to protect the city.

Major André was quartered, along with General Grey, in Benjamin Franklin's house. When preparing to leave he was found by a friend packing Franklin's books.

In spite of remonstrances he took valuable works, some belonging to public institutions, music, musical instruments, and one of Franklin's personal account books. He also lifted a portrait of Franklin ("the devilish philosopher who negotiated the French Alliance") by Benjamin Wilson, the English portrait painter and a friend to Franklin. This he gave to General Grey, who took it. (Major André's glitter becomes a trifle tarnished when one learns he was a looter.) In 1906 the portrait was returned to the United States Government by Albert Grey, 4th Earl Grey, Governor-General of Canada, on the bicentennial of Franklin's birth; it now hangs in the White House.

The British had occupied Philadelphia only nine months; the French alliance was paying off already. The party was over for the Loyalists. A number of them left hastily; others stuck it out and hoped for the best.

Some historians consider Sir Henry Clinton to have had the clearest head of any of the British generals in America, but it is difficult not to come to the conclusion that they all, from time to time, were decided dim-wits. Sir Henry was born in Newfoundland, and consequently was a colonial himself, if that makes any difference. At any rate he started off from Philadelphia, with his 17,000 men and a baggage train eight miles long en route to New York. His route lay through the sandy Pine Barrens of southern New Jersey.

His way led to Monmouth, and a famous battle.

35   MONMOUTH LEGENDS

> . . . *Washington,*
> *Whose every battlefield is holy ground,*
> *Which breathes of nations saved, not worlds undone.*
> —Byron, *Don Juan,* Canto VIII

In the middle of June, Washington learned through the washerwomen of Philadelphia, excellent spies, that the British officers had ordered their linen delivered at once whether ready or not. The indication was clear. On June 18, General Clinton and his army evacuated Philadelphia and crossed the Delaware en route to New York, which was still held by the British.

Washington was reunited with an old comrade in arms: General Charles Lee had been exchanged after a not-very-vile durance with the British in New York. Although Lee had been insubordinate after the Battle of White Plains, Washington accepted him as he was an acknowledged military genius. His "bubble reputation" had not yet burst.

Against great remonstrance at the plan Washington evolved, from Generals

Greene Wayne (called "Mad Anthony" Wayne for his foolhardy courage), and Lee, Washington set out in pursuit of Clinton. He hoped to catch up with him in the New Jersey Barrens before Clinton reached the protection of a range of low hills. According to military protocol Washington gave Lee, second in command, the leadership of a large detachment that was to attack Clinton's rear guard, with Washington close enough behind with the main army if needed. Lee refused the command, saying the whole plan was foolhardy, and Washington offered it to Lafayette.

On the night of June 27, Lee, apparently having changed his mind and taken charge, encamped within six miles of the enemy. Washington, with his troops, was three miles behind. He ordered Lee to attack in the early morning unless there were strong reasons to the contrary.

June 28 dawned, and it was a scorcher. The men stripped to the waist; some were overcome by the heat and collapsed. Washington pushed on, fearful that the British had eluded Lee.

He heard firing—a good sign—and then silence! Soon whole regiments appeared in retreat. Lee's confused officers said they were obeying orders.

Washington, leaving General Greene in command of his column, dashed ahead. And he saw the lanky Lee riding toward him. He was chatting amiably with his aides.

"My God, General Lee! What are you about?"

"Sir, these troops are not able to meet British grenadiers."

"Sir," said Washington in a towering rage, "they *are* able, and by God they shall!" And he ordered them to do so.

The cherished legend persists that the Father of his Country proved he had an hitherto unsuspected talent for profanity. General Charles Scott was a witness. He said, "He swore on that day till the leaves shook on the trees. Charming, delightful! . . . He swore on that day like an angel from heaven!" But General Scott, alas did not give posterity any sample of this angelic swearing, and we have to take it on faith.

After Lee's treacherous retreat, the British, instead of continuing their march towards New York, were in pursuit. Washington brought order out of the rising confusion. Otherwise the whole Army might have been lost. His troops, trained all winter at Valley Forge by Baron von Steuben, obeyed orders.

"General Washington," wrote Lafayette, "seemed to arrest fortune with a glance . . . His presence stopped the retreat. His graceful bearing on horseback, his calm and deportment which still retained a trace of displeasure . . . were calculated to inspire the highest degree of enthusiasm . . . I thought then as now I had never beheld so superb a man."

General Greene's regiment came on in good order. The men engaged in the delaying action appeared in formation. British horses came galloping . . . and the cavalry was annihilated by two regiments firing behind a low fence. Men and horses fell in horrible confusion. Next came an attack by British infantry. They had nowhere to turn. The Americans advanced like regular troops. The British retired to a strong position, and during the night they disappeared.

All day the weather had been roasting, and many on both sides were overcome. Amid whizzing bullets, the wife of artillery man John Hays brought pitcher after pitcher of cold water onto the battlefield to the sweltering men at the cannon, who gratefully called her "Molly Pitcher." When her husband, too, was overcome by the heat, she took his place at the cannon and continued there until the engagement was over–and gave America a heroine.

Some writers, who know all about Monmouth though they were not there, claim that the story of Molly firing a cannon is "apocryphal"; it was some other woman at some other battle. But there was an eyewitness. Joseph Martin, a native of Maine, left an account of Molly in action. While she was reaching for a shell a bullet whizzed between her legs, doing no more damage than ripping away the lower part of her petticoat. Looking down with apparent unconcern, she remarked that it was lucky that the bullet did not pass higher "for in that case it might have carried away something else," and continued her occupation.

In 1822 the Pennsylvania Assembly approved an act to "come to the aid of Molly McClolly" and granted her the munificent annuity of forty dollars. It was Molly Pitcher who had been twice widowed after Monmouth and moved to Carlisle, Pennsylvania, where she lies buried. In England she would have been called Molly Jug, which would have been a catastrophe.

And General Lee, the non-hero?

The day after the battle he wrote a letter to Washington demanding an apology, and suggesting that Washington was influenced by "dirty earwigs" close to him. Washington put him under arrest. He was court-martialed for disobedience of orders at Monmouth, misbehavior before the enemy and disrespect to his Commander in Chief. Found guilty on all three counts, he was suspended.

The controversy over Lee's actions at Monmouth went on (it still goes on among historians). In July 1780 he wrote a letter to Congress considered so insulting that he was dismissed permanently from the service.

But this was not quite the end of Charles Lee. Nearly a hundred years later a document was found among the papers of the Strachey family, whose ancestor had been secretary to General Howe when Lee was a prisoner of the British in New York. It was in Lee's handwriting and gave a plan for the conquest of the colonies.

"Washington at Monmouth" engraved by G.R. Hall after Darley. Reproduced by permission of the National Portrait Gallery, Smithsonian Institution, Washington, D.C.

36   THE EVIL GENIUS

Lee was not the only traitor in the Continental Army, and we must sully these pages with the now infamous name of Benedict Arnold, whom Washington considered one of his best and most courageous generals. He was second in command to Gates at the Battle of Saratoga, but he thought he should have been in command himself. He was cranky and disagreeable, and did not get on well with his superiors and peers.

Benedict Arnold was a Connecticut Yankee from the pleasant town of Norwich, while Horatio Gates was actually an Englishman, a godson of Horace Walpole; but Benedict Arnold's real trouble was that he suffered from vanity, jealousy, ambition, greed and a total lack of principle.

When Sir Henry Clinton evacuated Philadelphia, Washington had given Arnold the post of military governor of the city, and he was fêted by the rich Tories of the town. A poor man and a widower with several children, he was envious of the wealth around him. Though his position in the metropolis of Philadelphia might be the envy of other military men in less luxurious settings–battlefields, for instance–Arnold was dissatisfied with his lot. Like several others he felt unappreciated. In short he, like Lee and Gates, thought he could fill Washington's boots very well.

He managed to marry a rich belle, Peggy Shippen, age eighteen, who must have been dazzled by the man's position and reputation as a glamorous general. Peggy had formerly enjoyed a flirtation with our friend the glamorous André, and now as Mrs. Arnold she received a letter from the major, renewing their acquaintance and offering to do any little errands Mrs. Arnold might require in New York. There was more in this letter than met Peggy's eye.

In New York General Clinton had received a letter from Philadelphia in March 1779 signed "Gustavus." The writer said he was a patriot, he thought the war a great mistake, and the French alliance deplorable; and he could obtain information of value to the British. He included elaborate directions for addressing the reply. Sir Henry gave this letter to Major André to follow up. André wrote "Gustavus" assuring him he would like a longer letter, and signed it "John Anderson, merchant, New York."

Thus began the Gustavus-Anderson correspondence, and it continued for more than a year. Valuable information was supplied by Gustavus from time to time, and before long both Clinton and André became convinced that Gustavus was Benedict Arnold. No one else was in a position to know the facts he communicated.

It was then that André wrote the pleasant letter to Mrs. Arnold offering to do little commissions for her in New York. He spoke of dress materials, needles, ribbons–anything Mrs. Arnold required. These words were to convey to Arnold that John Anderson knew who Gustavus was.

Washington relieved Arnold of his post in Philadelphia at his own suggestion, and before long he maneuvered the command of the fortress of West Point.

West Point was a fortress with large installations and a garrison of three thousand men, fifty miles above New York. It occupied a bend in the Hudson and was supposed to command the river, which was the key to communications between New England and the South. Washington considered West Point of great strategic importance.

The Gustavus-Anderson correspondence continued, but now Gustavus became more explicit in his demands. On the surface the letters seemed merely business correspondence between merchants, but the message was that Arnold offered to surrender West Point to General Clinton for £20,000 and a generalship in the British Army.

Clinton sent André up the river in a small sloop called the *Vulture* which anchored off Teller's Point, seventeen miles below West Point, and late at night he met General Arnold in a thick wood on the banks of the Hudson near Stony Point. Arnold gave André maps, written descriptions of the forts, their armaments, their stores, the strength of the garrison, and copies of orders in case of attack, and he helped André conceal these papers in his stockings.

General Clinton had instructed André not to go inside the American lines and to wear his uniform at all times, so that if captured he would be subject to exchange, and not executed as a spy. Unfortunately he was persuaded to put on a civilian coat by a farmer hired to row him back to the *Vulture*; the farmer reneged. André was furnished a horse and directions for reaching the British lines. He set out, but attracted the attention of three low types who were playing cards by the side of the road near Tarrytown. André looked too elegant and was wearing expensive boots. When the men took off the boots for the purpose of robbing him of them, the incriminating West Point papers were found in his stockings.

These unsavory characters were illiterate, but not so ignorant that they did not know they had caught a whale. They took André to White Plains, the nearest American post. The Colonel in command there thought these papers were stolen, and sent the prisoner to General Arnold at West Point. A messenger rode on ahead with the news that a spy had been caught with the plans of West Point on his person.

General Arnold, who was at breakfast with his staff, read the message silently, rose from the table without change of expression, went to the riverbank, stepped into a barge which was moored there constantly, and had himself rowed down the river to the *Vulture*.

That morning, just after Arnold escaped, General Washington arrived at West Point. "Whom can we trust now?" he said.

Major André was executed October 2, 1780. He wrote a dignified letter to Washington, asking to be shot instead of hanged.

André went to his death to the sound of fife and drum playing a death march. He kept in step, with an agreeable smile on his face. The large crowd who had come to witness the show were overawed. The pious were shocked that a freethinker who had refused the attendance of a minister was "setting the Almighty at defiance at the time of his execution."

The officers who had pronounced the death sentence were on horseback. Major André bowed to each, still smiling. They returned the bow. Then André saw the gallows. His request to be shot had been denied. He stepped back and said, "Must I then die in this manner?"

"I am reconciled to my fate, but not to the mode," he said loudly.

Under the gibbet there was a cart hitched to two horses who were nonchalantly swishing their tails. André put one knee on the tailboard and lifted himself up. A murmur arose from the crowd.

He stood in his scarlet coat, his hands on his hips. Then he took off his hat, which he gave to his loudly lamenting servant, revealing "a long and beautiful head of hair which was wound with a black ribbon and hung down his neck."

Colonel Scammell, an old subordinate of General Arnold, read the death sentence with a shaking voice, and asked if the prisoner had anything to say. "I have nothing more to say but this: you all bear witness that I met my fate as a brave man." The crowd began to wail.

The executioner, his face disguised by grease and soot, leapt onto the wagon. André assisted him in fixing the noose. He tied the handkerchief over his own eyes without the slightest tremor. His arms were tied behind his back. Then the executioner shinnied up one of the poles and tied the other end of the rope to the beam. By now the crowd was screaming hysterically. Only the victim was calm.

The executioner jumped to the ground. He took a whip to the horses, they moved quickly forward, and "the world sprang out from under John André's feet."

Forty years later his bones were disinterred and reburied in Westminster Abbey.

The Americans put a price on Arnold's head. General Cinton gave him a command which included raiding New London, Connecticut, a few miles from his birthplace and the home of his childhood friends. Most of the town was burned after the explosion of a warehouse full of gunpowder. Eventually the Arnolds settled in London where they were received at court but hissed at the theatre. Arnold had been a traitor twice.

At 44 Benedict Arnold sailed to Canada in search of a new career in commerce. "He was received everywhere with astonishment and disapproval." He tried the West Indies, and ended by dying in England of dropsy in 1801, at the age of sixty.

His wife followed him three years later, carried off by cancer. Neither of these people had a very good time.

Those who say that Benedict Arnold was a great patriot must be unaware of the £20,000 price he put on his patriotism.

But the brave young English officer, Major John André, and his tragic fate, became a romantic legend in America, and prints and drawings of "The Capture of André" were produced in the country for the next hundred years.

When Sir Henry Clinton reached New York after the affair at Monmouth, he was favored with the first physical evidence of the French Alliance. A fleet, Charles Henri Hector, Comte d'Estaing in command, appeared off Sandy Hook, New Jersey. These were the very ships whose threatened approach had caused Sir Henry to evacuate Philadelphia. The French admiral was after Lord Howe's ships which had arrived from Philadelphia and were now drawn up in a fine defensive formation inside the Hook. Washington sent New York pilots to d'Estaing who told him his ships drew too much water to pass over the sandbars in the Narrows. He sailed away, avoiding any unpleasantnesses with Lord Howe's fleet. But the French fleet gave the Americans naval superiority in the coastal waters for the first time.

We next hear of the Comte d'Estaing heading for Rhode Island with four thousand French marines and a good force of Americans. But a fleet of thirteen British ships under the command of Admiral John Byron, known as "Foul Weather Jack" and grandfather of the poet, was headed for America. The Count landed his marines and the American troops near Newport, where there was a large encampment of Hessians. But then, suspecting the arrival of Foul Weather Jack, he gathered up his marines and sailed away again, abandoning the Americans to their fate. They managed to escape by their own efforts, and the Comte d'Estaing's reputation never recovered. When he sailed serenely into Boston harbor the outraged citizens began to riot against the French, and one French officer was killed.

Now Washington had his hands more full than ever. He wished, he said privately, that there "was not a single foreign officer among us, except the Marquis de Lafayette." He feared the French Alliance would collapse before it had begun. He succeeded in soothing the civilian leaders and commanded his men to "conciliate our powerful ally."

The Comte d'Estaing then sailed away, a thing he was good at doing—without deigning to tell Washington where he was going or whether he intended to return. He never did. Wherever he arrived he was just too late. He took part in the attack on Savannah in the attempt to dislodge the British who held that beautiful town. This also failed, and the ineffectual Count finally returned to France, where in 1794 he lost his head to the guillotine, possibly the only thing connected with the hapless nobleman that came off successfully.

37   THE SCOTTISH TAR

In 1774 or 1775 a young Scottish sea captain turned up in Philadelphia. His name was John Paul, to which he added, for reasons of his own, the name Jones. After much trouble he obtained a commission as First Lieutenant in the new Continental Navy, the first naval lieutenant's commission granted by Congress, and was assigned to a sloop named *Alfred*. With this and a small squadron Jones began preying on British shipping.

Prize money was what ships lived on, and the amounts taken made privateering highly profitable. The division of the money was rigorously adjusted. In the American Navy fifty percent went to the Congress, the rest was divided in various percentages among the captain, officers and crew. Privateering, in which Congress got nothing, was more profitable for officers and crew, even with the ship owner's take, and this is why it was difficult to get enlistments in the Navy.

John Paul Jones was highly successful with the *Alfred*, but he was the object of much jealousy; and since he had no well-placed relatives in an age of unbounded nepotism, he was demoted to number eighteen in the Navy's list of captains.

Finally, on November 1, 1777, he set sail for Europe in command of his own frigate, *Ranger*. He began to terrify British shipping and raid English coastal towns. Mothers kept their little ones quiet with threats of Captain Jones, and so great grew his fame, what with his daring, dash and successes, that he became a folk hero, even in Britain. When he found some Irish fishermen who had been impressed on a ship he captured, he had them rowed ashore in one of his boats and gave them money. He was a maritime Robin Hood, known for the concern he had for his prisoners.

Always battling for a better ship, through the influence of Benjamin Franklin and Lafayette (who was in France briefly to induce Louis XVI to furnish more aid to the American cause), Jones was finally given an antiquated merchantman, out of the China trade. He rebuilt her, outfitted her with cannon and renamed her *Le Bonhomme Richard* in honor of Benjamin Franklin and *Poor Richard's Almanack*, which in translation was very popular in France. With this, the largest vessel he had commanded, and three others, *Vengeance* (cutter), *Pallas* (frigate) and *Alliance* (a square rigger), to make up his little squadron, Jones set forth to terrify England and British shipping anew. At rumors of his approach as large a city as Liverpool almost went into hysterics, and the Liverpudlians made plans to build a fort on the Mersey. When his ships were sighted in the Firth of Forth, Edinburgh panicked. Drums rolled, bugles blew, and, doubtless, bagpipes added to the terror; women and children with their prized possessions took to the hills. But a storm came up, and John Paul and his ships sailed away.

"Bon Homme Richard & Serapis." Drawn by Wade. From
The American Revolution, The Picture Source Book, by John
Grafton, New York: Dover Books, 1975.

On September 25, 1779, Commodore Jones encountered a fleet of 41 British
merchantmen returning from the Baltic, convoyed by the frigate *Serapis*[1] with 44
guns, and the *Countess of Scarborough*, a sloop of twenty guns.

Very much in character John Paul sailed right up to the *Serapis* and did battle;
and what a battle it was. It continued for three-and-a-half hours; night fell and the
Serapis was afire in twelve places. The hull of John Paul's ship was pierced, her
decks ripped up, her hold filling with water, and fire consuming her unchecked.

But when the captain of the *Serapis* asked John Paul if his ship had struck her
colors, he replied with the words that capped his immortal fame, "Sir, I have not
yet begun to fight!"

It was the *Serapis* that surrendered. John Paul boarded her. Despite all efforts, *Le Bonhomme Richard* could not be saved, and sank in two days, the wounded being removed to other vessels.

This was one of the most memorable battles in naval history.

Jones now sailed his squadron, the *Serapis* and the *Countess of Scarborough* as prizes, the ships crowded with prisoners, to Holland. There he was the hero of the hour; he was followed in the streets; and a ballad (said to be still sung in Holland) was composed in his honor. France, too, went crazy over John Paul Jones. He was received by the King, presented with a gold-hilted sword. Decorated and lionized, he was initiated into the prestigious Lodge of the Nine Sisters which numbered Franklin and Voltaire among its members. The Lodge commissioned the famous Jean-Antoine Houdon to execute a bust of John Paul.

But at home he was always being passed over in the matter of promotions. Franklin, Adams, Jefferson and Lafayette knew his worth, but he had enemies in the Congress, among the most violent being Sam Adams. John Paul was the victim of a faction.

John Adams, as an American commissioner in France, was living at Auteuil with his wife, Abigail, who has left a description of John Paul:

"From the intrepid character he justly supported in the American Navy, I expected to have seen a rough, stout, warlike Roman—instead of that I should sooner think of wrapping him up in cotton wool, and putting him in my pocket, than sending him to contend with cannon-balls. He is small of stature, well proportioned, soft in his speech, easy in his address, polite in his manners, vastly civil. . . . He has been here often and dined with us several times."

In 1788 "the Father of the American Navy," out of a job, went to work for the greatest nymphomaniac and despot of the age, Catherine II of Russia, known as Catherine the Great. Russia was having trouble with Turkey in the Black Sea, and the Empress wanted John Paul for her navy. He stipulated admiral's rank, and this she bestowed. However, when he got to St. Petersburg, one glimpse of the insatiable lady, who was sixty, fat, with false teeth and swollen legs, made him more anxious than ever to go to sea. With the rank of rear admiral (at last!) and a Russian uniform of white with blue reveres and gold epaulettes and cuffs, he joined the Russian fleet and saw action in several battles in the Black Sea. But politics and jealousies made the service unsatisfactory, and he resigned his commission.

John Paul's dream was of a great American Navy. His precepts on naval discipline are, it is said, still part of the curriculum at the United States Naval Academy at Annapolis.

Jones died at the age of 45 in Paris on July 18, 1792, somewhat avoided. One senses that his egotism rendered him at the end a bit of a bore. He received little of the prize money due him from the American Government for his capture of over 300 British ships, not to mention the *Serapis* and the *Countess of Scarborough*.

In 1905, after a diligent search instigated by the American Ambassador to France, General Horace Porter, Jones' lead coffin was located in a long disused Protestant cemetery outside the walls of Paris. The body, preserved in rum, was recognizable from the Houdon bust and in such good preservation that an autopsy was performed on it.

President Theodore Roosevelt sent four cruisers to transport the body of "the Father of the American Navy" to America to enhance our naval prestige. Off Nantucket the four cruisers were joined by seven battleships under the command of Rear Admiral Robley D. Evans, Commander in Chief, North Atlantic Fleet. These eleven great ships sailed majestically along the American coast in single file toward the Chesapeake, destination Annapolis. How John Paul would have liked to be in command of this fine squadron! In a way he was.

John Paul was finally deposited in a tomb in the crypt of the Naval Academy chapel, and now the middies have something to hold ceremonies over, lay wreaths upon, and thus keep out of mischief.

They are also said to sing a song to the tune of "Everybody Works but Father":

> *Everybody works but John Paul Jones,*
> *He lies around all day,*
> *Body pickled in alcohol,*
> *On a permanent jag, they say . . .*

38   THE VICTORIOUS COWPENS

The Masterminds of Whitehall, "in stately conclave met," decided, as they weren't getting very far in their land war in America in the North, to shift activities to the South, subdue the rebels there, and then move gradually to the North and wipe that up. In the South there were said to be many Loyalists who would gladly come over to the right side as soon as they had the chance. Where have we heard that before?

To effect this purpose an expedition headed south, and Savannah, Georgia, was captured in December 1778. Georgia was overrun, the King's Governor reinstalled in his mansion, and the province declared again to be part of the British Empire.

Things moved slowly for a year. In the following December General Clinton sailed from New York with 8,500 troops to "pacify" South Carolina. In May 1780 he took Charleston, and General Benjamin Lincoln was obliged to surrender his force of 2,500 men. It began to look good for the British. But South Carolina refused to *stay* pacified. Georgia proved unruly too, even if it was once again part of the British Empire.

Clinton returned to New York, leaving General Cornwallis in charge of all this mess, with powers to pacify by any means whatever, including hanging. The houses and barns of the patriots were burned, livestock slaughtered, crops destroyed, and the people driven into prison camps.

Savagery increased in the Carolina Campaign. Banastre Tarleton, a young cavalry leader, "swift, thorough and bold," became celebrated for his brutality, even in a brutal age. He and his British Legion gave no quarter, bayonetted the fallen, and slashed to pieces those who surrendered. He was known as "Bloody Tarleton." A dashing portrait of this young fiend by no less a painter than Sir Joshua Reynolds is in the National Gallery, London, and much admired.

With General Lincoln's defeat at Charleston, our friend General Gates was sent by Congress to replace him, against the wishes of Washington, whose preference was for General Nathanael Greene.

At Camden, South Carolina, on August 16, 1780, Gates suffered the worst defeat of the war at the hands of Cornwallis. His men ran helter-skelter from the British charge, and Gates, "the Hero of Saratoga," kept up with them, and never stopped until he reached Charlotte, North Carolina, sixty miles away.

Cornwallis was a victor once again, but the country was sparsely settled and the coastal region full of swamps; there was no use conquering a swamp. Wherever the British turned they were harassed by snipers, who then disappeared into the woods.

On October 7, Colonel Patrick Ferguson, said to have been one of the cruelest of Cornwallis' officers, with a force of 1,200, was caught unaware at King's Mountain, near the border of North Carolina, by several regiments of backwoodsmen organized by the brilliant frontiersman John Sevier, and annihilated. It was the bloodiest battle of the war since Bunker Hill.

Throughout the Carolinas this seemed to be a signal for the patriots to rise. Cornwallis and his army were shaken. Snipers grew as numerous as mosquitoes in those swamps and marshes. It was guerrilla warfare, which was to become so popular in later times. These irregular bands of hit-and-run warriors were organized by three men: Thomas Sumter, "the gamecock of the Revolution," Andrew Pickens, who had already had successes at a place called Kettle Creek, and Francis Marion (known as the "Swamp Fox" for his habit of disappearing into swamps). They continued to make life miserable for Cornwallis.

Francis Marion, the Swamp Fox.

The work of the militia, and independent patriots unconnected with the Continental Army, has often been overlooked, yet some of the important battles of the American Revolution owe victories to these men, most of them anonymous.

Congress, coming to its senses again, replaced the swiftfooted hero of Saratoga with General Nathanael Greene, Washington's choice in the first place, and he and General Daniel Morgan, ready with his riflemen and his turkey-call, redeemed the Camden defeat with a resounding victory at The Cowpens, South Carolina, on January 18, 1781. ("The Cowpens" was the name given to a level stretch of land in the mountains used as a corral for herds of cattle being driven from one grazing ground to another.) Cornwallis was outmaneuvered with great skill until he found himself removed from his base of operations at Charleston. A year before he was in control only of the coast, and it was the same now. Nothing had advanced. It must have been discouraging to learn that Georgia was out of the Empire again, the King's governor removed, and the patriot governor and legislature back in power.

Second in command under Greene at the Battle of The Cowpens was a German soldier of fortune named Johann Kalb, calling himself Baron De Kalb. (The Continental Army was rich in bogus noblemen.) De Kalb had served France in several of her wars, and had been a secret agent for that country against the British in America. Commissioned a general, he served faithfully under Washington in the terrible winter at Valley Forge, but was mortally wounded at The Cowpens. Most people traveling these days by subway from Manhattan to Brooklyn are instructed to "change at De Kalb Avenue"–one of the many memorials to the general.

Another soldier of fortune, this time an authentic nobleman, who lost his life to the American cause, was a Pole, Casimir Pulaski, who had fled Poland for political reasons. In Paris he met Franklin, who gave him a letter to Washington and paid his passage to America. Pulaski joined the Revolution in 1777 and organized a cavalry unit, the Pulaski Legion, which saw much action. Pulaski was mortally wounded in an attack to dislodge the British from Savannah. In New Jersey the Pulaski Skyway attempts to keep his memory green as do towns that bear his name throughout the southern states.

39   THE FASHION-PLATE FRENCH

On July 10, 1780, another French fleet appeared in the harbor of Newport, Rhode Island, and debarked 5,000 troops under the command of the Comte de Rochambeau. Having only lately seen the last of Hessian occupation, the people of Newport were wary of these new and different foreigners and they locked their doors and peered out of windows. But the behavior of the Frenchmen was exemplary, and after awhile the suspicious, buttoned-up New Englanders forgave them for coming to their aid, and for being foreign, and relations grew warmer.

The Comte de Rochambeau was a very different sort from d'Estaing. Jean Baptiste Donatien de Vimeur, Comte de Rochambeau, was a most remarkable nobleman. He was fifty-six and had a fine paunch though the statue of him in Lafayette Square, Washington, depicts him as a young man with the figure of a ballet dancer. (He must have posed for it when he was very young.) Rochambeau preferred the company of his officers and troops to the splendors and boredom of court, to which his high rank entitled him. He referred to himself as Papa Rochambeau.

On his arrival the Comte wrote Washington, "The commands of the King, my master, place me under the orders of Your Excellency. I come wholly obedient and with the zeal and veneration which I have for you and for the remarkable talents you have displayed in sustaining a war which will always be memorable."

Rochambeau had secret orders not to agree to any strategy he thought wrong, and yet to appear to be subservient to Washington. After the unpleasantness d'Estaing's actions had brought on, the Franco-American entente was strained, but Rochambeau was a practiced courtier and a diplomat.

After two months of communicating by dispatches, the two generals met at Hartford on September 20. They were closeted for a day. "They separated," wrote the young Swedish Count Jean Axel de Fersen, an aide to Rochambeau, "quite charmed with each other. At least they said so."

On leaving Hartford, Washington journeyed to West Point, arriving there, as we have seen, the very day Benedict Arnold's treachery was revealed.

Louis XVI was persuaded to send the greater part of the French fleet to the aid of Washington and Rochambeau. Twenty ships of the line departed from Brest in March 1781, under the command of Rear Admiral François Joseph Paul, Comte de Grasse, his first destination the West Indies. Here de Grasse encountered an English blockading squadron, drove it off, and captured a couple of islands. At Cap-Haïtien, Santo Domingo (now Haiti and then under French rule), four more ships joined the de Grasse fleet, with 3,000 men from the Santo Domingo garrison under command of the Marquis de Saint-Simon. They then had to leave those waters in a hurry as it was July and the hurricane season was approaching. Rochambeau sent word to de Grasse by frigate, asking him where he intended to strike. De Grasse chose the Chesapeake, where there was room to maneuver, rather than New York harbor, where d'Estaing had been unable to break through The Narrows in 1778.

Conferences between Washington and Rochambeau—one in New London and one in Wethersfield—had settled on a plan of procedure. When de Grasse's reply arrived in Newport, Rochambeau had already left with his army, and was marching through Connecticut en route to a rendezvous with Washington at White Plains. The French army's long exile in Newport had come to an end.

Never in history did momentous events fall into place so neatly as those that now unfolded in succession and led to the end of the Revolution.

Rochambeau and the French army arrived in White Plains with vast wagon trains and bands playing. In this army were some of the oldest and proudest regiments of France. Each regiment wore collars and lapels in its own colors–green, pink, sky blue, crimson or rose. The infantrymen wore white coats and long waistcoats, the artillery were in gray trimmed with red velvet. Ostrich plumes waved on the hats of the sergeants. The hussars of the Duc de Lauzan's Legion had saddlecloths of tiger skin, the officers in scarlet breeches and coats of pale blue. There were noblemen in abundance: the Comte William Deux-Point, the Prince de Broglie, the Vicomte de Noailles, and the Comte Mathieu Dumas.

Astonishment was great among these fashion-plate military men at the sight of George Washington's little ragged army. Many of the men had no uniforms, some were barefoot, and nobody seemed ever to have brushed his hair. Among them there were old men and boys of twelve or thirteen. They were goggle-eyed in their turn at the sight of those who had come to aid them in scarlet and gold, and regarded them with suspicion. But soon suspicion was allayed, and officers and soldiers of both nations became friendly and commingled with their peers.

The French noblemen marveled at Washington. "I have never seen anyone who was more naturally and spontaneously polite," wrote one. "He asks few questions, listens attentively, and answers in low tones and with few words. . . . His modesty was very astonishing, especially to a Frenchman."

It had long been Washington's cherished dream to attack New York; there some of his most humiliating defeats had occurred at the hands of the British. But Rochambeau and his aides were dead set against this plan, which seemed impractical. Washington capitulated after a three-day cooling-off period, "The Navy must have the casting vote in this contest," he said. Rochambeau wanted to take the war into Virginia, and with the cooperation of de Grasse's fleet, trap Cornwallis. Sir Henry Clinton in New York was facing the alarming possibility of an attack on that city from all the combined troops gathered at White Plains with the two top generals. The knowledge that de Grasse's fleet was somewhere in American waters did not allay his fears. Washington, whose dismal reputation for being unable to tell a lie is undeserved, encouraged Sir Henry in these alarms. He left 4,000 troops in White Plains when, on August 19, he and Rochambeau broke camp and ferried 6,000 across the Hudson at King's ferry. He planted false intelligence, which pointed to an attack on the city via Staten Island, and set up fake ovens for baking hardtack in various spots in New Jersey, from which Clinton deduced that Washington's advance base would be there. Sir Henry swallowed the imaginary hardtack to the last crumb and dispatched not one soldier to reinforce Cornwallis, but instead sent word to fortify himself somewhere on the Virginia coast which would afford a port for the British fleet, and to send *him* reinforcements.

Cornwallis chose Yorktown, began building earthworks around it, and settled comfortably into his trap. Yorktown was a perfect place to harbor a fleet, and a perfect trap. The little town was built on the right bank of the York River, near its mouth. Opposite, on the other bank, is a place called Gloucester Point.The York River empties into the Chesapeake and a few miles south, where the bay empties into the Atlantic, it is less than two miles from shore to shore.

Rochambeau, in his letter to de Grasse, also informed him of the miserable state of affairs in America, and the critical lack of money. He had only enough to pay his troops till the end of July, and he urged the Admiral to pledge the French Navy's credit for money in "the Indies" (West Indies). As much as 1,200,000 *livres* were urgently needed. Four or five thousand troops were urgently needed too.

Though this information about the ragged, underfed and unpaid American army and the bankrupt government was discouraging, Admiral de Grasse went ahead readying his fleet, which had been marauding around the islands and heckling the British. By August 3 he had three infantry regiments, 100 dragoons, and 350 well-equipped artillerymen, but still no money for Rochambeau. The bankers of Santo Domingo were reluctant to advance money, even when the noble de Grasse pledged his plantation in Santo Domingo and château in France, estates worth far more than the loan. Angry at delays and quibbling, the Admiral then induced the director of the customs, Señor de Salavedra, to go to Havana and try to raise the money there.

In Havana the people were wildly enthusiastic. The 1,200,000 *livres* were raised in six hours, and ladies pledged their jewels to the cause.

Admiral de Grasse set out for Virginia with 28 ships, clumsy, tub-like hulks, blunt, top-heavy and difficult to maneuver. Most of them carried 74 cannon that had no sights and were elevated and aimed by guesswork. Two more of these clumsy but highly picturesque vessels joined the fleet two days later.

When Washington arrived in Philadelphia there was wild rejoicing. He was met with cavalry, which rode ahead to conduct the General to the City Tavern, where he drank rum punch and was greeted by all the notables of the capital. He was to stay at the residence of Robert Morris, "the financier of the Revolution," who with superhuman effort had been assembling boats to take 7,000 men down the Chesapeake. General Henry Knox was equally busy, pressing the Board of War for cannon, cartridges, flints, and powderhorns in vast quantities.

That night there was a banquet at the Morris house. Washington, Rochambeau, Henry Knox, Thomas McKean, the President of the Congress and other notables of the city were among the guests. Ships in the harbor fired salutes as the gentlemen drank toasts as though the war had already been won.

Next day the American Army entered the city to martial strains. They were ill-clad, many barefoot and in any kind of uniform or none at all. They marched, but they looked glum. They had not been paid for months, some never, and the sight of the prosperous citizens of Philadelphia, waving from balconies in all their finery, did not serve to comfort them.

The Philadelphians in turn were shocked at the appearance of their countrymen, and the poor fellows, discontented and perhaps humiliated, were marched right through the City of Brotherly Love and out the other side.

Washington reviewed his miserable-looking Army with aplomb, and sent out pleas to officials in Virginia and Maryland to gather supplies along the route the Army was to take, to improve the roads, and to collect as many boats as possible.

Though de Grasse had not been heard from for three weeks, a dispatch from Lafayette brought the great news that Cornwallis had occupied Yorktown, just as it was hoped he would. But Washington's continued fear that the British fleet would arrive before de Grasse and block the Chesapeake was not allayed.

A day or two later, after the American Army left Philadelphia, the French Army entered. It halted on the outskirts of the city for the men to change into their dress uniforms and Philadelphia gasped at the resplendent sight. One of the regiments gave a drill on the banks of the Schuylkill before an audience of gaping Philadelphians. The precision of the men was such as no one had seen before. The men were in spotless white and rose uniforms, with plumes of rose and pink in their hats. The ranking officers were entertained at lavish banquets.

On September 5 Washington left Philadelphia. The American Army was now encamped near Wilmington, Delaware, still grumbling over the lack of pay. Washington feared the men would mutiny and ruin the chances of victory. But while in Philadelphia Robert Morris was still trying desperately to raise money, word arrived that 2,500,000 *livres* in silver had landed at Boston, a gift from Louis XVI. It would be weeks before these coins could reach Philadelphia.

Rochambeau and his staff left by boat on the Delaware River to inspect fortifications downstream, and Washington, having arranged to meet them at the upper end of the Chesapeake, had passed through the village of Chester when, about three miles below, he and his officers were overtaken by a dusty, exhausted rider. He was a courier from Baltimore, and he handed the General a dispatch. De Grasse and his fleet had arrived at the Chesapeake on August 30 and had blocked the bay!

Nobody had ever seen the dignified Washington act as he did then. No longer the leader of an army and the hope of a nation, he was "a child whose very wish had been granted" as the Comte de Deux-Point described him. He could not have "revealed a livelier emotion."

In great excitement the party turned back toward Chester to find Rochambeau and give him the great news. They hurried to the wharf, and just at that moment Rochambeau's boat hove into view. The Frenchmen saw an extraordinary sight. There, on the wharf, Washington was waving his hat and a large white handkerchief over his head in wide circles. As Rochambeau stepped off his boat, Washington shouted the news, and clasped the Frenchman "in a fierce embrace."

Couriers, taking the news to Congress, found the city of Philadelphia in the wildest excitement–the news had already reached there. The streets surged with people, guns were being fired; it was happy pandemonium among the staid Quakers. And yet the war had not been won.

Admiral Graves, never too quick on the trigger, set sail in a leisurely fashion from New York for the Chesapeake with his fleet, for the purpose of protecting Cornwallis, if occasion warranted, on September 1, two days after Admiral de Grasse and his fleet had arrived there from the West Indies. Graves had nineteen ships of the line and a few frigates and smaller vessels, and he had no idea what he was getting into. He expected Washington to threaten New York or Staten Island, and had no notion that Cornwallis was in danger; he only knew that de Grasse's fleet and that of de Barras were *somewhere*.

It was an unpleasant awakening for Admiral Graves when he approached the Chesapeake and found de Grasse and all his ships already in possession. A battle, never clearly understood because of the confusion, took place off the Virginia Capes, de Barras' ships arrived to join de Grasse, and Admiral Graves was obliged to sail majestically away. By now even Cornwallis knew he was in a trap, a fact that his staff must have known for some time.

The American and French Armies sailed down the Chesapeake in the motley flotilla Robert Morris had assembled, and joined Lafayette and his troops at Williamsburg, seven miles from Yorktown. Ships from the West Indies landed three regiments under General Saint-Simon to join them at Jamestown, nearby, on September 2. They were eagerly welcomed, 3,500 big strong men in white uniforms with pale blue collars and lapels. They landed by torchlight amid clouds of mosquitoes. Lafayette now commanded 5,500 regulars and 3,000 militia. Everyone, including Lafayette, suffered recurrent bouts of fever. The heat was unbearable. On the 14th Washington himself arrived at Williamsburg. Lafayette embraced him like an effusive child.

Washington had a thousand arrangements to make for the siege of Yorktown. A dispatch from de Grasse informed him that he planned to sail to New York to see if the enemy would dare "come out." This would have ruined everything, and Washington wrote the Comte of the "painful anxiety" this caused him.

Three days later de Grasse sent a cutter captured from the British to Williamsburg, to bring the commanders down the James River for a meeting in Lynnhaven

Bay, where his fleet was assembled. They passed Yorktown, dozing in the sun. The party included Washington, General Rochambeau, General Henry Knox, and their aides.

The next day they were at Lynnhaven Bay and saw for the first time the overwhelming sight of the combined fleets of de Grasse and de Barras, commander of the Newport fleet–all told, 32 magnificent vessels riding at anchor. De Barras had brought the heavy ordnance from Newport which would have been impossible to haul overland. Everything was working out to a T.

Among all these vessels was de Grasse's flagship, the *Ville de Paris,* a gift from that city, sparkling with fresh paint.

Admiral de Grasse was a large, handsome, impressive man over six feet tall. He greeted Washington, who was even taller, in the French manner, a kiss on both cheeks, and cried, "My dear little General!" Everyone present exploded in laughter, and fat, jolly General Knox was convulsed. Washington's reaction is not recorded; one hopes at least he smiled.

After a consultation at which de Grasse promised to stay until November 1– the New York plan was scuttled–surely long enough to finish off Yorktown. Then the Admiral entertained his guests at dinner, a good time was had by all, and the Americans were rowed to another vessel, the *Queen Charlotte.* Salutes were fired, and the French sailors climbed all over the rigging of their ships to catch a glimpse of the great General Washington.

Due to storms and squalls Washington and his party had a difficult time getting back to Williamsburg; they had to change ships, and spent one night on a sandbar.

By September 28, plans were drawn up and the armies prepared to march to Yorktown. In order to look and act like conquerors, and not feel too inferior to the resplendent French, the men were ordered to shave. Uniforms had somehow been procured from Philadelphia, and each regiment was issued 12 pounds of flour so the men could powder their hair.

And at 5 A.M. on September 28, 1781, to the sound of fife and drum, the troops marched the seven miles to Yorktown to make history.

40   THE WORLD TURNED UPSIDE DOWN

The combined French and American forces, 16,000 strong, after stopping to build fires and cook a meal in spite of the heat, reached Yorktown at 3 P.M. The armies then divided, the French moving into position at the left, or river side, of the town, the Americans taking the right, encircling the town and hemming in Cornwallis and his 7,500 men. The British had built breastworks and a series of small forts or redoubts all about the town, but on the south side, occupied by the Americans, where the land was marshy, they had built bridges across the marsh, which the Americans now destroyed.

It was an uncomfortable night for everyone. Tents for headquarters had not arrived, and Washington slept under a mulberry tree. Water was scarce, and, when it was found, the buckets brought contained frogs. Now and then a desultory shot from a cannon marred the ominous quiet, or the American riflemen exchanged a few shots with the Hessians who were sniping from trenches.

Next day the tents arrived from headquarters, and the old worn canvas under which Washington had slept for more than five years was pitched. Everyone was waiting for something to happen.

Some pickets of the field officer of the day, Colonel Alexander Scammel, discovered an empty redoubt on the road to Williamsburg, and on further inspection it was found that Cornwallis had evacuated all three command posts of the outer line. The abandoned outer line was immediately occupied by the French and Americans without opposition, and they were that much closer to the enemy. Now, as soon as the big cannon Admiral de Barras had brought from Newport could be rolled up, they would have a clear field for firing into the town. Rochambeau had the earthworks reinforced. Pot shots to prevent this, or to destroy what was being done, casualties now and then on both sides, marked the passing days–clashes in attempts by the British to strengthen the garrison at Gloucester Point across the river, a sort of tuning up for the real music. They didn't hurry in the 18th century. It would have been unseemly for either side to jump the gun. Finally, on October 9 everything was ready, the last cannon in place, and the French and American artillery opened fire. Five days later the French and American troops stormed the weakened British fortifications by night.

The battle raged for three days. Washington, Lafayette, Hamilton, Rochambeau, men now immortal in history, were there. Ships in the river were fired and sunk, redoubts taken, men blown to pieces, heads, arms and legs scattered about.

At nine in the morning of October 17, the anniversary of the Battle of Saratoga, a redcoat drummer boy climbed onto a British parapet and began a steady roll on his drum. The shelling was so loud that he was unheard; infantrymen finally saw him, then the gunners. One by one the batteries fell silent.

A British officer appeared, holding a white handkerchief over his head. The drummer boy scrambled off the parapet to join him, still beating a roll. An American officer crossed the open line, torn to destruction by shells. He took the British officer's handkerchief, blindfolded him, and led him into the American lines, to a house at the rear. The infantrymen and the gunners stared.

Washington read the message from Cornwallis. It was a request for a cessation of hostilities to settle terms for the surrender of the posts at Yorktown and Gloucester.

The negotiations took two days. There were so many goings and comings under a flag of truce that the drummer gave up the formality of drumming. Every article of the surrender agreement was haggled over day and night. Cornwallis demanded concessions unacceptable to Washington, such as the return of his entire army to England at American expense! The etiquette of the formal surrender also took much time, the British demanding certain protocol that they had not allowed the Americans when they surrendered at Camden. In fact they did not act very nicely about all this, even though they were really not in a good bargaining position.

At 11 A.M., October 19, Washington and Rochambeau rode out with other officers to a captured redoubt. Admiral de Barras appeared as representative of de Grasse, who was "confined to his cabin with an attack of asthma." The surrender documents were delivered shortly, signed by Cornwallis and his chief naval officer, Captain Symonds. Washington and de Barras signed. There was a great silence.

At noon the American pickets occupied the posts—trenches, magazines, storehouses—which the British and Hessians had just relinquished. Troops with spades followed the pickets and filled in the trenches that had been dug across the road.

Washington and Rochambeau rode onto a large field, each leading his own men, who fell into lines facing each other, the French in their beautiful uniforms. Bands played desultorily to fill the time.

The British were late.

At last there was a roll of drums and they appeared, led by General O'Hara (Cornwallis had claimed a sick headache), the colorguard carrying furled flags and the band playing "The World Turned Upside Down," a dismal dirge. The drums were covered with black handkerchiefs, and the fifes had black ribbons tied around them. No wonder it had taken so long to get ready.

Comte Dumas rode out to indicate the surrender field to O'Hara. "Where is General Rochambeau?" O'Hara asked. Dumas nodded towards the French line, but then, realizing that O'Hara intended to surrender to Rochambeau instead of Washington, spurred his horse and tried to block his path, but O'Hara got to Rochambeau and offered his sword. The Frenchman shook his head and pointed to Washington, saying, "We are subordinate to the Americans. General Washington will give you orders." So O'Hara had to give his sword to Washington. He apologized for General Cornwallis, who had a sick headache, or so he claimed.

Washington refused O'Hara's sword, saying, "Never from such a good hand," the meaning of which escapes this historian. It was a decided breach of protocol, a thing Washington was strict about. He passed O'Hara to General Lincoln, his deputy commander, and it was probably he who accepted the sword.

Cornwallis' failure to appear at this solemn and trying event is in striking contrast to the behavior of Burgoyne in a similar situation, and the impression is inescapable that gentleman Johnny Burgoyne was a greater gentleman than Lord Cornwallis.

General Lincoln pointed to a field where the Duc de Lauzun's hussars had reined their horses in a large circle in the center of which the British regiments were to put down their arms and march back between the allied lines. These files of soldiers, and the crowds beyond, come to witness this momentous ceremony, maintained a deathly silence.

The platoons of British regulars, neat in new uniforms, could not conceal their emotion, and seemed overcome by the number of their victorious enemies. Their steps were irregular, the lines frequently broken. Colonel von Seybothen, tears streaming down his cheeks, could scarcely give the command, "Present arms! Lay down arms! Put off swords and cartridge belts!" Many of the men were weeping as they obeyed. "They manifested a sullen temper and flung down their arms violently." General Lincoln sent a brusque order, and then they stacked their arms more carefully. One of the New Jersey officers recorded that the British officers "behaved like boys who had been whipped at school. Some bit their lips, some pouted, others cried."

Admiral de Barras was a poor horseman but had said he would sit 48 hours in the saddle to see the British prisoners file past. He suddenly cried, "Good heavens! I think my horse is sinking!" The poor beast had stretched to relieve himself regardless of the solemnity of the occasion. This also helped relieve the tension. Bless the horse that pee'd at Yorktown!

The British, 3,500 strong, marched off between the files of their silent victors.

41   THAT EPICUREAN REPAST

What! Shall our feast be kept with slaughtered men?
—King John, Act III, Scene I

After the surrender there was a dinner at Washington's headquarters. General O'Hara attended in place of the invisible Cornwallis, still sulking in his tent. The British officers chatted with the French and Americans as if there had never been a war. All was easy and affable. But some of the Americans could not forget British atrocities—murder, arson, the inhuman treatment of prisoners—and were outraged by the spirit of brotherhood.

There were rounds of festivities amid the carnage as was the style of the times. Three days after the surrender Rochambeau gave a dinner for General O'Hara, an Irishman and the only member of Cornwallis' staff who spoke fluent French.

The random arms and legs had doubtless been swept up and disposed of by this time. O'Hara was garrulous and a braggart, and said in a stage whisper that he was glad he had not been captured by "the Americans alone." Lafayette, who was present, observed caustically, "It is obvious General O'Hara does not like encores." O'Hara had already been captured by "the Americans alone"–at Saratoga .

Rochambeau sent a loan of £150,000 in silver to Cornwallis, as he and his staff were impoverished. *Noblesse oblige.*

News of Yorktown reached London in due course. Lord North staggered backwards and cried, "Oh God, it is all over!" He should have been glad, except that his ministry wavered and finally fell, in spite of the King's efforts to shore it up, and never again did any British monarch wield the power George III had enjoyed.

42   GROWING PAINS

The world's great age begins anew,
The golden years return.
–Shelley, *Hellas*

When the smoke of battle blew away at Yorktown, a sorry mess was revealed. The British still held Savannah, Charleston and New York, and America was bankrupt. The new states owed huge debts to France and Holland, and the only way to pay these debts was for Congress humbly to beseech the states to pay. In the years 1771-1783 Congress asked the states for ten million dollars and it got one and a half million.

Forty paper dollars bought one silver dollar, and soon it would cost more. There being no national coinage, old pieces of silver and gold–English, Dutch, French, Spanish, Portuguese–circulated with no fixed values. The states were shut out of trade with the West Indies or any part of the British Empire, and since Congress could not make commercial agreements–all the states wanting to make their own–it was unable to function in the field of commerce.

The states treated each other as foreign countries. Taxes were levied in New York on firewood coming from Connecticut and eggs from New Jersey. There were continual quarrels over boundaries, riparian rights, currency values. Pennsylvania took up arms to drive Connecticut settlers out of the Wyoming Valley (The territory of Wyoming, which became a state in 1890, took its name from this valley in Pennsylvania.), and some died of exposure and starvation. Pennsylvania felt sorry about this later.

The Dean of Gloucester, Josiah Tucker, was accounted a leading English political thinker. "The mutual antipathies and clashing interests of the Americans," he announced, "their difference of governments, habitudes and manners, indicate that they will have no center and no common interest. They never can be united under any species of government whatever." End quote.

George III, too, had a clouded crystal ball. "The States will repent before long and beg to be taken back into the British Empire," he said. He added he was not sure whether they should be taken back.

Antipathies existed between the colonies, and rivalries and jealousies as well, but there was one thing the worthy Dean did not consider. The new nation was blessed with great and brilliant men such as were never before gathered in one place at one time: Washington, Franklin, Adams, Jefferson, Hamilton, Madison, to name the most prominent–the Founding Fathers–and there were many more. These men, who had held the infant country together by the combined power of their personalities, their devotion and their brains, finally achieved, through long and arduous deliberation, the very union the worthy Dean declared impossible.

Another thing the Dean did not realize: The men of the Continental Army came from all the colonies; they fought together for a common cause in each other's colonies, and this gave impetus to the growth of nationalism. The people of America *did* have a center and a common interest, thanks to Britain herself.

The Founding Fathers knew that a strong central government must be established. Alexander Hamilton outlined a plan for one, and became the mouthpiece for the group called "the Federalists." Washington wrote a letter to the governors in 1783 saying that there must be a supreme power, "without which the Union cannot be of long duration, and everything must very rapidly tend to anarchy and confusion."

Ever since the Second Continental Congress had convened the members had been struggling to come up with Articles of Confederation, but no state wanted to give up an iota of its freedom to anyone: It would be like returning to the Crown. The smaller states were naturally afraid of being overpowered by the larger ones and the difficulties would have been insurmountable were it not for the greatness of the deliberators, their tact, their shrewdness, their genius.

In March 1781 the Articles of Confederation were ratified. Mainly they gave a legal aspect to the authority Congress had been exercising all along. Each state retained its freedom, independence and sovereignty, and had one vote in the Congress. But the central government had no power to enforce its authority. The colonies were not yet a nation at all. The weak union was nothing more than a "league of friendship," but the Articles were a step in the right direction.

The Congress established departments of Foreign Affairs, War and Finance, which sounded respectable and gave prestige. The latter department, under the genius of Robert Morris, helped get the economy going.

And all this took place while the Congress was conducting the war–Yorktown was still seven months away.

John Adams, Benjamin Franklin, John Jay and Henry Laurens were the peace commissioners representing the Continental Congress to negotiate the final treaty with England. The matter was of extreme delicacy and involved the interest of all the great powers. The United States and France had pledged not to make a separate peace with Great Britain. Spain was allied with France, but not with America, and while eager to profit at British expense, she had ambitions involving parts of the Mississippi Valley; nor did France want America to become *too* powerful.

When the peace negotiators found that the Comte de Vergennes was not entirely to be trusted, they violated their instructions from the Congress and approached the British agent, Richard Oswald.

Vergennes was a friend of America, but was a pragmatic Frenchman first. "We ask independence only for the thirteen states," he wrote the French Ambassador to Spain, the Comte de Montmorin, explaining that France did not wish a new republic to become "the exclusive mistress of this immense continent."

Franklin was very deft and shrewd, and in the end the negotiators got about what they wanted with a separate peace, which took all Franklin's diplomacy to smooth over with Vergennes. His Britannic Majesty acknowledged the colonies to be free, sovereign and independent states. The borders were set at the Great Lakes, the Mississippi River and roughly the northern boundary of Florida. Of equal importance were the fishing rights on the Grand Banks.

Britain would withdraw her troops from America "with all convenient speed."

Restitution for seized Tory property was a thorny problem. The Congress, having no power over the states, could only "recommend" restoration. Most of the states saw fit to ignore the recommendations.

With such a weak government, the American colonies could not be respected in Europe. Jefferson, American Minister to France (1785–1789) wailed in a letter home, "We are the lowest and most obscure of the whole diplomatic tribe." When John Adams, the first American Minister to England (1785) attempted to negotiate a commercial treaty, the British Foreign Minister asked him witheringly whether England was expected to make thirteen treaties? European bankers refused to make loans to the new nation, for what chance had they of ever getting their loans repaid?

The new nation was in a difficult position. It had won its independence from one monarch with the help of another monarch. It was essential to make commercial treaties with yet other monarchs, from whom tender loving care for a set of upstart rebels, and republicans at that, on the fringes of a vast wilderness 3,000 miles away, could hardly be expected. The no-account but ambitious little nation, calling itself the United States of America, was more or less friendless.

Britain retained a string of trading posts between Lake Champlain and Lake Michigan, all on territory belonging to the Americans by the treaty of peace. She said, since the states had not kept their part of the treaty by paying their debts to British merchants or restoring the confiscated property of the Loyalists, it would continue to hold these posts. The fur trade was worth a million and a half a year, which may have had something to do with this implacable attitude.

More trouble was brewing. Twenty-five thousand settlers, led by Daniel Boone and other stalwarts, had crossed the Alleghenies in the early 1780s and inhabited the rich lands in the vicinity of the Mississippi. By the end of the decade this region had 100,000 settlers who had established farms and homesteads. The only outlet for their produce was the Mississippi, and this river, according to the Treaty of 1783, was open to American navigation. But Spain was in possession of New Orleans. Its strategic position, 107 miles from the sea by water and commanding the whole of the delta, gave Spain the upper hand, and Spain withdrew "the right of deposit" at that port. The Mississippi was useless to the Americans without New Orleans.

Some of the settlers were in favor of raising an army and driving the Spaniards out. As the eastern merchants were uninterested in the navigation of the Mississippi, and showed no inclination to aid the westerners, the latter then toyed with the notion of "throwing their allegiance" elsewhere. The new nation was on the verge of losing all the rich land acknowledged as hers in the peace treaty. Washington said, "The western states stand on a pivot. The touch of a feather will turn them any way."

The East was alive with war profiteers. A luxurious life, imported from France and England, was their lot, while the poor farmers who had fought the Revolution thinking a new era of equality was about to dawn, "went home without a farthing in their pockets." The words are Washington's.

With the phenomenal rise in prices these humble folk could not pay for the necessities of life, nor the interests on the mortgages on their farms, which were foreclosed, fat fees going into the hands of lawyers. Those unable to pay their debts went to debtors' prison.

Things were particularly bad in Massachusetts, and in the western counties of that state, in the summer of 1786, mobs began forcibly to bar foreclosures by preventing the courts from holding their sessions at Northampton and Worcester.

Captain Daniel Shays, a veteran of Bunker Hill, rose up as leader of these rebels. They marched to Springfield and blocked the meeting of the State Supreme Court; the judges fled in terror. The Shaysites defied the sheriffs and constables to seize property for debt, and attacked the Springfield arsenal.

It was then that the Governor sent 4,000 troops in pursuit of the Shaysites, and a battle took place at Petersham. The Shaysites were routed, several were killed, the rest taken prisoner, and Captain Shays fled to Vermont.

Everyone was shocked at this violent rebellion–everyone but Thomas Jefferson. The Spirit of '76 was still alive! "God forbid that we should have twenty years without a rebellion!" he said.

In the meantime John Hancock had become Governor of Massachusetts. He put his John Hancock on a pardon for all the Shaysites in prison, which included the absent Daniel Shays. Hancock had once been a rebel himself.

Shays' Rebellion did not help the American image in Europe, which sank even lower, if that were possible. But it did make abundantly clear what the Founding Fathers had known from the first, that the central government must be vested with more authority if it were to survive; this led to the creation of the American Constitution.

Part Two

FROM THE GREAT CONSTITUTION TO AN ANGEL AND EARTHLY CREATURES

1   THE GREAT CONSTITUTION

What men or gods are these?
–Keats, *Ode on a Grecian Urn.*

On May 9, 1781, shortly before sunrise, General Washington left Mount Vernon by coach to attend the great Constitutional Convention in Philadelphia. He arrived on May 13. The *Journal* reported, "Sunday last, His Excellency General Washington, a member of the grand Convention, arrived here. He was met at some distance and escorted into the city by the troop of horses and saluted at his entrance by the artillery. The joy of the people on the coming of this great and good man was shown by their acclamations, the ringing of bells, & c."According to his diary the mannerly General waited on the venerable Dr. Franklin as soon as he got to town. (Franklin died in 1790. In his long and detailed will he wrote, "My fine crab-tree walking-stick, with a gold head curiously wrought in the form of the cap of liberty, I give to my friend, and the friend of mankind, General Washington. If it were a scepter, he has merited it, and would become it.")

On the day appointed for the opening session of the Convention, May 14, only two states were represented, Pennsylvania and Virginia, Washington and James Madison representing Virginia. There was no quorum until May 25, when a sufficient number of delegates had trickled into town to conduct business, 29 men from 9 states.

Robert Morris of Pennsylvania proposed Washington for President, the motion seconded by John Rutledge of South Carolina and a foregone conclusion. Alexander Hamilton nominated Major William Jackson for secretary.

Washington, from the chair, said he had never been in such a situation, he felt embarrassed, and hoped his errors, as they would be unintentional, would be excused. A committee was appointed to prepare standing rules and orders, and the convention adjourned until May 28 to give the committee time to complete its task.

The Preamble to the Constitution is clear and precise:

"We the people of the United States, in order to form a more perfect Union, establish justice, insure domestic tranquility, provide for the common defense, promote the general welfare, and secure the blessings of liberty to ourselves and our posterity, do ordain and establish this Constitution for the United States of America."

The entire constitution is remarkably concise. It took four months to make it that way.

And it took as remarkable a group of men as ever assembled anywhere to accomplish the mighty task. Their average age was less than 43, but as Professor John A. Garraty has noted, they had escaped the weakness usually associated with the young: "instability, half-cocked radicalism, a refusal to heed the suggestions of others." Jefferson, who as Minister to France was absent, called these men "demi-gods."

Their task required the reconciliation of clashing interests. Fortunately they were basically pragmatic, having a unique sense of what was possible as distinct from what was ideally best.

"If all the delegates named for this Convention at Philadelphia are present," wrote Monsieur Otto, the French charge d'affaires to the Comte de Montarin, "we will never have seen, even in Europe, an assembly more respectable for the talents, knowledge, and patriotism of those who compose it."

A Frenchman, Baron de Montesquieu, had published in 1748 *The Spirit of Laws*—a book banned in France but read with enthusiasm in England—in which he propounded a separate and balanced government in order to guarantee the freedom of the individual. He proposed a three-branched government (Executive, Legislative and Judicial). Montesquieu was influenced by John Locke, and in turn his work influenced the delegates to the Grand Convention and thus had a profound effect on the American Constitution.

The delegates, anxious for a lasting government, were confronted with almost insoluble problems. There were two grand objectives. One was, as Madison put it, "How to substitute the mild majestracy of the law for the cruel and violent majestracy of force." Powers of a general nature, and powers of a local nature, must be assigned to their appropriate governments. *All depends on the correct distribution of these powers.*

The immediate objectives were to restore order, strengthen the public credit, and make it possible for the country to enter into commercial treaties and agreements with foreign powers so that trade might flourish. Problems abounded, such as the conduct of Indian affairs and the management of the western lands. The delegates were patricians, either by birth or attainment, and had a high, even an awesome, sense of their duties.

"We are framing a system," said Madison, "which we wish to last for ages." It might, he said, "decide forever the fate of Republican Government."

The dedicated delegates set themselves a rigid schedule–five hours a day, six days a week. To this was added the burden of writing notes and attending committees.

The Convention voted to guard against "licentious publication of their proceedings," and a remarkable secrecy was maintained.

James Madison was determined to keep a record of all that went on, and chose a seat in front of the presiding member. "The labor to which Madison committed himself was stupefying." Madison's *Notes of Debates in the Federal Convention of 1787* is a major treasure of the Republic and was a tremendous undertaking on which he worked most of the rest of his life.

One of the many seemingly insurmountable difficulties in carving a new Federal system out of such divergent material was the fact that the states were tenacious of their sovereign powers, and the small states had the added fear of being swallowed up by the larger ones. The concept that a government could have two powers, state and federal, was entirely new.

As to votes, slavery presented a problem. The northern states knew they could not abolish slavery and still have a Federal Constitution. Northerners wanted slaves to be counted in each state's share of direct Federal taxes. The Southern states wanted the slaves to be included in determining their representation in the House of Representatives, but with no intention of letting the slaves vote! Finally an agreement was reached with a three-fifths compromise. A slave would be counted as three-fifths of a person for both taxation and representation.

A powerful presidency was the most radical creation of the new constitution. The President has the responsibility of executing the laws, and is Commander in Chief of the armed forces, but only the Congress can declare war. The President has the power to appoint Federal judges and other officials, and to veto any law voted by congress, though a two-thirds vote in both houses can override his veto.

Representation in the lower house is based on population, each representative serving a two-year term, but each state, regardless of size, has two senators, each serving a six-year term.

Senators and Representatives are bound by oath to uphold the Constitution, but no religious test is required as a qualification to any office or public trust under the United States. Neither could any titles of nobility be granted. (No Dukes? No Duchesses?)

No duties or imposts of any kind are to be levied on goods moving from one state to another. (This assured the rapid growth of interstate commerce.)

Checks and balances are scattered throughout the Constitution. Congress has the power to impeach for "high crimes and misdemeanors," but the power is cleverly divided: the lower house impeaches, the upper house tries.

The third branch of government, a "Supreme Tribunal" of judges, finally emerged as the "Supreme Court" in Article III. Its powers and duties are defined, and the judges, or justices, are not subject to dismissal. Surprisingly, in Section 3 of this Article, treason is taken up, and a prohibition regarding its punishment: "No attainder of treason shall work Corruption of Blood." In more prosaic words, the innocent family of a convicted traitor may not be made to suffer. This seems to have been a new concept in law.

Trial by jury and the writ of *habeas corpus* are generally assured.

There existed a wariness on the part of the states that the Federal Government would suck away their traditional rights, and this fear proved well founded. But the rights of the states began to be eroded in a way scarcely foreseen–and that was by the national judiciary, Federal judges in Federal courts set up in the states to try offenses that were made Federal.

The going had been long and arduous, requiring almost superhuman patience. The debates over the fears of the larger states combining against the smaller ones at one time seemed perilously close to wrecking the convention. Madison pointed out that Virginia, Massachusetts and Pennsylvania had no common interest in point of "manners, religion or staple products," their staples being respectively tobacco, flour and fish, and hence had no motive for combining. But the small states, it was evident, were not to be moved by argument.

It was now that Dr. Franklin made his famous suggestion that the sessions be opened with prayer. Coming from the revered and venerable Franklin, a highlight of the Age of Enlightenment, and never noted for his piety, this was a surprising turn of events. The suggestion deserved serious consideration, but there was opposition on various grounds:

(1) It might offend the Quakers, and they were guests in a Quaker City.

(2) If it leaked out that after five weeks of deliberation the Convention was reduced to imploring aid from the Almighty it would look as though dissension had forced them to this measure.

(3) It would entail the extra expense of a chaplain's salary. This was a sobering thought!

But to vote down any suggestion of the revered Dr. Franklin, so long a national institution, was unthinkable. The delegates skirted the problem tactfully by adjourning the session without bringing the matter to a vote.

And they did very well, even without prayer. Gladstone described the American Constitution as "the most wonderful work ever struck off at a given time by the brain and purpose of man," and William Pitt said of it, "It will be the pattern for all future constitutions and the admiration of all future ages."

Taking this into consideration, and the fact that sessions of the Congress, which often achieve nothing, or pass ridiculous and sometimes outrageous laws, are opened with prayers offered by a chaplain (changed regularly, like the bill-of-fare at a table d'hôte), one cannot help wondering.

At about four o'clock on September 17, the Convention "dissolved itself by adjournment *sine die*." As the delegates left the State House a man in the anxious crowd leaned forward and asked, "Dr. Franklin, what kind of a government are we to have?" "A republic, if you can keep it," old Ben replied.

"Beyond all doubt the Convention was the most far-reaching political event in all the horologe of time. Never were more important problems submitted to any assembly for solution than were presented to the framers of our Constitution. Upon the result of their deliberations depended the destiny of a nation and the future happiness of unnumbered millions of people.[1]

That night the members of the Convention met for the last time, to enjoy a social evening. They dined together at the City Tavern. Let us hope that the food, the wine, and the entertainment were worthy of the great men gathered there!

It was ten months after the signing of the Constitution before the requisite number of state conventions (nine) had ratified it, making it law, during which time the rudderless country drifted along. There was strong popular fear of executive power; the people had had a long dose of it and many of the delegates had come to their state conventions opposed to ratification. But after endless debates the opposition gave way everywhere. It was the influence of Washington, waiting at Mount Vernon, that pervaded the conventions. He had presided over the making of the Constitution and was the first to sign it. Monroe wrote to Jefferson, "Be assured, his influence carried this government."

Not entirely satisfied with the Constitution, Washington knew it was the best that could be devised and accepted by so many differing factions, and that nothing here below is perfect.

2   LEVEES AND AMENDMENTS

When the Constitution became the law of the land Washington was, not surprisingly, the choice of the electors for President. John Adams, having the next largest number of votes, automatically became the Vice President. They took the oath of office in New York on April 30, 1789.

Congress had rented a house for the President, but it was hardly large enough for the entertaining he was obliged to do. With the burgeoning problems incident to office must be included social pressures. Everything was new and protocol had to be invented.

There were three official entertainments every week. A levee for gentlemen (Tuesdays, three o'clock to four o'clock) which anyone respectably dressed could attend; Martha's tea parties (bisexual) Friday evenings; and official Thursdays at four o'clock. At Martha's teas the gentlemen sat on one side of the long table, the ladies on the other, with Martha at the center. The President insisted that Mrs. Adams, wife of the Vice President, sit beside Martha.

Washington's aide arranged for the levee in what he called "the presence chamber." Throwing wide the door, he entered first and cried in a loud voice, "The

The Washington Family; painting by Edward Savage; National Gallery of Art, Washington, D.C.; Andrew W. Mellon Collection.

President of the United States!" Washington was so shaken by this that he did not recover his composure throughout the levee, and was furious with his aide when the function was over. After that he was "discovered" already in the room when the guests were ushered in, his sword at his side and his ceremonial hat under his arm. (This was a special sort of hat designed to be carried thus, and not to be worn on the head.)

When the first Congress met in New York, September 25, 1789, its chief act was to submit to the States twelve amendments to the Constitution. There was dissatisfaction that the Constitution included no clarification of individual and states' rights. Two of these amendments had to do with appointments and salaries of members, and were not ratified. Those ten original amendments are known as the Bill of Rights.

The first prohibited Congress from making any laws respecting the establishment of religion, or prohibiting the free exercise thereof; or prohibiting freedom of speech or of the press; or the right of the people "peaceably to assemble and to petition the Government for redress of grievances." The first is the most important of the Amendments.

Another gave the people "the right to keep and bear arms," explaining "a well-regulated militia being necessary for the security of a free state." (This amendment has come to be used by gunmen, criminal and trigger-happy destroyers of wildlife as an argument against registration of their lethal weapons.)

Other amendments guaranteed speedy trial by jury and prohibited cruel and unjust punishments.

There have been in the history of the United States, three or four periods when the Constitution has been tortured almost out of shape, and yet that document lives on to meet challenges of which its framers could not have dreamed.

3   GEORGE WASHINGTON'S HEADACHES

Frenchman, you are saucy.
—Thomas Otway, *Venice Preserved*, Act II

Washington proved an extremely conscientious President, cautious and non-aggressive. Taking the concept of the separation of powers very seriously, he did not think a President should propose or espouse legislation, and carefully avoided any mention of the subject in his annual messages to Congress. In picking his advisers (who developed into the Cabinet as it is known today) he chose men without regard to their factions and who did not necessarily agree with his own views.

Jefferson was made Secretary of State; Hamilton, Secretary of the Treasury; Edmund Randolph, Attorney General; and General Knox (who had begun his career as a bookseller in Boston), Secretary of War.

Alexander Hamilton, a far-sighted economic planner, was one of the most powerful of the Federalists and believed a strong central government to be essential to the growth of the nation. The Government owed more than $50,000,000 to foreigners and its own people, which Hamilton made plans to pay off, putting the country on a firm financial basis. He favored a Bank of the United States, and the President, somewhat dubiously, signed the bill. The Bank of the United States was successful from the start. Its banknotes were eagerly accepted at face value, and business found it easier to raise new capital.

In 1789 the French Revolution broke out, and by 1793 France didn't know where she was going, and Louis XVI had lost his head. Soon France was at war with Britain, and this gave the United States the opportunity, so desired by all nations, to play one off against the other. One little stickler was America's 1778 treaty with France by which she was obligated to defend the French West Indies "forever against all other powers." But nobody wanted to do this. Washington issued a proclamation of neutrality, and France sent Edmund Charles Gênet as special representative to the United States to seek American support against Britain. "Citizen Gênet" produced a considerable imbroglio.

The Americans were greatly excited by the French revolution: they had a special interest in this sort of thing. The ideas of democracy they had promulgated were taking hold in the Old World. Gênet, described as young, charming, ram-

"Washington and His Cabinet." Lithograph by Currier & Ives. Reproduced by permission of the National Portrait Gallery, Smithsonian Institution, Washington, D.C.

bunctious, concluded that the American people did not approve of Washington's neutrality, and began, illegally, to license American vessels to operate as privateers against British shipping. Washington forbade these privateers the use of American ports, and was backed by Hamilton, who was always pro-British. Gênet went so far as to challenge the president's authority and threatened to appeal over his head to the American people, who were indeed pro-French. The Government demanded his recall.

Before this could happen his party, the Girondists, fell, the Jacobins were in power, and his return to France would have meant the guillotine. Washington, returning good for evil, refused to allow the extradition of Gênet, who remained in America and married the daughter of Governor George Clinton of New York.

Graver issues confronted the President. The war in Europe greatly increased the demand for American goods, and both Great Britain and France began to attack American merchant ships. Great Britain, with her large navy, did most of the damage. About 600 American vessels were seized on the high seas in 1793 and 1794. A storm of rage rose, and Washington, in an attempt to avert another war with his old enemy, sent chief Justice John Jay as Minister Plenipotentiary to London to negotiate a settlement of the problem.

John Jay, after months of discussion, negotiated a treaty which caused dissension at home. Like Hamilton, Jay was pro-British, and perhaps had not struck as hard a bargain as he might have done. The main points were that great Britain agreed to evacuate her posts in the Northwest, to compensate ship owners for seizures in the West Indies, and to open up her colonies in Asia to American shipping. But she refused to concede American rights as neutrals on the high seas. Britannia ruled the waves!

Yet a "most favored nation" proviso prevented discriminatory duties on British goods, and the United States was committed to pay pre-Revolutionary debts owed to British merchants. But no mention was made of British payments for the slaves seized during the fighting in the South. The treaty angered many people, but Washington, though disappointed, submitted it to the Senate, which ratified it.

There were valuable results from this treaty. Spain wished to withdraw from the anti-French coalition but was afraid of British attacks on her American possessions, and suspected the treaty was a presage of a wider Anglo-American entente. So Spain agreed to a treaty negotiated by William Pinkney that granted the United States free navigation on the Mississippi, opened the port of New Orleans, and accepted the American version of the northern boundry of Florida.

The two treaties cleared the United States' title to the vast stretch of land between the Appalachians and the great Mississippi river. General "Mad Anthony" Wayne defeated the Indians at the Battle of Fallen Timbers (near the present Toledo,

Ohio) and they abandoned their claims. Settlers poured like an avalanche into this new territory. Kentucky and Tennessee were admitted to the Union. Mississippi Territory and then Indiana Territory became entities on the map. "The great westward flood reached full tide." America was on the march.

In 1791 Hamilton had clapped an excise tax on whisky, snuff, loaf sugar and carriages. In the counties of Pennsylvania west of the Alleghenies, where much grain was grown, this tax was resented even more than elsewhere. The settlers there who converted their grain into whisky in small distilleries, making it possible to transport their produce across the mountains, declared the tax detrimental to their liberty and economic welfare. By 1794 rioting broke out. The house of a tax collector was attacked by a band of small distillers, an army platoon attempting to rescue him was forced to surrender to this mob, and one man was killed. Next, government representatives were seared with hot irons. It puts one in mind of the Stamp Act riots of 1765. But these rebels went further. They appealed to like-minded inhabitants of Kentucky, and other places where whisky was distilled, to join in a general revolution. There was talk of establishing a new trans-Allegheny nation or of marching on the capitol, now transferred to Philadelphia.

Washington feared this insurrection would be the precursor of others. He called 12,000 troops, assumed command himself and invited Hamilton to go along—a surprisingly tactless move by Washington since it was Hamilton who had imposed the tax. But everyone can blunder; no harm was done. The rioters, confronted with such a huge force, dispersed. The army had met no opposition, nobody was hurt, no property damaged. Washington boasted to John Jay that the rebels "had been brought to a perfect sense of their misconduct without spilling a drop of blood." He pardoned two of the ringleaders condemned to death. The Government had shown that it was now strong enough to enforce Federal laws.

In September 1796 Washington's second administration was drawing to a close. He announced his retirement from public service in a Farewell Address to the nation. Now 64, he was tired and wanted to return permanently to his beloved Mount Vernon, having given his life to the nation he, more than anyone else, brought into being.

Washington's retirement set a precedent. Every succeeding president served no more than two terms until Franklin D. Roosevelt threw tradition to the wind and ran for four terms. After that a law was enacted limiting presidents to two terms.

The Farewell Address of Washington was destined to have a long influence on American thinking. So great were the man's popularity and prestige that during his terms in office party lines were not clearly drawn. He was a symbol of unity, above party. "The baneful effects of the spirit of party" disturbed him. He tended to agree with Hamilton on foreign policy and finance, thus incurring the displeasure of Jefferson, who dreamt of an agrarian and agricultural society with no big business, no rich landed gentry (like himself), no large cities—a bucolic happy land dotted with charming little farms, contented farmers and contented cows. Hamilton's ideal was a large, busy nation full of factories, banks, flourishing commerce, and rich, impressive cities. Neither of these men was adverse to almost any means to further his views.

Washington ended his address by warning his countrymen against "inveterate sympathies" or "passionate attachments" to any foreign power. He was greatly alarmed at a growing tendency he noted among his countrymen, to divide themselves into "French" and "English" factions. (This seems to be pointed at Jefferson and Hamilton.)

The historian, Samuel Eliot Morison, has pointed out that Washington, though an aristocrat in the best sense of the word, was "more nationalistic and less provincial than any other American of his generation." And his grim determination saved the country. He described himself too modestly as one who had inherited "inferior endowments from nature."

What he had inherited was character. He inspired respect; his influence was tremendous, and always used for good effect. He sowed the seeds of a Bill of Rights in his inaugural address; he put up with men who were devious or mutual enemies (Hamilton and Jefferson) because they had qualities he needed to run the country.

There was nothing at all little about the man.

Upon Washington's retirement the party races began. In the end Hamilton's political maneuverings to eliminate Adams from the ballot backfired, and John Adams drew 71 electoral votes against Jefferson's 68, and Jefferson became Vice President, as the Constitution then required.

4 JOHN ADAMS' HEADACHES

Welcome once more to Paris, gentlemen.
—Fletcher, *The Wild-Goose Chase*, Act 1, Scene 2

John Adams, the son of a New England farmer, was inaugurated second President of the United States on March 4, 1797, in Philadelphia, with the retiring President, George Washington, in attendance, seated among the private citizens.

Adams, whom we remember defending the redcoats at the Boston Massacre trial, was a man of enormous rectitude, courage and patriotism, and had devoted his life to public service. He had been a member of the First Continental Congress, 1774, a member, with Franklin, of the peace commission of 1783, America's first minister to Holland and to Great Britain; he had proposed Washington as commander-in-chief of the Continental Army, and Jefferson as draftsman of the Declaration of Independence. But he was said to be irascible, and lacking the patience and tact of Washington.

He made the mistake of retaining the Cabinet officers of Washington's second administration who were devoted followers of Hamilton.

Like all presidents, "Honest John Adams" inherited a bag of troubles, but the most serious one was America's deteriorating relations with France. The Directory, called "the most corrupt government of the French Revolutionary years," was angered at the Jay Treaty for favoring Great Britain. James Monroe was recalled as the American Minister as he was supposed to be too friendly to France, and this annoyed the Directory too. When his successor, C. C. Pinckney, arrived at Paris he was ordered to leave the country. (He apparently went to the Riviera for a vacation instead.)

At the news that the American envoy had been treated like a common spy, Adams called a special session of Congress and in his speech declared that the United States must convince France that the American nation was not a degraded people, nor would they humble themselves "under a colonial spirit of fear."

Talleyrand had never wanted a war with the United States, and he invited the President to send him new ministers. Adams, wishing to maintain Washington's policy of neutrality without submitting to indignity hoped to do so through diplomacy. To demonstrate that his intentions were peaceful, he appointed Elbridge Gerry, a staunch pro-French Jeffersonian to the post, but added John Marshall who, with Pinckney (summoned back from his holiday) could keep a weather eye on Gerry.

The commissioners arrived in Paris in October 1797, to join Pinckney at a very unpropitious moment. Bonaparte had brought Austria to the bargaining table that month (the Treaty of Campo Formio) and the Directory was riding high on that dangerous horse, Arrogance. Talleyrand again refused to receive the American ministers. The stage was set for the famous XYZ Affair.

The three American commissioners were visited in Paris by one of those mysterious, intriguing ladies who crop up now and then in French history. One pictures this one as being very decolletée (perhaps she was on her way to a ball), wearing purple satin and an enormous coiffure surmounted by a jungle of ostrich plumes (frigates under full sail on top of the head were apparently no longer the *dernier cri*). The lady's name was Madame de Villette, and not surprisingly she was a friend of Talleyrand. She suavely introduced the Americans to three gentlemen.

These three gentlemen bore a message from Talleyrand. No business could be transacted with the government until official apologies were made for the President's speech to Congress, a loan of $10,000,000 be forthcoming to the Directory, and $250,000 slipped into the receptive palms of the Directors themselves.

When the astonished Americans heard this outrageous proposition they enquired what the alternative would be. One of the gentlemen (it was said it was Monsieur Y) mentioned the power of the French party in America (the Jeffersonians), and noted the fate of the European nations who had tried to defend their independence. It was a not well-veiled threat.

"Our case is different from the minor nations of Europe," replied John Marshall, perhaps with a touch of *hauteur*. "They were unable to maintain their independence. America is great, and so far as concerns her self-defence, a powerful nation."

The bickering went on for some time, without any money changing hands, and then John Marshall and Charles Pickney went home. Elbridge Gerry remained in Paris, supposing his presence would prevent war.

When the dispatches recounting this whole unsavory episode reached America, Adams denounced the French for their insulting treatment of the United States and declared he would not send any more ministers to France until he had assurances that they would be treated with the respect due the representatives of a "great, free, powerful and independent nation!"

The pro-French Republicans doubted the President's charge, whereupon Adams turned the commissioners' report over to Congress, deleting the names of the three agents, and substituting the letters X, Y, and Z. The names of these pseudonymous gentlemen have not been lost to posterity. They were (X) Jean Conrad Hottingeur (a Swiss banker) and (Z) Lucien Hauteval, also Swiss, and, surprisingly, (Y) an American banker in Hamburg, a Mr. Bellamy.

The Republicans made a mistake in doubting the word of John Adams; no more upright man ever existed. The reaction to this revelation was much greater than Adams expected. Patriotic fervor and martial spirit rose like a geyser. John Adams, never a charismatic character, suddenly became a hero. He was the man of the hour. He cut off all trade with France, abrogated the treaty of 1778, and authorized American vessels to capture French ships whenever they could on the high seas.

The reaction to France's insults was violent. Charles Pinckney's reputed reply to the alphabetical gentlemen, "Millions for defence, but not one cent for tribute!" became the toast at every dinner. The pro-French Republicans left Philadelphia. Thomas Jefferson said he thought it his duty to remain silent. (How wise of him!)

Patriotism took a great leap forward. Frigates were fitted for sea, and more built, including the celebrated *Constitution* and the *Constellation*. The first national anthem, "Hail Columbia!"—more patriotic than poetic—sprang into being. Congress ordered the enlistment of 3,500 officers and men, and a provisional army of 50,000.

President Adams, that level-headed Yankee, thought all this excessive and put off the enlistment until spring of 1799. At any rate, few were interested in enlisting. George Washington was asked to accept a commission as Lieutenant General of this hasty army for purposes of prestige. Though he could not be expected "to leave his fig tree" as John Adams put it, he designated those who should and filled the various commands—inspector general, adjutant general, quartermaster general, etc.

The 3,000 men who were persuaded to enlist turned out an unpromising lot. Adams described them as "the riff-raff of the country and the scape-gallows of the larger cities."

A naval war with France had already begun on February 7, 1799. The *U.S.S. Constitution* captured a French frigate *L'Insurgente* off Nevis in the Caribbean. Sea battles between frigates occurred sporadically until October. Undeclared wars are not an invention of the 20th Century.

By this time the British had bottled up Bonaparte's army in Egypt, and France was incapable of invading anybody. However, the Secretary of War founded a school for gunners and sappers in the old fort at West Point, which Benedict Arnold had failed in betraying, and President Adams, on his last day in office, appointed the first faculty of the United States Military Academy to teach there.

There was another unfortunate result of the pugnacious spirit of the times. This was the Alien and Sedition Acts that Congress pushed through and Adams signed (though he should not have) in 1798. Adams approved building up American strength, but stopped short of war. The Republicans, still pro-French, wanted the buildup stopped, fearing this new strength would be used against France. Adams' brief moment of popularity was followed by virulent personal attacks in the press to a degree unimaginable today. The Federalists, expecting war, began to panic. Many refugees from the French Revolution and general European unrest had fled to America, and the Federalists began to see spies behind every bush.

The Alien Act gave the President power to arrest or expel aliens in times of "declared war," but as no war had been declared the measure had no importance. The Act also authorized the President to expel aliens he considered dangerous to the peace and safety of the United States. Adams never invoked the law but a number of aliens left the country in fear that he might.

The Sedition Act was a grave mistake. It made it a crime to impede the operation of any law or instigate riot or insurrection, which was reasonable, but it also made it illegal to publish or utter any "false, scandalous or malicious criticism of high government officials."

James Madison, "Father of the Constitution," had the best comment to make

U.S.S. *Constitution*, "Old Ironsides." "Ay, tear her tattered ensign down!" Reproduced from the Collections of The Library of Congress.

about this proviso. It rested, he said, on the exploded theory that government officials are the masters and not the servants of the people. To criticize a king is to undermine the respect for the establishment over which he rules, and that is seditious; to criticize an elected official is to express dissatisfaction with one's agent and the manner in which he is performing the task assigned him. But the Federalists could not, or would not see this fundamental difference.

The election of 1800 was approaching and the Federalists, with this law to back them, attempted to silence the opposition of the Republican press. Twenty-five persons were prosecuted and ten convicted, in unfair trials. It was a barefaced violation of the First Amendment to the Constitution, which guaranteed freedom of speech and press. Both Jefferson and Madison said as much.

Talleyrand, finally realizing how violent had been the reaction in America to his little attempts to replenish his coffers, sidled up to Adams and invited him to send yet another minister (or two) to Paris. The Federalists, terrified as usual of everything French, tried to block this appointment; Adams threatened to resign the Presidency—a clever threat for that would have made Jefferson, the pro-French Vice President, President, which would have been worse. The thwarted Federalists had to give in and the undeclared war with France fizzled out.

5   GEORGE WASHINGTON'S CITY

*There was no ruined image of Menkaura, there was no
alabaster head of Akhnaton.*
—Thomas Wolfe, *Look Homeward Angel*

On July 12, 1790, a joint committee of Congress had presented Washington an "Act for Establishing . . . the permanent Seat of the Government of the United States," as he recorded in his diary. It was to be located on the banks of the Potomac in the newly created "District of Columbia," a ten-mile square of land ceded to the Federal Government by the states of Maryland and Virginia. The selection of the site was made by Washington, Jefferson, and Hamilton, and, according to the Act, the Government was to be transferred thither, from Philadelphia, the second temporary capital, "on the first Monday in December 1800," ten years hence.

"Columbia," a beautiful lady symbolizing the newly established country, seems to have been dreamed up by Timothy Dwight (1752–1817), a Congregational clergyman and President of Yale, in a fervent and patriotic poem envisioning a great future. "Columbia, Columbia, to glory arise!" The name proved useful, from the District of Columbia and Columbia University to the space shuttle of 1981. (Should Columbia and Britannia ever meet, the fur would fly.)

It was Washington who chose a Frenchman, Pierre Charles L'Enfant, to lay out the city. The *Georgetown Weekly Ledger* of March 12, 1791, informed its Maryland readers that "Major Longfont [sic] employed by the President of the United States has arrived to survey the land . . . where the Federal City is to be built."

L'Enfant was enthusiastic about the place and had grand visions. He chose the commanding site, known as Jenkins Hill, for the Capitol, from which he planned a broad and splendid thoroughfare leading to the President's House. A competition for the design of the house, offered by the Commissioners of the future Federal City, was won by James Hoban, an Irish architect living in Charleston. He was awarded $500.

An amateur architect named Dr. William Thornton drew the winning plans for the Capitol, which were praised by Washington and Jefferson. Neither of the buildings was finished when, according to schedule, the Government moved from Philadelphia to the new Federal City. (Washington always referred to it modestly as "the Federal City.") The first session of Congress was held in the new Capitol, or what there was of it, on November 17, 1800. Both the Capitol and the President's house have undergone many changes since.

President Adams arrived to take up residence in the new presidential mansion on November 1.

John Adams was blessed with a highly intelligent and devoted wife. Abigail Adams arrived from the Adams' farm at Quincy, Massachusetts, somewhat after her husband, a tortuous ten-day journey in a springless coach over incredible roads. In a letter to her daughter she gave her impressions of her new home:

"The house is on a grand and superb scale, requiring about thirty servants to attend and keep the apartments in proper order . . . an establishment very well proportioned to the President's salary." She added more specifically, "There is not a single apartment finished . . . We have not the least fence or yard or other convenience. The principle stairs are not up and will not be this winter." Mrs. Adams did not mention it, but water had to be hauled in buckets from a pump five blocks away.

A city built from scratch requires a lengthy adolescence. It has no art, no amenities, no history, to anchor it to civilization.

Aside from the unfinished Capitol and the unfinished President's house, the city of Washington was in the future. There was one tavern near the Capitol, raised through a lottery and elegantly called "Blodgett's Hotel," using the modish French word. Most of the houses were miserable huts. Over a wide area one could see only a few brick kilns and temporary huts for laborers. Pennsylvania Avenue was a broad clearing "studded with stumps and alder bushes," and called, by the classically inclined, "the Great Serbonian Bog"—Milton's name for the swampy Lake Serbonia in Egypt where (for those who have not read their Herodotus lately) whole armies were engulfed—which led from the Capitol to the President's house, three miles to the West.

Senators, congressmen, government clerks and foreign ambassadors were all hard put to find a place to lay their heads. How everyone must have longed to be back in civilized Philadelphia!

George Washington died at Mount Vernon on December 14, 1799, of what is believed to have been diphtheria or a streptococcus sore throat. The doctors bled him four times, which doubtless hastened the end. He had only two years to enjoy the life he had so longed for. He was 67 years old.

Abigail Adams visited Martha Washington in December 1800, a year later (shortly after she reached Washington), and one would have liked to be present, a fly on the wall, to hear the conversation of the two first First Ladies of the Land as they sat together: Abigail Adams, so much a product of New England at its best, who had run the family farm for years, and Martha Washington, a Virginia lady, the owner of 300 slaves. Abigail's letters, with their astute and sometimes ironic comments on politics and the passing scene are still read, while Martha found it a chore to write at all.

The best known passage in Abigail's letters is in one she wrote her husband in Philadelphia while he and his colleagues were haggling over whether to declare Independence from Britain or not. "I long to hear that you have declared an Independency," she wrote at the end of March, 1776 adding "in the new code of Laws which I suppose it will be necessary for you to make, I desire that you would Remember the Ladies, and be more generous and favorable to them than your ancestors. Do not put such unlimited power into the hands of the Husbands. Remember all men would be tyrants if they could. If particular care and attention is not paid to the Ladies, we are determined to foment a Rebellion, and will not hold ourselves bound by any Law in which we have no voice or Representation." This was written 73 years before Elizabeth Cady Stanton stunned the country with her Resolutions and Declaration of Sentiments at Seneca Falls. But John Adams did not Remember the Ladies.

Besides being a commentator and running a farm, Abigail could gather and husk corn, but, as her husband observed, "she made a poor figure at digging potatoes."

Imagine Martha Washington commenting on public affairs, or digging potatoes in those billowing satin skirts!

Martha's biggest problem was her 300 slaves. According to the General's will they were to be set free at her death. But there were old and infirm slaves who begged to be kept, others ill-equipped to face the world, and others who had married Custis slaves. Martha "cloaked" (clothed) them all and set them free. She followed her husband in 1802.

The Government went on at a busy pace in the barren landscape that would one day be Washington. The election of 1801 was approaching, and the leading contenders were Adams, a moderate Federalist, and Jefferson, the head of the Republican party, a party which would now be called the Democratic party. The other leading "Republican" candidate was Aaron Burr of New York, a former senator and a rival of Hamilton in both politics and law.

The vote was close. Jefferson and Burr each received 73 votes against Adams' 65. The candidate with the second largest number of votes, as the law then said, became Vice President. In this dilemma it devolved upon the House of Representatives to decide between them. Even here there was a deadlock, and finally Hamilton, who hated Burr, threw his vote to Jefferson. The two men became even more bitter enemies, with fatal results for Hamilton. Fortunately nowadays President and Vice President run on the same ticket, and you cannot vote for one without voting for the other. This simple procedure has avoided many complications.

6   THOMAS JEFFERSON AND DOLLEY MADISON

Thomas Jefferson, who had spent the winter in Conrad and McNunn's boarding house ($15 a week American plan), forsaking the luxury of Monticello and all those slaves to be near the scene of action, was sworn in as third President of the United States on March 4, 1801. In ostensible simplicity he walked to the Capitol accompanied by two of Adams' cabinet officers, a few representatives and a few members of the Maryland militia. John Adams, outraged by the result of the election had left town for home by daybreak and did not hear Jefferson's inaugural address. (He could not have heard it anyway as it was inaudible.)

The Federalists had presided over the making of the Constitution and guided the country for its first twelve years. They had strengthened the Federal Government, established a fiscal system, boosted the economy and had come to an understanding with Great Britain. Now the opposition was in power. Jefferson's victory had been close in the Electoral College but was a landslide in the congressional elections.

In his inaugural address (printed copies were handed about) the new President set the tone of his administration. The people had spoken, he said, but the rights of dissenters must also be respected. To violate those rights would be oppression. "We are all Republicans—we are all Federalists." He promised a "wise and prudent government."

He also promised to pay off the national debt (a recurring Presidential promise) and to stimulate agriculture and its "handmaiden," commerce, demonstrating which one he put first. He repealed the hated Whisky Tax and other Federal excises; he cut military and navy spending.

In a continued effort to prove how republican he was Jefferson became spectacularly informal in the President's House, wearing old clothes and receiving the representatives of foreign powers, all arrayed in ribbons and medals, in his carpet slippers. Anyone who came to call no matter how high his degree, had to wait his turn as in a queue.

The President gave stag dinners for congressmen and served them himself from a dumbwaiter. For a man who at fourteen had inherited crowds of slaves and an estate of 2,750 acres—surely room to swing a cat—this pose was not convincing. He had a French chef.

When he gave formal dinners he dressed formally, but he was at a disadvantage. He was a widower and his two daughters were seldom able to serve as First Ladies, one because of ill health and the other due to family commitments. When the President's guests included ladies this posed a problem.

James Madison was Secretary of State, and he had a perfect wife. Dolley Madison was born Dorothea Payne and had a patrician background. Tactful, warm-hearted, diplomatic, a vivid personality, she was one of Thomas Jefferson's favorite people. Dolley "snuffed," but manipulated her snuff-box so gracefully that it was "an ornament in her hand." The President called on her many times to be his official hostess; if she was unable to do so, he asked for Dolley's sister.

"Thomas Jefferson begs that either Mrs. Madison or Miss Payne will be so good to dine with him today, to take care of female friends expected." And one of them had to go.

The fact that she was "put forward by Mr. Jefferson" embarrassed Dolley. Before a State Dinner studded with foreign diplomats the President stepped up and offered Mrs. Madison his arm, as the wife of the Secretary of State. Dolley said under her breath, "Take Mrs. Merry," who was the wife of the British ambassador. But the President, with an enigmatic smile, conducted Mrs. Madison to the seat at his right. (Possibly Mr. Jefferson did not care for the wife of the British ambassador.)

Mrs. Merry, furious, seized her husband's arm and marched in behind the President. No wonder Dolley was embarrassed. It must have been a cozy dinner party. The Merrys complained to London of ill-treatment and eventually Ambassador Merry was recalled.

Throughout Jefferson's two administrations Dolley sat beside the President at State Dinners, and presided whenever ladies were entertained at any function.

In his radicalism Jefferson had a few prejudices other than his hatred of monarchy and the British system. One of these was against entrenched judicial power;

Opposite: **James Madison, engraved by C. Cook, date unknown. Dolley Madison, engraved by Goodman & Piggott, c. 1818. Montpelier, the Madison's Virginia Estate. Reproduced by permission of the National Portrait Gallery, Smithsonian Institution, Washington, D.C.**

Jefferson despised *any* entrenched power. The biased behavior of Federalist judges at the Sedition trials increased his hatred, and he determined to rid the courts of the worst of them. He succeeded with one (District Judge John Pickering) who was obviously insane, but the Senate refused to convict Samuel Chase, an Associate Justice of the Supreme Court whose handling of cases under the hated Sedition Act had been arbitrary and high-handed, because his actions did not constitute "high crimes and misdemeanors" as provided in the Constitution.

A more momentous problem faced Jefferson when Spain ceded Louisiana back to France (the secret Treaty of San Ildefonso). She had received Louisiana in the Treaty of Paris in 1763 (that marked the end of the Seven Years' War and reshuffled so much of the world). Access to New Orleans and the mouth of the Mississippi was essential to the United States which might otherwise lose all the land beyond the Appalachians. While Spain, a feeble country, controlled Louisiana, the situation could be tolerated, but now Louisiana was suddenly in French hands again, and France was in the hands of Napoleon Bonaparte. This was quite a different story! New Orleans was the port through which the products of the western territories were shipped to the markets of the world. The city was vital to the United States.

In April 1802 Jefferson instructed the American ambassador in Paris, Robert Livingston, to attempt to purchase New Orleans. The summer went by with nothing happening. Then in October the Spaniards, who oddly were still in control of New Orleans despite the new treaty, suddenly revoked the right of deposit at that port. Jefferson dispatched his friend and disciple James Monroe as Minister Plenipotentiary to Paris, with instructions to offer Napoleon $2 million for New Orleans.

Talleyrand, the crafty and cynical, was still Foreign Minister, having survived the XYZ affair and the Directory, and was on the Napoleonic bandwagon, which was, at the moment, the bandwagon to be on. Finally on April 10, he, at Napoleon's instructions, summoned Livingston to his office and casually offered to sell not only New Orleans but the whole of Louisiana to the United States. Livingston must have been struck speechless.

Talleyrand asked how much America would give for the province, and poor Livingston, thinking wildly, offered something in the neighborhood of $4 million. His instructions said nothing about buying an area almost as large as the entire United States.

Too low, said Talleyrand, and suggested that Monsieur Livingston go home and think it over for a day or two. The American ambassador, one can assume, did not sleep a wink that night. In those days before quick communications, he could get no instructions for months, and Napoleon might change his mind.

Fortunately James Monroe arrived in Paris the very next day and Livingston had someone with whom he could share his burden. The two men decided to offer

Talleyrand $15 milllion on their own responsibility. The offer was accepted and on May 10, 1803, the historic treaty was signed. James Monroe came home with 828 thousand square miles in his pocket, the justly famous Louisiana Purchase. No real estate broker since has been able to pull off such a deal.

Napoleon had his reasons for unloading this vast expanse of territory so soon after having forced Spain to deed it back to him. He had lost Santo Domingo (Haiti) when significant numbers of his troops there had succumbed to yellow fever and were unable to put down a revolt of the slaves under that extraordinary character, Toussaint L'Ouverture, "the Black Napoleon." Contemplating a renewal in the seemingly never-ending war in Europe, and the impossibility of holding Louisiana if the British, with their powerful navy, had designs on it, or the probability of the Americans overrunning it in the course of time, Napoleon freed himself of the whole problem and gained $15 million.

There was wild rejoicing in America, but Jefferson's joy was tempered by a problem. Under the Constitution did the Government have the power to add new territory, or grant citizenship to the 50,000 inhabitants of the region by executive act, as the treaty required? Jefferson and his advisors knew it would be dangerous to delay ratification of the treaty until a constitutional amendment could be acted upon by three-fourths of the states. The President "acquiesced with satisfaction," and Congress sort of looked the other way over the niceties and subtleties of the problem, and ratified the treaty. Thus even Thomas Jefferson, staunch constitutionalist, knew when expediency was really the first law.

Though Jefferson, almost a Yankee in his frugal thinking, was averse to spending money on building up a navy, and sanctioned only a fleet of little gunboats, he had inaugurated the biggest land deal in history.

It was the behavior of the Barbary States of North Africa that turned his thinking nautical at last. The rulers of these kingdoms, Morocco, Algiers, Tunis and Tripoli, had been pirates for centuries, levying blackmail on the Venetians, the Genoese, Spaniards, English, French, Dutch, Danes, Swedes, and since 1785, the Americans. Any nation trading in the Mediterranean, was obliged to pay tribute to the Barbary Corsairs, and the nations were willing to do so only because it was cheaper than waging war. Many prisoners were taken and held for ransom, including, in 1575 Miguel Cervantes, the author of *Don Quixote*; and this practice was still going on.

American trade was increasing, making more plunder for the barbaric corsairs, and Jefferson determined to put a stop to them. Not one cent for tribute!

A squadron of ships was sent to deal with the problem, money being raised by a special "Mediterranean Fund" tax of 2½ percent on all imports.

On the night of February 16, 1804, a young lieutenant, Stephen Decatur, in an act of daring bravery reminiscent of John Paul Jones, rowed with a few men into the harbor of Tripoli in a small craft, boarded the American frigate *Philadelphia*, which had been captured by the pirates, overpowered her crew, set fire to her hull, and rowed back to his ship unharmed under a terrible bombardment from the Tripoli batteries. Thus Stephen Decatur became another naval hero.

Peace was made with Tripoli in 1805 after more exploits by the intrepid Decatur, and this signaled the end of the Barbary pirate raids on Mediterranean shipping, which had been going on since Barbarossa defied the powers of Charles the Fifth in the 1530s.

All the nations of Europe that had been paying tribute to the Barbary pirates for three hundred years benefited, but there is no record that any of them ever said, "Thank you."

The acquisition of the huge Louisiana Territory had delighted almost everyone, but brought on reactions that seemed to threaten the Union. The diehard Federalists of New England were outraged. Their section of the country would inevitably lose in importance as the new West grew, and anything would be better than that! The most extreme of them, known as the Essex Junta, led by former Secretary of State, Timothy Pickering, concluded that the only solution was to secede from the Union and form a "Northern Confederacy." They believed that to be successful this Confederacy would have to include New York.

But Alexander Hamilton, the most prominent and powerful of the New York Federalists and one of the authors of the Constitution, rejected the Junta's proposals forthwith and so did other prominent men. The Junta then turned to the Vice President, Aaron Burr, who was running against the Republican candidate for Governor of New York. Burr did not promise anything, but he won their backing and was soundly defeated at the polls. Hamilton accused Burr of treason, and even after the election which Burr did not win, continued to cast aspersions upon the man's character, not a difficult thing to do. Burr's political morals were shady and the suspicions of his traitorous leanings had some foundation.

Burr challenged Hamilton to a duel, which took place on the Palisades at Weehawken, New Jersey, July 11, 1804. Hamilton disdained to fire, but Burr took careful aim. Hamilton, the fiscal genius of the Constitution, and a great if erratic man, died the next day, cut off in his prime at 49. Burr was indicted for murder in both New Jersey and New York, but continued to preside over the Senate as Vice President until his term expired in 1805. He had certainly been guilty of "high crimes and misdemeanors" but there was no move to impeach him.

The vast area of land that the United States had so unexpectedly acquired remained for the most part a wilderness trod only by Indians. Even before the acquisition Jefferson was interested in this no-man's-land, its geography and its potentials, particularly in the prospects of Indian trade.

Jefferson's private secretary was Meriwether Lewis, aged 32, a veteran of Indian wars at home in the wilderness. The President put him in charge of an expedition, and Lewis chose as his colleague William Clark, aged 28, who was likewise an experienced frontiersman.

Lewis had knowledge of minerology, astronomy and some botany; he could take latitudes and longitudes. Jefferson wrote to the famous botanist, Dr. Barton of Philadelphia, he has "the firmness of constitution and character, prudence, habits adapted to the woods, and familiarity with Indian manners and habits requisite for this undertaking."

Meriwether Lewis was well liked by the ladies of the Cabinet, and particularly by Mrs. Madison. They fluttered about "providing everything that could possibly be needed in such a perilous journey."

Lewis and Clark, with a company of 48 valiant men, set up winter quarters in St. Louis, and in the spring of 1804 started up the Missouri River. As guide they had a Shoshoni squaw named Sacajawea, who embarked with her papoose on her back. It is of some comfort to learn that her French-Canadian husband was also in the party.

By autumn they reached what is now North Dakota, where they spent another winter. Not having been frozen to death, they set out again in April 1805. They passed the Great Falls of the Missouri and the Continental Divide in southwest Montana, and reached the Pacific in November, via the Clearwater, Snake, and Columbia rivers. They spent another uncomfortable winter there. They started back in the spring of 1806 and reached St. Louis September 23.

It was a tremendous undertaking and the news of its successful conclusion was greeted with joy. The men brought with them an enormous amount of information about the country—accurate maps, geological and botanical specimens, even fauna, including two grizzly bear cubs that so delighted the President that a den was constructed for them on the White House grounds.

Jefferson sent out other explorers to furnish further information about the great unknown region, including an expedition in 1805 headed by Lieutenant Zebulon Pike. He and his party ascended the Mississippi in an unsuccessful attempt to discover its source. The following summer Pike and his men proceeded up the valley of the Arkansas and attempted, but failed, to climb the mountain that bears his name. Later Pike unfortunately entered California, then part of Mexico, ran into a bit of the Spanish army and was obliged to surrender all his maps and papers. Less lucky than Lewis and Clark, he returned with only his memories.

7   THE THOUSAND AND ONE NIGHTS

—telling me of the moldwarp and the ant,
Of the dreamer Merlin and his prophecies,
And of a dragon and a finless fish.
—Henry the Fourth, Part One, Act III, Scene 3

At the end of his term as Vice President Aaron Burr disappeared. He was up to some kind of mischief, in fact so many kinds of mischief that they have never been straightened out. In Washington he approached the British Minister with a most indecent proposal—for half a million dollars and British naval support, he offered to liberate Louisiana from the Union and hand it over to Britain. Britain was not interested at the moment.

Burr had an old friend in the person of General James Wilkinson, Commanding General of the United States Army, whom Jefferson made Territorial Governor of Louisiana. What the President did not know was that Wilkinson enjoyed at the same time the role of secret agent for Spain, in the pay of that country. During the troubles over closing the Mississippi to American vessels he attempted to sway the disgruntled settlers into the Spanish orbit.

Burr next appears at an island called Blennerhassett at the headwaters of the Ohio River, where dwelt a romantic Irishman named Harman Blennerhassett. Mr. B. was charmed with Burr's plan to conquer Mexico, make Burr Emperor, and himself Grand Chamberlain! People entertained grand ideas in those days.

In a luxurious flatboat the party sailed down the Mississippi, stopping here and there to visit prominent gentlemen, to whom Burr outlined various flamboyant projects—a different one to each, it is said. Money was forthcoming, for Burr could charm birds off the trees and money out of anyone's pocket. The Southerners were fascinated by the polished and glamorous gentleman from New York, who had been Vice President of the United States and fought a duel, which was a gentlemanly thing to do, even if he had killed one of the Founding Fathers of the Republic. People seem to have hung fascinated on his words, and to believe his flights of fancy, however improbable.

In Tennessee, Burr met Andrew Jackson, who promised to get him elected to the Senate if he would settle in Tennessee. Burr had bigger fish to fry.

In New Orleans his varied plans charmed disgruntled Creoles, who did not want to live in a territory of the United States, and American filibusterers who wanted to invade Mexico. The Roman Catholic Bishop of New Orleans gave him his blessing. So did the Mother Superior of the Ursuline convent in that town. It would appear that nobody ever spotted Aaron Burr for a phony.

Back in Washington Burr wheedled $2,500 out of the Spanish Minister, presumably to get Louisiana back for Spain, and in the summer of 1806, now with headquarters in Lexington, Kentucky, he signed up recruits for his expedition, wherever it was bound. This time it was to take up a claim for 400,000 acres in Louisiana, there perhaps to be summoned to be President of Louisiana when his supporters declared Louisiana free. (Surely this was much better than giving it back to Spain!)

Burr and his Irish henchman, the dazzled Blennerhassett, and General Wilkinson, the two-faced, commanding a flotilla of ten flatboats, reached the mouth of the Cumberland River by the end of the year. And it was at this juncture that the treacherous Wilkinson, deciding that Burr was "worth more betrayed than befriended,"[1] wrote President Jefferson of Burr's "deep, dark, wicked and widespread conspiracy." Jefferson issued a proclamation to the nation and ordered Burr's arrest for treason, specifically for levying war against the United States. Burr attempted to escape to Spanish Florida, was caught and brought to Richmond for trial. Jefferson did not act in a very statesmanlike way, offering a commission in the Army to one witness if he would testify in a manner "not averse to the Administration," which sounds dangerously like bribery. Chief Justice Marshall, who heard the case, gave so narrow a definition of treason that the jury found the accused not guilty in less than half an hour.

Burr departed for Europe and dreamed up more Arabian Nights entertainments, such as a plan to restore Canada to France, for which purpose he charmed money out of prominent French pockets. Guileless Britons with more money than brains contributed to a plan for hiring sailors, out of work because of Jefferson's shipping embargo of 1807, to march on Washington and set up Burr as dictator.

But Burr's further adventures are outside the scope of this history. General Wilkinson, "a traitor to every cause he embraced,"[2] remained in the good graces of Jefferson and retained his command in the Army.

If Charles Lee of Monmouth is the second nastiest man in American history, surely Aaron Burr is a close contender.

8   JEFFERSON'S AND MADISON'S HEADACHES

There may be a brief misunderstanding between England
and America, but that will not last.
—Charlotte Brontë, *Shirley*

Nelson's victory over the allied French and Spanish fleets, at the Battle of Trafalgar (October 21, 1805) had given great Britain's naval power tremendous prestige and Britannia herself a swelling in the head that took generations to reduce. Napoleon, whose navy was no match for Britain's, resorted to the only thing he could do—levy economic warfare. He blockaded Britain and Britain replied with her "Orders in Council," forbidding trade with continental Europe. (Orders in Council were measures decided by the British cabinet and then debated in Parliament.)

Jefferson's great aim was to keep the Republic, new, weak and poor, out of the conflict. American commerce was brought to a standstill. Even the West Indies were now off bounds, and where could America get her rum? The French seized any American ship that touched a British port, and if she touched a French port she was seized by the British.

Britain then overreached herself and roused America to a pitch of excitement unequaled since the first shot was fired at Lexington in 1775. The frigate *Chesapeake*, commanded by Captain James Barron, left Norfolk, Virginia, June 22, 1807, bound for the Mediterranean, her guns not mounted, her decks littered with tackle. Off the Virginia Capes she was overhauled by the British warship *Leopard* and ordered to heave-to and be searched for British deserters. When Captain Barron replied that he had no deserters the *Leopard* opened fire. Three men were killed outright and eighteen wounded. Barron, unprepared, struck his colors after giving a single token shot lighted by a coal brought from the galley. The *Chesapeake* was boarded, four alleged deserters seized (one English, the others American) and the *Chesapeake* limped back to Norfolk with her dead and wounded, her hull riddled, her rigging shredded. The reaction throughout the nation can be imagined.

Jefferson could do nothing more than issue a proclamation excluding British shipping from American ports, and instruct James Monroe, now American ambassador in London, to demand an apology and reparations for the attack on the *Chesapeake*.

An apology! A Tory government laughed. "An insignificant and puny power," observed the Tory press, "to mitigate Britain's proud sovereignty of the ocean!"

That this violent act should be committed on the vessel of a country with which Britain was at peace can only be explained by the Battle of Trafalgar and the swollen-head syndrome it produced. In such cases that rarest of the senses, called for some reason "common," is the first thing to go. The British Foreign Secretary, George Canning, sent a message to Jefferson saying he was willing to discuss reparations for the action against the *Chesapeake*, and the admiral whose orders were responsible for it had been dismissed from his command on the American coast. But Britain remained firm in her rights to search and to impressment on the high seas. Another of those Orders in Council made every neutral vessel that did not touch a British port and pay duties subject to seizure. Britain was acting very like the Barbary pirates. Jefferson had the choice of submission or war, both of them abhorrent, and the second foolhardy.

The tragic *Leopard* and *Chesapeake* affair ended in another tragedy. Captain

James Barron was court-martialed for having put to sea unprepared, and for having surrendered so meekly, he was found guilty and sentenced to suspension from the Navy without pay for five years. The sentence was approved by President Jefferson. Captain Barron led a dark life thereafter. Even after the five-year suspension he could get no commission, and blamed all this on the vindictive hostility of Decatur, who had been a member of the court-martial. In 1819 he challenged Decatur to a duel, and killed him. Such was the end of the dashing hero Stephen Decatur.

The old Decatur house, where his wife grieved to death, still stands in Lafayette Square in Washington. From a window, now blocked up, Stephen's ghost is said to peer out on certain nights, or perhaps it is that of his grieving widow.

The British policy of impressment went merrily on and was the greatest cause of the War of 1812.

Britain continued to build up her navy, but it was impossible to corral the requisite sailors, who being ill-paid, ill-fed and ill-handled, preferred to ship on American vessels where conditions were better. As Britain did not have enough sailors to man her 700 warships she continued to halt unarmed American vessels on the high seas. A party then boarded, lined up the crews and selected the most likely, claiming they were British subjects. Naturalized Americans were deemed still British subjects, and native-born Americans were impressed along with the rest.

Shortly before assuming office, Madison sent Congress a detailed report of 6,057 Americans who had been kidnapped off American ships in the three previous years. Jefferson, in an attempt to make the British acquire a little common sense, (a hopeless task as it turned out) induced Congress to pass an Embargo Act which forbade foreign commerce entirely. It was a poor move. The shipping interests were ruined, and this outraged the maritime states of New England and New York. Southern and western farmers lost their best markets and they also were enraged, for in spite of all the seizures, shipping was still profitable.

The Embargo Act was repealed and the Nonintercourse Law substituted. This forbade commerce with Britain and France, the law to be suspended for either country when that country ceased attacking neutral shipping.

Jefferson wanted his Secretary of State, James Madison, to succeed him, and though Madison was thought in New England to be a Federalist and was now thoroughly hated, so great was Jefferson's popularity that Madison was elected by a large majority.

James Madison was very different from Thomas Jefferson. He lacked Jefferson's flair and was incapable of receiving diplomats in his pantoufles—besides, Dolley would not have let him. He lacked the little streak of insincerity of the *poseur*, and was a deeper thinker than Jefferson, but he had no better solution for the manifold troubles with England and France than Jefferson had.

Poor Madison! There were troubles on land as well as at sea. Settlers in the west were land-greedy and kept driving the red men from the rich Ohio Valley, their ancestral hunting-grounds. They suffered Indian raids in retaliation. One's sympathy is with the Indians.

General William Henry Harrison, Governor of Indiana Territory, wrested land from one tribe by promising it concessions against a rival tribe, pitting one against the other until it looked as if the Indians would annihilate themselves.

It was then that a great man rose among the Indians, the Shawnee chief, Tecumseh. Even General Harrison thought him a genius. With the help of his brother Tenskwatawa, who was called the Prophet and had magical powers, he united the tribes against the whites, to drive them off the land.

The Indians had their encampment in Indiana Territory at the spot where Tippecanoe Creek joins the Wabash. It was called Prophetstown. While Tecumseh was away uniting the tribes and recruiting men, the Prophet, most inadvisably, ordered an attack on Harrison's camp, outside the village. Unfortunately the Prophet's magic deserted him at this point, the white men held their ground, the Indians were disillusioned about the prophet, and Harrison, after the indecisive Battle of Tippecanoe, burnt Prophetstown. But the Indian fighting continued with the old traditional scalping.

The settlers blamed the trouble on British scheming, instead of their own insatiable greed. What they were doing was grabbing land they did not own, just as the British were grabbing American sailors. Since this putative British scheming was based in Canada, they reasoned, parts of Canada should be annexed to the United States. And since annexation was in the air, there were Southerners who thought it would be a fine idea to annex Florida by grabbing it from Spain. Spain was (at the moment) an ally of Britain, which made such a scheme logical.

Henry Clay, a member of the United States Senate from Kentucky and sometime Speaker of the House, was a mouthpiece for these expansionists and the leader of a group of men called the War Hawks. They were disgusted and ashamed at the supine attitude of Congress toward the repeated insults of Britain. The national honor needed vindication, so they demanded war against the most powerful navy in the world, the United States having no navy to mention. The shipping interests of the East were more pragmatic. They could see no sense in taking on the most powerful navy in the world.

Two weeks after his Inauguration in 1809, Madison informed the British Government that if it would rescind the Orders in Council, which authorized attacks on American shipping, he would ask Congress to enter upon immediate hostilities against France. At the same time he informed the French Government that if France would cease her "commercial aggression against the United States" and Britain did not, he would advise immediate war with the latter.

Finally on November 2 of the following year, 1810, Madison proclaimed non-

The Battle of Tippecanoe, November 7, 1811. Reproduced from the Collections of the Library of Congress.

intercourse with England and told the British ambassador that continued interference with American trade "will necessarily lead to war." It did.

Madison's first action in national defense was to lay up Jefferson's little gunboats
as wasteful of men and money, and ordered laid-up frigates refitted. Congress
stopped most of the work. He called for preparations for possible war. But Congress,
holding the purse-strings then, as later, was thinking of its own politics. To vote
more taxes would be suicidal, and preparations were not allowed.

Undeterred, Madison started a national debate on the question whether the
Republic should have a Navy "such as to make the American flag respected." It
was a clever move. It took the question away from politicians and state jealousies

of Federal power, to appeal to national pride.Madison asked for the construction of ten frigates and the repair of six of the ten remaining frigates. The construction of new ships was stopped and the repair of the remaining frigates limited to three. Madison persisted. He wanted a quick build-up of military strength too. If war came, troops could march on weakly defended Montreal and Quebec before the enemy could cross the ocean. He wanted the old regiments brought to full strength, 10,000 additional men recruited, and a call for 50,000 volunteers. But Congress was again the stumbling block. Leaders of the anti-Madison Whigs declared these figures puny; Madison couldn't please anybody. There should have been 35,000 regulars with five-year enlistments that would have required the build-up of a large and costly officer corps before any men could be recruited, and an army of 50,000 volunteers might have meant a military that would refuse service on foreign soil. Congress squabbled most of the winter, and won. Madison skeptically signed the bill for the regulars and the volunteers. Captain Charles Stewart was offered the command of a Great Lakes fleet, as yet only on paper. (The Great Lakes were controlled by the British.) But Captain Stewart scorned fresh-water fishing; he was a deep sea man.

At the end of March, Madison told the House Committee on Foreign Affairs that he was ready to ask for a shipping embargo—a prelude to war. The Congress declared the embargo. It took effect on April 4, "but the Executive will not take upon itself the responsibility of declaring we are prepared for war." Congress declared war on Britain June 18, 1812, nevertheless, and continued to hamstring every effort of the President to prepare the country for war.

The War of 1812 has been called "the second War of Independence," incurring the displeasure of Sir Winston Churchill. It has also been called "the least known to the most people" of all the major events of American history.

9   BRITANNIA FAILS TO RULE THE WAVES

> *Britannia needs no bulwarks,*
> *   No towers along the steep;*
> *Her march is o'er the mountain waves,*
> *   Her home is on the deep.*
> —Thomas Campbell, *The Mariners of England.*

The day war was declared Madison ordered all available frigates to sea.

Governor William Hull of Michigan Territory, a grizzled veteran of the Revolution, was offered a commission as Brigadier General. That was one of Madison's most grievous mistakes; the appointment seemed logical at the time, and even the

President's enemies approved. Both General Hull and Madison, urged the building of lake squadrons, but with Captain Stewart refusing the command, a thing military and naval officers seemed allowed to do—weren't there any other captains?—and Congress hostile to naval construction, Hull assured the President he could lead an army over the Detroit River and along the northern shore of Lake Erie to the Niagara River. This would restrain the Indians of the region, deliver much of Upper Canada (Ontario) into American hands and win control of the lakes in much less time and at much less cost than building a fleet.

This Detroit campaign was forced on the Government not only by a dearth of regulars but by the refusal of the New England governors to furnish militia for Federal service. By the Congress that had declared war, and by the uncooperative Yankees, Madison was forced to fight the whole war with one arm tied behind his back.

But all went well for the Americans at sea. The American frigates were now larger, tougher and faster than their British counterparts. The U.S.S. *Constitution*, Captain Isaac Hall, outmaneuvered H.M.S. *Guerrière* in mid-ocean and "gunned her into submission" in two and a half hours. The U.S.S. *United States*, Stephen Decatur in command, forced H.M.S. *Macedonian* into submission off Madeira. Then the *Constitution* was at it again off Brazil. The British frigate *Java* had her mainmast shot away and was battered past salvage.

Action popped up in unrelated places like popcorn from a popper, on sea and land. Delaware Bay and Chesapeake Bay were blockaded throughout the winter of 1812–13. The Royal Navy's Admiral Cockburn ("a tough and ruthless old salt") had a busy time of it from Lynnhaven Bay where he devastated the countryside to Havre de Grace at the upper end of Chesapeake Bay, and then spent the summer off the Delaware coast cruising about and having fun landing here and there, burning buildings and replenishing his stores—while the Americans were busy in Canada, far from home.

There had been a battle on Canadian soil early in July, at Chippewa, in which the British force "broke and ran," but the most stubbornly contested fight of the war was fought on July 25 near Niagara Falls.[1] This contest rejoices in the most charming name a battle can boast. "The Battle of Lundy's Lane," despite which it was unusually bloody.

General Winfield Scott, later crowned with glory in the inglorious Mexican War, commanded a brigade. Beginning in late afternoon, the fighting went on until midnight. Colonel James Miller, ordered to capture the enemy's artillery, said, "I'll try, Sir," and did. British officers who had fought in the Peninsular War said later that Colonel Miller's change surpassed anything they had ever seen. The British finally retrieved their guns, but this battle prevented an invasion of the United States from the Niagara front. Both generals were severely wounded, and over 40

Colonel Miller at the Battle of Lundy's Lane. Reproduced from the Collections of the Library of Congress. "I'll try, Sir."

percent of the men involved were killed, but Colonel Miller's feat gave the American Army something to be proud of. They were not to have much more reason for pride for some time.

This odd war reached as far as Cape Horn and the South Pacific. Off the coast of Africa the U.S.S. *Constitution* captured two British ships and added to her glory. Indeed the good ship *Constitution* had so sensational a career on the element Britannia ruled she became famous as *Old Ironsides*. When in 1830 the Navy planned to scuttle the old frigate, Oliver Wendell Holmes wrote his stirring "Old Ironsides," beginning "Ay, tear her tattered ensign down!" Taken up by every newsaper in the land, protests poured into the Navy Department, for everyone knew the history of glorious "Old Ironsides," and the battered frigate was preserved for posterity. This may be the only instance of a ship being saved by a poem.

Britain was pitted against Napoleon, conqueror of most of Europe, who intended to conquer the whole of it. This war in America was a piddling affair with little attention paid to it, although it didn't seem that way to the Americans. News of these American victories was received in England "with amazement and indignation." Did not Britannia rule the waves? The "spoiled children of victory"—Trafalgar, Cape St. Vincent and the Nile (where that retarded boy "stood on the burning deck")—considered American victories an impertinence. ("The Battle of the Nile" was fought on the Mediterranean, by the way.)

10   REVERSED DIRECTIONS

Go not to Wittenberg.
—*Hamlet*, Act 1, Scene 2

One can readily understand how welcome these sea victories were when one learns what was happening meanwhile on land.

General Hull, in command of 2,500 regulars from Kentucky, Ohio and the Michigan territory, crossed into Canada on July 12, 1812, had a slight skirmish with an enemy inferior in numbers, and hastily retreated to Fort Detroit. There, on August 12, without firing a shot and without consulting his officers, he surrendered his entire garrison to the British General, Isaac Brock. Brock had 300 regulars, 400 Canadian militiamen, and "several hundred Indians whooping in the woods" who must have frightened old General Hull.

He said he was out of supplies, which his surprised officers denied, and had only one day's supply of powder. When the victors, as surprised as Hull's men, showed him a large supply of powder found in the fort, "it did not create a blush." One of the British officers said that "his actions stamp him either a coward or a traitor."

Hull was court-martialed for cowardice, found guilty, and condemned to be shot. Madison pardoned him for his service in the Revolution—and his grey hairs.

The President's reaction to the disaster was courageous. New forces must be counted on to redeem the country's honor: it was now necessary to speed up the building of a fleet to gain control of the Great Lakes. This would have been done sooner if Hull's promise of an easy conquest by land had not misled the Administration.

Indians under General Brock captured Fort Dearborn (now Chicago) and massacred 85 helpless captives. All that the Americans could do was try to keep the Canadians out of Ohio.

With the fall of Fort Dearborn the British controlled the entire frontier from Lake Erie to the Mississippi, and victorious General Block hurried back to Canada. His dearest wish now was to attack the enemy on the New York side of the Niagara River. But on October 13 it was the Americans who took the initiative and attacked the heights at Queenston, and here General Brock lost his life. The attack, however, was futile. Several thousand New York militia on the other bank (General Stephen Van Rensselaer in command) refused to cross the river to aid their countrymen. They said they had turned out to defend their homes, not to invade Canada, so their countrymen on the other side, in full view of them, surrendered.

As General Van Rensselaer proved a hopeless leader, command was given to Brigadier General Alexander Smyth, known as "Apocalypse Smyth" because he had written an explanation of the Book of Revelation. He was a grandiloquent type. On a cold and sleety night he embarked his troops for a crossing of the river with magnificent oratory: "Hearts of War! Tomorrow will be memorable in the history of the United States!" But on a closer look, not liking what he saw on the opposite bank, he returned his troops to the American side. The astonished troops, 4,000 strong, "broke into wild disorder" and fired their muskets in every direction, showing a preference for the direction of General Smyth's tent.

The War of 1812 is the most helter-skelter, higgledy-piggledy war of which there is any record.

A month after the day that would be memorable in the history of the United States, Major General Henry Dearborn, a veteran of Bunker Hill, now 62 years old, stationed at Plattsburg on the New York side of Lake Champlain, marched his militiamen northward; their objective the trunk road to Montreal. After they had progressed twenty miles the men refused to go further, so General Dearborn marched them back to Plattsburg.

Stern notices posted all over Canada warned United States citizens to quit the country in a few hours or be subject to arrest and imprisonment, but people who lived on both sides of the border continued to journey back and forth as they had always done, to go shopping and take tea with friends.

Forays and battles went on sporadically by land and water in many places for the next three years. Confidence in generals began to wane in both countries; there were frequent reshuffles in all commands.

Troops numbering nearly 600 were ordered by General Dearborn to attack the Beaver Dam post. A woman in Queenston named Laura Secord learned of this, and set out to warn Lieutenant James Fitzgibbons at that post. It was a 12 hour hike. Acting in a leisurely manner reminiscent of the British, the Americans appeared at Beaver Dam two days after Laura had arrived with her warning. They were attacked in the rear by some 400 Indians of the Caughnawaga tribe under the command of Captains Dominique Ducharme and William Kerr, and were unnerved. They shot wildly at the war whoops and rustling trees for three hours. Finally Lieutenant Fitzgibbons rode up at the head of fifty troops and called upon the Americans to surrender, which they were only too glad to do. Ducharme had been unable to call for surrender because he couldn't speak English. Thus the Americans were protected, as Fitzgibbons said, "from the tomahawk and the scalping knife."

Laura Secord was a pedestrian Paul Revere and her name is preserved on Canadian candy boxes.

It will occasion little surprise to learn that General Dearborn received a message from Secretary of War Armstrong conveying orders from the President to retire "until your health is reestablished."

11   CROSSED SIGNALS

Tripping hither, tripping thither,
Nobody knows why or whither.
—W.S. Gilbert, *Iolanthe*, Act 1.

General Harrison, "the hero of Tippecanoe," attempted to turn the tide but was hamstrung by the British squadron on Lake Erie, which threatened his communications. Madison assigned Captain Oliver Hazard Perry the task of building a fleet to challenge the British. This he did, but the struggle on the lake went on; when one side was ahead the other retired to the protection of its base to catch breath and come out again.

In April 1813 the Americans burned the little red brick Parliamentary buildings and Government House at York (now Toronto), then the Canadian capital, for no valid reason. The arsonists then left in a storm and got drenched and seasick on the lashing waves of Lake Ontario. It was perhaps heavenly revenge.

In September a decisive battle was fought at Put-in-Bay on Lake Erie. Eighty-five men of the 103 on Perry's flagship, many of them blacks, were casualties. Perry sent the laconic message, "We have met the enemy and they are ours." Since the British had lost control of Lake Erie, General Harrison could advance against them but they burned Detroit before retreating to Canada. Tit for tat. Harrison followed them up the Thames River in Ontario. Here occurred a battle in which the great Tecumseh was killed (October 5, 1813). The Indian empire he had established crumbled, but the American forces were thrown back. The

British captured Fort Niagara and burned the town of Buffalo. Another tit for the same tat.

On March 31, 1814, Paris fell to Wellington and his "Invincibles" and Napoleon was obliged to abdicate on April 11. He who had owned most of Europe was exiled to the miniscule island of Elba in the Mediterranean and the British fatuously thought they were free of the upstart Corsican for good. Now they could devote their entire attention to the "saucy Americans," who objected to their sailors being kidnapped and their peaceful merchant ships seized on the high seas.

In May the British issued a proclamation calling for a general uprising of the Southern slaves. None of them rose. Madison wrote Secretary Armstrong that this meant a campaign of "ruthless devastation" and that without doubt the National Capital would be a target. How right he was! But it was not until July that the Congress skeptically accepted Madison's proposition that 10,000 militiamen be called to guard Washington and Baltimore. When General Winder, commander of the lately set up 10th Military District which included the District of Columbia, wanted to do this, Secretary of War Armstrong, who suffered from a severe case of inertia, said a militia was "best used upon the spur of the occasion." Madison seemed unable to overcome this man's sloth and laissez-faire.

But now, with success seeming to accelerate for the British, and Napoleon tucked away on the island of Elba, the time had come to put into effect a grand Master Plan for crushing the United States, or at least "giving Jonathan a good drubbing." ("Brother Jonathan" designated the people of the United States, and had a humorous belittling connotation.)

Vice Admiral Sir Alexander Cochrane, Commander of the North American Station, was the leader of this venture. He had various schemes up his sleeve for proceeding. Though he knew no Americans, he knew all about them. "They are a whining, canting race much like the spaniel, and require the same treatment—must be drubbed into good manners." (Heaven help the spaniels!)

The Admiral's first scheme was to kidnap the leaders around Madison, working from within. "A little money well applied will attain almost any object among such a corrupt and depraved race."

One would like to know whose palms among the Madisonians the brave Admiral intended to grease, and who was on the kidnap list. James Monroe, Secretary of State? Vice President Elbridge Gerry? Perhaps Dolley?

But he changed his mind. There were so many glittering possibilities. He could recruit the Blacks ("All are good horsemen," he averred), who would steal their masters' horses and turn into a fine brigade of Black Cossacks. (In three months he was able to recruit 120.) He could take his army to New Hampshire, destroy the Portsmouth Navy Yard, and then march over the mountains somehow or other and join General Prevost's forces in Canada . . . but the prospect of New Orleans was the most alluring.

Intelligence sources (the same old reliable sources) informed him that thousands would flock to the British colors—and what riches abounded in that port! There for the taking were £4,000,000 worth of cotton, sugar and such, and the Admiral calculated that his share of this prize would amount to £125,000.

Wellington said later of this expedition, which turned out so badly for the British, "Plunder was its object." The Iron Duke did not much care for this war.

But there had to be an overall strategy before any of the Admiral's plans could be put into action.

Strategies must be great fun to devise on paper. This one formed itself into a three-pronged design!

Prong One. An army of 10,000 was to march south from Montreal via Lake Champ—but Stay! Is there not something *déjà vu* about this? If memory serves it appears to be the same route followed by Gentleman Johnny Burgoyne in 1777 with a notable lack of success. The masterminds, wherever situated, had not learned a thing in 33 years. There must have been something the matter with their brains.

Prong Two. Another, smaller, army was to assemble in Jamaica, sail to New Orleans and bottle up the Mississippi, choking the West.

Prong Three. An amphibious force was to destroy coastal towns around Chesapeake Bay, and then deal similarly with Washington and Baltimore.

But even the best laid plans of mice and men are apt to go wrong, which everyone knew but the British.

Before the 10,000 men set out from Montreal bound for wherever they could get, 4,000 men under General Robert Ross sailed from Bermuda for the Chesapeake, destination Washington. They landed in Maryland at the mouth of the Patuxent River on August 19, 1814 to the intense surprise of everyone.

A squadron of gunboats, meant to protect the capital, scurried away up the river, and was sunk to keep it out of the enemies' hands.

For a week the Washington papers assured their readers that there was no cause for alarm, it was improbable that the enemy would advance nearer the capital. (Why improbable?)

Advance the enemy did, and by the 22nd the British invaders were at Upper Marlboro, Maryland. By the 23rd they were four or five miles further, and within fifteen miles of the city.

The defenders of Washington were poorly prepared—in fact they apparently were not prepared at all. This was thanks mostly to secretary Armstrong and his congenital inertia, and partly to rather feckless General Wilder, and perhaps partly to President Madison who seemed unable to stir them up. One feels that Dolley might have been better at this.

James Madison asked Dolley if she had the courage and the firmness to remain in the President's House until his return next day. She assured him she "had no fear but for him and the success of our army." He left for the battlefront beseeching her to take care of herself and the Cabinet papers.

Later she received a note scribbled in pencil telling her to be ready at a moment's notice to enter her carriage and leave the city. The enemy was stronger than at first supposed and it might happen that they would reach the city with the intention of destroying it.

Dolley had once entertained 24 Indian chiefs with five interpreters at dinner—a prospect that would have daunted any hostess in the world—except Dolley; and she was not daunted now. She dashed off a letter to her sister with the news. "I am accordingly ready," she wrote. "I have pressed as many Cabinet papers into trunks as to fill one carriage. Our private property must be sacrificed as it is impossible to procure wagons for its transportation."

Dolley did not want to leave until she saw her husband safe. "Dissaffection stalks around us," she wrote. "I hear of much hostility toward him."

Most of her friends were gone now, and most of the servants. "Even Colonel C. with his hundred, who were stationed as a guard at this inclosure." Mrs. Madison was abandoned even by the White House guard! But the Madison's faithful doorkeeper, Jean Pierre Sioussa, "French John . . . with his usual activity and resolution," Dolley wrote, "offers to spike the cannon at the gate and lay a train of powder, which will blow up the British should they enter the house. To the last proposition I positively object without being able to make him understand why all advantages in war may not be taken." (Dolley Madison was born Dorothea Payne, of Quaker parents.)

By the next day, the 24th, the enemy had gathered at Bladensburg, a Maryland village six miles northeast of Washington, and the battle began.

The President and the Secretary of State galloped here and there in an effort to reform the lines. Such was not their *metier*. Madison was 63 and somewhat frail. The Secretary of War, John Armstrong, listless as usual, could not bring himself to believe the British intended to enter Washington; he could hardly believe it when they did. The lines were reformed, and had to give way, and reform again. Finally it was a rout.

As some of the populace was fleeing westward toward Georgetown, Stephen Pleasonton, a clerk in the State Department, began feverishly packing papers into large sacks. Armstrong, chancing to see him at this work, suggested it was all foolishness, but Stephen begged to differ, and hauled the bags away in an ox cart. And thus were saved some of the nation's most sacred documents, including the Declaration of Independence and Washington's commission in the Continental army.

Dolley Madison awaited news, standing in an upper window of the White House with a spyglass. The table was set for dinner, in case the President and his followers might return and be hungry. As the populace continued to stream up Pennsylvania Avenue with their loaded wagons, Dolley was urged to flee before being caught in the mainstream of the retreat; but she hung on.

Then the President's freedman servant, Jim Smith, galloped up waving his hat and crying, "Clear out! Clear out! Secretary Armstrong has ordered a retreat!" And he handed the First Lady another note scribbled by her husband, "The battle is lost—fly at once!"

But the indomitable Dolley was not one to panic. Her sister and brother-in-law (Richard Cutts) were with her now and two gentlemen from New York, Jacob Barker, a banker, and a young man named Richard de Peyster. Charles Carroll, a presidential aide, was there to aid. ("Aides" seldom helped in unhooking curtains.)

They all set to work gathering up what could be saved. The red velvet curtains from the East Room, books and papers, were loaded into a wagon.

And the great, full-length portrait of General Washington by Gilbert Stuart that hung in the State Dining Room, must on all accounts be saved. But it was screwed so tightly to the wall it could not be budged. "Forget the picture!" cried Mr. Carroll. "You must leave at once!" He left himself, in search of the President.

Dolley was not ready to give up yet. Consumed with anxiety over the fate of her husband, she stuck to the matter in hand. On her order French John ran for an axe, the frame of the painting was hacked apart, the painting, unharmed on its stretcher, lifted from the wall. The two gentlemen from New York later carried it away to safety. "Don't let it fall into the hands of the British!" cried Dolley. "Destroy it first!" And seeing to the rescue of four remaining boxes of the President's papers, and the ornamental gold eagles from the East Room, and cramming a few odds and ends of White House silver and doubtless her jewels, into her reticule, the First Lady clambered into her waiting carriage, followed by her faithful maid Sukey. The Cuttses came next in their carriage, and the procession was completed by John Freeman, the Madisons' butler, driving the "coachee" with his family crammed inside and a featherbed lashed on behind. They all made their way toward Georgetown.

Dolley Madison rescuing the portrait of Washington on the approach of the British is one of the few well-known incidents of the War of 1812, but she rescued much more.

12   PAVILIONS AND PALACES

*As they know we object
    To pavilions and palaces,
How can they respect
    Our republican fallacies?*
—W. S. Gilbert, *The Gondoliers*, Act 1

For the victors now came the pleasure of destroying the Capitol, "that citadel of Republicanism." Once the doors were broken down awed redcoats surged through the building. It was all so grand in a nation that boasted republican simplicity and an abhorence of royal trappings: the 21 Corinthian columns in the Hall of Representatives, for instance.

At first it was decided to blow up the great, uncompleted pile, but the few remaining citizens protested the explosion would wreck their houses, and they had done nothing against the British. So General Ross kindly decided to burn the building instead.

Admiral George Cockburn is reported to have stood on the House Speaker's chair and cried, "Shall this harbor of Yankee democracy be burned?" (He was misapplying the word 'Yankee' which is continually misapplied in England to this day.) All were in favor of the Admiral's excellent proposal, but it was a difficult thing to accomplish since the building was stone. A fire was finally set by piling the mahogany desks, chairs and tables of the Hall of Representatives in the middle of the room, adding gunpowder, and firing rockets into the pile. The same procedure was followed in the Senate wing.

The Library of Congress was housed in the Hall of Representatives. Though consisting of only 4,000 volumes it included 740 rare and important works bought for its nucleus in London and Paris in 1804. All these made fine missiles to hurl into the mounting flames. The redcoats had a deal of fun!

Up went everything, the portières, the clock with its gold eagle over the Speaker's chair, which stood at ten o'clock precisely. Flames soon surged through the doors and windows, and the sandstone walls of the building began to crack. Fanned by the wind, the fire started to burn other buildings including two houses George Washington had built in North Capitol Street.

Admiral Cockburn, regaining his civilized behavior, sent a note to Mrs. Madison gallantly offering to conduct her to any destination she chose, but Mrs. Madison was no longer in residence.

Dolley spent the night at Rokeby in Virginia, the estate of her friend, Mrs. Matilda Love Lee, who took in the exhausted First Lady and presumably Sukey and the coachmen. Dolley sat long at an upper window gazing at the red sky over Washington, which was "wrapped in a winding-sheet of flame."

Half an hour after Dolley's flight, President Madison arrived at the White House with Attorney General Richard Rush. Madison had suffered an exhausting day, enlivened by several shells that fell near him. He needed refreshment. Jacob Barker and Richard de Peyster needed refreshment too, and had already been re-freshed by some of the President's brandy.

We learn from Louis Sérurier, the French Minister, in a letter to Talleyrand, how different it was from the scurrilous stories circulated by Madison's enemies, who had the President flying in panic to Frederick in Maryland. Madison remained in the White House until after the militia, acting on "the spur of the occasion," as Secretary Armstrong thought the militia should, "streamed by in confused flight toward Frederick."

Then the President and the Attorney General set out to cross the river into Virginia. Some learnéd historians say they went by ferry, others by the long bridge, which is more likely as they were mounted. Then began a frustrating search for Dolley. They missed her in several places and night fell. The next day, August 25, Jemmy and his Dolley were reunited at Wiley's Tavern on Difficult Run, near Great Falls, a series of dangerous rapids.

The bumpy road over which the First Lady was bounced and jounced in her carriage, fleeing the British with the remaining Cabinet papers, has undergone a metamorphosis and is now the Dolley Madison Highway.

13   THE HOSTS ARE ABSENT

Pray enter;
You are learnéd Europeans, and we worse
Than ignorant Americans.
—Massinger, *The City Madam*, Act 111, Scene 3

When Admiral Cockburn, General Ross, and a number of other officers strutted into the abandoned "President's Palace," having taken care of the Capitol, they found to their delight the dining table set for forty, wine in the coolers, crystal goblets and platters of cold cuts, prepared for the President and his followers on that hot August day. During this *dejeuner à la fourchette* toasts were drunk to the Prince Regent and "success to His Majesty's arms by sea and land." Captain Harry Smith noted particularly "the super-excellent Madeira."

It is painful to think that these elegant British officers and gentlemen were probably obliged to *wait on themselves*, as the flunkies had fled. (War is war!) French John, thwarted in his sensible wish to blow the British up (one cannot help wishing

French John had *not* been thwarted!), had taken off for Octagon House, the French Legation, with Madame Madison's macaw, to consign the bird to the care of Monsieur Sérurier's chef, a friend of his.

James Madison's medicine chest, George Washington's portrait, and Dolley Madison's macaw were among the few things that escaped the ensuing holocaust. The medicine chest was restored to the White House long after by a Canadian whose ancestor had looted (and saved) it.

After being sufficed, General Ross personally supervised the piling up of all that beautiful late 18th-Century furniture as kindling to start the conflagration. Orders from the barbarian Cochrane were "to destroy and lay waste public property," but Admiral Cockburn expansively permitted the taking of a few souvenirs. He himself modestly chose an old hat of the President's. Among other articles lifted were a pair of rhinestone buckles, a brace of pistols and a ceremonial sword. Captain Smith, more practical, changed his shirt for a clean one of President Madison's, doubtless found upstairs in a dresser drawer. But this was not the limit. All the silver from the dining table was spirited away by the redcoats in tablecloths when the officers were not looking—a rich haul.

(The studious Reader is urged to take pains not to confuse *Vice* Admiral ("Lay waste and destroy") Sir Alexander Cochrane, with *Rear* Admiral Sir George Cockburn, who looted President Madison's hat. Sir Alexander (the Vice) was noted for his scorn of Americans, while Sir George (the Rear) was the jaunty type who loved a good time and got it by following the Vice's orders to "lay waste and destroy." He did a splendid job.)

The gentlemen, now fortified and restored, strutted out of the President's Palace, consigning it to the flames.

The arsonists were disgusted at finding not one plugged nickel in the Treasury Building, but it, the State Department and the War Office, fed the flames nicely. On orders from the Secretary of the Navy, the Navy Yard had already been fired on to deny its use to the enemy. That night the flames could be seen in Baltimore, forty miles away.

Afterwards, Admiral Sir George Cockburn was in a happy, joshing mood, as befitted a victor, but General Ross was subdued. He said he never would have burned the President's house if Mrs. Madison had been in it. He mourned the loss of some of his men and listened sympathetically to appeals of the few frightened citizens who had not fled the city.

There exists a fine, full-length portrait of the doughty Admiral Cockburn, hand on sword, cocked hat, haughty mein and enormous feet, with Washington in flames behind him. This historic painting is in England at the National Maritime Museum at Greenwich; its spiritual home is, of course, the British Embassy in Washington, and one can't understand why it doesn't hang there!

The following morning a thunderstorm broke over Washington, too late to do any good, followed in the afternoon by a terrific wind storm which blew the roof off the Patent Office and the Post Office in Blodgett's Hotel, the only public building to escape the flames, and rolled cannon about the streets. By this time the Nation's capital must have been something of a washout.[1]

On August 30 the city of Alexandria, across the river in Virginia, surrendered to the enemy, who removed all the stores and merchandise. On September 3 the British Navy started down the river with 21 prize vessels loaded with 13,768 barrels of flour, 756 hogsheads of tobacco, and untold amounts of cotton, tar, beef, sugar and other commodities. As a future general, Andrew Jackson, was to observe on another occasion, to the victor belong the spoils.

The British were now bent on polishing off Baltimore. Fortunately, they moved at a leisurely pace, and the redcoats did not land at North Point, near the end of the peninsula jutting into Chesapeake Bay, at the head of which stood the city, until September 12.

But in the meantime things were happening in other places. News of the burning of Washington caused a profound shock throughout the nation. There had been high feelings against the war and poor "Jemmy" was blamed for all the trouble; editorials had been fiery. But things had now progressed above party lines. The National capital had been put to the torch; and the country united.

14   "THE BOMBING OF FORT McHENRY"

better known as
"THE STAR SPANGLED BANNER"

The opposition press rallied in this national crisis, but the people were ahead of the press. The Citizens' Committee of a remote section of South Carolina raised 100 men and $3,000 to buy supplies. "Conflagration and rapine will never bow the spirit of the American people!" the Committee stoutly wrote the War Department, and added that they needed a bugle. The day after the burning of Washington a company of 85 was raised at Frederick, Maryland, and left for the ravaged capitol in four hours. (They were too late.)

In Philadelphia and all the big cities there was a huge outpouring of men eager to enlist. Some 15,000 from every walk of life began digging entrenchments to protect the city. The women were busy making military uniforms. It was the same all over the country, even in recalcitrant New England.

Of course every city and town thought it was next on the British agenda, and besieged the Government for forces to protect it. The Administration was desperate with swarming Committees of Safety.

But Baltimore *knew* it would be next on the list. It was believed to be the richest town in the country; with over 45,000 inhabitants it was third in size, and it was a bustling seaport and shipbuilding community. The frigates that had sent British vessels to the bottom were built here.

The Baltimore deal was to be a two- rather than a three- pronged Master Plan, so dear to the heart of British military men. While a force landed at North Point to march up the peninsula and attack the city, the gunboats prepared to sail up the Patapsco River to bombard and storm Fort McHenry which guarded the city. (Named for James McHenry, Secretary of War in the administrations of Washington and Adams.)

There was action when the British landed at North Point. Their advance on Baltimore was blocked. In the seventeen days since the destruction of Washington an army of nearly 20,000 had been raised. Men poured into the threatened city from all the nearby states—Virginia, Pennsylvania, Delaware, New Jersey, as well as from all over Maryland. It must have been a surprise for the British after the walk-over in Washington.

While on the way to attack, General Ross was shot and killed by a sharpshooter. (The British press was indignant at this dastardly deed. Wars should be fought by one side only.)

In the meantime British gunboats sailed up the Patapsco River, and on September 13 began bombarding Fort McHenry. They found they could not approach nearer the fort than a mile and a half.

The bombing of Fort McHenry began about seven o'clock in the morning. The British squadron, which consisted of sixteen vessels—frigates, bombing vessels and rocket ships—could not approach near enough to the fort to make direct hits. The water was shallow and the defenders had sunk twenty-two vessels in the channel. Major Armistead, in command of the fort, found that he couldn't reach the ships with his guns either, and after about three hours silenced his guns.

Dr. Beames, a civilian from Upper Marlboro, Maryland, who had graciously received General Ross and Admiral Cockburn when they called uninvited at his house, subsequently had half a dozen stragglers from the British army rounded up and arrested. This logical action on Dr. Beames' part so infuriated Ross that he sent a detachment of cavalry to arrest his former host in the early morning of August 28. He and several other Americans found in Dr. Beames' house, including Robert Bowie, a former governor of Maryland, were confined in the brig of one of the vessels of Admiral Cockburn's squadron.

J. S. Skinner, a U.S. agent for the exchange of prisoners of war, and Francis Scott Key, a young lawyer, carried a note from President Madison to the Admiral under a flag of truce, asking for the physician's release. The Admiral consented to the request but detained them on one of his vessels. This was shortly before the squadron sailed up the river to bombard the fort.

The bombing of Fort McHenry continued, with intermissions, for 25 hours. It is estimated that over 1,500 shells, weighing over 220 pounds each, were fired during this time.

Mr. Skinner and Mr. Key passed the night pacing the deck of the small supply ship on which they were detained, and as the bombs arched and "the rockets' red glare" lighted the night, now and then in the distance they caught a glimpse of the huge flag waving over the fort, "still there."

It was a stirring sight, and Key, by avocation a poet, felt a poem stirring in his head. On the back of an envelope he scribbled the opening lines of "The Star Spangled Banner" (though he never gave the poem a title). He finished it at the Indian Queen Tavern in Baltimore when the two men had accomplished their mission and, with Dr. Beames, were released.

The poem is a good one, and as dramatic as might be wished. In fact it is one of the best of national anthems. (The bombast of the last line must be overlooked: Bombast is endemic to patriotic songs.) The poem was printed in a broadside and was called "The Bombing of Fort McHenry" with a notation that it could be sung to the tune of "To Anacreon in Heaven," an English drinking song. No author's name was given. Within a few weeks it was printed in newspapers from one end of the land to the other. It was sung from New Hampshire to Georgia in taverns and everywhere Americans gathered. After the burning of Washington, something of this sort was needed in the country.

15   THE TIDE TAKEN AT THE FLOOD

At seven in the morning of September 14 the bombardment of Fort McHenry ceased and the bombing squadron started down the river. By nine o'clock the last of the frigates followed. The enemy had given up the Fort McHenry project. Very few bombs had hit the fort and these had done little damage. Neither side had been effective.

By land things were not going well for the British either. The redcoats were unable to advance closer than within two miles of Baltimore and had to retreat.

Soon came news of another American victory. The reader will recall the prong of the plan to crush the United States by sending troops down from Montreal via Lake Champlain with Sir George Prevost in command. These were troops released from the Peninsular War by the downfall of Napoleon.

At the town of Plattsburg, at the northern end of the lake, General Prevost encountered a force of 3,300 Americans under the command of General Alexander Macomb, aged 32. Though vastly inferior to the British in numbers, they had a well designed plan of defense.

Prevost called up his supporting fleet which consisted of four ships, including the *Confiance*, and a dozen gunboats. But there was an American fleet on the lake under the command of Captain Thomas Macdonough, also 32. The nation had Madison to thank for this. (Thomas Macdonough had already proven himself a hero. He was with Stephen Decatur at the boarding and burning of the captured American frigate *Philadelphia* in the harbor of Tripoli, in defiance of the Barbary Corsairs.)

Macdonough's flagship, the *Saratoga* (26 guns) had been launched 35 days after the laying of her keel, and then came news that the British were building the *Confiance* (37 guns), far more powerful than the Saratoga. Macdonough said he thought that by building a light brig the loss of the lake could be averted. The Secretary of the Navy protested that there was no money to do this. Madison ordered the ship built. The keel was laid when the cautious Secretary of the Navy again got cold feet about the lack of funds. The President reaffirmed the order that the ship be built, and with the utmost speed.

Captain Macdonough was a resourceful young man. The timbers of the brig *Eagle* were trees in the forest July 15, and the *Eagle* was launched August 11.

There were not enough sailors to man this vessel, the Secretary of War now complained. Fill out the crew with soldiers! said Madison. He explained to the protesting Secretary that naval efficiency was essential for his own land operations: Control of the lake must be won to prevent the landing of an army in the American rear. Elementary.

The Battle of Lake Champlain occurred on September 11, 1814, and was a murderous engagement. Small vessels with no bulwarks to protect their crews attempted at pistol range to pound each other to pieces. The *Confiance* silenced the starboard battery of the *Saratoga* and killed one-fifth of her crew. Macdonough wheeled his ship around on her anchor, or "wound ship" as it is called, and with her port battery forced the *Confiance* and three other ships to surrender. The British Commodore was killed.

General Prevost, with all his fine plans disrupted, and the Americans now controlling the lake and menacing his flank, was obliged to withdraw his troops to Canada, and they never returned. The hardy veterans of the Peninsular War ("Wellington's Invincibles") met their Waterloo at Plattsburg, New York. "A lamentable event for the civilized world" mourned *The London Times*. (Figure that one out.)

The Battle of Lake Champlain is one of the most significant battles of U.S.

naval history. The guns of Fort McHenry fired a salute to the victory when the news reached Baltimore on September 18. Gentleman Johnny Burgoyne had done better in 1777 than Sir George Prevost in 1814: Saratoga is a hundred miles south of Plattsburg. (In the old town of Plattsburg stands a monument to Captain Thomas Macdonough, that valiant and resourceful young man.)

Nobody, but nobody, ever got to Albany.

16   A COLD DOUSE AND PLUM PUDDING

News traveled slowly over the Atlantic in those days, and in London they were still rejoicing over the burning of Washington and listening to those highly reliable sources that declared that Baltimore was reduced to rubble and President Madison had shot himself. It was delightful to think that New York, Philadelphia, Boston and all the other cities would soon share the fate of Washington and Baltimore. That was the public attitude, but the British Government was not so optimistic. The cost of the war was already prodigious, and perhaps it was a little difficult to remember what it was all about.

The press assured its readers that the Americans were savages, "dirty-shirts" and other unattractive things, and since most were illiterate (it said), what did it matter—burning the Library of Congress? President Madison, who stood five feet five inches tall and wore a plain but neat black suit, a scholarly little gentleman by then 63, "the Father of the Constitution" (which Gladstone later admired so highly), was transformed by the magic of the British press into a reincarnation of Attila the Hun.

But on October 16 dreadful tidings began to pour in. Baltimore was intact and untaken, Prevost and his whole army had retreated to Canada, President Madison had not shot himself, and General Ross was dead. All the bright visions abruptly faded.

"It is to be *borne* that an officer in command of 11,000 British troops shall retreat before a handful of Banditti?" wrote a certain colonel to a friend who was a marquis. To this fastidious colonel anyone not born in Britain was a poltroon or a bandit. Lesser breeds without the law.

The destruction of Washington was disapproved in Europe, especially of course in France. There it was the British who were banditti, pirates—their's "an act of atrocious vengeance, a crime against humanity," in the words of the *Journal de Paris*.

The French journalists found the destruction of Washington wonderful grist for their journalistic mills. The glory that was Greece and the grandeur that was

Rome could not hold a candle to poor scrubby little Washington, still in its birth throes, "a city whose riches and beauty formed one of the valuable monuments of the progress of the arts and human industry." One can imagine how the eyes of Washingtonians would have popped out of their heads if they could have read that! It was wonderful anti-British propaganda.

There were Englishmen who disapproved too. Captain Harry Smith (he with the fine palate for Mr. Madison's Madeira) was shocked at what he was called upon to do. "It made me ashamed to be an Englishman. We felt more like a band of Red Savages from the woods." (Note the word "we.") He was convinced it was Admiral Cochrane who ordered the burning, and of this one can be certain. "Wellington would never have done it," the Captain said.

In the House of Lords, Lord Grenville deplored the destruction. In Commons, Samuel Whitbread declared that the burning of buildings was "abhorrent to every principle of legitimate warfare." (The Americans themselves had done a little building-burning in Canada.) The *Statesman* commented, "The Cossacks spared Paris, we spared not the capital of America." (Washington must have been flattered to be compared to Paris.)

The British were stumped and turned to the great Duke of Wellington in some desperation. He was offered command of the King's Forces, with the power to make war or peace. The Duke as usual was on top of the situation and informed the Prime Minister, Lord Liverpool, (whose name was Robert Banks Jenkinson) that what was needed in America was "naval superiority on the Lakes" and the question was whether this could be accomplished. Without this, he said, he would be going to America only to sign a peace treaty "which might as well be signed now." He added, "I think you have no right from the state of the war to demand any concession of territory from America."

Macdonough's victory at Plattsburg was a decisive battle, if not of the world, at least of the War of 1812.

The Iron Duke's grim attitude toward the feasibility of gaining control of "the Lakes"—or eliminating them—ended the fighting in America, and this could not have been more providential. Within the next six months the course of European history was altered. (Wellington seems to have been the only British general who ever bothered to study a map.)

The American peace commissioners—John Quincy Adams, Henry Clay, Albert Gallatin, James Bayard and Jonathan Russell—had been whiling away the dull time since August at the Hotel Lovendeghem in Ghent, Belgium, bickering with their not very brilliant opposite numbers. As long as the news was favorable to the British, the British demands were severe. They demanded, among other things, a buffer Indian state in the northwest and control of the Great Lakes. This the Americans rejected. Then the British demanded a parcel of Maine to unite Halifax and Quebec, both sides of the St. Lawrence, and ports on the Great Lakes. (The British already had ports on all the Great Lakes except Lake Michigan which lies entirely within the boundaries of the United States. These gentlemen were weak in their geography.) Again rejection by Mr. Adams and his colleagues.

Things were very depressing, the only comfort being that sympathy in Europe favored the "insignificant and puny power"—because Britannia was the top power. The British Government was sick of the war and its enormous cost, but the public still demanded that the enemy be "chastised." Then Whitehall began to grow a little touchy about the destruction of Washington and the Library of Congress. Though it is acceptable to destroy people in warfare, it has always been considered an act of barbarism to burn books.

But when the awful news of Baltimore, the death of Ross and the American victory on Lake Champlain began to trickle in, the British comissioners were no longer in a strong position.

After a great deal of give-and-take, and consulting the powers in London, the Treaty of Ghent, or "The Treaty of Peace and Amity between His Britannic Majesty and the United States of America" was signed in the old Carthusian Monastery at Ghent at 6 P.M. on Christmas Eve, 1814. The church bells rang out, and John Quincy Adams said he hoped it would be the last treaty of peace between Britain and the United States and it was.

The British commissioners dined next day on roast beef and plum pudding sent from home.

The Treaty, however, was not yet ratified and Whitehall had two sets of plans in its pocket (despite Wellington's advice): one if the Treaty was ratified, and one for a new and better offensive against America if it wasn't. President Madison was distrusted. He had turned from Attila the Hun into a wiley, scheming gnome. "The Americans always cheat us," complained a pessimistic member of the British delegation.

The month of December 1814 saw other events belonging to this history, and brief mention should be made of the Hartford Convention.

The New England Federalists had opposed government measures that interfered with foreign trade (like the Embargo Act of 1807), and the expenses of the war now in progress caused much bitter pain. These men were Yankee to the core and opposed to all unnecessary expense. The New England states had refused to surrender their militias even when New England was threatened with invasion, and continued to trade with Canada, which might be called seditious. Extremists even contemplated a separate peace between New England and Britain, and a conference was called by the Massachusetts Legislature. The convention met in Hartford on

December 15, 1814, and the sessions were held in secret. Fortunately George Cabot, head of the Massachusetts delegation, was a moderate man, and said, "We are going to keep you young hotheads from getting into mischief."

A proposal to secede from the Union was rejected, and the final report merely called to account Madison's administration and proposed several constitutional amendments which would favor New England.

So the Federalists, supposedly the party favoring a strong central government, paradoxically found themselves on the side of states' rights. The Hartford Convention was suspected of treason (not without reason) and has had a bad name in the history books. Its concepts would return to curse the nation in the years to come.

When commissioners from the Hartford Convention arrived in Washington to lay their grievances before Congress and say what they thought of the President and how impossible it was to win this war, they were stunned by the news that peace had been declared. The war was over; their cause was gone, the wind sucked from their sails; the Federalist party had received its *coup de grâce*. The gentlemen from Hartford presumably went home with their tails between their legs.

Two months after the Treaty of Ghent was signed on March 1, 1815, Napoleon, bored with ruling a tiny island off the coast of Italy, instead of half of Europe, suddenly landed at Frejus on the French Riviera with 1,050 troops and started for Paris. The old charisma worked for awhile and shouts of "Vive l'Empereur!" rose skyward.

But in Paris there was near painic when the news reached the city on March 5. The King, Louis XVIII, brother of the guilliotined Louis XVI, departed with a few horsemen, for Lille near the Belgian frontier. Finding he was not wanted there, the poor fat fugitive, now 60, crossed the frontier. Napoleon was again master of Europe.

But not for long. A force of 120,000 Prussians under Marshal Bloucher, and a mixed bag of Belgians, Dutch, Hanoverians and English under Wellington was assembled in Belgium when Napoleon advanced to meet the same number of troops instead of the 600,000 he had called up. Inertia, and a disinclination for any more fighting were contributing causes: the world's most colossal ego was running out of glamour.

On June 18, 1815, at the village of Waterloo, the emperor made his last stand. The Prussians seemed to slink away, and Napoleon faced the fact that he was alone and it was now or never. Moreover, innumerable Russians were hovering in the background somewhere. The battle became a rout and Napoleon's army emulated the Prussians. La Grande Armée wasn't so grand anymore. Napoleon was obliged to abdicate for the second time, and soon he was en route to another tiny island—

this one St. Helena, a British possession in the South Atlantic. When he returned to Paris in 1840 he was entirely harmless in his coffin, having died in 1821.

17   THE BRITISH ARE SWAMPED

What was he doing, the great god Pan,
Down in the reeds by the river?
—Elizabeth Barrett Browning,
A Musical Instrument

Unfortunately communications from Ghent were poor and nobody in America knew in 1814 that a peace treaty had been signed. The creeks and inlets of the Chesapeake were still being raided. British frigates were sailing into the innumerable coves and inlets of the Maine coast and demanding ransom, or burning a farm or two and slaughtering cattle before sailing away.

And Sir Edward Pakenham (Wellington's brother-in-law) in command of 5,700 men sailed from Jamaica to put action into that third Prong of the good old Strategy and take New Orleans. He had all kinds of trouble on the way, and when he reached New Orleans, worse troubles.

Major General Andrew Jackson, known to his men as "Old Hickory" though he was only 47, the district military commander at New Orleans, had received a warning of British intentions from James Monroe in September, and Jackson was expecting trouble. But "the possible approaches to the city were too many, too varied and too widespread to permit defensive positions to be established."[1] Meandering bayous, creeks and cypress swamps were a confusion to everybody.

Sixteen hundred British troops (soon augmented by a great many more) landed and were within eight miles of the city when they were detected. "By thunder, they shall not sleep on our soil!" Old Hickory cried fiercely when the news was brought him. The first skirmishes began December 23, 1814 but it was not till January 8, 1815 that the decisive battle took place.

Because of the treacherous terrain, the problems for the British were almost insurmountable. The Mississippi was low and they had great trouble launching their boats through a cut in the levee to get them into position. The banks of the cutting fell in and the seamen worked, reported Lieutenant Colonel Alexander Dickson, "in a deep Mud into which they frequently sunk up to the Middle." The men moving the guns for the center batteries could find no direct route to the position and were obliged to drag them back to the levee road and start all over again to get them

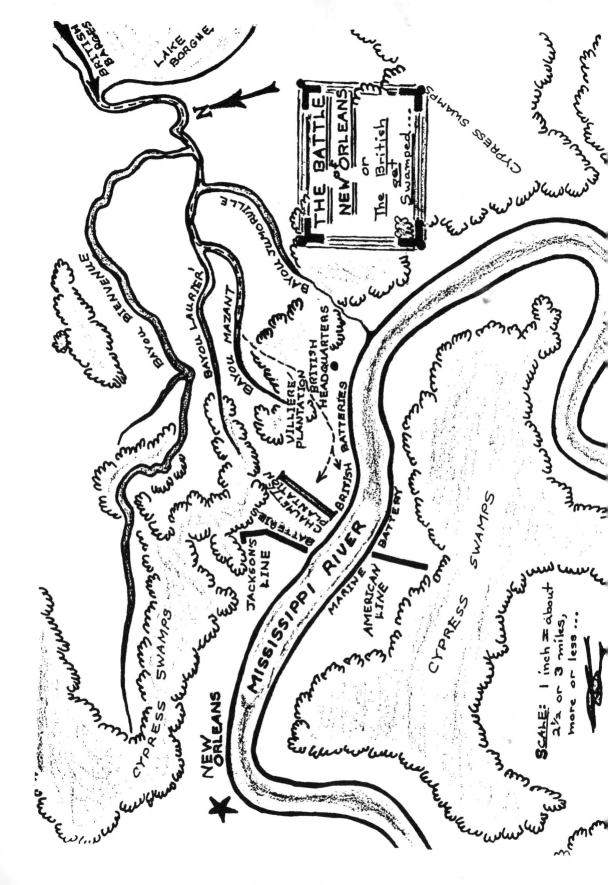

properly placed. Two hours later the batteries were not yet half finished. It was one of those days—or nights.

Through all this turmoil General Pakenham was slumbering soundly at his headquarters. Nobody thought to rouse him. Had he been awake and alert, he *might* have postponed the attack until his forces were prepared, or done one of several other things. But plans once made must be carried out; and so the Battle of New Orleans was lost to the British—as it might have been otherwise, but without the incredible loss of life which shortly took place.

Picture a long, flat field, with nothing on it behind which to take cover; only the Mississippi, and breast-high bulwarks along the far side, with the defenders entrenched behind them. This was the Chalmette Plantation.

The doomed British assault columns advanced bravely over the field, because ordered to do so. A British Lieutenant Colonel said, "My regiment has been ordered into execution. Their dead bodies are to be used as a bridge for the rest of the army to cross over." He was perfectly right. The order coming from the general in command makes it clear that none of Wellington's military genius had sloughed off on his brother-in-law. In less than half an hour, more than 2,000 men perished, General Pakenham himself, three major generals, eight colonels, six majors, 18 captains and 54 subalterns among them. It was a mighty prelude to the Light Brigade's charge at Balaklava, but there was no Tennyson to make this heroic tragedy immortal. It is forgotten everywhere, except in New Orleans. Nations are not prone to treasure the memory of their fiascos.

When what was left of the British forces withdrew, over 300 men lay wounded among the dead on the battlefield, and it is pleasant to learn that these were brought into the city and laid in the barracks, and were succored by the inhabitants of New Orleans at an appeal from Jackson, furnished with blankets, pillows, bandages and care. There was no Red Cross then.

The British buried their dead on the spot, assisted in their gruesome task by their erstwhile enemies. Sir Edward Pakenham and a few others of high degree enjoyed the privilege of being shipped home in casks of rum. Sir Edward, his monument, at least, ended up in St. Paul's Cathedral.

A horrid story went about that when General Pakenham's cask reached England it was shipped back to America by mistake, and the rum was being quaffed in a general provisions store in Charleston, South Carolina, when it was discovered that there was somebody's body inside the cask. Grisly as well as absurd—for who would ship a cask of rum back to America whence it came in the first place? And what was the General's military secretary, Wylley, doing, who had charge of the cask? And surely there would have been some identification on it:

CONTENTS
SIR EDWARD PAKENHAM IN RUM
THIS END UP

Jackson himself was shocked at the dreadful toll of the battle. He was moved by the incredible slaughter of "so many gallant soldiers."

This frontal attack on an entrenched enemy seems to have been an aberration exhibited at times by various generals, some of them intelligent. It happened at Bunker Hill and at New Orleans as well as at Balaklava. Something of the sort took place at Fredericksburg. The great Lee himself succumbed to this insanity at Gettysburg in spite of the protestations of some of his generals. Every one of these maneuvers was a disaster.

An interesting sidelight on the defense of New Orleans is the part played in it by Jean Lafitte, the famous pirate, who offered his services and his men to Jackson. Jackson accepted the offer of "the hellish Banditti" because he needed all the help he could get. Lafitte furnished artillery, men and all the ammunition necessary. Then too, his knowledge of the geography of the region was of great value. He doubtless hoped he would be rewarded by a pardon for his plundering and the restitution of his seized property. (He was pardoned by President Madison because he had refused overtures of the British to join them in the capture of New Orleans and had thrown in his lot with the Americans.)

In spite of the disastrous Battle of New Orleans, more properly the Massacre of New Orleans, Admiral Cochrane without bloodshed seized Fort Boyer in Mobile Bay and was on his gladsome way to wreak havoc in Chesapeake Bay. Little ransom could be expected from the humble fishing villages and oystermen along those shores, but surely there would be farms to burn and cattle to slaughter.

Alas! On February 11 the British sloop *Favourite*, flying a flag of truce, entered New York harbor. On board were Henry Carroll, Clay's secretary, and the secretary of the British Peace Commission, Anthony St. John Baker, with copies of the Treaty of Ghent. When good Admiral Cochrane heard this news he was "most amazingly cast down," reported Captain Edward Codrington. His spirits had been buoyed up ever since Washington at the thought of all that lovely loot waiting in New Orleans, those endless barrels and bales of cotton, sugar, tobacco and what not, worth £400,000, of which £125,000 he calculated, would rightly be his. *Ah, fuyez, douce image*!

Henry Carroll reached Washington on February 14, 1815 with the Treaty. He arrived at Octagon House, where the Madisons were living until the President's house could be rebuilt, in the late afternoon. The President, Secretary of State Monroe and others retired to an upper room to dissect the Treaty, word by word.

The house was soon full of excited people, Cabinet secretaries and officials.

The Battle of New Orleans. Reproduced from the Collections of the Library of Congress. The agonized figure lower right and the wooden commander holding his sword as if signalling a taxi-cab, are doubtless stage props.

A radiant Dolley was receiving congratulations in the middle of the room. Nobody doubted the ratification of the Treaty.

At eight o'clock the President appeared and announced to his assembled guests that the Treaty was satisfactory. "Peace!" cried Dolley, and everyone echoed the cry. Long-time enemies embraced. The butler poured the wine; and here we take leave of her who remains one of America's (and Thomas Jefferson's) favorite people, and the helter-skelter War of 1812.

18   PEACE OF GHENT, 1814, AND THE TRIUMPH OF AMERICA

In the cluttered but lofty allegory here reproduced, Minerva can be seen at left dictating the conditions of peace which Mercury presents to a cowed Britannia suffering from a headache—and no wonder—but is obliged to accept due to the proximity of Hercules clad in a lion's pelt and holding a truncheon. (He represents the overwhelming power of America before which the whole world quails.) An angel on a pedestal inscribed with victories is writing the names of heroes on an obelisk. At right, America, in a chariot and wearing a headdress borrowed from an Aztec king or possibly from an Egyptian deity, passes through an arch on her way to the Temple of Peace, attended by a hovering Angel of Victory holding a laurel wreath, and a numerous train. In the distance can be seen the gutted ruins of the Capitol. (Some may think this allegory a trifle overdrawn.)

The War of 1812 seems to have been inevitable, and the causes went further than free trade and sailors' rights, repeated violations of American territorial waters by the British Navy (declaring an enemy coast blockaded when it was not blockaded), and matters connected with British activities with Indians in the West. It was the arrogant and contemptuous attitude of the British Government toward the upstart Americans that made the war inevitable. The humiliated worm finally turned.

After the war the contempt was gone, to be replaced by a patronizing attitude perhaps even more difficult to bear. But the little United States had proved that she was a nation to be taken seriously. The upstart Americans had fought Britain, a great power, twice, and won twice, the second time without outside aid. The fact could not be ignored by any court in Europe. The war made the United States more of a nation. It had taken the lives of 2,260 Americans and 3,430 Britons to accomplish this.

The war gave the nation a National Anthem, though it was not officially so designated by Act of Congress until 1931, generations after it had become so in the popular mind. (One wonders how many who attempt to sing the Anthem—on or off key—know where those bursting bombs and glaring rockets exploded, or when, or why.)

In 1812 Madison was sneered at by the Federalists as a puny, weak creature. In 1814 they were calling him a dictator. He was obliged to fight the war with an uncooperative Congress, incompetent generals and a seditious New England, but he refused all advice that would have impinged on any of the constitutional rights of those who gave vocal aid to the enemy, and when he left office the Citizens' Committee of Washington addressed him in part: "We cannot resist offering you our own and the nation's thanks for the vigilance . . . the energy . . . and the safety with which you have wielded an armed force of 50,000 . . . without infringing a

"Peace of Ghent 1814 and Triumph of America." Reproduced from the Collections of the Library of Congress.

political, civil or religious right." (On February 19, 1942, after Pearl Harbor, President Franklin D. Roosevelt, by executive order, caused 112,000 American citizens of Japanese descent to be removed from their homes on the West Coast and thrown into concentration camps. They had done nothing to aid and abet the enemy. James Madison whirled in his grave.)

19 AN ENIGMATIC TREATY

The whole subject must, I think, remain vague.
—Darwin, *The Origin of Species*.

Nobody won the War of 1812, in spite of the magnificent allegory with which our readers have been favored. The British commissioners had instructions to admit neither impressment nor neutral rights as subjects of discussion. Thus the question of free trade and sailors' rights, which had started the war in the first place, were not even mentioned in the Treaty! One wonders why President Madison declared it "satisfactory." "One can only conclude that the Treaty was as dogged by illogicality as the war itself had been."[1]

All the Treaty did was conclude hostilities and restore prewar boundaries. And before the next war impressment was abandoned as a method of manning the Royal Navy. There were no war reparations: The destruction of Washington, the devastation, the looting of Alexandria and other places, were ignored along with towns and villages set afire, ships seized or sunk, crops laid waste, cattle slaughtered. Britannia seems to have gotten away with murder!

Another casualty of the war, and one that need not be regretted, was the Federalist Party. Far from supporting the Government, the Federalists had secretly dealt with the enemy, who, they argued, could not be defeated, and had threatened to break up the Union. But after Jackson's victory at New Orleans a great wave of patriotism and confidence in the future covered the land, beneath which the Federalists vanished.

There were some odds and ends to clear up. Since no land had changed hands the two signatories could meet in a pleasant atmosphere without grudges. Discriminatory duties were abolished, making it possible for America to trade freely with the British Empire, except for the West Indies.

Nevertheless the British began at once to build up their shattered naval strength on the Great Lakes. This could have been the beginning of an arms race, but the United States suggested a mutual demilitarization of the lakes, including Champlain, and His Majesty's Government agreed. Perhaps nations were beginning to see reason.

The Rush-Bagot agreement of 1817 allowed both powers one armed vessel of a specific size, with one 18-pounder each, on Lakes Champlain and Ontario, and two each on the other lakes. Gradually the entire border was demilitarized, the 49th Parallel was agreed upon as the northern boundary of Louisiana Territory, and the Oregon country was put under joint control for ten years. Finally, by 1872, the Canadian-American boundary, more than 4,000 miles long, became the longest unguarded frontier in the world.

20   A HERO ONCE AGAIN

While the problems of the Canadian-American boundary had been resolved, there remained a Spanish-American boundary between Florida and Georgia. Slaves, who could not be legally recaptured continued to escape into Florida; they were often recaptured illegally, which angered the Seminole Indians particularly. Worse yet, marauding Indians crossed into Georgia and on one or two occasions pounced on White Americans and scalped them.

There were two British subjects in Florida, a Scot named Arbuthnot who owned a trading schooner, and a carefree type named Ambuster. This latter adventurer joined a group of Seminoles whose chief enjoyed, as did so many Indian chiefs, an unforgettable name. It was Bowlegs.

President Monroe, who had succeeded Madison, ordered through his Secretary of War John C. Calhoun, that General Andrew Jackson "adopt the necessary means" to end the border troubles. No sooner said than done. Andrew Jackson and a force of Tennessee militia "burst into Florida," marched to the fortress of St. Marks, hauled down the Spanish flag, arrested Mr. Arbuthnot, and had two Seminole chiefs who had sought refuge there hanged. Old Hickory had a rough and ready style.

He then traced Bowlegs through a forest "festooned with Spanish moss" and found him and his braves at the Suwanee River. The braves fled, but who should come crashing through the woods but the adventure-bent Ambuster with a letter from Arbuthnot warning Bowlegs of the approach of Jackson, and offering him ten kegs of gunpowder, a fatal error.

Jackson ordered both Ambuster and Arbuthnot court-martialed, one for espionage, the other for leading Indians to war with the United States. Both were found guilty and executed. Then, after a double-quick march to Pensacola, Jackson took the fortress there, removed the Spanish governor, and had it garrisoned by Americans.

Jackson, the hero of New Orleans, then went home, a hero again. But in Washington there was consternation. What would Britain say? What the British press said was that the "ruffian" Jackson had murdered "two peaceful British traders." Public opinion demanded (1) instant apology and reparation, or (2) war!

Lord Castlereagh, the Foreign Minister, who had proved just and firm on other occasions, examined the documents from Washington and concluded that the victims of Jackson's high-handedness had been engaged in practices as to have "deprived them of any claim on their own government for interference." The belligerence simmered down. Samuel Eliot Morison said of Castlereagh, "He did more for Anglo-American friendship than any other statesman of the century."

The Spaniards have always been noted for a streak of realism that exists side by side with their mysticism as evinced in their art. Madrid knew that its hold on all its American possessions was slipping. Jackson's raid demonstrated that the United States, or almost any power, could seize Florida without half trying. Spain, the country that had once been given the whole New World on a platter by Alexander VI, found her empire tottering. She was willing to cede Florida to the United States in return for a clearly marked boundary to Louisiana as far east of the Rio Grande as possible, to preserve Mexico.

Negotiations were opened by the Spanish ambassador to Washington, Don Luis de Onís, and ended with the King of Spain ceding "all territories which belong to him situated to the eastward of the Mississippi and known by the name of East and West Florida." (Florida then extended as far west as the great river.) In return the United States assumed the claims against Spain held by inhabitants of this region to the tune of $5 million. The United States gave up all claims to Texas, one of Mexico's three provinces, the other two being New Mexico and Upper California. The King in question was Ferdinand VII whose hideous phiz was immortalized by Goya.

This settlement got out of the King an even more vast tract of land. For giving up Florida he accepted a boundary to Louisiana Territory that followed the Sabine, Red and Arkansas rivers to the Continental Divide and the 42nd parallel to the Pacific. This parallel is the present boundary between California and Oregon. The addition of Florida to the United States so delighted Americans that the gain of the vast tract of land westward which included access to the Pacific attracted little attention. But John Quincy Adams knew its significance. "The acquisition of a definite line of boundary to the Pacific forms a great epoch in our history," he wrote in his diary. How right he was, and how nearsighted everyone else.

James Monroe had presided over the Louisiana Purchase; now he was in charge of the annexation of Florida and another vast tract of land that gave the United States access to the Pacific. History loves to bestow titles—the Great Emancipator, the Great Compromiser, the Great Commoner—and James Monroe should receive the title, "the Great Realtor," if good usage contenances such a styleless word.

Between 1818 and 1822 most of the Spanish colonies lying between the Rio Grande and the Strait of Magellan, encouraged and excited by the French Revolution and the Napoleonic wars, had thrown off the crumbling yoke of Spain. Then Russia, Prussia and Austria, later joined by France, dreamed up an absurdity called the Holy Alliance. It was anything but holy in its aim, which was to restore the whole area, a large part of a large continent, to the Bourbon Dynasty, in the interest of Legitimacy. This would mean sending vast armies across the sea to conquer a continent full of rebels, and mountains among the highest in the world, and no more unfeasible plan was ever devised by man. The Bourbons were doubtless legitimate, like many of us, but had little else to recommend them, and it would have required innumerable Bourbons to sit squarely on those phantom thrones, whose number rose to the neighborhood of seventeen by 1830. There were surely not enough Bourbons to go around.

At the other extremity of the New World there was more trouble brewing. The first white settlement in Alaska was made by Russian fur traders on Kodiac Island, off its southern coast, in 1784. This of course made the whole of Alaska a Russian possession, but not until 1821 was any attention paid to the vast place, sparsely inhabited by Eskimos and polar bears. In that year Czar Alexander I suddenly issued a ukase forbidding any foreign power to venture north of the 51st parallel, which is in the vicinity of Vancouver Island, British Columbia. Non-American powers were beginning to flex their muscles in all reaches of the American continents.

"Ukase" sounds more awesome than "imperial command" but it didn't much awe John Quincy Adams. However, with this menace to the north and the faint prospects of Bourbons in the south, Adams was uneasy. In particular he didn't relish the idea of his old friend the Czar dictating where American ships could and could not go; and evidently Mr. Adams and Mr. Monroe thought the only good Bourbon came in a bottle.

Adams was concerned likewise over Great Britain's ambitions in the northwest part of North America which had to be contained, if his vision of American territorial extensions was ever to materialize. He therefore made a suggestion to the President, which Monroe thought a good idea.

In a secret communication Adams informed the Russian ambassador, Baron Tuyll, of a new policy the Government was adopting, to the effect that "the American continents are no longer subjects for any new European establishments," and that any attempts to extend their system to any portion of this hemisphere would be viewed "as dangerous to our peace and safety, and any interposition against the sovereignty of existing American nations an unfriendly act." This announcement was aimed in several widely different directions.

The American Government likewise pledged itself not to interfere in European affairs, and this is the part of the policy that got the attention at home. Nobody wanted to go to fight in Europe! European statesmen dismissed the whole thing as contemptuous saber-rattling.

At the same time that Adams talked to the Russian baron he sent a communication to the American ambassador in London, Richard Rush (who had accompanied President Madison to the Battle of Bladensburg) in strictest secrecy, to inform the British Foreign Secretary (still George Canning), of the American Government's new policy. Neither Baron Tuyll nor Mr.Canning made any objection to this policy. Mr. Canning thought it was aimed at Russia and therefore to the advantage of the British holdings in Canada, and Baron Tuyll thought it was aimed at Great Britain and thus to the advantage of Russia. And it was Baron Tuyll who was right. Any extentionist plans Great Britain might have had, went no further.

How devious are the ways of diplomacy! Russia had no interest in Canada. The frozen wastes of Alaska were frozen wastes enough.

President Monroe included the new policy in his annual message to Congress in December 1823. Little noticed at the time, the policy grew in importance with the passing years, but it was not till about 1850 that it came to be known as the Monroe Doctrine, and it was still operating when the United States prevented Russia from setting up missile bases in Cuba in 1962 under the wise guidance of President John F. Kennedy.

As for the Bourbons, that whole fantasy had been abruptly squelched before it could do any harm.

In 1822 Monroe had already informed Congress that four American nations—Argentina, Peru, Chile and Mexico—had applied for recognition by the United States as legitimate governments (even without Bourbons) and requested appropriations for sending ministers there. This would mean a great increase in commerce when diplomatic relations were established.

The United States was the first nation to recognize the new republics in defiance of the Holy Alliance. As early as 1828 Monroe had sought the cooperation of Great Britain in recognizing these new nations, but Great Britain turned thumbs down on the proposal. Russia, Prussia and Austria, holy or not, were best left to their own devices. Thus the United States got there first.

21   THE GREAT LAFAYETTE, OR THE NATION'S DARLING

In 1824 the Marquis de Lafayette, now 67, returned to visit the United States, accompanied by his son, George Washington Lafayette (who was a dud), a secretary, a valet, and a red wig. As he came ashore at the Battery in New York he was confronted by a huge crowd and a tense silence. The people were seeing a figure step out of history; they were looking on Lafayette plain. They were awed.

Then the cheering began. Cannon roared, bands played, flags, French and American, fluttered from every building. Lafayette was conducted to an open barouche through dense crowds, a space cleared by troops, and escorted by the Lafayette Guards to City Hall, where he shook hands for two hours. No one arriving in America has ever received such an ovation. After four days in New York the Marquis left for Boston in a cavalcade of carriages and horses.

Lafayette spent fifteen months in the United States. Crowds, balls, banquets, triumphal arches, maids strewing flowers before his carriage—from Portland,

Maine, to Savannah, Georgia—were his lot. When he came to Richmond, Virginia, the "Junior Morgan's Riflemen," a volunteer company of Richmond boys, served as an honor guard for the great hero, commanded by a fellow of fifteen, "Lieutenant" Edgar Allan Poe. Lafayette called on old John Adams at Quincy, spent a week with Thomas Jefferson at Monticello, and four days with the Madisons at Montpelier. President and Mrs. Monroe wanted him to stay in the White House, but this was thought too exclusive, and he went to Gadsby's Hotel, the guest of the nation.

June 17, 1825, was Bunker Hill Day, and Lafayette made the trip to Boston again to lay the cornerstone of the Bunker Hill monument. He had visited every state in the Union but Maine and Vermont, and at the request of the inhabitants of those states he made a hurried trip to both.

The new frigate *Brandywine* was almost completed, and the government wanted to put her at Lafayette's disposal for the return to France. He consented to wait until she was ready. President and Mrs. John Quincy Adams, now inhabiting the White House, induced him to stay with them, and aside from a great State Dinner, were able to give him a little rest at last, which perhaps he did not want. He visited the tomb of Washington at Mount Vernon, and prints of this highly charged scene emerged from the lithograhers.

Congress voted Lafayette $200,000, gave him 2,300 acres of land in Florida, and made him and his posterity honorary citizens of the United States. His descendents, when they visit America, enter the country to this day on United States passports.

Lafayette, when he returned to France on the *Brandywine*, took with him cases of earth so that he could one day be buried in American soil.

22   JOHN C. CALHOUN IS FURIOUS

James Monroe's two administrations had been successful ones, due in large measure to John Quincy Adams, the best Secretary of State any President ever had. But when it came time in 1824 to elect a new President the political situation had vastly changed. The Federalists had uttered their last gasp, a casualty of the War of 1812, and the Republican party (read "Democratic") stood unopposed.

What had happened was the rapid rise of sectionalism. The North, the South and the West, rather than political parties, now vied for control of the government.

The New England states put forward John Quincy Adams. Tennessee offered Old Hickory, the Hero of New Orleans, popular as successful generals are so likely to be; and from Kentucky there was Henry Clay, the former War Hawk; South

Carolina had John C. Calhoun, another of the War Hawks and President Monroe's Secretary of the Treasury.

No candidate won a majority in the Electoral College, and as directed by the Constitution, the choice was thrown to the House of Representatives, which had to choose between the three candidates with the greatest number of votes. Clay, who was not among the top three, threw his vote to Adams, whose views agreed with his own on the issues of the day. Thus Adams won, and made Clay his Secretary of State.

The Jackson faction seized on this. "A corrupt bargain!" they cried—as if John Quincy Adams could ever be corrupt. Clay had announced two months before the election that he was an Adams man.

John Quincy Adams' presidency was as unhappy as his terms as Secretary of State had been successful. Jackson resigned his seat in the Senate and spent the next four years fighting to oust Adams and Clay and the whole "dynasty of secretaries" from power. His able lieutenants kept pounding the big drums of Collusion and Corruption, shouting that "the people's choice" had been unjustly deprived of the presidency. Jackson was hardly the people's choice as in six states, with a quarter of the population of the country, there was no popular vote; the electors were chosen by the legislatures, and only one of them (South Carolina) had voted for Jackson. Rabble-rousers, as has been noted before, are rarely meticulous about facts. Jackson had been unjustly deprived of nothing. But he thought he had a grievance— so did all his cohorts—and they made the whole of Adams' administration as miserable for him as possible.

Supreme among John Quincy Adams' headaches was the tariff. There is nothing duller to read about, nor to write about, than the Tariff, so suppressing a yawn, we must try to be brief.

Every section of the country had its own ideas about a protective tariff, depending on what it produced and wanted to have protected. The manufacturers of the North wanted high tariffs; the South did not. Fearing its side would lose, the South resorted to a ruse: it joined with the western farmers in demanding duties on raw materials (wool, flax and iron ore) needed by the manufacturing North, thinking this would cause the northern industrial interests to vote against the bill. But the North, used to and devoted to high tariffs, voted for the bill in spite of all. The bill passed both houses of Congress and President Adams reluctantly signed it in 1828. They were the highest tariffs imposed before the Civil War.

"The Tariff of Abominations!" Calhoun cried.

The Senate held up Adams' appointments, Congress turned down his plans for internal improvements, and in Georgia the Governor defied him when he tried to defend the claims of the Cherokees for their treaty lands. Rabble-rousing southern orators urged boycotting the protective states and even the resignation of southern congressmen. Talk of secession began to float about.

23   A NATION AWED

All the things we ever knew
Will be ashes in that hour.
—Edna St. Vincent Millay, *Mariposa.*

John Adams was ninety years old. Paralyzed and scarcely able to communicate, he knew he was dying. For 49 years he and Thomas Jefferson had carried on a correspondence, though there had been hiatuses springing from those "inveterate sympathies and passionate attachments" to foreign powers Washington had so wisely warned against in his Farewell Address. The Federalists (pro-British, including Adams) and the Republicans (pro-French, including Jefferson) were at swords' points most of the time, each party accusing the other of everything short of treason. One Thomas Callender of Richmond, Virginia, published what Adams called "the basest libel and vilest slander which malice could invent or calumny exhibit" against him. Adams' quill was both vitriolic and fluent. Mr. Callender was sentenced to jail under the Sedition Act. But when Jefferson succeeded Adams as President he pardoned him. That made irascible John Adams boiling mad. He took it as an endorsement of Callender's libels against him rather than a repudiation of the unconstitutional Sedition Act. But this was not enough to feed Adams' ire. Adams' son John Quincy had been appointed commissioner in cases of bankruptcy by the Federal Court of Massachusetts. When the law made this appointment a permanent one at the behest of the President, Jefferson removed John Quincy and appointed somebody else. It seemed clear that Jefferson nurtured a personal animosity toward the Adams family, and showed it in petty ways. Washington himself had deemed John Quincy worthy of being appointed Minister to the Netherlands when he was 27.

Birds in their little nests agree, but the Founding Fathers in their little nest did not. Adams and Jefferson were on opposite sides of most fences. Jefferson hated Hamilton and Adams distrusted both. They said dreadful things about each other in private. Madison appears to have had a more equable disposition. Washington kept these warring factions in line for the good of the country by his tact, diplomacy and the enormous prestige he so justly deserved.

But for John Adams all the quarrels had receded. He and Thomas Jefferson were part of history now, and there was still much to talk about. Instead, there would be silence. Abigail was gone, and their son was President and had inherited a heavy burden. Those around the old man listened attentively, hoping to understand what he was trying to say. His last words were, "Thomas Jefferson still lives."

But Jefferson had died four hours earlier. It was the Fourth of July, 1826.

Fifty years before, to the day, the Declaration of Independence had been adopted by the Continental Congress. The last of the Founding Fathers were gone together. The strange and prophetic coincidence awed the nation.

24   THE DOCTRINE OF INTERPOSITION

Even the damned may salute the eloquence of Mr. Webster.
—Stephen Vincent Benet, *The Devil and Daniel Webster.*

John Marshall, who as an American commissioner in Paris faced up to those XYZ gentlemen, became the fourth Chief Justice of the United States, and is known in history as "the Great Chief Justice." By the width and wisdom of his interpretations of the Constitution he raised the Supreme Court to its present awesome power, and made certain the right of the Court to review state and federal laws and pronounce on their constitutionality. Thus the Federal Government gained power and the states lost power.

In 1819 a legal battle convulsed the placid groves of Academe. Dartmouth College, at Hanover, New Hampshire, was founded and chartered in 1769 (with funds provided by the Earl of Dartmouth with the worthy aim of instructing the Indians in the Christian Gospels, a course dropped from the curriculum long ago). In 1816 the New Hampshire legislature, without the consent of the trustees, amended the Charter to make the college public. The trustees brought suit and the case was heard before the Supreme Court. Daniel Webster, one of the most colorful characters in American history, won the case. Born in a log cabin in New Hampshire in 1782, he was now a senator from Massachusetts. Handsome, imposing, with beetling brows, glittering eyes ("like anthracite furnaces," said Thomas Carlyle), dowered with a magnificent voice and overwhelming oratorical powers, he argued that the amendment was unconstitutional because the state had impaired "the obligation of a contract." (Webster, an alumnus of Dartmouth, said, "It is a small place, but there are those who love it.")

Chief Justice Marshall announced the opinion of the Court: a contract was inviolable. This decision made the contract clause of the Constitution the instrument by which private property rights are protected against state abridgements, guaranteeing their security.

When Marshall died in 1835 the Liberty Bell in Philadelphia tolled his knell—and cracked. Perhaps this was symbolic. (The bell was never recast.)

As for Daniel Webster, a mighty future awaited him. Among other accomplishments, he came close to annihilating John C. Calhoun.

In the election of 1828 Jackson gained the presidency by a landslide and John Quincy Adams left the White House and did not attend Old Hickory's inauguration. The first six Presidents were not only intellectuals but aristocrats. Three of them were Founding Fathers. But now there was in the White House a frontiersman, an Indian fighter with no experience in politics, reeking of the "Untamed West" though he owned a fine plantation in Tennessee.

After the inauguration the "common people" invaded the White House to shake the new President's hand, and wrecked the place. Footmen appearing with trays of food and drink were knocked down in the rush. Tables of viands were upset. Backwoodsmen in muddy boots climbed all over the damask furniture, bric-a-brac was brushed off the mantels, pictures crashed to the floor, the carpets were covered with food and drink. It was a saturnalia. After an hour Jackson was rescued by his entourage and slipped out through a side door and went to his hotel. Old Hickory had had enough of egalitarianism for one day.

Jackson began his administration with no clearly defined program to carry out. He was all for the common man (still), but under strong leadership (his). Jackson was perhaps the most opinionated President who ever sat in the White House, and some of his opinions were good. Though he believed in the legitimate rights of the states, he was above all devoted to the Federal Union.

The new President picked for his Secretary of State Martin Van Buren, Governor of New York, where he was born (in the Dutch town of Kinderhook, on the Hudson) in 1782. Van Buren's early career in law, and then in New York politics, had sharpened his natural abilities for analyzing complex problems and producing clear, concise conclusions. He was a subtle thinker, deft and witty, far removed from the oratorical and sometimes bombastic flights of Daniel Webster. He was referred to as "the Red Fox."

The President had, beside his official family, an unofficial coterie of political cronies who acquired the name of the "Kitchen Cabinet"—a camarilla—and it was with them that he did his consulting, scarcely troubling with his official family. (He rarely called Cabinet meetings.) Martin Van Buren was a member of both groups and soon became the most important man around Jackson.

It was not long before John C. Calhoun, the Vice President, realized that he was not the number one man, nor the favorite to succeed the President. This put him in a contentious mood.

Jackson's first troubles stemmed from that old *bête noir*, the tariff. Calhoun had been a strong protectionist (high tariff) man in 1816, but since then South Carolinians had changed their minds, and so had John Calhoun.

Carolinian cotton plantations were not as profitable as formerly—the land was depleted and the new fertile soils of the Southwest produced better yields and higher profits. But the Carolinians blamed it all on that whipping boy, "the Tariff of

Portrait of Daniel Webster, "Black Dan." Painted by
Francis Alexander. Gift of Dr. George C. Shattuck, Class of
1803, Hood Museum of Art. Reproduced by permission of
Hood Museum of Art, Dartmouth College, Hanover, New
Hampshire.

Abominations." Protective tariffs raised the price of things they needed, and lowered the price, they seemed to think, of the cotton they exported.

Calhoun developed an ingenious theory to circumvent the tariff laws and yet remain (he thought) within the law. Briefly, his theory was this: If Congress enacted a law a state thought to be of doubtful constitutionality, it could hold a convention, and if the delegates decided that Congress had indeed overreached its legal powers, these delegates could declare the Federal law null and void, and go on from there— ultimately in secession from the Union, if necessary.

Calhoun's "nullification" theory was based on the premise that the national government existed at the state level, because the national government was the creation of the states, and depended on the states for its existence—hence sovereignty never left the states. In other words, the Union, which had taken the effort of so many knitters to knit, could be unraveled at will by any knitter who chose to do so. Calhoun called his theory "the Doctrine of Interposition" and it certainly interposed a new and ingenious interpretation of the creation of the Constitution.

Jackson declared nullification to be treason. Privately he threatened to hang his Vice President. No single state could hope to defy the Federal Government. Yet for Calhoun, who would not budge from his position, it would be a face-losing proposition to yield, and nothing is more valuable than one's face.

It was then that Henry Clay came to the rescue of South Carolina, and Calhoun's face. He devised a simple plan. This was a compromise by which the tariff would be gradually lowered each year until it reached the 1816 level. Calhoun accepted this, but now busied himself working for southern solidarity and power to resist Federal authority in the future.

South Carolina bided its time, Calhoun elaborated on his theory as the months went by, and when Congress gave little relief in the Tariff Act of 1832, a convention was called, it adopted an ordinance of Nullification declaring the tariff acts of 1828 and 1832 null and void, and forbade the collection of duties within the state of South Carolina.

In the meantime the question of the sale of public lands came up, and was linked to the tariff in a peculiar way. Southerners contended that with a lower tariff there would be an increase of foreign imports, bringing more money into the Treasury, and thus making it possible to sell public lands at a cheaper price.

Senator Samuel Foote of Connecticut proposed that the sale of public lands, on the other hand, be restricted. This proposal was denounced by Senator Robert Y. Hayne of South Carolina as a plot designed by Eastern manufacturers to check the flow of Westward migration and keep their factory workers at home. Southerners hoped for Western support in their drive to lessen the tariff and were willing to see western land sold in exchange for such support.

Dartmouth's champion, Daniel Webster, now again takes center stage. He rose in the Senate (his oratorical powers doubtless sharpened by his successful defense of his Alma Mater) and accused South Carolina of advocating disunion. Hayne took the bait. He launched into an impassioned and emotional exposition of the doctrine of States' Rights, and this seems to have been the cue Webster wanted to hear. Webster undertook to answer Hayne more fully on another day. He was setting the stage for a major effort.

On the appointed day the gallery of the Senate was crowded with the elite of Washington.

Webster's speech, which lasted for two days, is known as "the Second Reply to Hayne." The Senator took for his theme the issue of States' Rights versus the Federal Government, and his speech is the great oration in defense of the American Constitution, and one of the most powerful speeches ever delivered in Congress.

After defending his State against Hayne's charge of selfish sectionalism, Webster proceeded in defense of the government. It was not a mere league of states as the Southerners claimed. Not the States, but the People, had made the Union.

"It is, Sir, the people's Constitution, the people's government, made for the people, answerable to the people." If Congress exceeded its powers, there was an arbiter appointed by the Constitution itself, namely, the Supreme Court, to declare a law void. This authority could not be given to a state or a group of states. Pennsylvania would annul one law, Alabama another, Virginia a third, and so on. Congress would become a mockery, the Constitution, "a rope of sand." The Union would fall apart, the states would return to the frightful anarchy which followed the Revolution, while our flag, now "the gorgeous ensign of the republic" would droop, its stripes erased, its stars obscured, over the "broken and dishonored fragments of a once glorious Union!"

This seems to have silenced Mr. Hayne for the nonce.

On April 13, 1830, the anniversary of Thomas Jefferson's birthday, there was a great banquet to honor his memory. President Jackson proposed the first toast. He raised his glass, looked grimly at the Vice President, who was at the forefront of all this nullification nonsense, and said, "Our Federal Union—it must be preserved!"

Calhoun rose and offered his toast: "The Union—after our liberty, most dear!"

Senator Hayne resigned his seat in the Senate to become Governor of South Carolina and Calhoun resigned the Vice Presidency to enter the Senate where he could promote his nullification notions. He became a more and more outspoken exponent of states' rights, and more and more a champion of slavery and its extension. Later, as Secretary of State under John Tyler, he negotiated the admittance of Texas as a slave state, and later in the Senate, opposed the admittance of California as a free state. He had been one of the War Hawks in 1812 and espoused a strong

Army and Navy. He encouraged manufacture, internal improvements, a national bank. Later he opposed most of these measures.

Calhoun was deemed a statesman and a philosopher, and was a towering figure in the political life of his time. But because of his pro-slavery stand, long a subject deplored and dead, and his constant efforts to weaken the Federal Union, he is not generally considered a sympathetic figure in American history. National thinking long ago went against him.

25   THE GREEK TEMPLE IN PHILADELPHIA

The Nullification issue had scarcely been put to sleep by Webster's great defense of the Constitution when another battle had to be won.

Alexander Hamilton had urged the creation of a national bank to serve the Government for short-term borrowing, and to increase credit for expanding business. The bank bill was passed in 1791 by a House vote of 39 to 20, though James Madison himself had declared that the Constitutional Convention had denied to Congress the power to charter companies and the proposal was therefore unconstitutional— and he should know.

President Washington consulted Jefferson, who upheld Madison's view, but Hamilton said that the power to regulate the currency carried with it the implied power to establish monetary agencies. Washington, with perhaps some misgivings, signed the bill. And so the First Bank of the United States opened its doors in 1791. The bank had a 20-year charter and soon eight branches in various cities; the main office was located in Carpenters' Hall, Philadelphia's hallowed place where the first Continental Congress had sat.

In 1811 the Bank's charter expired and the same political party that had chartered it refused to renew the charter. So the bank wound up its affairs and disappeared.

Five years later, in 1816, the same party voted to establish a new and even larger institution. The War of 1812 had left the national finances in a chaotic state; the credit of the country had fallen to its lowest ebb. The Treasury did not have the funds to pay the interest on the public debt held by banks in New England. Banks had multiplied during the war, extending their note issues until by the autumn of 1814 most of the banks not in New England were forced to suspend specie payments, and prices rose to be the highest in the 19th Century. Thus sentiment grew for the establishment of a new national bank, to assist the Government in financing the war and to bring order out of chaos. A flood of banknotes circulated at different discounts, including United States Treasury notes with similar fluctuating values.

Madison, overcoming his constitutional scruples, approved the bill on April 10, 1816, and the Second Bank of the United States opened for business in 1817—in Carpenters' Hall left vacant by the First Bank. The Second, like the First, was *not* a national bank but a private banking corporation, privately controlled, but enjoying "unique and profitable relations with the Government" and also the undying hostility of the states. Many thought states' rights were being infringed, and there were loud and continued cries that the bank was unconstitutional. The concentration of capital was in the Northeast, while the expanding South and West needed more capital.

The Bank boasted a capital of $35 million, of which one fifth had been subscribed by the Government. It served as a repository for the public funds that it could use for its own banking purposes, and without payment of interest. It could issue unlimited bank notes. Furthermore the bank could not be taxed by the states, and no similar bank was to be chartered by Congress.

Obviously, the Second Bank of the United States was in an enviable position with its tidy little charter, and the state banks were heavily disadvantaged. Even those who were advocates of the bank agreed that it had too much power. It enjoyed a virtual monopoly of the currency and almost complete control over credit. Its banknotes circulated throughout the country and were accepted everywhere as a dependable medium of exchange. It had 25 branches scattered far and wide, and paid handsome dividends to its stockholders. Its shares sold far above par. Furthermore it could boast as its head office a Greek temple in Philadelphia, modeled after the Parthenon (Doric columns without, Ionic columns within) and Nicholas Biddle of that city was the president of this sumptuous bank.

Andrew Jackson, "the People's President," was out to get it. It was too rich and powerful, and it used its resources to aid with loans and credit those businessmen and politicians of whom it approved, employing the public funds to make money for the rich who could afford its shares.

The charter of the bank was due to expire in 1836, and it was now 1832 and a presidential year. Henry Clay was nominated for the presidency at the Republican Convention, and he and Nicholas Biddle cooked up a neat little scheme. Clay was to introduce a bill to recharter the bank before the old charter had expired, and he pushed such a bill through Congress. As hoped, Jackson vetoed the bill. Reintroduced in the Senate, a two-thirds majority could not be mustered to override the veto. Clay and Biddle were jubilant. Jackson would surely lose enough eastern votes to cost him the election—and hand it over to Clay.

How can wise men be so foolish? What did the "common people," Jackson's constituents, care about Mr. Biddle's bank? Old Hickory had defied the money kings and their reputed power, and state after state eagerly voted for him. Clay carried six states with an electoral vote of 49; Jackson's total was 219. The Hero of

New Orleans could do no wrong. And now he was out to get "Emperor Biddle's Monster."

A clause in the charter allowed the Government to withdraw its deposits in the bank, and the Secretary of the Treasury was told to do this, and to discontinue depositing any more of the Government's balances. The Secretary did not obey; Jackson dismissed him and appointed Roger B. Taney, who would do what he was bid—boycott the bank.

The Government's money was now deposited in various banks that were called "pet banks." Jackson wanted the small people to be able to borrow money easily, contending that Mr. Biddle made loans only to the rich and mighty, of money that belonged to the people. Though the Senate tried to censure the President, it had no power to do so. But the Bank of the United States faltered. When its charter expired in 1836 it was chartered by the state of Pennsylvania, but the panic that developed in 1837 did not help, and in 1841 it closed its doors.

Andrew Jackson succeeded in almost everything he undertook. He negotiated successfully with Great Britain for abolition of tonnage duties on trade with the West Indies; he managed to wheedle 23,500,000 francs out of Louis Philippe (the "Citizen King") in payment of claims of American citizens whose property had been seized by Napoleon. He was constantly triumphant.

There are those who contend that making credit easier and more available caused the weakening of the dollar. By the late 20th century the country was living on credit; the dollar was a lowly thing, while during the reign of Nicholas Biddle it had a stability it has never enjoyed since.

Henry Clay, in revenge for his defeat in 1832, influenced the Senate in rejecting Taney for secretary of the Treasury. Two years later, on the death of Chief Justice John Marshall, Taney became Chief Justice of the Supreme Court. In revenge for seeing his friends excluded from Jackson's cabinet, John C. Calhoun, with a deciding vote in the Senate, defeated Martin Van Buren's appointment as Minister to Great Britain. The next year he saw Van Buren occupying his former position as Vice President, thus presiding over the Senate that had rejected his appointment to London.

Jackson was worn out by his eight vigorous years in the White House, and wanted to retire to his plantation, The Hermitage, in Tennessee. His handpicked candidate to succeed him, his Secretary of State Martin Van Buren, was nominated.

The opponents of Jackson, whom they called "King Andrew the First" began to call themselves "Whigs" after the party in England that traditionally stood for limiting the power of the king. They had three candidates to put forward: Daniel Webster for the North, one Hugh Lawson White of Tennessee to seek the Southern votes, and General William Henry Harrison, former governor of Indiana Territory who had fought Tucumseh in various places and was in consequence a man of the

West. None was a match for the Democratic candidate, and Martin Van Buren became the eighth President of the United States.

These were boom times. There had been a surplus in the Treasury divided among the states for the building of roads, canals, and those new-fangled railways. Money from the land offices had been pouring into the Treasury when Van Buren took office, but it was paper money issued by various state banks backed only by the credit of the issuing bank. Jackson had issued a "Specie Circular" stating that in the future only hard money, or the notes of specie-paying banks (i.e., gold and silver) would be accepted in payment for public lands.

Van Buren was in office scarcely three months when the bubble burst. The distribution of the Treasury surplus had weakened the state banks ("pet banks"), the Specie Circular caused a run on the banks, since everyone wanted to change his paper dollars for precious metals, and the states had over-extended with their roads and canals and were forced to default their debts. It was the Panic of 1837. Van Buren was gathering the crops sown by Jackson.

In those days there was no precedent nor thought of the government coming to the aid of the people in bad times, but Van Buren favored the borrowing of $10,000,000 to meet expenses during the emergency. By presidential order he cut the length of a workday down to a mere ten hours for workers on all federal projects. He urged Congress to reduce the price of public lands and to pass a bill giving settlers the right to buy 160 acres at a set price before they were opened for public sale. This pleased the farmer-labor segments of his party.

Van Buren's greatest contribution was his proposal for a new fiscal system. Mr. Biddle's bank was destroyed, Jackson's "pet banks" were unreliable. Something new was needed. Though the United States had been minting coins since 1792 when the first mint was established in Philadelphia, and paper money began to be issued by banks in 1815, the Government had never printed paper money. Possibly memories of those worthless "Continentals" of the Revolution lingered on.

Van Buren's plan was basically a simple one. Government funds were to be deposited in an independent treasury at Washington and in sub-treasuries in various cities—an Independent Treasury or Sub-Treasury system. Treasury agents were to handle the funds themselves, and no private banks would have the advantage of using the people's money as a basis for loans with which to earn money for themselves and their shareholders.

In 1840, Van Buren's last year in office, he succeeded in driving this sensible and just measure through both houses of Congress.

26   THE LOG CABIN ON WHEELS

The election of 1840 approached, and this time the Whigs were better organized. Then, too, there was a depression—always grist to the mill of an opposition party.

Henry Clay, ever hopeful, was passed over. His views were known, he had been defeated too often, and in his long public career he had garnered the usual crop of enemies. Webster was out of the running too, for the same reasons. It would be much more savvy to have a new candidate without any views.

Jackson, a popular general, had come to power on a populist wave, and was elected without making any of his views known. The Whig Convention had the ideal candidate. Harrison was the Hero of Tippecanoe, the enemy of Tecumseh, the Indian fighter, the erstwhile Governor of Indiana Territory, but, despite having served as a Congressman and Senator, he was an unknown quantity.

To balance the ticket the convention nominated for Vice President John Tyler, a Virginian and a strong states' rights man. Then the Whigs had a lucky break. A Democratic paper called Harrison a simple man who should retire to a log cabin on a pension and drink hard cider. A large proportion of the population lived in log cabins, or had once done so, and drank hard cider too, when nothing better was available. The Whigs had been handed the election on a platter.

Yes! they said. Our man *is* a simple man of the people, and lives in a log cabin, and loves hard cider, and grits and chittlins too, whereas Mr. Van Buren luxuriates in "the regal splendor of the President's Palace" (just where they wanted to put their own candidate), "drinks foreign wines, and fattens on the rich concoctions of a French chef," and pursues other such un-American activities.

The fact that William Henry Harrison was a member of a distinguished family, the son of Benjamin Harrison, a Signer of the Declaration of Independence and once Governor of Virginia, was well educated, and lived in no log cabin but a handsome house, was all a carefully kept secret.

A log cabin became the symbol of the Whigs. Log cabins on wheels were pulled through the streets in political parades, and America had its first dose of the carnival approach to campaigns. Hard cider was consumed at Whig rallies by the barrel; it was the patriotic thing to do.

Some genius thought up the slogan, "Tippecanoe and Tyler, Too." There is nothing to equal the mysterious power of alliteration, and General Harrison was swept into the White House.

President Harrison's Inaugural Address was full of classical allusions, lasted nearly two hours, and was the cause of his death. His Secretary of State, Daniel Webster, attempted to pare it down a bit (much against Harrison's will) and told a friend, "I have killed seventeen Roman proconsuls as dead as smelts," but it wasn't enough. Harrison caught a cold delivering his address on the steps of the Capitol. It developed into pneumonia, and he was dead in just a month.

There is no record of how many others at the ceremony succumbed to the same malady.

27   THE FACE OF THE WATERS

As a beam o'er the face of the waters may glow
While the tide runs in darkness and coldness below.
—Tom Moore, *Irish Melodies.*

Having put it off too long, we must now squarely face the terrible tragedy of human slavery.

Slavery in America began in the most casual way.

In 1619 a Dutch privateer arrived at Jamestown, twelve years after the settlement of the place. The ship's cargo consisted of twenty Blacks who had been lifted off a Spanish slave ship, and the Dutch didn't know what to do with them. They were anxious to get rid of them and offered them dirt cheap.

The settlers didn't know what to do with them either, but they were a bargain and bargains are often irresistible. The settlers decided to buy them and pay for them with tobacco.

The status of these wretched chattels was ambiguous. Slavery was not a recognized institution, thus they were looked upon as indentured servants. The indentures, however, instead of being worked out after a term of years, proved in most cases to be permanent, though some gained their freedom and even became landowners.

Other slave ships arrived from time to time, and after 30 years there were some 300 black indentured servants in the colony and the number was rising. Though some of these blacks owned land, others, the records show, were sold by one planter to another, still without the label of slaves.

The Virginia House of Burgesses cleared up the status puzzle in 1662. Slavery was legally recognized.

In time there were slaves in all the American colonies. (The humanitarian William Penn owned slaves.) Slavery was not historically considered reprehensible.

In the North slavery was not successful. The climate was cold for these Africans, their cost was high, and white labor was cheap and plentiful. But they met the needs of the South very well. There was plenty of land in cultivation, and the blacks were needed to work it. The South lived on cash crops. Tobacco was grown from the beginning in Jamestown and brought huge profits on the London market. Rice was introduced from Madagascar in 1696 and flourished in the swampy coastal areas. This meant more need for labor. Indigo came along in the middle of the 18th century and was in great demand for the mills of England.

Then in 1793 an ingenious Yankee from Massachusetts named Eli Whitney invented the cotton gin. It had taken the work of many slaves to handpick all the seeds out of the cotton bolls. The cotton gin was a remarkably simple machine and revolutionized the economy as well as influencing history. It consisted of a toothed cylinder which revolved against a grate that inclosed the seed cotton. The cylinder pulled the fibres out of the grate, leaving the seeds behind. This simple invention caused cotton to become the great and profitable crop of the South, encouraging the growth of the slave trade as well as feeding the cotton mills of the world.

Between 1816 and 1819 four new states were admitted to the Union—Indiana, Mississippi, Illinois and Alabama, all of them with rapidly increasing populations as the great Western migrations continued. The West was in the ascendant and the older eastern states found this distasteful.

When Louisiana became a state in 1812, the rest of the huge western territory was called the Missouri Territory, and it was rapidly filling with fur traders. The Mississippi was alive with boats plying up and down and two and a half million dollars worth of business was being done annually. Missouri applied for admission as a state in 1818.

But there was a rub. There were now 22 states in the Union, half of them free and half of them slave states. With Missouri admitted as a slave state the balance would be disrupted in favor of the South. There were all kinds of technicalities involved too that would be wearisome to go into. Representative James Tallmadge of New York proposed an amendment to the bill admitting Missouri into the Union, but prohibiting the further introduction of slavery. This amendment passed the House but was defeated in the Senate.

That gave legislatures, mass meetings and frequenters of taverns a whole splendid summer to orate, debate, shout, and fan the flames of discord. By December, when Congress reconvened, passions were so high over the issue of Missouri that words like "disunion" and "civil war" filled the air.

And then the possibility of a compromise arose. Maine, which had been a part of Massachusetts since it was bought from the heirs of Sir Ferdinando Gorges in 1677, induced Massachusetts to consent to separation. With an antislavery constitution already worked out, Maine applied for admission to the Union as a new state. Senator Thomas of Illinois introduced an amendment to the bill admitting Missouri and Maine together which would exclude slavery forever from the Missouri Territory *except for Missouri itself*. Thus, any new states to be carved out of the Missouri Territory in the future would be free.

The House accepted this compromise by a close vote, and in March 1820

President Monroe signed the bill. Thus Maine became a free State, free from Massachusetts (as well as free from slavery), which is perhaps why she is often referred to as "the State of Maine" instead of merely "Maine," like other states; and Missouri entered as a slave state, planting the seeds of later troubles. The Missouri Compromise entered the history books and was the bane of school children for years, until the mid-20th century when American history was dropped from the curriculum in favor of an ersatz social history concocted by committees and as bloodless as stones.

Although the invention of the cotton gin greatly encouraged slavery, slavery was firmly established in the South by 1700 when the black population numbered 150,000. Of these 18,000 lived north of Maryland.

The American Colonization Society, of which some southern planters were members, had been granted land in western Africa by local chiefs in 1821, for colonizing freed Blacks. The place was called Liberia, and became an independent country in 1847. But it solved no problems for the vast numbers of blacks in America.

Both in the North and in the South the going was tough for them, but tougher in the South. Slaves were forbidden to hold property, were denied the right to testify in court against a white person, and it was illegal to teach them to read and write (except in Maryland, Kentucky, and Tennessee). If a slave was killed in the course of being punished, it was no crime. A slave could not leave his master's property without permission, could not be out after dark, was not allowed to congregate with other slaves except in church, and of course was forbidden to carry firearms.

The transatlantic slave trade was closed in 1808, but the good old American activity of smuggling flourished until mid-century.

Slaves in the North were in a different situation, especially if they worked as domestic servants. Chain gangs and labor in the fields were not a way of life in the North, and during the long, cold winters there was nothing to do in the frozen fields. In the cities the master could not keep so close a guard over his slaves, some of whom were hired out and mingled with other blacks, enslaved and free, and even with the humbler whites.

There were in the North as well as in the South those who believed that human slavery was immoral, and the number kept growing. By 1789 slavery was legally abolished in New England, and soon in the other northern states, New York, New Jersey, and Pennsylvania. But the South refused to join the North on this issue; its economy was based on slavery, and the only way it had joined the Union had been at the price of excluding slavery as an issue in the Constitution.

But the free black in the North did not have a very pleasant time. He could vote only in New England (except Connecticut) and in New York if he owned a certain amount of property. But prejudice restricted his activities and he could find only the most menial work.

At about the time of the Missouri Compromise the movement to abolish slavery took on new momentum. Benjamin Lundy, a Quaker, published a weekly paper called the *Genius of Universal Emancipation,* in Baltimore. Being a Quaker, Mr. Lundy had a mild, reasonable approach to the problem. His associate editor was William Lloyd Garrison, who was not so mild and reasonable, and the two parted over policies, Garrison founding a new weekly, the more fiery *Liberator,* in 1831. A year later Garrison founded the New England Anti-Slavery Society, and a year after that, the American Anti-Slavery Society.

But even before 1830 there was a movement for Abolition, and, surprisingly, more anti-slavery societies rose in the South than in the North. It was southern slaveless farmers as well as northern abolitionists, and the slaves themselves, who threatened "the peculiar institution."

There were slave uprisings as early as 1800 and probably before, the most famous being one organized by a slave preacher named Nat Turner. In Southampton County, Virginia in 1831, a band of blacks armed themselves, went from house to house, and slaughtered sixty white men, women and children with axes and guns. A hundred slaves were executed.

The movement grew, aided by orators both white and black. Of the latter the most famous was Frederick Douglass, an escaped slave from Maryland who had spent some time lecturing in England (where he was a sensation).

His white counterpart was Theodore Weld, a displaced Connecticut Yankee, who at Lane Seminary in Cincinnati indoctrinated the whole faculty to abolition. He organized anti-slavery debates among the students and was dismissed from the seminary. Almost the whole student body requested honorable dismissal. This became the "Lane Revolt." Seventy of the students, as agents for the American Anti-Slavery Society, spewed all over the countryside in their incendiary campaign against slavery. They met very mixed receptions.

Weld received eggs, rocks and other missiles and was knocked almost unconscious by a stone thrown through the window of a church in which he was speaking. When he recovered he went calmly on with his speech. "The lion-hearted, invincible Weld," Garrison called him.

Women entered the movement early, in spite of strong prejudice against their speaking in public in mixed company.

The noted Lydia Maria Child, whose works with such blameless titles as *The Frugal Housewife* and *The Little Girl's Own Book* went through innumerable editions and were household words both North and South, suddenly stunned her public by publishing a work called *An Appeal in Favor of that Class of Americans Called Africans*

(1833). It was a strong and lucid attack on slavery. In the South it and all her previous innocuous works were publicly burned, and even in the North, where the anti-abolition population was large, the lady was reviled. At the Boston Atheneum, where she had the unprecedented honor of a free library card, the card was withdrawn. Such was the status then of free speech in the Land of the Free. An irate member of the Atheneum took her book in a pair of tongs and threw it out the window.

Two sisters, Sarah and Angelina Grimké, of Charleston, South Carolina, born into the highest circle of slave-holding aristocracy, rebelled against slavery in their childhood. When they grew up they "deserted the South and invaded New England like screaming banshees." Angelina addressed a committee of the Massachusetts Legislature in 1838, before an immense mixed crowd. It was a world-shattering event and, at that time, an act of superhuman courage. The two sisters spoke every-where, often to hostile crowds. Most church pulpits were barred to them because they were female. There were riots and packed houses wherever they appeared.

"We Abolition women are turning the world upside down," said Angelina, and she was not far wrong.

By now there were more than 2,000 local abolition societies in the nation with more than 200,000 members.

In 1840 the Antislavery Society experienced a schism. Garrison insisted that women be allowed to speak at antislavery meetings even if there were men present. Some felt this was going too far. There *was* a limit.

That year there was a World Antislavery Convention in London, and delegates from all civilized nations were invited. But when they arrived at Freeman's Hall the female delegates were rejected. Among them were two American women, Lu-cretia Mott and Elizabeth Cady Stanton, accompanied by their husbands James Mott and Henry B. Stanton, who were also delegates. The Motts were Quakers.

Women were excluded by Scripture from sharing equal dignity and authority with men, they discovered.

"The clerical portion was the most violent in its opposition," Mrs. Stanton wrote in her autobiography, explaining with a sardonic note to be heard throughout the country for the next 62 years, "their all-sustaining conceit gave them abundant assurance that their movements must necessarily be all-pleasing to the celestials whose ears were open to the proceedings of the World's Convention. Deborah, Hulda, Vashti and Esther might have questioned the propriety of calling a world convention when only half of humanity was represented there; but what were their opinions worth compared with those of the Rev. A. Harvey, the Rev. C. Stout, or the Rev. J. Burnet who, with Bible in hand, argued woman's subjection divinely decreed when Eve was created?"

Mr. Stanton made an impassioned speech in favor of the women; so did William

Lloyd Garrison; and when this was of no avail they refused to take part in the convention, and sat with the spectators.

"It was really pitiful to hear narrow-minded bigots pretending to be teachers and leaders of men, so cruelly remanding their own mothers, with the rest of woman-kind, to absolute subjection," Mrs. Stanton observed.

Mrs. Mott and Mrs. Stanton knew that not all the slaves were black.

In Elizabeth Cady Stanton's heretical breast grew a lifelong antipathy to the Church.

28   ROADS AND WATERWAYS

There isn't a train I wouldn't take,
No matter where it's going.
—Edna St. Vincent Millay, *Travel.*

The great expansion westward raised issues other than that of Slavery. In 1805 President Madison had called to the attention of Congress "the great importance of establishing throughout our country . . . roads and canals." Turnpikes were being constructed at a rapid rate, and had been since 1790, but water routes for the transportation of produce were used wherever possible. The great rivers were used too, but the rivers flowed in a north-south direction. In 1816 there were only a hundred miles of canals. More waterways were needed going east and west, to link the Atlantic with the Mississippi. The Appalachian Mountains, which lay between, were the big problem.

De Witt Clinton, a son of the Revolutionary hero James Clinton, a former Senator, and then Mayor of New York, had in 1810 traveled across New York State as a Canal Commissioner, and thought it would be feasible to dig a canal to link Buffalo, on Lake Erie, to the Hudson. He convinced the New York Legislature, money was voted, and the construction of a canal 363 miles long through much dense wilderness was completed in 1825. In the days before bulldozers, this feat accomplished by manual labor and animals, seems comparable to the building of the Great Pyramids, and took much less time. The boon to the economy was tremendous. Goods brought to New York for shipment to Europe from as far away as the Mississippi made that city the business and commercial center of the country, and the cities all along the canal profited and grew.

The Erie canal was a financial success from the start. With another canal linking Lake Champlain to the Hudson, also sponsored by Clinton, it made half a million dollars the first year. Soon the entire expense was paid for, and the canals were making $7 million a year in profits.

The canal boom was on. The Delaware and Hudson Canal linking northeast Pennsylvania to the Hudson was completed by private capital in 1828. Ohio farmers demanded a link between the Ohio River and the Great Lakes. The result was the Ohio and Erie Canal to Cleveland. A canal from Toledo to Cincinnati was begun in 1832. The state of Indiana undertook to build the Wabash and Erie Canal, 450 miles long. Thus, by inland waterways it was possible to ship goods all the way from New Orleans to New York. Traveling lake, canal and river, goods could be shipped from Chicago to New York. Shipping greatly increased.

As was to be expected in this land of boom and bust, there was overexpansion. Innumerable little feeder canals were constructed everywhere which did not carry enough commerce to make them profitable; and then came the railroads.

In England the Stockton and Darlington Railway began to operate in 1825 over a short length of track, with engines propelled by steam. America pricked up her ears. The Baltimore and Ohio Railroad opened a 13-mile stretch of track in 1830—the first spadeful of earth being turned in ceremonies on the Fourth of July, 1828, by John Carroll of Carrolton, the last surviving Signer of the Declaration of Independence. In the same year the Charleston and Hamburg began operating in South Carolina, and by 1833 it boasted the longest track in the world—136 miles. In 1831 the Mohawk and Hudson began service between Schnectady and Albany, the state capital.

The state of New York became alarmed, and prohibited the encroaching railroads from hauling freight in competition with its own Erie Canal. The Chesapeake and Ohio Canal Company did all it could to block the advancing Baltimore and Ohio Railroad, which gave signs of proceeding up the Potomac past the narrow gorge at Harper's Ferry with the terrible threat of competition.

But the railroads had three advantages over the canals: costs were lower, service was quicker, and, unlike canals, they did not freeze over in winter. By 1851 the Erie Railroad could boast of being the longest in the world (537 miles), and linked New York with Lake Erie. In 1852 the Baltimore and Ohio reached the Ohio River at Wheeling in what is now West Virginia. Eight short lines were consolidated and called the New York Central and linked Albany to Buffalo. In 1858 the Pennsylvania Railroad pushed from Philadelphia to Pittsburgh and it was now possible to travel from the East Coast to Chicago in two days, the cost being between $20 and $30. The impetus to industry and agriculture was enormous.

In the mid 1840s, when steamships began to ply the Atlantic the time consumed by the voyage was greatly reduced, larger ships meant larger cargoes, and another boost to industry and agriculture.

Before long steamships brought human cargoes. The great wave of immigration began. The Potato Famine in Ireland ("the Great Hunger" of the 1840s) forced thousands to leave that then unhappy land, and people from all the countries of Europe began pouring into the land of opportunity and were absorbed—those who survived the dreadful conditions of steerage.

29   THE MADMAN FROM MASSACHUSETTS

Ex-President John Quincy Adams had the longest and most distinguished public career of any American. He accompanied his father on a mission to Russia in 1781-83; he was a protege of George Washington, who appointed him Minister to the Netherlands when he was 28; in his father's administration he was Minister to Prussia; then he ran for the Senate and served five years, during which time he approved the Louisiana Purchase. In 1808 he resigned his seat and was appointed Minister to Russia, his second trip there.

Czar Alexander I took a great shine to Mr. and Mrs. Adams (and the latter's unmarried sister). They all spoke fluent French, the language of the Russian court. Though the poorest of the diplomatic corps, and in the second rank of diplomatic precedence, the Czar accorded them privileges given only to the French ambassador. This caused "a Buzz of astonishment in Court circles," Louisa Adams wrote home. The Czar of All the Russias and Mr. Adams walked together along the quay of the Neva and in the Nevsky Prospect, and the Czar unburdened his woes (the approaching war with Napoleon) to Mr. Adams in the Imperial Gardens.

Twenty-three American ships held in Russian ports, and 53 held in Danish ports, were released through Adams' deft and unofficial handling, thanks to this friendship with the Czar.

In 1814 he was the chief American commissioner (with Henry Clay) at the Treaty of Ghent.

Adams was President Monroe's Secretary of State, and the chief architect of the Monroe Doctrine. In 1824 he was elected President, but served only one term. A great statesman but a poor politician, his administration was a troubled one. Andrew Jackson won the presidency by a landslide, as we have seen, and ex-President Adams retired to his farm at Quincy and to his books and nursery of seedling oaks and fruit trees.

In 1831, when John Quincy Adams was 64, there was a movement in and about Boston to induce him to run for Congress as the representative of the District of Plymouth. Suspicious and cynical, Adams suspected dark ulterior motives in the promoters of this strange scheme. He was finally convinced it was sincere.

But to run for the House of Representatives and become a Congressman after having been President! Everyone told him it was beneath his dignity. He didn't think so; he was elected and spent the last seventeen years of his life in the House, championing the cause of justice everywhere.

Adams was a frosty, crusty character, without a visible spark of the warmth of his remarkable mother, Abigail. He had hardly any friends (except, perhaps, for the Czar), no charm, and a rasping voice. But he had unassailable integrity, and the courage of a lion.

In the House, Adams was often called to order. He embraced unpopular causes; this a good politician should never do. The Creek Indians on the Georgia-Alabama border were resisting efforts, both state and federal, to oust them from their ancestral lands and transplant them to new lands beyond the Mississippi. Adams sided with the Indians. This roused the hatred of the people of both those states. When he attempted to present petitions to abolish slavery in the District of Columbia he roused a hornets' nest.

As the yeasty ferment of abolition began to seethe over the North, the yeast of antiaboliton kept pace with it. The more vigorous and incendiary the abolitionists became the more warlike became the pro-slavery faction. William Lloyd Garrison barely escaped with his life from an angry mob that dragged him, by a rope, through the streets of Boston in 1835.

Elijah Lovejoy, a Yankee from Maine domiciled in St. Louis, Missouri, and editor of a religious paper, began attacking slavery. His office was sacked and his press thrown into the Mississippi. A new press bought for him by his admirers was also destroyed. He continued his crusade, defending blacks who had been accused of various things. The violence grew; the intrepid Lovejoy refused to be silenced. Finally, he was killed by the blast of a shotgun.

With tempers flaring in the country it is not surprising that they flared also in the houses of Congress.

Henry Laurens Pinckney of South Carolina proposed a resolution, the gist of which was that all petitions regarding abolition be referred to a select committee instructed to report that Congress had no constitutional authority to interfere with the institution of slavery; it was an affair for the individual states. Representative Pinckney himself headed this Select Committee on abolition petitions, which was appointed February 8, 1836, and did not report until May 18.

The report contained three resolutions, the salient one being that all papers relating in any way to abolition be laid on the table and no further notice be taken of them. This was the famous "Pinckney Gag Rule" and it was clearly unconstitutional. The First Amendment to the Constitution reserves to the people the right of petition. Adams fought the gag rule for eight years.

And he precipitated one of the most lively battles the House ever housed and earned various cognomens: the Madman from Massachusetts, Old Man Eloquence, and more besides, depending on which side of the controversy one favored.

When, on a certain Monday (the day petitions were read) his turn came, the Madman from Massachusetts said he had 30 petitions to present. One by one they were tabled. When he came to the 29th, he explained it was from nine ladies of Fredericksburg, Virginia, praying like the others for abolition in the District of Columbia. Adams said he would not read the names as, judging by the disposition of the country, he did not know what might happen to them. The House tabled the petition of the ladies.

Then came the 30th petition. This one, he explained, was from Fredericksburg too, but before he presented it he wanted the decision of the Speaker. It was, he explained, from 22 persons declaring themselves to be slaves, and he wished to know if this would be considered as coming within the gag rule. "I will send it to the Chair," he said. This was violently objected to, by a member from Tuscaloosa, Alabama. The Speaker, James K. Polk, said, since the circumstances were so extraordinary, he would take the sense of the House.

Pandemonium broke loose in the House of Representatives! Some of the members were shouting, especially one Charles Haynes of Georgia. Adams was no gentleman, he shouted, to make a question of a paper of this kind. Dixon Hall Lewis of Alabama shouted that members from slave-holding states demand the punishment of the gentleman from Massachusetts. Julius Alford of Georgia demanded that the paper be removed from the House, as an act of justice to the South, and burned. "Along with the member who presented it!" another voice shouted. Mr. Adams was unperturbed.

Representative Patton of Virginia had meanwhile gone to the clerk's table to examine the petition of the ladies of Fredericksburg (the 29th). "The name of no lady is attached to this paper!" he cried indignantly. He was from Fredericksburg. He knew only one name on the petition, that of a free mulatto "of the worst fame and reputation." The others he believed were free blacks too—all bad.

The House was in an uproar again. Thompson of South Carolina offered a resolution to call Mr. Adams to the bar of the House for censure; others thought this was not strong enough.

The representatives raged throughout the next day. Cries of "Expel him!" rent the air from all sides. Mr. Adams remained unperturbed.

"Let the petition be as the gentleman from Virginia has said. Prostitutes, I suppose," he conceded.

Patton denied he had said they were prostitutes. There were heated arguments as to whether Mr. Patton knew these ladies or not.

"I am glad to hear that the honorable gentleman disclaims knowledge of them," said Adams, "for I have been about to ask: if they are infamous women, who made them so? I have heard it said that in the South there exists great resemblance between the progeny of the colored people and the white men who claim possession of them."

"*Great confusion*," reported the *Register of Debates*, a staid sheet. (This was an understatement.) The fracas in the House of Representatives began to receive national coverage. The public crowded into the place to enjoy the circus.

The character of the ladies of Fredericksburg did not concern him, Adams said, and asked: "*Where is the law that says that the mean and low, and the degraded, shall be deprived of the right of petition? Where in the land of free men was the right of petition ever placed on the exclusive basis of morality and virtue?*" He pointed out to the embroiled members that there was no monarch on earth who is not compelled by the constitution of his country to receive the petitions of his people. "The Sultan of Turkey cannot walk in the streets and refuse to receive the petitions from the meanest and vilest in the land!"

The debate had begun on Monday, and was still raging Thursday. When the House prepared to vote on censuring Adams, he got the floor in his own defense. He said if the House would read the 30th petition they would find it the reverse of that which the resolution stated it to be. "My crime has been for attempting to introduce the petition of slaves that slavery should not be abolished."

Of course he realized that the petition was a hoax concocted to discredit him, but he had cleverly turned it to his own advantage and made it into his trump card.

On the resolution of censure, only 21 voted for; 105 voted against it.

Year after year, John Quincy Adams was on the front line in battles. Though an expansionist, he fought the annexation of Texas as a slave state because it would bring on war with Mexico. Again and again he presented petitions regarding slavery. By the time he was 71 he found himself "the genius of the antislavery cause." His health was poor; he had bouts of illness—still he labored on, writing long reports of 20,000 or 30,000 words. He rose daily at 4 A.M. and was always at his desk in the House unless severe illness prevented; his working day took almost all his waking hours.

James Smithson, an Englishman, had left a peculiar will and a sum of $100,000, which was now available to the United States to found in Washington "an Establishment for the increase and diffusion of knowledge among men." This was in the days of Andrew Jackson who doubted the propriety of accepting it, and left the matter up to Congress. Nothing was done by that body. President after President ignored the matter or said the Congress had no power to accept it. John C. Calhoun, who had the distinction of being on the wrong side of every question, declared it was beneath the national dignity to accept "the gift of an illegitimate foreigner"— Mr. Smithson being the illegitimate son of the Duke of Northumberland.

"John Quincy Adams Seized with a Fit in the House of
Representatives" February 21, 1848. Kellog & Comstock.
From the author's collection.

Adams, who had a great interest in science, had backed a proposal to build an observatory at Harvard, and regretted the country's indifference to scientific research, fought for acceptance of the Smithson legacy, and a bill to accept the money was finally passed in 1846, eleven years after it was made available.

In 1848, to jump ahead of our story, the war with Mexico ended triumphantly and inexcusably, for the United States. A bill was introduced in the House to bestow lovely gold medals on eight meritorious generals. This was on February 21. When the Speaker asked if the main question should be put, Adams cried, "No!" but the bill carried, and as the clerk began to read the resolution a reporter at the press table saw Mr. Adams grasp the edge of his desk. Representative David Fisher of Ohio, whose desk was next to his, jumped up and caught him as he began to slump from his chair. Representative Grenell of Massachusetts called to a page to bring water.

From desk to desk the word spread, "Mr. Adams is dying!" The Speaker called for a motion to adjourn and it was quickly made and passed *viva voce*.

Adams was placed on a sofa and carried into the rotunda of the Capitol. Senator Benson, who had just emerged from the Senate chamber, turned back and cried out the news. The Senate adjourned.

Five members of the House were physicians. They bent over the old man. He was unconscious and breathing loudly. Since the rotunda was cold and drafty he was carried into the Speaker's room and laid on a mahogany sofa. His right side was paralyzed, there was only involuntary motion of the muscles of his left side. He was bled, as was the terrible custom of the day. His wife arrived. At a few minutes past three o'clock he regained consciousness for a moment and looked at the circle of anxious faces.

"This is the last of earth," he whispered. And then, after a pause, "I am content."

He lingered unconscious for two days. Every day at noon the Senate and the House met and immediately adjourned.

John Quincy Adams died at seven in the evening of February 23, 1848, "by destiny's design under the old copper-roofed dome of the Capitol where for 17 years he had done his finest work—the champion of the muted slave and the Bill of Rights."[1]

30   AN AGREEABLE EPISODE

William Henry Harrison died unexpectedly, a victim of his own verbosity. He was the first president to die in office, presenting a new problem. The Constitution provides that in case of the death of a president his duties and authority "shall devolve on the vice-president." This seems to mean that the vice-president is to fill the unexpired term in the capacity of surrogate. But John Tyler would have none of that. He insisted on being sworn in as President, setting a precedent still followed. He kept Harrison's entire Cabinet.

John Tyler was a courteous, elegant gentleman from Virginia and a strong states-righter, who had left the Democratic party in protest against Jackson's high-handed procedures and egalitarianism. He was expected to follow Whig policies.

One of these was the abolishing of the Independent Treasury system set up under Van Buren, and the return to a National Bank. The bill was passed and Tyler signed it. But when Congress passed a new Bank of the United States bill of its own devising, Tyler vetoed it. The entire Cabinet, with the exception of Webster, resigned. Tyler replaced these indignant statesmen with more malleable ones.

The squabbling continued unabated. And the issues that fired the squabbling—sectional rivalries, the right of squatters to occupy unsurveyed lands (the United States still had hundreds of thousands of square miles of unsettled territory to sell), problems in raising the tariff, or lowering it—make very dull reading.

An agreeable episode comes along at this juncture. The reason Webster had not joined the exodus of disgruntled cabinet secretaries is that negotiations were proceeding with Great Britain to settle a number of vexing and unrelated problems, and Webster had high hopes of solving them. The British Foreign Minister, Lord Palmerston, nurtured in his crabbed breast a rabid hatred of America, but there had been a change of government in 1841, and the new foreign secretary, Lord Aberdeen, was fortunately not so prejudiced. He sent Lord Ashburton to America in 1842 as a special minister, to try to solve the problems.

Lord Ashburton was unique among British politicians and statesmen at this time; wonder of wonders, he liked America. Webster admired the British, and the two men liked each other. They met in an informal and friendly atmosphere, and the difficulties were ironed out amicably.

Rebellion having broken out in the eastern provinces of Canada in 1837, the rebels chartered a small American ship, the *Caroline*, to carry supplies, sold at a profit by Americans, across the Niagara River from the New York side. While the *Caroline* was moored one night on the American side, the Canadian authorities came across the river and burned her. In the ensuing fight one American was killed. There was great turmoil on both sides of the river.

Then there was trouble over the Maine-New Brunswick border. The boundary had been set at the Treaty of Paris, so deftly drawn by Franklin in 1783, but it was impossible to locate and, as it is difficult to settle a boundary that cannot be located, a new one was needed. In 1838 Americans and Canadians, mostly lumberjacks, began to move into the disputed area and snarl at each other, and the snarls developed into the "Aroostook War." More trouble between the two countries was threatened. (Aroostook County, Maine, is now famous for its potatoes.)

Turmoil arose also over the slave trade. A shipload of a hundred slaves sailed, entirely legally, from Virginia to New Orleans in 1841. Enroute the slaves mutinied, took over the ship, and put in at Nassau in the British West Indies, where they claimed asylum. The British authorities there declared the bondsmen free, for they were now on British soil. Americans, mostly Southerners, were infuriated.

Lord Ashburton and Daniel Webster were both willing to compromise. The disputed area in Maine was divided almost equally, Canada receiving about five twelfths of it, or 5,000 square miles, strategic to Canada for connecting Halifax and Quebec. It was a huge terrain of unbroken forest, of little use for anything else.

There were minor adjustments over boundaries in the Lake Champlain region and elsewhere, and an extradition treaty between Canada and the United States was likewise arranged. Seven crimes were carefully listed as subject to extradition.

Lord Ashburton, in unofficial notes, expressed regret for the raid on the *Caroline*, and pledged there would be no future "officious influence" with American ships forced to enter British ports by untoward circumstances, such as storms or, one assumes, mutinies.

Surveyors had been less than accurate when the Americans built a large fort at a cost of $1 million, at the northern end of Lake Champlain on land that turned out to be Canadian. (Snafus are not confined to the twentieth century.) Lord Ashburton ceded this strip along the New York and Vermont border to the United States as a friendly gesture.

Anglo-American relations looked rosier than they had for many years.

31   BETTER FORGET THE ALAMO

Texas, enormous to the point of absurdity, comprised but the northern part of Mexico's state of Coahuila, and had been included as part of the Louisiana Purchase. But in the transcontinental treaty with Spain the United States had renounced any claims to Texas in exchange for Florida and the huge extra slice of the continent which extended to Oregon and the Pacific.

Mexico struck off her Spanish shackles in 1822, but, just as Spain had, she found herself unable to handle her own vast territory, which included Texas. Rich and valuable though the land was, and capable of supporting a large population, it was a waste, losing revenues, and of no aid to the Mexican economy.

Mexico, with fatal results, offered land grants to anyone who would settle the country, swear allegiance to Mexico, and renounce that pact with the devil, the Protestant faith. Many Americans, largely from the Southern states, accepted this excellent deal with alacrity and by 1835 there were some 35,000 Americans in Texas, ten times the number of native Mexicans.

Between the Mexicans and the settlers no love was lost. The easy going and mostly illiterate natives, who were there first, found themselves a minority in their ancestral land, looked down upon by the newcomers who were, one may be sure, insufferably arrogant.

The Mexican government began to see its mistake. It was losing control of the country, and, in an effort to shore up its waning authority, it passed restraining laws. Although slavery had been abolished in Mexico after 1829, settlers had brought their slaves with them and were lax about swearing allegiance to Mexico and renouncing the pact with the Devil. A new law prohibiting slavery (already prohibited) after 1842 was passed, demonstrating the government's powerlessness to enforce laws already on the books. One of the settlers, Stephen Austin, went to Mexico to protest and was promptly thrown into jail.

The Texans, as soon as they began to be restrained, began to want independence, which follows as the night the day. There were skirmishes that soon developed into full-scale armed rebellion.

Antonio Lopez de Santa Anna, the Mexican president (read dictator) set out for Texas with a force of 6,000 to subdue the rebels. The battle was joined at San Antonio. The Americans, under Colonel William B. Travis and a mere 187 men, defended the town heroically, but were obliged to seek refuge in an old mission called the Alamo, where they held out for ten days.

While this seige was going on the Texans declared their independence, and on March 6, 1836, Santa Anna's forces stormed the walls of the mission, slaughtered everyone within, including the wounded, soaked the corpses in oil and burned them. Among the victims were Jim Bowie, inventor of the Bowie knife, and the famous frontiersman, David Crockett.

The rebellious Texas Army, commanded by Sam Houston, a former governor of Tennessee was finally numerous enough to make a stand and attacked the Mexicans on April 21. (Their battle-cry, "Remember the Alamo" is still repeated in Texas. But where were Sam Houston and his rebels when they were needed at San Antonio?)

The Mexicans were driven from Texas, and Texas applied for annexation to the United States. But Andrew Jackson was leary. Not only would it lead to war with Mexico, but the old slavery issue would again rear its ugly head. On his last day in office, Jackson recognized the Republic of Texas and relegated all future problems to his successors.

Left out in the cold by the United States, Texas turned to Europe. She dreamed of a huge new republic stretching to the Pacific, a rival to the United States. This idea delighted Britain. A new, rich independent republic would cut the comb of the cocky, expanding United States, furnish cotton for European mills at a competitive price, and become a new market for European goods. It might even be that some sort of arrangement could be worked out by which England would gain another foothold in the New World. Both France and Britain made haste to recognize the new Republic of Texas, and concluded trade treaties with her. Britannia smacked her lips and the sound was heard in Washington.

Henry Clay, the perennial Whig candidate, and Martin Van Buren, for the Democrats, had both straddled the Texas issue, having failed to sense the expansionist sentiment growing in the country. For this reason they were both passed over by their parties. The Whigs nominated a nonentity, and the Democrats, a dark horse named James K. Polk, 14 years in the house of Representatives, a Jackson Democrat, and an avowed expansionist. Tyler in his last days in office, pushed a bill through Congress, and Texas was annexed to the United States in the secondary role of territory, to save it from Britain, or worse.

This was in February 1845. In the following December, Congress voted to admit Texas into the Union as a state.

James K. Polk was a unique President and a marble statue should be raised to him in every state in the union, bearing on its pedestal in letters of gold, the words, "He kept his campaign promises."

These were four, and enough to make any presidential head swirl. (1) To lower the Tariff of 1842. (2) To restore the Independent Treasury. (3) To oppose federal internal improvements. (4) To obtain Oregon and the whole Southwest.

His opposition to internal improvements, possibly sprang from a desire for no higher federal taxes. The thorniest immediate problem was to be Oregon. "The whole Southwest" was no small matter, either.

Expansion was in the air, and Oregon was a major goal. In 1841 the caravans of covered wagons began setting out on the "Oregon Trail." Accompanied by great herds of cattle they faced a trek of 2,000 miles, through Indian territory, over high mountains, and across rivers; it was a six or seven months' journey facing every kind of hardship. It is surprising how many of these pioneers made it, and how many heads of cattle and horses; it is one of the great heroic sagas of American history.

The boundaries of the Oregon country were defined as: the northern parallel of 54.40, on the east the crest of the Rocky Mountains, on the south the 42nd parallel, and on the west the Pacific. This was a tidy parcel of real estate, of a half million square miles in which can now be found the states of Oregon, Washington, Idaho, parts of Montana and Wyoming, and half of British Columbia. Five nations had at various times laid claim to this vast terrain—Russia, Spain, France, Britain and the United States but the first three countries, as time went on, surrendered their claims to Britain or the United States, who were left alone in the field, glaring at each other. Both these nations had claims that were valid, or depending on the point of view, invalid, so by the Treaty of 1818 the citizens of both were given access to the region for ten years. In 1827 the agreement was renewed, with the proviso that either nation could terminate it with one year's notice.

President Polk, in his inaugural address did not mince matters about Oregon. He boldly stated America's claims to the whole territory.

It seems that Polk was a wily president. The British minister in Washington, Richard Pakenham by name, was sent reeling, and, before he could regain his equilibrium, Polk informed him that the United States would accept a boundary at the 49th parallel, which is now the boundary between the state of Washington and British Columbia. Mr. Pakenham rejected this proposal without even informing London.

The next move was for the President to demand the whole place again, up to the *54th* parallel, and when Congress convened in December 1845 he asked for authority to give Britain one year's notice. "The only way to treat John Bull is to look him straight in the eye," observed Polk to a Congressman friend.

John Bull saw reason. The Hudson's Bay company was becoming alarmed at the great influx of Americans along the Willamette Valley (north of Eugene, Oregon) where by 1845 there were 5,000 settlers and trappers, whereas north of the Columbia River (present boundary between Oregon and the state of Washington) there were less than 800. The Hudson's Bay company prudently moved its base of operations to Vancouver Island, informing Britain that, in case of a conflict, the Oregon country would be impossible to defend.

When Britain had been given notice to end the Treaty, Polk hinted that there might still be a possibility of compromise. The British foreign secretary (still Lord Aberdeen) with scarcely concealed eagerness, suggested the 49th parallel again, which Mr. Pakenham had rejected out of hand. Mr. Polk had gained his goal by very clever maneuvering.

The boundary in question is now the frontier between the United States and British Columbia. Vancouver Island, the lower part of which juts below the parallel, was left to Britain, and thus both nations had access to the Strait of Juan de Fuca, and to Puget Sound and the present cities of Seattle and Tacoma—a very sensible arrangement.

32   AN ANGEL INTRUDES

. . . methinks an angel spake.
—*King John*, Act V, Scene 2

At Palmyra in northern New York lived a family named Smith, just as everywhere else, but Joseph Smith, a son of the family (one of eight children) was markedly different from all other Smiths and had a unique experience. An angel appeared to him and described a spot on a nearby hill ("The Hill Camorah") where, if he dug, he would find a book of golden plates; and sure enough. . . . They were written in undecipherable hieroglyphics, but when one looked through a pair of stones called Urim and Thummim, attached together with bows in some fashion (also explained by the angel, who was clothed in white, as angels should be, had a trumpet and answered to the name of Moroni), these heiroglyphics translated themselves into English.

Joseph transcribed the golden plates with the aid of the stones, behind a curtain, and produced the "Book of Mormon" which was the history of an ancient tribe who peopled America in the dim past—the lost tribe. Joseph produced three witnesses who had seen the golden plates and who had signed affadavits to that effect; and if this were not sufficient, he drew up a statement about seeing the plates that eight more witnesses had signed. Then the plates seem to have been wafted away by the angel Moroni. But, after a believer mortgaged his farm to pay for printing it, everyone could read the book who could keep awake long enough to do so. ("Chloroform in print," Mark Twain called it.)

This happened in 1827, when Joseph was 22. He was described as tall, with light brown hair, blue eyes with long thick lashes which gave his glance a dreamy look suitable for a prophet, and a prominent nose. He was considered handsome. Further celestial revelations caused him to found a religion, "The Church of Jesus Christ of Latter-Day Saints" which attracted many followers. But most of the local population had known Joseph too long and were skeptical.

Joseph and his latter-day saints moved west in the face of local opposition, first to Kirtland, Ohio, and then to Missouri, where they again met such opposition and caused so much strife that the Governor of the state ordered their expulsion. They then settled at Nauvoo, Illinois, where things were better at first. The state granted them a charter which gave them almost complete autonomy, including the right to their own militia, their own courts, and their power to make laws as long as they did not infringe on Federal laws.

While still in Ohio, Joseph received a new revelation: the one way to salvation was in the practice of polygamy like those stalwarts of the Old Testament, Abraham, Isaac, Moses, David, Solomon et al., and he had been secretly following this doctrine.

By the time the Mormons were in Nauvoo the practice was no longer a secret, and this increased the hostility.

Converts poured into Nauvoo, the result of missionaries whose ardent words proved irresistible. With polygamy and the resulting abundant progeny the town grew so fast and the Mormons so prosperous that the inevitable fear, envy and hostility among the original inhabitants, led to armed conflicts. Finally Joseph Smith was imprisoned; the mob broke into the jail, and he and his brother Hyrum were killed.

The Saints realized that the choice was between exodus and massacre.

They chose for their new leader, Brigham Young, one of the twelve "Apostles" of the Church, a powerful, ruthless man whose word was law. He and his 2,000 followers set out on February 15, 1846, and crossed the Mississippi en route to the promised land. Young was not sure where this would be found, but he said he would recognize it when he saw it. California was still part of Mexico and Oregon was in dispute between Great Britain and the U.S. Surviving tremendous hardships, on July 24th, five months after he left Nauvoo, Brigham Young found the promised land. It was in the country of the Ute Indians. Emerging from a cañon he saw a vast plain surrounded by snow-capped mountains and in the distance an azure lake. In the cañon green trees nestled, but the plain was arid. In spite of this, the Saints stayed and built Salt Lake City.

In 1850 Utah was constituted a territory and Young appointed governor. Petitions to join the Union as a state were turned down. Congress viewed the practice of polygamy coldly. Federal judges appointed to the territory were not Mormons and so were unsympathetic. Clashes began again and President Buchanan sent troops to proceed against the Saints. Young defied the Government in the "Utah War" (1857–1858). By diplomacy he avoided an outright break with the government, but he had to step down as governor.

Brigham Young died in 1877. Most of his surviving 17 wives and 44 children attended his funeral. (Where were the rest?) In 1896 Utah was admitted to the Union as the 45th state, after polygamy was officially banned by the Mormon Church. It all began with Joseph Smith, or possibly the angel Moroni.

33   THE BEAR-FLAG REPUBLIC

Mexico did nothing about Texas when she declared herself a republic in 1838, but when the American Congress voted to annex Texas in 1845, Mexico was outraged and broke off diplomatic relations with the U.S.

President Polk, who would have preferred to achieve his aims without fighting (and he had quite a few aims), sent General Zachary Taylor into Texas to "protect her border." But which border? Texas always claimed the Rio Grande as her border, but the Mexicans said it was the Nueces River, 150 miles east of that, which flows into the Gulf of Mexico at Corpus Christi, and this made a trifling difference of some 30,000 square miles.

Zachary Taylor reached the Nueces with 1,500 troops, but prudently went no further.

In November 1845 Polk sent a secret envoy, John Slidell, to Mexico City to negotiate the disputed territory. Mexico owed American citizens $2 million for losses suffered by them in skirmishes and upheavals, and Polk offered to shoulder this debt in return for recognition of the annexation of Texas and for acceptance of the Rio Grande boundary. Polk also authorized his secret envoy to offer up to $30,000,000 for New Mexico and California, or as much of them as he could get.

John Slidell got nowhere. The President of Mexico at this time, José Herrera, was afraid even to receive Slidell because the Mexicans were in an unruly mood over the terrible conditions in their country and had a strong dislike of the present regime. The situation was touchy. The news that an American envoy was in the city—perhaps to grab more of the country—caused the speedy overthrow of Herrera.

The new indispensable man was General Mationo Paradez, a blowhard type with a drinking problem, who likewise refused to see Slidell and in trumpet tones (after having had a few) claimed for his country the whole of Texas. Slidell hurried home and told President Polk he was convinced the Mexicans would never negotiate until they had to.

General Taylor, known to his men as "Old Rough-and-Ready," now crossed the Nueces and advanced to the Rio Grande; the Mexicans captured one of his cavalry patrols, and blood was spilled. "For some strange reason legal minds always consider this a just provocation to spill more blood."[1]

Congress declared war, and authorized raising 50,000 troops.

Poor Mexico! There was no doubt from the start about the outcome of this war. It was one victory after another for the Americans. The Mexican army, with a surprisingly large percentage of generals in resplendent uniforms, lacked good direction—perhaps it was a case of too many generals spoiling the consommé.

At Palo Alto, north of the Rio Grande, over 5,000 Mexicans fled before half that number of Americans. Then 7,500 Mexicans were routed by 1,700 Americans at Rescola de las Palmas. Zachary Taylor and his army were well established south of the Rio Grande, and the war hadn't been going on a week. Old Rough-and-Ready was on the march. He defeated the Mexicans again at Matamoros ("Kill-the-Moors"), and then farther south at Monterey.

President Polk had a wide-ranging plan to achieve his aims, which were to

"James K. Polk, The People's Choice." Currier & Ives.
Eleventh President of the United States. He kept his
campaign promises! From the author's collection.

force the Mexicans to make peace on American terms by seizing key areas on the Texas-Mexican border, to grab New Mexico and California at the same time—a sort of three-pronged design or Strategy the British were so fond of in times past, but Polk's Strategy worked.

General Stephen W. Kearny was dispatched from Fort Leavenworth, Missouri, to subjugate California with 1,800 men. Among them were 500 Mormon volunteers who, Brigham Young thought, would be handy to have there if the Mormons decided to take over the country.

When Kearny arrived in sunny California it was not so sunny. He learned that Captain John C. Frémont, a U.S. Army officer, had beaten him to it. An American Navy squadron, under the command of Commodore Sloat, was off the California coast. Frémont joined with Sloat and the American settlers, and the Mexican officials departed in haste.

Kearny was furious at having been beaten at the game. Frémont said *he* was conqueror of California and had organized a government (with himself at the head). The flag of the "Bear Flag Republic" was waving in the breeze.

Kearny was Frémont's superior and he ordered him back into the military service. Frémont refused. He was then ordered east, tried by court-martial for mutiny, and dismissed from the Army. President Polk pardoned him and reinstated him to his former rank. Haughtily he refused the pardon and resigned.

Such was the petty military squabble that launched the great State of California.

34   THE SPOT RESOLUTIONS

Poor Mexico, so far from God and so close to
the United States.
—Profirio Díaz

Things were not going smoothly in Mexico either. The Mexicans refused to be reasonable and hand over everything the U.S. wanted. Polk was anxious to end the war, which was growing more and more unpopular at home, especially the farther one got from Mexico. Just as there had been a "Mr. Madison's War" in New England, now there was talk of "Mr. Polk's War."

Polk, in a worthy effort to have done with hostilities as soon as his aims were achieved (and he had everything he wanted from Mexico), sent for the Chief of the Army, General Winfield Scott, known to his men as "Old Fuss-and-Feathers," and they worked out a plan to make Mexico come to her senses and do as she was told. General Scott was to land at Vera Cruz and with this conquering army move to Mexico City and occupy it.

Scott and his forces landed in due course at Vera Cruz.

The game of musical chairs, forever going on in Mexico, had landed Santa Anna in the seat of power. He, thinking to take advantage of the division of the American Army, decided to crush Old Rough-and-Ready first, and then hurry south and do likewise to Old Fuss-and-Feathers.

The battle of Buena Vista was lost by both sides, and Santa Anna had to retreat to protect Mexico City.

The bombardment of Vera Cruz went on for four days, when the city and the castle of San Juan de Ulloa capitulated. (The latter was known as "the Gibraltar of America.")

But General Scott, in spite of his feathers, was a great general. He started on the 260 mile stretch to Mexico City (all the way up hill), and by clever flanking actions avoided head-on collisions with Santa Anna's troops; and in "one of the most brilliant campaigns in American military history," as some historians say, conserved the lives of his men.

At Cerro Gordo (Fat Ridge) Santa Anna sought to annihilate the invaders, but Scott's forces cut a swath through the jungle, making a path for the artillery, and once in position sent the Mexicans fleeing under a savage bombardment.

When Scott reached Puebla he encountered a welcoming committee of priests and town officials who invited them all to a banquet. This seemed a little odd, and the plan to poison the American Army was foiled when General Scott insisted that the priests taste the rich viands first. Scott marched on towards the capital.

The next battle occurred at a small village called Contreras. Santa Anna and his General Valencia withstood the American advance, and Santa Anna, sensing victory and wanting all the glory himself, ordered Valencia to fall back and leave the stage to him. General Valencia paid no attention to this order, and Santa Anna, in a fury at seeing the laurels destined to go elsewhere, withdrew his troops to the town of Guadalupe, where he had a tent he could sulk in. General Valencia and the City of Mexico were thus left to their fate.

Another battle occurred nearer the city at a place called Churubusco where Scott encountered, of all things, a battalion of Irish immigrants in battle array. To them it was a holy war against "that dirty Protestant Scott." After a furious charge by the Americans, fifty Irishmen were captured and hanged from a gallows in front of Chapultepec Castle. (This, like Bloody Tarleton's tactics in the Carolina Campaign of 1780, is not considered a *comme il faut* treatment of prisoners of war.)

Chapultepec Castle, perched on its rocky eminence, and the guardian of the city of Mexico, now had to be breached. It was defended by a handful of young cadets. For three days they held Scott and all his forces at bay, and when obliged to capitulate, some wrapped themselves in their national flag and leapt from the parapet crying, "Viva Mexico!"

On the anniversary of that day, September 15, there are patriotic speeches in Mexico City and the laying of wreaths. Santa Anna is a national hero, but he abandoned Mexico City and the cadets in a fit of pique, and is the most unheroic hero any nation ever had.

In a message to Congress on May 11, 1846, President Polk declared that the Mexican Government had "at last invaded our territory and shed the blood of our fellow citizens on our own soil." But *was* it our soil? The boundary had for a long time been in dispute.

In the following December Polk again referred to Mexico as "invading the territory of Texas, striking the first blow and shedding the blood of our citizens on our own soil."

A tall and lanky freshman congressman from Illinois, name of Abraham Lincoln, wanted more facts. Congressman Lincoln offered a set of resolutions to the House on December 22, 1847. The gist was stated in the first: "That the President of the United States be respectfully requested to inform this House whether the spot on which the blood of our citizens was shed, was or was not within the territory of Spain, at least after the Treaty of 1819 until the Mexican Revolution."

Second Resolution: "Whether the spot is or is not within the territory which was wrested from Spain by the revolutionary Government of Mexico."

The third Resolution had to do with this mysterious spot too: "Whether that spot is or is not within a settlement of people which settlement had existed . . . long before the Texas revolution, and until its inhabitants fled before the approach of the U.S. Army." These were uncomfortably pointed questions. There were five more, all on the same theme.

Little attention was paid to the congressman's resolutions at the time, and it was only after Lincoln became a great figure in history and his slightest utterance was resurrected, pondered and analyzed by generations of historians, that these were, not surprisingly, named the "Spot Resolutions."

A freshman congressman was supposed to be seen and not heard until he had been in the House a respectable length of time. That fellow from Illinois did not follow tradition. Lincoln was an active representative from the start.

President Polk was not obliged to answer any of these embarrassing questions, though with the enviable ability politicians enjoy to reply to questions without answering them, doubtless Mr. Polk would not have been incommoded.

With the fall of Chapultepec the Mexican Government fell. In the peace demands Mexico was to hand over Texas (already taken), Arizona and New Mexico for $15,000,000; a swindle if there ever was one. The new president, Peña y Peña, signed the Treaty of Guadalupe Hidalgo on February 2, 1848. There was nothing else he could do.

When a country is invaded, one's sympathy goes to the invaded country. The Mexicans are bitter about this war, and with good reason. The U.S. with its magic phrase "manifest destiny" (which excused anything), does not come off well in Mexico. The invaders sang an old song, "Green Grows the Lilac," as they went conquering along, and Mexicans call Americans "gringos." The term is pejorative.

35   THE FATEFUL YEAR

Between 1845 and 1848 the U.S. added (by foul means or fair) 1,200,000 square miles to her territory, and was almost twice as large as she had been before. With the new additions came new problems, and they were based on the slavery issue.

While the Mexican War was in full swing Polk had asked Congress for an appropriation of $2,000,000 for the negotiations of the boundary settlement that would be made with the peace commission, whenever it came. A congressman from Pennsylvania, named David Wilmot, a Democrat and anti-slavery man, offered an amendment to this appropriation bill to the effect that "neither slavery nor involuntary servitude should ever exist in any part of the territory which might be acquired by the war." This was the Wilmot Proviso.

The Wilmot Proviso passed the House several times, only to be defeated in the Senate. It became the standard of the Abolition North, and engendered the Free Soil party of 1848, from which sprang the Republican party of 1854.

Of course the South rejected the Wilmot Proviso. Calhoun and his followers denied that Congress had the right to interfere with slavery anywhere. Slaves were property, like houses and horses, and were the state's concern, not the federal government's.

Between two extremes, total slavery or total abstinence from slavery, there had to be compromises. The Missouri Compromise of 1820 might be extended straight across the country to the Pacific, dividing New Mexico and California in the middle, half slave and half free! Or, the question could be left to the settlers of the new territory themselves. This last proposal is known as "popular sovereignty" or "squatter sovereignty" and caused a great deal of trouble.

Polk refused to run for a second term, and died three months after leaving office, worn out by keeping promises. (Later Presidents have generally avoided this perilous policy.)

As if hearing distant thunder, both political parties sought a candidate who would please all sections of the country to put off the coming storm. The Democrats chose Governor Lewis Cass of Michigan who, though a northerner, was sympathetic with the South. Such people were sarcastically called "dough-faces," meaning they could be molded into any desired shape and had no convictions of their own.

The country was blessed with *two* military heroes, our friends Old Rough-and-Ready (Taylor), hero of the Rio Grande, and Old Fuss-and-Feathers (Scott), ditto of Vera Cruz. But the latter was considered too cantankerous, and Zachary Taylor was the nominee. Though the general had no political experience, hadn't voted in years, and owned a sugar plantation in Louisiana and 300 slaves, he was not so extremely pro-slavery as Calhoun, not to mention his own son-in-law Jefferson Davis. When asked his opinion on the bank issue and the tariff problems, the good man was franker than any politician. He said he had had no time to investigate these subjects.

Military glory counted more than opinions. "Old Rough-and-Ready" was an unbeatable campaign slogan with its magic alliteration and Zachary Taylor was swept into the White House.

36   THE SQUEEZED STONE

I was, being human, born alone;
I am, being woman, hard beset;
I live by squeezing from a stone
The little nurishment I get.
—Elinor Wylie, *Let No Charitabel Hope*

While Polk was in office many significant things were taking place in the country, and 1848 was a particularly busy year.

In January a fellow named James W. Marshall was at work constructing a saw-mill on the American River in the Sacramento Valley east of San Francisco. He noticed some yellow specks in the bed of the stream. They tested out pure gold. The rest is history.

On February 23, John Quincy Adams died in the Capitol in Washington, as has been recounted.

In July occurred the Seneca Falls Convention, and that is history too.

Judge Daniel Cady of Johnstown, New York, was a man greatly respected in his community, a former member of Congress, and a lawyer. He had a little daughter Elizabeth, however, who when she grew up organized the Seneca Falls Convention that caused pain and suffering to a large portion of the population of the United States.

As a child of ten, Elizabeth's greatest pleasure was to creep into her father's office and listen to the cases his clients brought him. Little Elizabeth had very big ears, and a good sized brain too.

Many of Judge Cady's clients were poor farm women, and they had their troubles. It was unfair for a husband to take the money his wife earned at the washtub and spend it on drink. But a wife's wages belonged to her husband. It was the law.

Poor old Mrs. Brown! Her husband willed her farm, where she had labored all her life, to her stepson, and now she was out in the cold. A wife's property belonged to her husband. It was the law.

Flora Campbell was a butter-and-egg woman and had long supplied the Cady family with these and other commodities, and Elizabeth loved her. Now she sat in the Judge's office in tears. Flora's husband, without her consent, had mortgaged the fine farm her father had left her, and the creditors were taking over. The Judge explained that the law stated that on marriage a woman's property became her husband's. It was perfectly legal; nothing could be done.

Little Elizabeth Cady decided she would get rid of such unjust laws. She stole into her father's library and turned the books that held these laws upside down. She planned to come back later when no one was looking and cut those wicked laws out. She whispered her design to Flora Campbell to comfort her.

Flora warned the Judge, and the books were saved. The Judge explained to his precocious daughter that there were many copies of these books, and that cutting out the laws would not change them. The only thing to do was for her to grow up and go to the Legislature in Albany and tell the legislators all the unjust things she had heard, and maybe the legislators would change those laws. The Judge was speaking in the spirit of pure whimsey.

When she grew up Elizabeth Cady did just that.

In 1840 she married a fiery and liberal-minded young lecturer named Henry B. Stanton. On their wedding trip they traveled to London where they attended the Anti-Slavery Convention from which women delegates were excluded on account of their sex. It was at this meeting that she met Lucretia Mott.

Now, in 1848, the Stantons were living in the peaceful little village of Seneca Falls, New York, in a house Judge Cady had given them. Seneca Falls is scarcely twenty miles from Auburn, and when Elizabeth received a letter from Lucretia Mott, announcing her arrival in Auburn, she was delighted. She would meet again her fellow reject from the Anti-Slavery Convention whom she greatly admired; she found running a household and taking care of a rapid succession of little ones, mostly boys, in a sleepy country village after the excitements of the great world, on the dull side.

What sort of person Lucretia Mott was, and why Elizabeth Stanton so admired her, is clear when one learns of her voluble opinions and protestations. Lucretia

Mott, Quaker of Philadelphia, had journeyed to northern New York State that summer of 1848, which was a year of great unrest in Europe. There were revolutions in France, Germany, Austria and Italy, and a revolution now began in the tranquil village of Seneca Falls, New York, the consequences of which turned out to be more drastic and lasting than all those revolutions in Europe.

Being members of the Indian Committee of the New York and Philadelphia Yearly Meetings of the Friends, Mrs. Mott and her cooperative husband James (who had met prosperity in the woolen business) were on a tour of inspection of the Seneca Indians at the Cattaraugus Reservation in northern New York. The Friends had set up a modern farm and school on the reservation, but unfortunately some of the Friends had been unable to resist the temptation to convert the Indians to the Christian faith, and now there were Christian and Pagan factions bickering on the once peaceful reservation. Religion thus demonstrated its undeniable ability to beget every kind of discord from local dissentions to bloody wars.

Lucretia Mott was impressed by the deep religious fervor of the pagans. "Far be it from me to say that our silent, voiceless worship was better adapted to their conditions," she wrote. (It seems that Mrs. Mott rather favored the "pagans.")

At the Yearly Meeting in Philadelphia it was suggested that the women be taught to "stay home and cook" while the men labored in the fields. Mrs. Mott protested, saying that a council of squaws must first be convened about this. She was thought to be joking.

An Anti-Sabbath Convention, under the leadership of William Lloyd Garrison, had been held in Philadelphia to challenge penal enactments to compel strict observance of the Sabbath, depriving working men of any day of recreation (Abby Kelley and Stephen Foster—not the songwriter—had been arrested in Ohio for distributing anti-slavery pamphlets on the Sabbath). At the Convention Lucretia Mott spoke, saying she would no longer hide her sewing when callers arrived on "First Day" (Sunday) as long as it was regarded a greater crime to do an innocent thing on the first day of the week "than to put a human being on the auction block Second Day." Mrs. Mott was too sensible to appeal to the devout. She became an excoriated heretic, so much so that a Quaker doctor refused to treat her when ill, saying, "Lucretia, I am so deeply afflicted by thy rebellious spirit that I do not feel I can subscribe for thee." (How "Christian" can one be?)

Having visited the Indians the Motts next visited several settlements of escaped slaves who were clearing the land, establishing farms, and who were determined that their children receive the education they had been denied. Then, duty done, the Motts journeyed to Auburn to visit Lucretia's sister, Martha Wright, and her husband David.

Lucretia Mott. Reproduced from the Collections of the
Library of Congress. Too sensible for the devout.

Jane Hunt, a Quaker friend of the Wrights, precipitated history by inviting Martha Wright, Lucretia Mott and Elizabeth Stanton to tea at her house near Waterloo, four or five miles from Seneca Falls, with another Quaker friend who had liberal views, Mary Ann McClintock. It was a small tea party, consisting of five mere women, but was destined to have longer repercussions than the Boston Tea Party. These women were happily married and had no personal grievances, but they deplored the inferiority of women before the law, before industry and education. They talked volubly on the subject, Elizabeth's favorite, and soon she proposed that they hold a convention to consider what could be done to improve the status of their sex.

The five women sat eagerly down at a small mahogany table and began to make plans. (This little historic table is preserved somewhere in the vast reaches of the Smithsonian Institution in Washington.) That very day a notice was sent to the *Seneca County Courier*.

WOMAN'S RIGHTS CONVENTION

A convention to discuss the social, civil and religious conditions and rights of women will be held in the Wesleyan Chapel at Seneca Falls, New York, on Wednesday and Thursday, the 19th and 20th of July current; commencing at 10 o'clock A.M. During the first day the meeting will be exclusively for women who are earnestly invited to attend. The public generally are invited to be present on the second day, when Lucretia Mott, of Philadelphia, and other ladies and gentlemen, will address the convention.

It was only a five days' notice, and there was much to be done. When the women met next day to formulate their plans and draft their resolutions there were difficulties—the insurgents had so much to be insurgent about. Finally Elizabeth picked up a copy of the Declaration of Independence and read it aloud. It was the solution to the problem. Mrs. Stanton set out to write her "Declaration of Sentiments," using it as a model. From Jefferson's famous opening line, "When in the course of human events," to the list of grievances, it fell together beautifully. But a startling part of the new Declaration came after the opening line, by the insertion of two little words in a sentence everyone knew by heart: "We hold these truths to be self-evident, that all men—("and women" were Elizabeth's new little words)—are created equal."

In the Declaration of Independence there are listed 28 grievances of the colonies. It was decided to limit the number now to eighteen. Henry Stanton helped his wife look up eighteen substitute grievances, laws unjust to women, and the problem was which ones to leave out. Henry had studied law in his father-in-law's office.

By substituting the word "man" for "King George" it seemed like plain sailing.

"The history of mankind is a history of repeated injuries and usurpations on the part of man towards woman, having in direct object the establishment of an absolute tyranny over her. To prove this, let facts be submitted to a candid world." And Elizabeth read her list of grievances:

Women were deprived of their property rights, of rights to their persons, of rights over their children. Married women were civilly dead, and single women property owners without representation. Women were deprived of educational opportunities and opportunities for employment in any but the most ill-paid labor, women were victims of a double standard of morals—and so on.

When it came to the Resolutions, Elizabeth had a great big surprise up her sleeve: "RESOLVED, That it is the duty of women of this country to secure for themselves their sacred right to the elective franchise."

Henry Stanton was stunned. He begged his wife not to introduce anything so revolutionary into the convention and said if she did he would have to leave town. (His liberalism did not go *that* far.)

Lucretia Mott protested too when Elizabeth read her resolution to her. "Oh Lizzie! If thou demand that, thou will make us ridiculous! We must go slowly." But Elizabeth was not easily discouraged. Frederick Douglass, an ex-slave and the star attraction of the Massachusetts Abolition Society, was coming to the convention, and she would ask his opinion.

"What," she asked when he arrived, "do the Negroes need more than anything else to put them on the right plane?" "The ballot," he replied. She read him her resolution, and he said he would speak for it.

Frederick Douglass was born in Maryland, the son of a slave mother and an unknown white father. He seems to have been owned by a succession of sadists. "In the South everyone wants the privilege of whipping somebody else," he wrote. He learned the alphabet by himself and how to read and write. After escaping, being recaptured and lashed to within an inch of his life he finally escaped successfully. He became the star attraction of the Massachusetts Abolition Society because he was a remarkable speaker. But always under the threat of being recaptured as a fugitive slave, he fled to Britain and became a sensation in England, Scotland and Ireland. English friends raised the money to buy his freedom ($700).

Back in America he continued to lecture, and established and edited the first all-negro newspaper, *The North Star,* in Rochester, New York, with a press given him by his admirers. He edited it for seventeen years. Later he became marshal of the District of Columbia, recorder of deeds for the District, and minister to Haiti.

On July 19, 1848 there was an unusual amount of traffic on the sleepy country

General Washington, always the gentleman, ignores the
fact that Susan B's wings are totally inadequate.

roads leading to Seneca Falls, every sort of vehicle from farm carts and democrat wagons to surreys and chaises, converging on the Wesleyan Chapel. Surprisingly, these vehicles were not entirely filled with members of the female sex either. There were a number of men coming to a meeting called for women only. (One can't help wondering if the men were coming to check up on their women folk to see what they were up to now.)

They found the chapel locked. Evidently the minister regretted his hospitality. A young nephew of Mrs. Stanton's climbed in through an upper window and unlocked the door. The chapel was soon filled to overflowing.

James Mott took the chair and opened the meeting at 11 o'clock. (The women were unaccustomed to conducting meetings and unfamiliar with the Rules of Order.) Then Lucretia Mott, the only woman among them who was used to public speaking, explained to the assemblage the reasons for calling the convention, drew a vivid picture of the humiliating status of women all over the world, and said that it must be raised. Mrs. Mott, quiet and soft-spoken in her Quaker manner, dignified and every inch a lady as could readily be seen, urged the women present to set aside the notion that it was unladylike for women to speak in public, and to take part freely in the discussion.

And then Elizabeth read her Declaration of Sentiments in a loud, clear voice. There were discussions by Lucretia Mott, Frederick Douglass and Ansel Bascom. This gentleman was a member of the New York State Constitutional Commission which had passed the Married Woman's Property law in April of that year. Married women were now allowed to own property in New York State. Mr. Bascom was a neighbor of the Stantons and one senses that they may have had some influence on Mr. Bascom, and thus on the Constitutional Commission. But it was not until 1854 that Elizabeth Cady Stanton spoke before the New York Legislature, the first woman to do so. Her speech caused a sensation, but the legislators did nothing.

On the second day of the convention the resolutions were voted on and passed until it came to Number Nine. Elizabeth read this out boldly, and spoke for it, surprised at her own eloquence. So did Frederick Douglass, as he said he would.

Then came the debate. In the end this resolution was passed too, but by a narrow margin. Though the people were not against the "elective franchise" for women, they wanted more time to think over so revolutionary an idea.

The first demand for equal suffrage ever heard in America or anywhere else, was made by Elizabeth Cady Stanton with the disapproval of two people she revered. And the resolution was seconded by a black man, an ex-slave.

"The Hen Convention" was the mildest term applied to the little meeting in Seneca Falls. It drew a tremendous amount of publicity because nothing like it had ever happened anywhere before. Clergymen thundered: the very foundations of civilization were threatened, the commands of Jehovah defied! Editors from Maine to Texas sharpened their pens and dipped them in vitriol and ridicule. Hyenas, atheists, hermaphrodites, had gathered at Seneca Falls. Sixty-eight women and 33 men signed the Resolution, but many withdrew their names when the storm burst. They did not have the courage of their convictions. Undaunted, the women decided to hold a second convention in the large city of Rochester, New York, two weeks later. The ball had started rolling.

A young, ill-paid teacher at the Canajoharie Academy, at Canajoharie, New York, read of the Seneca Falls convention in the local paper. Susan B. Anthony was a native of South Adams, Massachusetts, and was born in the Quaker faith. She was also a born reformer. Temperance and Abolition were her missions, but she agreed heartily with all the resolutions of the Seneca Falls Convention until she came to the one demanding the "elective franchise" for women. Then she laughed. What a hopeless idea!

Two years later Susan B. Anthony met Mrs. Stanton at an anti-slavery meeting,

Frederick Douglas, from his autobiography *My Bondage and My Freedom*, **1855.**

"Mrs. Stanton and Her Children, About 1848, the Time of the Seneca Falls Convention." From *A Life of Susan B. Anthony,* by Rita Childe Dorr, New York: Fred A. Stokes, 1928.

and not long after that Mrs. Stanton convinced her that women would get nowhere, their influence of little account, until they had the ballot. Susan B. Anthony gave up work on every issue but equal rights for women, and became Elizabeth Cady Stanton's great disciple.

Woman was a frustrated creature in small ways as well as large ones. A woman could not enter a restaurant alone, be conducted to a table, sit down and order a meal. She had to be accompanied by a man—any man. Having studied the menu she could not tell the waiter, standing there with pad and pencil, what she wanted to eat. She told her male escort who relayed the information to the waiter. When Susan B. Anthony remarked to a waiter that she would like a lamb chop and a baked potato—or whatever it was—he stood frozen until the gentleman repeated Susan's words to him. Then he was able to write the order down.

No woman could enter anything more respectable than a bordello and hire a room. When Susan arrived at a hotel and asked the clerk for a room the terrified manager finally capitulated, but ordered a member of his staff to sit all night outside her door (with a loaded gun?) guarding—what? Susan? No, the reputation of the hotel.

When those notorious sisters, Victoria Woodhull and Tennessee Claflin (notorious for running a brokerage firm backed by Cornelius Vanderbilt and advocating in their paper, *Woodhull and Claflin's Weekly*, free love and perhaps even more outrageous things such as equal rights for women) entered a restaurant and sat down at a table, they were informed they could not be served unaccompanied by a gentleman. This is what they expected, and they were ready. They sent out for their coachman. He may not have been technically a gentleman, but he was a *man*. Diners craned their necks and some stood on chairs to witness the excitement.

In the early part of the present century a woman lit a cigarette in a restaurant. Men were smoking, but a waiter respectfully told her, "Ladies are not permitted to smoke."

"Who told you I was a lady?" she inquired, doubtless emitting another puff.

"Ladies" have come a long way from Seneca Falls.

37   THE LID IS OFF

"Over the Mountains
Of the Moon,
Down the Valley of the Shadow,
Ride, boldly ride,"
The Shade replied,—
"If you seek for Eldorado!"
—Poe, *Eldorado*

The Compromise of 1850, proposed by Henry Clay, who also begot the Missouri Compromise of 1820, and has earned (as one might expect) the title of "the Great Compromiser," was the direct result of those specks of gold Mr. James W. Marshall found in the river in the Sacramento Valley in 1848.

The Gold Rush is the most boisterous, raucus, bawdy and colorful episode in the history of North America.

When President Polk confirmed the "extraordinary character" of the gold strike in his annual Message to Congress in December of that year, the lid was off.

Who has not heard of the "Forty-niners?" There was no containing them. They were rough, they were tough—and they poured into California like locusts. In that one year it is estimated 55,000 crossed the plains in covered wagons, hell-bent for gold; faced hostile Indians, starvation, death from freezing in the mountains, death from thirst in the arid wastes and alkali flats of California and Nevada—to stake out claims and make a fortune in a day, and likely gamble it away in a night. Twenty-five thousand came by ships around the Horn, a voyage which could take six months. Some crossed the Isthmus of Panama and were likely to perish of fevers. With these rough, tough men came camp followers, and these soiled doves were rough and tough too.

In one year the population of California rose from 6,000 to 85,000.

A government was desperately needed, and President Taylor suggested a simple solution: admit California as a state at once, and let the people themselves decide about slavery—the "squatter's sovereignty" policy. The rest of the land lifted from Mexico could be made into another state. This would neatly skip the territorial interlude and the slave-or-free problem, since a *state* could of course do what it liked about slavery. However it was obvious that both California and New Mexico would be free states. The new inhabitants of California were mostly northerners, and neither there nor in the other parts of the new lands would slavery be practical.

The hitch was that a free California would destroy the balance of slave and free states—that delicate balance that was forever about to be unbalanced—and to allow all the new land to be free would overwhelm the South entirely. So the South was up in arms against a free California and the whole idea. There was an *impasse*.

Henry Clay was 74, and far gone with consumption when he returned to the Senate after an absence of seven years and made his great effort at conciliation. The bill he presented was called the "Omnibus Bill" and it was the prelude to what all historians, however they may disagree on other matters, agree on calling "the greatest debate ever heard in the halls of Congress." It went on for six months!

Clay's Omnibus Bill had five separate parts briefly summarized thus:

(1) California should be admitted as a free state.

(2) Territorial governments should be set up in the rest of the former Mexican lands (New Mexico at the south and Utah at the north) without restrictions as to slavery.

(3) Texas, a slaveholding state, should be pared down from 379,000 to 246,000 square miles, in return for $10,000,000 to pay her war debts contracted before 1845.

(4) The slave trade should be prohibited in the District of Columbia but slavery itself not prohibited without the consent of Maryland.

(5) A new law would authorize Federal marshals to capture fugitive slaves in the North, who would have no right to trial by jury; and these marshals were to be empowered to force citizens to aid them in the capture or incur a heavy fine.

This last condition outraged the North and was never successfully enforced. The citizens refused to aid in the capture of fugitive slaves, and the Underground Railroad was the result: another dramatic saga of American history.

(In 1764, due to a boundary dispute between the heirs of Lord Baltimore in Maryland and William Penn's heirs in Pennsylvania, two English surveryers, Charles Mason and Jeremiah Dixon, were brought to America to increase the number of competent American surveyors. They drew the line between Pennsylvania and Maryland, later extended westward between Pennsylvania and western Virginia, now West Virginia. This "Mason-Dixon Line" has long been used to differentiate the North [free states] from the South [slave states]. This is but one explanation for the name Dixie, signifying the South.)

Clay's aim was to preserve the Union, the great achievement of the Founding Fathers. At this time everyone wanted to preserve the Union, which indicates that both sides knew it was threatened. Every important senator took part in the debate. John C. Calhoun, old and likewise dying of consumption, sat huddled in blankets while his speech was read by his colleague, Senator James Mason. (No relation to Mason of the Mason-Dixon line.) The Union was no longer a guarantee of the liberties of the South, he said, and accused the North of aggression.

Daniel Webster, still around, spoke on March 7. (The debate had now been going on since January 29.) Webster was an anti-slavery man, but now, to preserve the Union, he spoke in favor of the Compromise, and thus earned the hatred of the abolitionists. John Greenleaf Whittier, the great abolitionist poet, wrote a scathing attack on poor Webster, beginning:

So fallen! So lost! The light withdrawn
Which once he wore!
The glory from his gray hairs gone
Forevermore!

He called it "Ichobad."

It was now July, and sweltering in Washington. The debates went on and on. No advance seemed to be made. President Taylor still clung to his simple plan and would do nothing to further the Omnibus Bill. Then Old Rough-and-Ready suddenly died in the White House, of cholera morbus, on July 9.

The new President, Millard Fillmore, a lawyer from Buffalo, New York, favored the Compromise. During July and August all five bills passed both Houses and the President signed them. The Compromise of 1850 was the law of the land.

At the next Whig convention President Fillmore was passed over in favor of General Winfield Scott (Old Fuss-and-Feathers) who was judged to have more glamor than Fillmore (which almost anyone could). The Democrats were in a deadlock over James Buchanan (who had his innings next time round) and Lewis Cass (the 'northern man with southern sympathies,' or 'doughface') who had lost before to General Taylor. And so they lighted on a politician named Franklin Pierce. This gentleman was from New Hampshire, in spite of which his sympathies were southern. He had served both in the House and the Senate, was affable and well-liked and is thought to be the handsomest of American Presidents, his only distinction. (Some give the beauty prize to Warren G. Harding.)

The Democrats won. In President Pierce's first message to Congress, December 5, 1853, he spoke of the Compromise and how its passage had brought a sense of repose and security to the nation. If so, the United States was a fool's paradise.

The makeup of President Pierce's Cabinet was revealing.

In spite of Compromise, which both parties favored, the issue of slavery still hung over the country like a lowering cloud, but Secretary of State Marcy (a New York man) "held aloof from the slavery question." Perhaps he thought it would go away. Pierce's Secretary of War, Jefferson Davis, was destined for the lofty fate of President of the Confederacy. (He was the late lamented President Taylor's son-in-law.) He and the Attorney General, Caleb Cushing of Massachusetts, were both strong states-righters and pro-slavery men. The Secretaries of the Treasury and the Navy were conservative Southerners. Such was the complexion of President Pierce's cabinet.

Senator Stephen A. Douglas of Illinois was chairman of the Senate Committee on Territories. Five-feet-four and rather wide, he was known as "the Little Giant."

He had an expansionist view and was the spokesman for the "popular sovereignty" doctrine. Slavery, as an issue itself, he thought ridiculous.

He introduced a bill in the Senate for the territorial organization of a tract of land that, though nearly 500,000 square miles in extent (part of the Louisiana Purchase of 1803 that James Monroe had brought home from France in his pocket) had been rather ignored. It was occupied by nomadic Indians and less than a thousand white settlers in scattered military posts.

But now with Oregon opening up and California in a frenetic state over gold—the whole Pacific region suddenly come to life—this vast ignored tract took on new importance. Some kind of administration was necessary, especially as it was essential to the development of railroads, and Douglas was a director of the Illinois Central, and hoped to make Chicago the terminus of the line.

After a conference with President Pierce and Secretary Davis, Senator Douglas reworked a bill he had already presented to the Senate, having in aim the organization of the Territory of Nebraska. This bill made no mention of the Compromise of 1820, in which (it may be recalled) that region was forever dedicated to "free soil."

But the new bill, lovingly concocted with the help of President Pierce and Secretary Davis, differed fundamentally.

The southern faction in Congress would never accept the original Nebraska Bill (Nebraska lay north of latitude 36.30, a district from which slavery was excluded by the Missouri Compromise of 1820). Douglas proposed to divide the territory in two, Kansas and Nebraska, and to repeal the Missouri Compromise. The question of slave or free could be left to the settlers—Douglas's old "popular sovereignty" deal again.

Nothing could stop the bill from passing. The southern senators and northern pro-slavery faction voted for it, regardless of party lines. Douglas, his fighting instincts roused, pushed and propounded. President Pierce added what influences he had for passage. The Kansas-Nebraska Bill became law in May, 1854.

The repeal of the Missouri Compromise, long considered sacred, and the opening up of the western lands, thought free, to slavery, was like the exploding of a bomb in the North. According to some historians, no such indignation and rage had been known in the country since the Stamp Act and the Intolerable Act of colonial times; and these had led to the Revolution.

38   BLEEDING KANSAS

We have put laurel crowns on lousy heads.
—Dostoevsky, *The Possessed.*

It was the Fugitive Slave Act that enlarged the split between North and South. When southerners invaded the free states in pursuit of fugitive slaves, the hostility intensified. The sight of human beings, some settled for years in the North, being dragged off in chains made the northern gorge rise, and stuck in the northern gullet. Mobs tried to impede enforcement of the law, and often succeeded. In Boston a crowd rescued a runaway slave from a Federal marshal, and helped him escape to Canada. The tune had changed since William Lloyd Garrison was dragged through the streets on a rope. A man was chained and dragged away without being allowed to see his wife and children. A southerner claimed a free black woman and her six children, all born in the North. Free Negroes who had never been slaves were terrified, and some fled to Canada.

Harriet Beecher Stowe's novel, *Uncle Tom's Cabin,* appeared in 1852 and sold 300,000 copies in a year. Melodramatic, highly colored and emotional, the book was an overwhelming indictment of slavery, and intended to show its brutalizing influence on whites and blacks alike. Dramatized versions were played by traveling companies in every nook and corner of the North before enthusiastic, weeping audiences. In 1853, Mrs. Stowe visited England. She was received by Queen Victoria who, like everyone else, had wept at the account of Eliza crossing the ice to freedom in Ohio, her child in her arms and pursued by bloodhounds. The vivid account of the slave warehouse in New Orleans was even more moving.

Several states passed "Personal Liberty Laws" in an attempt to nullify the Fugitive Slave Act. The Supreme Court of Wisconsin declared the national law void, the Supreme Court decided against the state, and Wisconsin defied the Supreme Court. It sounded like anarchy.

The South, counting on the Fugitive Slave Act as its best hope, was outraged at the unlawful North. How Stephen A. Douglas, who was born in Vermont, could have been so blind to the emotional and moral issues of slavery and to the reaction of the North to his Act, or how Franklin Pierce, from the sister state of New Hampshire, could have been so unperceptive, is inexplicable. Politicians are supposed to have a sense of the public pulse.

The Underground Railroad came into being with the Fugitive Slave law. Runaways were secretly moved from one "station" to the next in a network that was quickly organized by abolitionists at risk of severe fines and imprisonment. Since it was secret, not much is known about the Underground Railroad or where the "stations" were located—in people's houses, places were constructed where these hunted creatures could be concealed until it was safe to whisk them away, usually in the dead of night, to the next station, en route to Canada.

The valiant souls who led slaves out of the South, outwitting the law in various ways, were called "conductors." The most famous of them was a slave named Harriet Tubman, born in Maryland. She led over 300 of her people to freedom, using various ruses and disguises, sometimes encouraging the more timid along with a revolver.

Sea captains smuggled slaves onto their ships in southern ports and brought them to northern ports. With the passage of the Kansas-Nebraska Bill almost the entire North opposed the return of fugitive slaves. Messrs. Pierce and Douglas had never contemplated this.

The ranks of the Democrats were severely thinned by the Kansas-Nebraska Act, and two new parties emerged. One was reactionary and had nothing to do with slavery. It was opposed to immigration and Roman Catholics. Orignally a secret society with the password "I don't know," it became the Know-Nothing party and could not have been more aptly named.

The other party was made up of those who deserted the Whigs (now moribund), those who were Free-Soilers, and anti-Nebraska Democrats. It was the result of a spontaneous uprising all over the country. They called themselves Republicans and they were particularly active in New England. Their main objective was to keep slavery out of the territories. In 1854 they won more than a hundred seats in the House of Representatives.

Both the South and the North were determined to have Kansas. It had the blessings of popular sovereignty, and who ever got there first with the most, would win. So Kansas became a battleground; and the prelude to a terrible war. The place began filling up with pro-slavers and abolitionist settlers, battling for control. The issue was red hot, and got hotter and hotter.

In 1854 an election was held in Kansas to pick a territorial delegate to Congress. Missourians began pouring in and helped elect a pro-slavery candidate. Then in the following March 5,000 more inundated the state ("Border Ruffians" they were called) and elected a territorial legislature which immediately enacted a slave code and strict repressive laws against abolitionist agitation.

The antislavery inhabitants held elections of their own and elected a legislature with just the opposite views. And so there were two rival governments in Kansas.

The first territorial governor had complained to Washington of the illegal manner in which the pro-slavery Legislature had been elected. President Pierce, instead of seeing to it that a legal election be held in Kansas, protected by federal troops if necessary, as was his duty, replaced the governor with a thoroughly proslavery man. No more *complaints* of illegality!

The next thing was that a posse of pro-slavers sacked the anti-slavery town of

Lawrence. The scene was set for the entrance of the most fanatical character in American history.

John Brown was 55 years old. Failing at everything else, he devoted his life to freeing the slaves, and failed at that too. In 1855 he went to Kansas with four of his sons to help save that territory from becoming a slave state. John Brown's sons were as fanatic as their father.

After the sacking of Lawrence, he, his sons, and two other men of the colony he had founded at Osawatomie Creek, crept into a little pro-slavery settlement on the banks of the Pottawatamie River, dragged five sleeping men from their rude cabins, and slaughtered them in cold blood. Brown said he was an instrument in the hand of God. God must have told him to mutilate the bodies too. It is peculiar what God tells people to do.

For this exploit in God's name he was known as "Old Brown of Osawatamie," though he hailed from Torrington, Connecticut. He became a sort of folk hero to the abolitionists.

As a consequence of this, sporadic fighting broke out all over the territory and in the next year and a half more than 200 people were killed. The territory earned its name of "Bleeding Kansas." So much for popular soverignty.

39   CONGRESSMAN BROOKS' CANE AND DR. EMERSON'S DRED

The day after Brown and his cohorts murdered the five men at Osawatomie in retaliation for five who had died in the sacking of Lawrence, a disgraceful and bloody act was performed within the sacrosanct walls of the U.S. Senate. That august body was losing its temper. Senators shook their fists at each other. Insults flew thick, faces got redder and redder.

Senator Charles Sumner of Massachusetts, who had an eloquent tongue but no restraint, and was undoubtedly more psychotic than most men, was roused by the Kansas issue to heights of vituperation. He launched into personal attacks on Senator Douglas for his popular sovereignty theory, and on Senator Butler of South Carolina, who was absent that day.

Butler's nephew, Congressman Preston S. Brooks, entered the Senate Chamber when the Senate was not in session and Sumner was at his desk doing his homework. Without warning and with a wide swing he slammed his gold-headed cane down on Sumner's head opening a wound to the scalp and sending a gush of blood over the Senator's face. Brooks slammed the cane down at least fifteen more times before anyone interfered. Sumner never completely recovered and it was four years before he was able to return to the Senate, a broken man, during which time Massachusetts sent no one to replace him.

When the House censured Brooks he resigned, went home, and was triumphantly reelected. He was the recipient of many souvenir canes. (Query: Is there Congressional immunity to crimes such as Assault and Battery?)

Between the war in Kansas and the Brooks incident, the country was in greater turmoil than ever. Everyone was outraged at something—and it was time for a new presidential campaign.

The Democratic platform endorsed the Kansas-Nebraska Act and popular sovereignty, in spite of the fact it was working so poorly. Franklin Pierce was let go without a murmur. A leader was needed who had made no enemies on either side, which reduced the potential candidates to almost zero. But there was one man left who seemed to fill the bill. He was James Buchanan of Pennsylvania, a tall, dignified gentleman 65 years old, cautious, intelligent, a reverer of the Constitution; and he could hold his liquor: all desirable attributes. Some Republicans called him a doughface and more forceful politicians held him in some contempt. He had been a congressman, a senator, Minister to Russia, President Polk's Secretary of State—and best of all, he had been absent from the country for the last four years as American Minister to England, and thus had escaped all the Kansas-Nebraska imbroglio, and consequently had made no enemies. He seemed the man to steer the ship of state into calmer waters.

The new Republican Party, being on the other side, denounced the Kansas-Nebraska Act and the expansion of slavery and embraced a policy of internal improvements. It chose for its candidate John C. Frémont, the explorer of the Far West who once had some trifling difficulties in California with Colonel Stephen W. Kearny. The Far West was as good to him as England was to Buchanan—being in those places had kept both men from making enemies.

The Know-Nothing Party quietly expired and their candidate Millard Fillmore went home.

Buchanan won the election, carrying all the southern states but Maryland, and five northern states. It looked as though the country had decided to be conservative.

In his Inaugural Address the new President said that since the whole territorial question had been settled on the principle of popular sovereignty "everything of a practical nature has been decided." One wonders if he really belived this. If so, it was wishful thinking.

Only two days after Buchanan's inauguration, the Supreme Court handed down a decision, years in the making, which was supposed to settle, *once and for all,* the question of slavery in the territories: the Dred Scott Decision.

Dred Scott was the slave and body servant of a certain Dr. John Emerson of St. Louis, an Army surgeon. When assigned to a post at Rock Island, Illinois, and later to Fort Snelling in Wisconsin territory, Dr. Emerson took his body servant with him. When the surgeon died in 1846 Dred brought suit in the Missouri courts for his freedom, of course through abolitionists who sought to make a case. The argument was that residence in Illinois, where slavery was barred under the Northwest Ordinance, and in Wisconsin, where it was outlawed by the Missouri Compromise, had made him a free man.

Of the nine justices of the Court, seven were Democrats (five of them from the South), one a Whig, and one a Republican. Chief Justice Taney read the majority opinion. (1) Scott was not a citizen of Missouri and could not bring suit in the Federal courts. (2) Scott's residence in territory north of the Missouri Compromise line did not make him free. Slaves were property, and the Fifth Amendment prohibited Congress from taking property "without due process of law." Congress had no authority to pass a law depriving persons of their property in the territories. The Missouri Compromise had always been null and void!

The reaction to the Court's ruling in the Dred Scott case was the greatest ever stirred up by a Supreme Court decision. The South was jubilant, the North denounced the decision as a partisan opinion by a partisan body. The irony of using the Bill of Rights to keep a man in chains was not lost in the North either.

Andrew Jackson had appointed Taney Chief Justice in 1836 as a reward for his help in dismantling Mr. Biddle's bank. Supreme Court Justices have life tenure and are apt to be long-lived, in Taney's case too long. The decision he aided and abetted in the Dred Scott case—declaring black people to be property, not people—was a great boost forward for the menacing Civil War which came close to destroying the United States and cost more than half a million lives.

We must now return to Kansas, where we have spent so much time already.

The pro-slavery legislature of that territory called an election to chose delegates to a constitutional convention. The free-state settlers refused to participate. The delegates met at the town of Lecompton and went merrily ahead and framed a constitution establishing slavery as the law of the territory, but refused to submit it to a vote of all the people.

Governor Walker, a Southerner, who had been appointed by Buchanan, was an honest man. He denounced this travesty of the law and hurried to Washington to report the situation to the President. Now was Buchanan's chance to be a statesman. Instead he asked Congress to admit Kansas to the Union with this pro-slavery document as its frame of government!

Senator Douglas, outraged at this flouting of the whole principle of popular sovereignty, so close to his heart, broke with Buchanan. In his home state of Illinois 56 papers were published, and 55 of them denounced the Lecompton Constitution. Douglas was coming up for reelection, and saw how the wind was blowing.

In October a new legislature was chosen in Kansas in a fair election at last. A referendum on the Lecompton Constitution was submitted to the people, and the Lecompton Constitution was rejected, 10,266 to 122!

The fraud attempted in Kansas, heavily backed by the President, was plain for all to see.

In the closing months of Buchanan's administration, when a number of southern states had seceded from the Union, with their senators and representatives, Kansas was admitted to the Union—as a free state.

The senatorial election in Illinois in 1858 attracted national attention. These were again the times that try men's souls. There seemed no solution to the ever tightening deadlock of the slavery issue. The Union faced dissolution.

Senator Douglas of Illinois was up for reelection. The Little Giant was the most prominent northern Democrat, and to many he seemed the only ray of hope.

The Republicans chose as their candidate Abraham Lincoln, who had begun as a country lawyer, had served one term as a Congressman in Washington, where it will be recalled, he smelled something fishy about the Mexican War; and had served in the Illinois Legislature. He was a former Whig who joined the new Republican Party after the Kansas-Nebraska Act and was now the most prominent Republican in the state. Mr. Lincoln challenged Senator Douglas to a series of debates, to be held in various congressional districts of the state, and the Senator accepted the challenge.

The prospect of hearing two challengers face each other in debate over national issues, was a new experience. The debates were heavily attended, closely followed, and reported throughout the country.

It would be hard to imagine two more dramatically opposed individuals. The great Senator Douglas fostered his public image with some thought. He arrived in town by special train, dressed in the latest fashion in a fine broadcloth suit, stunning waistcoat, black silk four-in-hand and batwing collar. He was met by a brass band and rode to the appointed place at the head of a parade.

Abraham Lincoln, who was six-feet-four and wore a stovepipe hat that made him look taller (used, we are told, as a repository for letters, notes, etc.), came in the day coach with a few advisers, and preferred to walk with them through the streets to the scene of the debate.

The Lincoln-Douglas debates were on a remarkably high intellectual level, in spite of the fact that they were political speeches to gain votes.

Douglas concentrated on defending popular sovereignty, the theory of which sounded so logical and just, although it hadn't worked yet. He insisted it was the formula for keeping slavery out of the territories, but he said nothing about the institution of slavery itself.

Lincoln wanted to bar slavery from the territories, and to call it wrong. Were slavery prevented from expanding it would in time die a natural death. "If slavery isn't wrong, nothing is wrong." Mr. Lincoln had a knack for putting issues in a nutshell.

Douglas accused the Republicans of favoring *racial equality* by not abiding by the Dred Scott decision. Lincoln tried to show that Douglas defended that decision. "Judge Douglas is blowing out the moral lights around us when he contends that whoever wants slaves has a right to hold them."

The most famous of the debates took place at the town of Freeport, northwest of Chicago. It was here that Lincoln presented Douglas with a poser. Can the people of a territory exclude slavery prior to the formation of a state constitution? In other words, is Popular Sovereignty still legal in spite of the Dred Scott decision?

Douglas was not only battling for his return to the Senate: he was cocking an eye at the presidental election of 1860, and a sojourn in the White House. However he answered this question he would lose votes. If he rejected Popular Sovereignty he would undoubtedly be rejected by northern Democrats. If he reaffirmed the formula, southern Democrats would be offended and his chances for the presidency would vanish.

Douglas met the issue head on. He said the people of a territory could lawfully exclude slavery before adopting a state constitution, since slavery could not exist without laws supporting slave ownership. If a legislature failed to enact such laws slaveholders would stay out of the territory. This was an entirely new wrinkle and became known as the Freeport Doctrine. In the South, of course, it was called the Freeport Heresy.

It was, however, good enough for Senator Douglas' followers. They returned him to Congress. For Abraham Lincoln a greater fate was waiting.

40   HARPER'S FERRY, or, THE MEETING OF THE WATERS

There is not in this wide world a valley so sweet
As that vale in whose bosom the bright waters meet.
—Tom Moore, *Irish Melodies*

Where the Shenandoah joins the Potomac and both rivers flow amicably together towards the Federal City of Washington sixty miles to the southeast, stands the little town of Harper's Ferry, Virginia (now West Virginia). Guarded by the two rivers and hemmed in by high, rocky cliffs on the Maryland side, and a long spur of the Blue Ridge Mountains on the Virginia side, Harper's Ferry with its abundant water supply had attracted industry since 1796. A vital link in the transportation and communication lines between Ohio and the Shenandoah Valley and the East, Harper's Ferry flourished. In the 1830's the Baltimore and Ohio Railroad and the Chesapeake and Ohio Canal reached the town in their headlong dash to get to the Ohio Valley. In 1859 there were nearly 3,000 people living in and about the town. Twenty workshops employed more than 400 men. It was President George Washington who had insisted that the Government establish an armory and arsenal at this picturesque spot in 1798.

"John Brown of Osawatomie" chose this place as ideal for carrying out his next wild plan to free the slaves. He wanted a mountain stronghold in the South: throughout history mountains have enabled small bands to hold out over vastly superior forces. Such a stronghold would provide a refuge for slaves who, supplied with arms from the arsenal there, could fight for their feedom.

Virginia was a slave state in a mountain region, but only forty miles from Pennsylvania, a free state. With the armory and arsenal captured, and the slaves armed, there would be a general uprising (Brown did not doubt) in which free blacks from the North and Canada would flock to his banner and join their bondsmen brothers and set them free.

Such was John Brown's mad plan. It was heartily endorsed by his followers, as impractical as himself. Money was supplied by abolitionists, though whether they knew the details of his wild scenario is doubtful. Frederick Douglass, that very intelligent man, apprized by Brown of his scheme, warned him not to attack Harper's Ferry, and predicted he would be caught in a trap there.

Notwithstanding, Brown and his eighteen followers, two of them his sons, after weeks of hiding in a farmhouse a few miles out of town, set out in a wagon for Harper's Ferry. The historic date is October 16, 1859. They crossed the Potomac on the Baltimore and Ohio Railroad bridge about 10:30 P.M., taking a watchman prisoner. Once inside the town, the U.S. Arsenal was quickly occupied, the surprised night watchman also taken prisoner.

Brown then sent several of his men out to capture more hostages. One of these was Colonel Lewis Washington, great nephew of the great General, who lived a few miles out of town. He had prestige value, a sword presented to his great-uncle by Frederick the Great inscribed "From the oldest general in the world to the greatest," and a brace of pistols, a gift from Lafayette. (Brown wanted these for symbols.)

With three of his slaves the Colonel calmly climbed into the vehicle provided. The hostage-takers then stopped at the farm of another slave-holder, took the man, his eighteen-year-old son and four more slaves, and added them to their haul.

While hostages were being gathered in, the Baltimore and Ohio passenger train, eastbound for Baltimore, pulled into the station. It was now 1:25 A.M. A clerk from the Wager House, a hostelry next to the station, informed the engineer of the startling events taking place in the town. When the engineer and station-master went to check the tracks, they were halted by Brown's guards and returned to the train at gunpoint. The station master was shot for not moving fast enough— a free black and the first to fall in an attempt to free the slaves.

By early morning the hostages at the armory had increased to near forty; they were kept in the fire engine house, just inside the entrance to the armory grounds. The count had been made up of unsuspecting employees reporting for work.

Two of the raiders returned to Maryland with their wagon loaded with captured weapons to supply the hundreds of slaves confidently expected to joint the fight. (None did.)

Most of the inhabitants of Harper's Ferry were unaware of events and slumbering in their beds, in spite of the sporadic gunfire that had been going on for hours. They were awakened at daybreak by the ringing of the bell of the Lutheran Church by Dr. John Starry, a local physician who had been attending the dying station master. Messengers were dispatched to the nearest towns, Charles Town and Shepherdstown, with news of the armed seizure of Harper's Ferry, to summon the militia.

At about 8 A.M. Brown permitted the Baltimore and Ohio train to continue to Baltimore. At the first station from which he could send a message, the engineer telegraphed his superiors, quoting Brown as saying this was the last train to be permitted to pass the bridge at Harper's Ferry, going east or west. The president of the railroad telegraphed President Buchanan and the Governor of Virginia, and the commander of Maryland's Volunteers.

President Buchanan sent a detachment of marines to the scene, the only fighting men available at the moment, under the command of Colonel Robert E. Lee. The order came so quickly that the Colonel did not have time to go home and put on his uniform.

At 7 A.M. the residents of the town discovered a supply of guns in a building overlooked by the raiders, and a group approached to within a hundred yards of the armory. One of them, who fired on a group of men standing in front of the arsenal, was felled by a bullet and shortly died. After this shooting there was a lull in the morning's occupations.

Since Brown had made no provisions for food for the raiders or the hostages, he released "an infirm bartender from the Wager House," captured earlier, in exchange for 45 breakfasts. But when they came few dared eat the breakfasts for fear they were drugged or poisoned.

The firing continued. One of Brown's men sent word to him to leave Harper's Ferry while there was still a chance. Brown ignored this advice without apparently realizing that outside forces would certainly soon be converging on the beseiged town.

The first to arrive were the militia from Charles Town, Colonel John T. Gibson in command. Gibson divided his forces, and one group captured the B. & O. bridge and drove its defenders back towards the armory. One of these was Brown's son Watson. Another was an ex-slave who had joined Brown to free his wife and children. He was killed.

When Gibson and his contingent arrived he deployed it—some secured the Gault House Saloon which was at the rear of the arsenal and commanded the Shenandoah bridge and the armory yard. Another detachment took up positions in houses along Shenandoah Street which bordered the river on that side and from which one could fire into the armory grounds.

Brown knew at last that his situation was hopeless. He sent a hostage with one of his men, Thompson, from the engine house with a white flag. Thompson was dragged away.

Brown tried again, sending another hostage with two of his men. The raiders were promtply shot and lay bleeding on the ground. One of them was Watson, who dragged himself back to the engine house.

Around 2 P.M. George W. Turner, a prominent and respected citizen of the town was shot. When the popular Mayor of Harper's Ferry, Fontaine Beckham, was mowed down from the engine house the fury of the people was unleashed on the hapless Thompson. They shot him and threw his body into the Potomac.

The battle continued. Shots were exchanged from the engine house with the enraged townspeople, the Charles Town militia, and the Shepherdstown troop when it arrived, joined soon by a company from Winchester and five companies of Maryland Volunteers. No attempt, however, was made to capture Brown. All these men added to the confusion and hysteria, and a number got drunk at the Wager House.

Finally ninety U.S. marines marched into town, led by Colonel Robert E. Lee in unavoidable mufti. By 11 P.M. they entered the armory yard and the disorganized militia was relieved of its duties. Lee did not want to attack the engine house for fear of endangering the lives of the hostages, and wrote a surrender note. By 7 A.M. it was light enough to see and Lieutenant Stuart approached the engine house. Brown opened the door a crack, a cocked rifle in his hand. There was a parley, but Brown refused to surrender. The terms he offered were that he be given safe conduct out of the town with all the hostages.

Stuart stepped back and waved his hat, a pre-arranged signal for the marines to attack. As Brown slammed the door they did so. A heavy ladder used as a battering-ram finally shattered the door. Lieutenant Green was the first man in, Major Russell the second. The third, a Private Quinn, was shot dead. The rest came storming in safely. Colonel Washington pointed at Brown, and Green felled him with his sword, cutting a wound in the back of his neck. Two more of the raiders were killed, one pinned against the wall with a bayonet, the other run through with a saber. It was all over in a minute or two. None of the hostages were harmed, though they were gaunt from fear and hunger. The wounded, the dead and the dying were carried out of the building and laid on the ground. Colonel Washington pulled on his green kid gloves before leaving the engine house. He had an image to maintain.

John Brown's trial began October 27 in the Jefferson County Court House in Charles Town, and lasted three and a half days. Brown, suffering from his wounds, was carried to court on a cot. He was accused of treason against the Commonwealth of Virginia, conspiring with slaves to rebel, and for murder. He was of course found guilty on all three counts. Though there was abundant evidence of insanity in his mother's family he refused to use this plea. He was sentenced to be hanged December 2.

His wife had an interview with him the day before his execution, and then waited at Harper's Ferry for his body. She had lost three of her sons as well as her husband.

An open wagon drew up to the jail next day, the coffin of the condemned man in it. On this Brown sat as he was driven to the gallows, between rows and rows of mounted and foot soldiers. They formed a great ring around the place of execution.

John Brown's last words were, "Be quick."

John Brown's raid caused intense excitement from one end of the nation to the other. Among the abolitionists Brown was a martyr, and in many places in the North church bells tolled the day of his death. In the South he was Satan personified. So emotional and irrational were people everywhere that the fact that the man was a megalomaniac and belonged in an institution was missed. In the South, where there was always a haunting fear of slave insurrection, the conviction grew that the South was unsafe in the Union. Encouraged by Northerners, particularly Republicans, a general slave insurrection looked possible. John Brown's raid hastened the inevitable war.

John Brown did not end on the gallows. A spirited marching song of uncertain origin soon proclaimed:

"John Brown's body lies amouldering in the grave,
His soul goes marching on."

It was an excellent, rousing march, popular with the Union troops in the war that soon engulfed the country. Julia Ward Howe, a reformer and editor of an abolitionist paper, saw troops march through Washington to this tune on their way to battle in 1861 and wrote more elevated words to the melody: "The Battle Hymn of the Republic." (Sir Winston Churchill requested that the "Battle Hymn of the Republic" be played at his funeral. This took place in St. Paul's Cathedral, but the choirmaster conducted the stirring marching song like a dirge, and missed the music and the point entirely. Sir Winston might not have recognized it. Such is the curate mind.)

Part Three

THE GREAT DIVIDE

1   THE SIDES ARE DRAWN

"We can talk," said the Tiger-lily, "when there's anybody worth talking to."
—Alice Through the Looking-Glass.

Three days after John Brown was hanged at Charles Town, December 5, 1859, Congress met and spent two months battling over the choice of a Speaker. Then, on February 2, Jefferson Davis, Senator from Mississippi, introduced a set of Resolutions that were the ultimatum of the South—the terms to be met that would keep it from seceding from the Union. The Fugitive Slave Law must be enforced; slavery would have to be protected in all the Territories; and Douglas' Freeport Doctrine (or Heresy) repudiated.

Senator Davis launched some accusations along with his resolutions. He said the Republican Party was behind the John Brown affair and declared there was a vast conspiracy which stretched from New England to Britain to stir up insurrection and "overturn the institution of slavery," and that the Republican Party was "organized on the basis of war." Obviously none of this was true.

Senator Davis then quit the Senate and went home to Mississippi.

It is hard to understand how anyone could think that a large political party, though political parties are capable of much, would be quite foolish enough to back a madman in such folly as Harper's Ferry. But there were those who did not think John Brown was mad. Emotion can cloud intellects as high as those of Emerson and Thoreau, who compared John Brown to a martyr and the gallows on which he suffered to the Cross. Poor John Brown! His heart was in the right place, but his head was not.

Fate willed Jefferson Davis, a graduate of West Point and a military man in his thinking and desires, to be a politican and to attempt to be a statesman.

It seems as though some giant hand was moving pieces on a chessboard. Jefferson Davis delivered his ultimatum and left the Senate on February 2. Twenty-five days later, under the auspices of the Young Men's Central Republican Union of New York City, Abraham Lincoln made a speech at Cooper Union. Despite a snowstorm, 1500 people were on hand. On the platform in full view sat Horace Greeley, the famous editor of the *Tribune,* and William Cullen Bryant, the editor of the *Evening Post* and one of the country's revered poets. As Lincoln was escorted down the aisle there were cheers for Douglas' formidable rival.

The famous Cooper Union Address definitely altered the course of American history. It put Lincoln in the White House. At last people were hearing a voice that did not falter.

Lincoln cited proof that Congress had made repeated laws to control slavery in the territories, and the South had accepted them; that the threat to break up

the Union if a Republican President was elected had no justification, and he denied
that the Republicans had anything to do with the events at Harper's Ferry. He said,
"Let us be diverted by none of those sophisticated contrivances such as groping for
some middle ground between the right and the wrong, vain as a search for a man
who should be neither a living man nor a dead man—such as Union appeals beseeching true Union men to yield to Disunionists, reversing the divine rule and
calling not sinners but the righteous to repent—such as invocations imploring men
to unsay what Washington said, and undo what Washington did."

In April the Democrats held their convention in Charleston, South Carolina.
Every delegate was determined that the platform adopt measures providing federal
protection for slavery in the territories.

Some of the delegates left in a huff at provisions of a proposed platform that
was too mild to suit them. Stephen A. Douglas led every ballot taken by the remaining
delegates, but as he could not gain a two-thirds majority the Convention adjourned.

In Chicago in May the Republicans had their innings. They adopted a broad
and shrewd platform that avoided the stamp of being purely an abolition platform.
High tariffs, a homestead bill, plans for internal improvements including the building
of a railroad to the Pacific—everything was agreeable to most. Each state would
have the right to control its own institutions, but the platform denied that territorial
legislation or Congress had a right to legalize slavery in the territories.

The obvious choice of the Convention was Abraham Lincoln and he was nominated on the third ballot. He was prominent enough through the Lincoln-Douglas
debates to be respectable, but obscure enough to have few enemies. His Cooper
Union address was the one clear voice in the uncertainties of the time. He had
other qualifications too. He was radical enough to please, or not to alienate, the
radicals, and conservative enough to please the ex-Whigs. Furthermore, his political
charisma (as we would say now) was ideal: he was "Honest Abe, the Rail-splitter"—
and he was born in a LOG CABIN! He had everything. In fact he had far more
than the nominators realized—a rare thing at nominating conventions.

Those Democrats who had left their abortive Convention in Charleston in a
huff in April reassembled in Baltimore in June, only to leave again in a second
huff. This time they knew they would have to meet that fellow with the stovepipe
hat who had proved pretty adroit when he debated Douglas.

Those who had not gone to Baltimore were now wrangling in Richmond, and
the bolters from Charleston and Baltimore joined them there. In Richmond they
ended up with two nominees, instead of with none: the Northern Democrats chose
Douglas and their Southern brethren chose John C. Breckinridge of Kentucky. The
Democratic party, the party of Jefferson and Jackson, was split asunder before the
first shot was fired at Fort Sumter that split the nation.

There was another candidate for the Presidency, making four. John Bell of

Tennessee, a man of intelligence and integrity, was nominated by a newly formed party, the National Constitutional Unionists. Their platform was "the Constitution, the Union, and the Enforcement of the Laws"—a Southern unionist party.

Election Day was November 6. Lincoln walked to the courthouse in Springfield about 3 P.M. and was cheered by a large crowd. Cutting the names of his own electors from the top of the ballet, he voted a straight ticket.

He spent the evening in the telegraph office. When the returns began coming in, the outcome did not remain long in doubt. Lincoln had 1,866,452 votes, Douglas 1,376,957, Breckinridge 844,781, and Bell 588,824. But in the electoral vote, due to the curious electoral system in the U.S., Lincoln carried all the Northern states except New Jersey, which went for Douglas. He had garnered 173 electoral votes to Douglas' 12.

Threats of secession had long rumbled in the South, and during the campaign the threats had grown more specific: if a Republican President were elected the South would withdraw from the Union. Now a Republican President was elected, and the Southern states one by one proceeded to make good their threat.

South Carolina was by far the most fiery and rebellious of all the Southern states. The legislature of that state, meeting in Charleston on December 20, passed an "Ordinance of Secession," and the vote was 169 to 0. South Carolina had shown the way; she had put the first rip in the Union so carefully and painstakingly knit at the Constitutional Convention in Philadelphia in 1787.

By early February 1861, the new Confederacy had been sufficiently organized to get down to business, by which time six more states had followed South Carolina's lead: Mississippi, Florida, Alabama, Georgia, Louisiana and Texas. Jefferson Davis was proclaimed provisional President of the new nation, and Montgomery, the capital of Alabama, the new nation's provisional capital. The Capitol had a neo-classic façade and a cupola before which it would be quite suitable to take the oath of office, but there were only two hotels in the town, both filthy, popular with insects, and exorbitantly expensive. The food was inedible, the service bad. The town was noted, too, for its voracious mosquitoes, even, it was said, in February.

In this depressing place Jefferson Davis took the oath of office as provisional President of the Confederacy on February 8. His Vice President was Alexander F. Stephens of Georgia, a little fellow weighing less than 100 pounds, who had voted against secession in the Georgia legislature and had consistently opposed the policies of Davis, especially conscription and the suspension of the writ of habeas corpus. The two Southern gentlement didn't get along: in fact few of Davis' associates could get along with him.

There was a committee to draft a constitution, but we need not go into its provisions except to say, as Bruce Catton pointed out, it established a nation founded on slavery and dedicated to the proposition that all men are not created equal.

President Davis was of course as strong a states' righter as John C. Calhoun and he considered slavery a sacred institution. Later when things looked dark he wrote his wife gloomily, "I fear we will lose all our slave property." (His fears were confirmed.)

The President was authorized to raise an army of 100,000 and a loan of $15 million, which was a lot of money then. Commissioners were to be sent to seek the friendship of European courts. The great trump card was King Cotton, for which the mills of England and France were forever thirsting.

It was their "peculiar institution" of slavery that caused the Southern states to attempt to secede from the Union. Slavery was looked on with disfavor or hatred in the North, and new states were being admitted to the Union as free states. The South was losing her power in Congress and her "institution" was more and more menaced.

There were many in the South who deplored slavery, some on moral grounds, and others because they saw that slavery was a drag on the Southern economy. The "lowly hay crop" of the North was more valuable than all the cotton the South produced with free labor.

In a large group uniformity of opinion is impossible. The popular notion of the "Solid South" is false. In the days of John C. Calhoun many prominent Southerners were opposed to his Nullification doctrine. On the very verge of war tens of thousands in the Deep South were against a break with the Union, and in the elections of delegates to the state secession conventions those opposed were a very substantial minority—but still a minority.

North Carolina turned down a call for a secession convention. In Virginia, on April 4, 1861, the convention voted against a secession ordinance by an almost two to one majority.

In Georgia 37,123 voted for delegates against secession to 50,243 in favor; in Arkansas 17,000 against to 22,000 in favor. In Alabama it was 28,000 against to 35,700 for. There was an even larger vote against secession in Louisiana—17,296 against to 20,448 in favor. In Texas 22 percent of the voters, despite intimidation, voted against secession.

All during the war there were in the South areas of strong opposition to the Confederacy. In eastern Tennessee Union sentiment was so strong that the courts could not function without military support, and sometimes not even then. Northern Alabama and the mountainous counties of Arkansas and Virginia were strong pro-Union regions.

It has been estimated that some 48,000 Southerners served in the Army of the United States. Charles Galloway of Arkansas led two companies to Springfield, Missouri, where they were mustered into the Union Army, and then led them back to Arkansas to fight the Confederates.

2   THE RESHUFFLE

As the Southern states seceded from the Union one by one they seized the Federal property within their borders—post offices, armories, forts with their installations, Federal prisons. Flames of hatred rose high in the North.

But there were two off-shore Federal installations the South lacked the power to seize: Fort Pickens in the harbor of Pensacola, Florida, and Fort Sumter (named for Thomas Sumter, the gamecock of the Revolution) which occupied a small, man-made island in the harbor of Charleston, South Carolina. Fort Sumter soon became the spark that set the tinder off.

The North was bewildered by the turn of events which it had hoped would never really happen, and so was James Buchanan in the White House. He didn't know what to do, and neither did anyone else. He upheld, though feebly, the principle of the Union and the Government's right to its seized property in the seceded states. In his last annual message to Congress, now depleted of so many of its members, the President denied that states had a right to secede, but also doubted that the Government had the power to force them back into the Union.

Desperate, last minute attempts were made by various committees to come up with some sort of compromise, but all plans invariably collapsed over the subject of slavery in the territories, about which the South was absolutely hipped, to the exclusion of everything else.

As James Buchanan fidgeted in the White House and hoped there would be no open clashes before he could get out of it on March 4, and Abraham Lincoln, back home in Springfield, Illinois, worked on his inaugural address, pondered the makeup of his Cabinet, and grew a beard at the behest of a little girl, the country rumbled on its fateful course.

In Washington, March 4, 1861, at noon, the President-elect walked arm in arm with President Buchanan out of Willard's Hotel while a band played "Hail to the Chief." Seated in an open barouche the incoming and outgoing Presidents led off the long parade, surrounded and accompanied by prancing cavalry, bands, regiments of foot-soldiers, and a float with 34 little girls in white, representing all the states, including the Deep South.

What must Lincoln have felt as he was about to assume charge of a crumbling nation?

Buchanan said to him, "If you are as happy a man entering this office as I am leaving it, you will be the happiest man in the world."

The new President, in his Inaugural Address, remained conciliatory. He declared that the Union was older than the Constitution, no state could leave the Union on its own volition, that secession was illegal, acts of violence insurrection.

He said he intended to execute the laws in all the states, and to "hold, occupy and possess" the federal property seized in the seceded states. He was speaking directly when he said:

"In *your* hands, my dissatisfied fellow countrymen, and not *mine,* is the momentous issue of civil war. The government will not assail *you.* You can have no conflict without being yourselves the aggressors. *You* have no oath registered in Heaven to destroy the government, while *I* have the most solemn one to preserve, protect and defend it."

His concluding words transcended prose:

"I am loath to close. We are not enemies, but friends. We must not be enemies. Though passion may have strained, it must not break our bonds of affection. The mystic chords of memory, stretching from every battlefield and patriot grave, to every living heart and hearthstone, all over this broad land, will yet swell the chorus of the Union, when again touched, as they surely will be, by the better angels of our nature."

The problems awaiting Lincoln on his first day in the White House would have staggered Atlas. As has been observed, "He paused, but he did not stagger."

As the three Lincoln boys rushed around exploring their commodious new home, and Mrs. Lincoln decided what must be done to brighten up the rooms, grown somewhat shabby, Lincoln was consulting with the holdover War Secretary from the Buchanan Cabinet, Joseph Holt. Before him was a pile of communications from Fort Sumter, and the picture they presented was a startling one.

When South Carolina seceded, Major Robert Anderson, the fort's commander, had moved his troops out of Fort Moultrie on Sullivan's Island into Fort Sumter, which was a more defensible site; but he was now for the first time expressing doubts about his ability to hold Sumter. His little garrison of 83 men had rations for only a few days.

Sumter occupied a man-made island just within the harbor entrance and about three miles from Charleston. Its guns faced the sea, and several points of land faced it: Sullivan's Island to the north, on which stood Fort Moultrie, dating from colonial times, and James Island and Morris Island to the south, on the former of which stood Fort Johnson. Sumter, exposed in the harbor, stood exactly between them.

A commission from South Carolina went to Washington to persuade President Buchanan to order Major Anderson back to Fort Moultrie, and he had for once stood firm. In January he sent an unarmed, unescorted vessel, *Star of the West,* with provisions (and troops below decks) to Sumter, and she had been fired on by the Charleston batteries. The *Star of the West* abruptly changed directions, turned into the *Star of the North,* and headed home.

Thus Lincoln knew how trigger-happy they were at Charleston.

The subject of Sumter occupied Cabinet meetings through the month. Lincoln was determined that, if there was to be a war, the South should fire the first shot. He informed Governor Pickens of South Carolina on April 8, that he would send provisions to the fort.

Scholarly historians have written numerous books about Lincoln's motives in pursuing this course, and there are as many opinions as books. But these need not detain us here; only the unfolding facts.

President Davis, in Montgomery, on learning of Lincoln's message to Governor Pickens, ordered General Beauregard, who was in command of 7000 troops at Charleston, to send an ultimatum to Major Anderson to surrender or . . . Major Anderson refused to surrender, and so, on April 12, shortly before dawn, the batteries on Sullivan's and James Islands opened fire on Fort Sumter.

The South had fired the first shot, and the great American Civil War began.

The Confederates claimed that this act was not aggression. Major Anderson's act, in moving his men from Fort Moultrie into Fort Sumter, was. And hence it was the North that started it all. The phrase "Northern aggression," is still occasionally heard in the South, perhaps a little wryly.

The bombardment of Fort Sumter continued all day, and intervals during the night while crowds lined the waterfront at Charleston and cheered and cheered.

But there were those in South Carolina who did not cheer. Benjamin F. Perry, a lawyer of that state, wrote in his diary, "My heart is rent by the destruction of my country. The American people are demented . . . they are exulting over the destruction of the best and wisest form of government ever sacrificed by God to man."

Another native South Carolinian said bitterly, "South Carolina is too small to be a nation and too large to be a lunatic asylum."

At 8 A.M. on the 13th, after 24 hours of almost constant bombardment, the officers' quarters at Sumter were ignited by shot heated in the furnaces of Fort Moultrie. By 11 o'clock the conflagration was out of control. Captain Abner Doubleday (later famed as the alleged inventor of baseball), who had fired the first shot from the fort, reported, "The roaring and crackling of the flames, the dense masses of smoke, the bursting of the enemy's shells, and our own which were exploding in the burning rooms, the crashing of the shot and the sound of masonry falling in every direction, made the fort a pandemonium."

During this pandemonium a strange distant sound was heard over the water. The enemy was cheering its former compatriots—who continued to fire from the fort—for their gallant persistance in this hopeless situation. Such are the anomalies of war.

In the afternoon Anderson ran up a white flag. The fort was enveloped in flames, the men half choked by smoke and tortured by heat; but all were alive.

On Sunday afternoon the Union flag was run up, saluted by Anderson and his men, and hauled down. The men marched out of the fort with the honors of war and boarded federal vessels that had been tossing on the waves outside the harbor. The Union Navy had done "exactly nothing" to come to the aid of the fort, but took Anderson and his battered garrison to New York, where they received a hero's welcome.

On April 15, Lincoln called for the Union States to supply 75,000 militia to "suppress resistance to the laws of the United States by groups too numerous and powerful to be dealt with by the civil authorities."

"The first gun at Sumter," James Russell Lowell said, "brought the free states to their feet as one man."

Stephen A. Douglas hurried to the White House, clasped Lincoln's hand and pledged his support. Lincoln had destroyed his political ambitions, and Lincoln was greatly encouraged by his loyalty now. Ex-President Pierce, who had done what he could to aid the Southern cause, turned himself overnight into a strong Unionist, and ex-President Buchanan stiffened in the Northern cause.

There was the problem of the border states, particularly Virginia. Virginia ("the old Dominion") was the richest of all the Southern states, and Union sentiment stronger here than farther south. Yet Virginia joined the Confederacy on April 17, two days after Lincoln called for troops "to suppress resistance to the laws of the United States," and she was followed by Arkansas (May 6), Tennessee (May 7) and North Carolina (May 20).

The mountainous counties of western Virginia had voted against secession in May. There were no plantations there, few slaves (no cotton nor tobacco grown), and the people refused any longer to accept the decisions of the slave-holding aristocracy of the eastern counties who would always call the tune because of that three-fourths of an extra vote for any slave an owner claimed.

The governor of Virginia sent troops to coerce these western counties back into the fold, but mountain people are tough and independent. Instead, they "seceded from secession" and set up a new state of their own which they called Kanawha, after a river. Lincoln sent General McClellan of the Department of the Ohio to drive the Confederates out of the region, which he did with success. (This proved about the only success McClellan was destined to have.)

In 1863, Congress, with deft handling by Lincoln, admitted the new state to the Union under the unfortunate name of West Virginia. It was unconstitutional to do this (Article IV, Sect. 3, par. 1) "The bastard daughter of political rape," they said in the South. But Virginia had rejected the Union and its Constitution, and had no claim to the protection of its laws.

The four remaining slave states, Maryland, Delaware, Kentucky and Missouri, stayed with the Union, though there were many pro-Confederacy people in all of them. Lincoln kept a close watch on these states. It was essential that they remain in the Union, and in the case of Missouri and Maryland he did not hesitate to insure their loyalty with military force. Virginia was across the Potomac from Washington, and if Maryland seceded the capital would be surrounded by the enemy.

Maryland being a border state, allegiances were sharply divided there. In Baltimore, strongly southern in its sympathies, the 6th Massachusetts Regiment and some troops from Pennsylvania, attempting to pass through the city on their way to Washington in April, 1861, were jeered at by mobs who finally attacked them with stones, and then with guns. In spite of the efforts of the police and the heroic mayor of Baltimore to protect the soldiers, uphold the law, and calm the rioters, four soliders were killed and 36 wounded. Fighting in self defence, they killed twelve Baltimorians and wounded a number. It was the first casualty list of the war.

The press, North and South, made the most of this incident—from opposite points of view. A Marylander teaching in a college in Louisiana, read the highly colored accounts. James Ryder Randall was inspired to embark on the perilous seas of poetry-making.

> "Avenge the patriotic gore
> That flecked the streets of Baltimore,
> And be the battle-queen of yore,
>   Maryland, my Maryland!"

Mr. Randall grew fiercer and fiercer:

> "I hear the distant thunder hum,
>   Maryland!
> The Old Line's bugle, fife and drum.
> She is not dead, nor deaf, nor dumb;
> Huzza! She spurns the Northern scum!
> She breathes! She burns! She'll come! She'll come!
>   Maryland, my Maryland!"

This deplorable effusion based on erroneous reporting, became a great rallying cry in the South; and though Northerners might be scum, thunder never hums.

3   THE EMERGENCE OF THE RAIL-SPLITTER

When he came to Washington as the newly-elected President, Lincoln was considered "a small-town politician" by those who thought themselves professionals. His unpretentious air, long and lanky legs and his clothes, strengthened the impression, so the Cabinet he chose thought to lead him into professional ways. But the backwoods rail-splitter proved a better and stronger man than any of them. William H.

Seward (State) was one eager to be guide, mentor and friend. He took charge of the President-elect when he came to town to be inaugurated, introduced him to the right people, and guided him about. But once Lincoln was President, Seward found that he was no longer a guide. During the Fort Sumter crisis he wrote his wife, "Executive force and vigor are rare qualities; the President is the best of us."

William H. Seward had served in the New York State Legislature and later was Governor of New York for two terms, where he worked for educational improvements, better conditions for immigrants, and to protect fugitive slaves. He served two terms in the U.S. Senate where he opposed the Compromise of 1850; he was an implacable foe of slavery. He had lost the Republican nomination to Lincoln, who was now his boss, and to whom he was always loyal.

Within a month of taking office, under the pressure of tremendous decisions to be made, Lincoln grew with astonishing rapidity. In the national crisis, though far from a dictator by nature, he exceeded the limits of presidential power. He expanded the Army without congressional authority, and suspended the writ of habeas corpus when it seemed necessary to the national security.

After Sumter there was a pause while the border states were in suspended animation and both sides gathered their forces, awaited events, and took a long, close look at their war potential.

The North had the larger population—about 22 million, the South had 9 million, of which about three and a half million were slaves. The Northern economy was vastly superior: 80 percent of the factories of the country were in the North. The transportation system was vastly superior too, the North having more and better inland waterways, more and better roads, more wagons and animals. It had 20,000 miles of railroads while the South, with as large a land area, had half that amount. The North also commanded the sea power.

In the South's favor was the fact that she would be fighting a defensive war, within her own borders, and in control of her interior lines. The North would have to command long supply lines and communications, capture the enemy capital, and convince the civil population that the war was hopeless.

Another thing in the South's favor was King Cotton. Europe could not do without Southern cotton and would be obliged to take steps . . . King Cotton was the South's ace-in-the-hole, or so it was thought. This thought turned out to be a fallacy, largely thanks to Lincoln.

July was drawing to a close. It was three and a half months since Sumter, and armies were assembled north and south of the Potomac.

General Winfield Scott (Old F. and F.), aged and experienced Commander-in-Chief of the Army, had lost his best solider to the Southern cause in the person of Robert E. Lee of Virginia. Patrick Henry had cried at the First Continental Congress in 1774, "I am not a Virginian—I am an American!" But Robert E. Lee did not feel that way in 1860, and neither did most, but not all, living in the Southern states.

Robert E. Lee was a gentleman. He was the son of Light-Horse Harry Lee, the dashing cavalry officer and friend of Washington, and occupied an imposing mansion with pillars, at Arlington, Virginia, acquired through his wife who was a descendant of Martha Washington.

Englishmen especially—and Englishmen have written many excellent books on American history—fall in love with Robert E. Lee. His gifts of mind, his charm, his poise, the nobility that all in his presence felt, his honorable feelings—in short he sounds too good to be true. In any case, he wasn't true to his country.

It is said that Lee's decision to take up the cause of his native state and against his country was an agonizing one. But his vision was not as broad as that of the Founding Fathers, a number of them Virginians, whose wide views crossed state lines. Robert E. Lee chose to cast his lot with the slave owners, even though he disapproved of slavery. His view was parochial.

If Lee, with his military gifts, had not taken the course he did, and had commanded the Army of the Potomac instead of McClellan, the Civil War might have been over in half the time. His beloved Virginia would not have been so ravaged by war, and many thousands of lives would have been saved. Lee's "loyalty" cost the nation an untold amount in destruction and over 618,000 lives.

Lee's horse Traveller was about as famous as his master. The animal had "amazing speed" and could tire out the horses of Lee's staff. Only twice was he frightened by bursting shells. The second time he reared a cannon ball passed harmlessly under his girth. It reminds one of Molly Pitcher's experience at Monmouth. Lee, reviewing his troops on Traveller, inspired frantic enthusiasm in his men. Perhaps some of it was for Traveller.

Seventy-five thousand men from the ambiguous state of Kentucky fought on the Union side—as many as from New Jersey or Iowa. Allegiances separated many families. Mrs. Lincoln's three half brothers died fighting for the Confederacy. Mrs. Jefferson Davis' brother was an officer in the Union navy, and her father had been governor of New Jersey. Robert C. Breckinridge, a strong Union spokesman had four sons—two were in the Union Army and two in the Confederate Army. One of the Confederate brothers captured one of his Union brothers at the battle of Atlanta; the reunion was said to have been affectionate. There were other cases. Not only were General Winfield Scott and General George H. Thomas, "the Rock of Chicamauga," Virginians, like Lee, but "Damn-the-Torpedoes" Farragut, the captor of Mobile and New Orleans, hailed from Tennessee. Major Anderson, the hero of Sumter, hailed from Kentucky. The name "Civil War," which some Southerners prefer to call "the War Between the States" is tragically correct for this doubly tragic war.

The North, cheered by McClellan's success in the western counties of Virginia, began to feel expansive. "On to Richmond!" cried the press, and the public felt the same. The Confederate Congress was due to convene in Richmond on July 20, and it would be a triumph to bring the war to an end before that date.

General Irwin McDowell, in command of the Union Army at Washington, had 30,000 troops, and though they were not well trained, their three months' enlistments were running out. There were demands for action from all sides that could no longer be withstood. So "On to Richmond" prevailed.

General McDowell led his army into Virginia to follow the railroad line south. It must have been a most unusual invading force, and has been described as having the air of "a political club marching to its annual outing and clambake." There were streamers on the caissons and on saddles, flowers sprouting from cannon and gun barrels, there were bottles of whisky passed from mouth to mouth, and songs and sightseers. Among the latter were congressmen driving in carriages with lunch baskets and bottles of champagne for the picnic ahead. They were rejoicing already at what they would soon see: the rebellion "crushed by a single blow."

General P. G. T. Beauregard, who had fired the first shot at Sumter, was stationed with 22,000 troops at a place called Manassas Junction, some twenty miles southwest of Washington. Here he made the farmhouse of Mr. Wilmer McLean his headquarters, and it was towards this spot that all that motley conglomeration was bound.

At Manassas there was a broad stretch of cultivated land dotted with groves of trees through which ran a brook called Bull Run. It was here the two Armies met, and the picnic was abruptly over. It was the meeting of raw troops with no experience of war and little training.

At first the battle seemed to favor the Union, and reports of a glorious victory in the offing were sent back by the newsmen present. But by late afternoon the tide suddenly turned. Fresh Confederate troops arrived. Then the horrors of war became apparent. The Union men had had enough. They threw down their arms and fled. Fleeing soldiers took the horses from their traces for a swifter flight. Carriages and gun caissons were overturned in the scramble.

Among the fleeing were the congressmen, and perhaps a sprinkling of senators, all in tall black silk hats and elegant black broad-cloth suits heading, in undignified haste, for the Long Bridge over the Potomac, which presented an indescribable spectacle when the frantic soldiers and civilians reached it that night. This was the real "run" in the Battle of Bull Run. The southern belief that "one Southerner is worth a dozen Yankees" (i.e., Northerners) seemed confirmed.

The way to the capital was open; Beauregard did not take it. But Mr. McLean, on the other hand, finally took his. There was to be a Second Battle of Bull Run, and after that Wilmer McLean had had enough. He removed his family and himself to a nice, peaceful little farm two hundred miles to the southwest, far from war's alarms, near a place called Appomattox Court House. . . .

The Battle of Bull Run, or Manassas, left 1,984 Confederate dead, wounded or captured. The Union Army counted 1,584 dead and 1,312 captured. Thus some 3,500 did not survive that picnic.

Both sides were disorganized by the Battle of Bull Run—one side by defeat, the other by victory. The Confederates were low on supplies, the men got drunk, there were no facilities to transport what would be necessary for an assault on Washington. The North was in a state of shock, Washington was in terror, and there were no more battles for awhile.

Lincoln replaced McDowell with General McClellan, who had done so well in western Virginia, and who proceeded to build up the Army of the Potomac until it numbered 100,000 men.

This gentleman was a graduate of West Point, 34 years old. He excelled at organization more than at action, was a charismatic character with a flair, a high regard for himself, and some contempt for others, including his Commander-in-Chief, Abraham Lincoln. However, after the war, Robert E. Lee said McClellan was "by all odds" the best general he encountered. It must be because McClellan retreated so well. Grant, on the other hand, had beaten him.

Before we proceed to the nightmare of the next four years the present chronicler must confess that he has not read *The Official Records of the Union and Confederate Armies and Navies in the War of the Rebellion,* which fill more than 130 large volumes. Over a thousand engagements are here recounted, of which about 150 are important enough to be called battles. Most of this will be passed over in silence, and an attempt made to see the forest in spite of the trees.

It is difficult to follow clearly the fortunes of the North and South during the "War of the Rebellion" because different activities and long-drawn campaigns in different places, and unconnected with each other, were going on at the same time. In recounting these activities of vast armies historians refer to the various scenes of action as "theatres," and follow them separately. It is as if *Hamlet* was playing at one theatre and *Macbeth* at another simultaneously.

4   SHILOH AND THE CHEESE BOX

In 1862, after a period of comparative calm following the Battle of Bull Run, the curtain goes up on the "Western Theatre" of the great conflict, in the busy little river town of Cairo, Illinois, built on a precarious spot (subject to floods) at the junction of the Ohio and Mississippi Rivers. And it is here that a man, hitherto unkown to fame, but destined for great renown, first steps upon the national stage.

Ulysses S. Grant was a West Point graduate, and had seen action in the Mexican War. But he resigned his commission and appeared to be headed for oblivion. At the outbreak of the Civil War he was 39 and earning $800 a year as a clerk in his father's hardware and leather store at Galena, Illinois. He did odd jobs, such as delivering stove wood. He had "habits of intemperance," as they used to say, lounged about, smoked a good many cigars, and was a sloppy dresser.

Suddenly we find him commanding an army, where all his hidden talents blossomed. He had a knack for sensing the weak spot of the enemy, cool courage that rose under mounting difficulties, and a grim determination. These qualities ended by putting him in the White House, and eventually in a large granite tomb on Riverside Drive, New York, along with Mrs. Grant.

From picturesque Cairo (pronounced Care-o) General Grant set out in early February with 40,000 troops to capture a couple of strategic forts—Henry and Donelson—Confederate strongholds on the northern border of Tennessee. These installations guarded the lower Tennessee and Cumberland rivers and were built when Kentucky was trying to maintain her neutrality.

It was phase one of a concerted plan to gain control of the Mississippi with a combined military-naval strategy.

Fort Henry, on the Tennessee River, was favored with its first glimpse of riverboats sheathed in iron plates. A squadron of these terrifying vessels (flag officer A. H. Foote) appeared in the river in conjunction with Grant's forces on land, on February 6.

The defenders of Fort Henry surrendered with almost no resistance.

Grant then proceded to Fort Donelson on the Cumberland River. Here the defenders put up a struggle, but they were forced to capitulate to Grant's "unconditional surrender" on February 16, and the garrison of 20,000 men were Grant's prisoners.

For the South this was a disaster. The Confederates were forced out of Kentucky and lost half of Tennessee.

As Grant started moving South to a railroad junction called Cornith, in Mississippi, the scene shifts East for a day or two.

The Confederacy, in an ingenious attempt to break the blockade of her coast, which extended from Virginia to the Gulf of Mexico, raised a frigate called the *Merrimac*, which had sunk in the Norfolk Navy Yard, covered her sides with iron plates, installed a heavy ram in her bow, and rechristened her the *Virginia*.

On March 2, 1862, this odd-looking vessel entered Hampton Roads, and began destroying the astonished wooden ships of the Union fleet. She rammed and sank one ship, set another aflame with red-hot cannon balls and then, in spite of being impervious to the Union guns, was forced to return to Norfolk because of an adverse tide. She intended to return the next morning, finish off the Union vessels—and perhaps proceed up the Potomac and have a go at Washington itself.

But the next morning an even odder looking vessel suddenly appeared in Hampton Roads, proving that the Northerners were ingenious too. This apparition was a small ironclad vessel designed by a Swedish engineer named John Ericsson. It was called the *Monitor* and was described as looking like "a cheese box on a raft." From her deck, almost flush with the water, rose a revolving turret from which protruded two eleven-inch guns.

The battle between these two absurd-looking crafts was spectacular. Neither did much damage to the other, and finally the *Virginia* returned to Norfolk harbor. The blockade was saved.

This is claimed to be the first appearance in history of ironclad vessels, though ironclads had terrified the defenders of Fort Henry a month previous. But wooden ships were, within a few days or hours, rendered "as obsolete as Noah's Ark."

As has been noted, Grant and his Army, with his division commander William Tecumseh Sherman, after the capture of Fort Donelson, set out up the Tennessee River with the object of destroying the Confederate railroad connections at Corinth, Mississippi. (The Tennessee River here flows in a northerly direction, like the Nile, and Grant was moving South against the current. Very confusing.)

Grant debarked his troops near a place called Pittsburgh Landing, and established his headquarters at Savannah, Tennessee. Five divisions were placed at Pittsburgh Landing and one nearby at Crump's Landing. In this vicinity Grant was caught unaware by General A. S. Johnston, the able commander of Confederate operations in the West, with General P. G. T. Beauregard as second in command.

General Buell, commanding the Army of the Ohio, was marching with 20,000 men from Nashville to join Grant, and Johnston hoped to get there before Buell did.

On April 6 Johnston, who did get there first, fell upon Grant. Grant, expecting no attack, was taken by surprise. Confusion was great.

Later both Grant and Sherman hotly denied there had been any surprise, though history thinks there was.

The famous battle lasted two days. It was wooded, marshy country, intersperced with little ravines and knolls, bordered by the Tennessee River. Grant's forces were driven back from a log meetinghouse of the most humble description, called Shiloh Church ("Place of Peace"). This primitive building, scarcely larger than a hut, has given its name to one of the famous battles of the war.

On the second day General Buell arrived with his 20,000 men, and with the division from Crump's Landing, drove the enemy from the field, and at the height of the action General Johnston fell victim to a minnie-ball. Beauregard, outnumbered, and without fresh troops, resisted for 8 hours, and then withdrew to Corinth—which he abandoned to Union troops a month later.

Both sides lost more than 10,000 men, making Shiloh one of the bloodiest battles of the war, and General Johnston's death was an additional grievous loss for the South.

5   PURITANS KEEP OUT

And much of madness, and more of sin,
And horror the soul of the plot.
—Poe, *The Conqueror Worm*

Another staggering set-back for the South was the loss of New Orleans. Commodore Farragut took the famous (and infamous) little city on April 25, 1862. To accomplish this he had to run the gauntlet of two forts that guarded the river ninety miles below the city at Placquemines Bend and elude armed steamers and rams. He had eight steam sloops and fifteen gunboats to do it with—all of them made of wood. New Orleans was already abandoned by Confederate forces when it was taken, and Farragut proceeded up the Mississippi, received the surrender of Baton Rouge and Natchez, ran by the Vicksburg batteries, and joined the gunboat fleet upstream.

Due to the fact that General Halleck refused to release troops for a joint attack on Vicksburg, "the Gibraltar of the Mississippi," the city held out for another year and the Confederacy was able to maintain communications with Arkansas, Missouri and Texas. Halleck was busily doing his work for the Union cause.

New Orleans early became "the wickedest city in the world," and the giddiest. Masquerades and fancy dress balls were held almost nightly. The Quadroon Balls, where gentlemen paraded their beautiful quadroon mistresses in all their finery, were a feature of New Orleans life, though of course white ladies did not attend (and were not missed). Rich proprietresses of luxurious bordellos, thieves, vagabonds, vigilantes, Voodoo Queens, crooked politicians, gamblers, prostitutes, duelists, gulf and river pirates on holiday—all made life exciting, though often it ended suddenly.

Restraining laws never functioned long. No puritan ever got a toe-hold in New Orleans.

New Orleans was a great theatre town too. By 1803, plays in English were being performed and a real theatre built. By 1806, the Theatre d'Orleans was the third to be completed, and it was here that French opera had a long and brilliant career. The little Louisiana city could boast the most cosmopolitan air of any city in the country, and the most famous actors and actresses of the English-speaking world appeared there. Shakespeare—particularly the tragedies, oddly enough—were constantly performed.

Jenny Lind, on her famous tour with P. T. Barnum, spent a month in the city in 1851, and gave 13 concerts, all sold out. The Creole cuisine of New Orleans was celebrated, and the elite of French society spoke a classic 18th Century French no longer spoken anywhere else in the world.

6   THE AGONY OF CHARLES FRANCIS ADAMS

The men of Lincoln's Cabinet were 'scarcely a mutual-admiration society,'[1] but political considerations forced the appointment of some of them. Lincoln was obliged to name Simon Cameron Secretary of War. A self-made man from Lancaster, Pennsylvania, he was known to be tricky and corrupt, but he was the political boss of Pennsylvania and could split the Republican party in that state. When Lincoln asked Thaddeus Stevens, deep in Pennsylvania politics, if Cameron was really as corrupt as he was given credit for being, Stevens did the best he could for the man: "I don't think he would steal a red-hot stove," he said.[1]

Cameron became Secretary of War, and corruption in the war department set in at a rapid rate. (Some Army shoes were made of paper.) Finally Lincoln got rid of Cameron by appointing him minister to Russia, where he could try his hand at the Russian Crown Jewels.

The way was open for Edwin M. Stanton, who had been Buchanan's Attorney General and was now in Washington criticizing with scorn and vituperation the slow movement of the war. Mr. Stanton was very good at vituperation. Though he had once been contemptuous of Lincoln when the latter was a lawyer in Illinois and was briefed to appear in a case with the eminent Mr. Stanton, Lincoln offered him the War Department.

Historians agree tht Edwin M. Stanton was an excellent administrator, ended corruption in the War Department, put the railroads under military control, and got men and materiel where they were needed, but he proved to be treacherous, conniving, and power-mad.

Lincoln sent Charles Francis Adams as American Minister to the Court of St. James' in May, 1861.

Adams, whose father and grandfather had both been President of the United States, was presented with a very delicate job, and he was well qualified by background, education and brains, to handle it. Britain's sympathies were Southern, and Adam's business was to prevent her from recognizing the Confederacy.

John Henry Temple, 3rd Vicount Palmerston, now Prime Minister, remained as antagonistic to the United States as he had been in the 1830's, when he was Foreign Minister. Lord John Russell, now Foreign Minister, was a more uncertain factor, but was known for his antislavery sentiments. Palmerson's government was a coalition.

On arriving in Liverpool on May 13, Adams learned to his consternation that a Proclamation of Neutrality had just been issued by Her Majesty's Government, which conferred belligerent rights on the Confederacy. This did not mean that Great Britain recognized the independence of the Confederacy, but that she could be treated according to the rules of warfare. Great Britain was within her rights to do this, but coming "with unseemly haste" just before the new American Minister's arrival in England, and before he had the chance to explain Lincoln's theory of secession, it was evidence of Britain's unfriendliness and diplomatic discourtesy.

Britain justified the Proclamation on the grounds that Jefferson Davis had declared that the Confederacy would issue letters of marque (allowing privateers to prey on neutral shipping) and that two days later Lincoln declared a blockade of southern ports. Ships attempting to break the blockade would be subject to search and seizure by Union vessels. Thus the United States claimed the right of war against neutrals aiding the enemy. It was irrefutable that a state of war existed.

(It transpired that Her Majesty's Government had been discussing issuing the Proclamation before news of Davis' and Lincoln's Proclamations reached England. The explanation thus appeared to be an afterthought.)

A fact that did not ease tensions was that the American Secretary of State William Seward was thought to have "a belligerent hostility to all things English," in which he appeared to be the exact counterpart of the British Prime Minister, Lord Palmerston.

Charles Francis Adams was in a very difficult position. The job of keeping England from recognizing the Confederacy was walking a tightrope, and he walked the tightrope for four years.

Though England leaned strongly towards the Confederacy there were members of the Cabinet who did not, including the Duke of Argyle "probably the staunchest

Charles Frances Adams. He didn't shed a tear. Reproduced from the Collections of the Library of Congress.

pro-Northern of them all" though he characterized Secretary of State Steward as "the very impersonation of all that is most violent and arrogant in the American character." (A reversal, for usually Americans found the English arrogant.)

Mr. and Mrs. Adams, within three weeks of their arrival, were invited to dine by five members of the Cabinet. Adams detested these stiff and formal dinners (though he was rather stiff and formal himself). The Tory Opposition, including its leader, Lord Derby, appeared friendly, but the bulk of the aristocratic and commercial classes remained strongly pro-Southern. The commercial classes wanted a Southern success in order to gain a Southern market for their wares, and to "avoid the rigors of the Northern tariff."

Adams had to endure social life from a sense of duty, and though treated civilly, an added unpleasantness to be endured was "the patronizing tone used by the Upper Classes when referring to things American," and "the ill-concealed satisfaction with which the Aristocracy viewed America's troubles." (This does not seem unduly civil in the presence of the American Minister.)

All of England, wherever her sympathies lay, thought that a division of the U.S. was inevitable—even desirable. In England nobody cared about the integrity of the Union, nor realized that its preservation was linked with the progress of free institutions all over the world.

Then news of the Battle of Bull Run arrived. The Union forces had been put to ignominious rout. England seemed confirmed in her opinion that the Northern cause was desperate, if not already lost, and that the Confederacy should be recognized. C. F. Adams was most desperate of all.

Led by the *Times* of London, much of the press became openly friendly to the Confederacy, though a few important papers remained friendly to the Union.

By the fall of 1861 new troubles to disrupt relations appeared. British ships were departing regularly with clothing and supplies for the Confederacy, and these ships seemed to succeed in eluding the blockade. Adams made representations to Lord Russell, but his Lordship blandly said that the Government had no responsibility for these private activities.

Confederate ships were being received in British ports too. Having the privilege of belligerancy they enjoyed the right to obtain supplies and repairs, but not the right of increasing their armaments—which was surreptitiously granted. Adams feared that indignation at home, if the British Government did nothing about this matter, might lead to disastrous consequences.

To add to Mr. Adams' hypertension, there was tension in Mexico, which had failed to pay its debts to England, France and Spain. Intervention by these three powers was threatened. Napoleon III in particular was itching to get his foot in the Mexican door, and enlarge his empire. Intervention in Mexico would be a violation of the Monroe Doctrine, and the U.S. at present had troubles enough. Furthermore, foreign occupation of Mexico would weaken the blockade which was weak already.

At home the war appeared to have reached an impasse. What was desperately needed in the North was some sort of Union victory. France and Britain were growing impatient with the blockade, and wanted cotton. The British manufacturers had a large inventory and had not yet pressed the Government for action, but in France the need was greater, and in the fall of 1861 France suggested to Britain recognition of the Confederacy and refusal to respect the blockade. This idea pleased Russell, but Palmerston, who was a wilier politician in spite of his aversions, had his coalition government to think of, and wanted no dissensions. There were men in Parliament who still sided with the North.

Adams was personally respected. His tact and prudence were noted, and every politician must have realized the difficulty of his position. Adams knew that his major contribution was an avoidance of blunders, and that any important Confederate victory might bring the South rapid recognition.

At this delicate juncture news arrived of the *Trent* affair.

President Davis had sent two Commissioners to Europe, James B. Mason and John Slidell, the former to Britain, the latter to France to woo Napoleon III. They eluded the Northern blockade, reached Havana, and there boarded the British mail packet *Trent*.

On November 8 the American sloop *San Jacinto*, Captain Charles Wilkes, overtook the *Trent* on the high seas, and removed Messrs. Mason and Slidell without authorization. They were brought to New York and thence sent to Boston to be held prisoners in Fort Warren.

James Mason and John Slidell. They weren't worth going to war over.

The North was delighted at this illegal act—so was the South. Such an act would surely force Britain to declare war on the United States! Charles Francis Adams spent some dark days in London.

The British Government's letter demanding immediate release of the prisoners was stiff. But through the efforts of the Prince Consort the tone of the letter was softened—it was one of the Prince's last acts before his untimely death—leaving the way for the American Government to save face.

This Lincoln took, though the Northern public had been delighted at the capture of the Southern commissioners and the act of releasing them might have an adverse effect on public opinion. The halting of a neutral ship on the high seas was a flouting of international law and could lead to war.

But *was* it flouting international law? The written opinion of the law officers of the Crown declared that Captain Wilkes had done wrong to remove the envoys instead of taking the entire vessel for adjudication before a prize court. It was a question of the legality of neutrality. Adams noted the paradox: "Great Britain would have been less offended if the U.S. had insulted her a good deal more."

Secretary Seward's letter was an apology for a "rash act" and assured the Foreign Minister that the prisoners would be "cheerfully liberated" and sent on their way. "One war at a time," said Lincoln.

One wonders if Lords Palmerson and Russell had ever heard of the War of 1812, fought for this very principle of freedom of the seas? But "I can do it to you but you musn't do it to me," is a widely held belief.

Russell and Adams congratulated each other on the peaceful solution of the affair, and Lord Russell proved his sincerity by giving a cold shoulder to Mr. Mason on his belated arrival in London.

Mason and Slidell were scarcely worth going to war about anyway, and Mr. Mason would not have got very far in England. He constantly chewed tobacco and slobbered tobacco-juice all over his chin and shirt.

The settlement of the *Trent* affair had a good effect. It showed that Secretary Seward had no intention of forcing a quarrel with Britain. British pride was soothed and there began a remarkable about-face in public opinion; nobody advocated intervention for the moment. Earl Russell announced in Parliament the Government's determination to maintain its neutral policy, and the Opposition leaders remained silent.

The war in America seemed to be getting nowhere. Lincoln, frustrated, attempted to stir up a fighting spirit in his top generals, and one evening he, his secretary John Hay, and Secretary of State Seward called at McClellan's house. The servant told them that the General was attending an officer's wedding. They waited an hour. McClellan finally returned, and his servant informed him that the President was waiting in the parlor. The General stomped upstairs.

Half an hour later the servant was sent to remind the General that the President was waiting to speak to him, and returned to say that the General had gone to bed.

On the way home John Hay fumed at this incredible insolence towards the President. Lincoln replied that now was no time to bother about etiquette. "I would hold the General's horse if only he would bring us victories." (But after that, when Lincoln wanted to consult McClellan he summoned him to the White House.)

McClellan finally could no longer ignore Lincoln's and Stanton's orders to do *something* with this huge and trained army assembled in Washington—to advance on Richmond—and obeyed with some reluctance at the end of March.

7   TWO GENERALS AND AN OLD WOMAN

Put out more flags.
—Evelyn Waugh

McClellan's plan of advancing on Richmond is reminiscent of General Howe's method of reaching Philadelphia in 1777; he went by water. He ferried his huge army down the Potomac, into the lower Chesapeake, and established his first base at White House Landing about 25 miles east of Richmond. Then he paused and thought.

He thought that he would have to fight an army of 100,000 and though he had more than that number himself, he clamored for reinforcements. He never had enough reinforcements, he was insatiable. Lincoln, harrassed by a general who demanded more and more and never seemed to meet the foe, said that sending men to McClellan was like shoveling fleas across a barn floor—half of them never got there. He likewise said that the Army of the Potomac was a very fine army, and if McClellan did not want to use it he would like to borrow it.

Early in 1862, when Lincoln was trying to stir the reluctant McClellan up to advance on Richmond, a personal sorrow was added to the besieged man's heavy burdens. His second son, Willie, fell ill, and after many anxious days—with the poor father slipping away from meetings and inevitable receptions to see the boy—little Willie died at five o'clock one afternoon. The mother could not control her grief, but the father had to.

Among the many letters of sympathy and condolence received by the Lincolns, only a few were preserved among the President's papers, including a tender one from—George B. McClellan.

McClellan, now proudly bearing the title of "Commander of the Army of the Potomac", once on *terra firma* at White House Landing, instead of heading for Richmond, his best chance of winning the Confederate capital, spent a month laying siege to Yorktown where there were a mere 16,000 Confederate troops, thus giving Lee time to build up his Army by conscription, and to give Stonewall Jackson time to get his Army out of the Shenandoah Valley. Then McClellan started cautiously up the Peninsula towards Richmond, until he was within five miles of the Confederate capital, whose church spires looked beautiful against the sky.

The first clash began May 31, at the Battle of Fair Oaks with the Confederate Commander General Joseph E. Johnston. It was a drawn battle and Johnston was severely wounded. General Lee took over, and an inexplicable month later the series of engagements called The Seven Days' Battles began: Mechanicsville on June 26, next day Gaines' Mill, Savage Station on the 29th, Frazier's Farm on the 30th, and Malvern Hill on July 1—five battles in a week. At Malvern Hill, McClellan stood firm while Lee hurled his divisions one after another over wheatfields swept by artillery and fire from the Union gunboats on the James River. A glance at the map shows that McClellan, on June 26, within sight of the church steeples of Richmond, was in the course of a week driven in a semicircle farther and farther away from it. The people of Richmond heaved a great sigh of relief. Lincoln said McClellan was a sick man—he was suffering from "the slows."

The historian, Samuel Eliot Morison, claims that McClellan, at the Battle of Malvern Hill "proved himself a tactical commander second to none." This must have been the only time.

The Confederate losses during the Peninsula Campaign are set at 20,614, the Federal losses at 15,849, killed, wounded or missing.

Lincoln lost faith in the glamorous McClellan, and so did others. General Halleck had been placed in control of operations, thus relieving Secretary Stanton of these responsibilities. What General Halleck did was to call off the Peninsula Campaign entirely. So, by skillful maneuverings, McClellan gathered his forces about him and brought them to the James River at a place called Harrison's Landing. (McClellan was very skillful at retreats.)

He and his still powerful army, unconquered and full of fight, with morale still high, and the church steeples of Richmond still unimpaired, packed their rucksacks, boarded the ships awaiting them on the James River, and, like the Owl and the Pussycat, sailed away.

The sole result of all this was 36,460 young men and boys dead, wounded or missing.

What McClellan had missed was a great opportunity. (He was to miss another.) When he and his troops disembarked at White House Landing a swift thrust might have ended the war. But McClellan never could make up his mind to attack. He had 80,000 men in striking position, and large reserves. He always thought the enemy had thousands more than he did.

Lincoln relieved this General of command of the Army of the Potomac and gave it to General John Pope. General Halleck was made General-in-Chief of the Union Army.

General Pope said to his men, "I come from the West, where we have always seen the backs of our enemies." He was a bombastic number, a blood-brother of "Apocalypse Smith" of the War of 1812. He announced to newspapermen, "My headquarters will be in the saddle." On reading these grand words Lincoln observed, "A better place for his hindquarters."

General Thomas J. Jackson, known to fame as "Stonewall" Jackson, had been sent by Lee to the Shenandoah Valley where there were 17,000 Union troops, his mission being to prevent the Union Army from approaching Richmond from the rear. Stonewall Jackson believed that attack was the best defense; he was a modern Napoleon in this regard. The Union forces were driven from the Valley, and Richmond was safe for the time being.

Lee, now freed of worries about Richmond, thanks chiefly to Halleck and McClellan, marched north to meet Pope, who was leading a second invasion of Virginia over the same ground lately trod by McClellan. The battle was joined at Manassas, and history repeated itself. The Union troops were driven from that field again.

Lincoln put McClellan back in command of the Army of the Potomac because there was no one else. Grant was engaged on the Mississippi; General Braxton Bragg was keeping General Buell occupied with his invasion of Kentucky. Nobody knew quite what to do.

General Lee thought he knew. An Army 100,000 strong was guarding the Nation's capital, General Pope in command, headquarters, hindquarters and all. No chance there. So Lee decided to invade Maryland, and if possible go on to invade Pennsylvania, bringing the war to the North. He crossed the Potomac scarcely 25 miles from Washington.

The unfortunate men of Lee's Army, now dressed in homespun and rags, their spruce grey uniforms a thing of the past, took off their trousers, and those who had shoes took them off and tied them around their necks to ford the Potomac.

The Confederacy up to now had it all over the North in the way of excellent generals, two or three of whom were military geniuses. Even in the matter of whiskers they excelled their opposite numbers two to one.

At Frederick, Lee issued a proclamation to the effect that they had come, not as invaders, but as liberators, and urged enlistment in The Cause. But the young men thereabouts, seeing the ragged and often shoeless Army of Northern Virginia come to liberate them from their lush and smiling countryside ("apple and peach tree fruited deep," John Greenleaf Whittier described it), were disinclined to be liberated; it is said that less than 100 joined up.

Victor Hugo's *Les Miserables* was published in 1862, and the men of the Army of Northern Virginia began to refer to themselves as "Lee's Miserables." A sense of humor can survive anything.

Union sentiment was stronger in the western counties of Maryland, and it was at Frederick that the minister of the Dutch Reformed Church prayed for the President of the United States in the presence of Stonewall Jackson; but fortunately General Jackson was sound asleep, "as was his wont in church." Stonewall thus avoided not only the prayer but the sermon and (one hopes) the congregation's rendering of "The Stoutest Rebel Must Resign."

Far more famous is the episode of Barbara Fritchie who, "bowed with her four score years and ten," waved the Stars and Stripes from her attic window as the Confederate troops marched by, and when the men took pot-shots at it, is supposed to have said (according to Whittier):

> "Shoot if you must this old grey head,
> But spare your country's flag!"

(The fondest caper of historians is to attempt to eliminate all dramatic incidents and quotable lines throughout history: Molly Pitcher never fired a cannon; Ethan Allen did not say, "Open in the name of the Great Jehovah and the Continental Congress!"; the Charter of Connecticut was not hidden in a hollow oak; William Prescott at Bunker Hill did not say, "Don't fire until you see the whites of their eyes!" and you may be sure, according to these people, Barbara Fritchie never waved a flag.)

Lee's plan for his whole army was to move westward from Frederick and cross two low ranges of mountains—Catoctin and South Mountain—while Jackson was to cross the river back into Virginia, capture the garrison at Martinsburg, and then turn and swoop down on Harper's Ferry, which due to its geography was of great strategic importance. Co-operating with him, General Walker was to occupy the heights across the river on the Virginia side, and General McLaws the opposite heights in Maryland.

After sweeping all this up, these Generals would lead their troops westward again to a rendezvous in the town of Boonsboro, and all would rejoice. It was a ring-around-a-rosy caper.

Lee wrote out this plan carefully, and it went into effect. By September 12, all troops were out of Frederick, and by September 13, had reached Boonsboro. A division led by General Longstreet started north towards Hagerstown, close to the Pennsylvania line. No sooner was Frederick free of the Army of Northern Virginia than along came the Army of the Potomac to fill up the place again.

By about noon that day Lee's entire scenario was known. A private of the 27th

Barbara Fritchie. Did she or didn't she? Here is the answer. Reproduced from the Collections of the Library of Congress.

Indiana volunteers, B. W. Mitchell, picked up three cigars someone had carelessly dropped, wrapped in a paper on which was written "Special Order No. 191." Private Mitchell was an intelligent fellow, and he gave this paper (but presumably not the cigars) to his sergeant, who took it to the colonel of his regiment, who took it to headquarters. The Order was directed to General D. H. Hill and was signed by Lee.

Never did a general have such luck as McClellan had that day, and he planned to make use of it, with due deliberation. But by the time he made up his mind, Lee had already learned that McClellan gave signs of preparing for a march westward towards South Mountain. Had he been quick about it, McClellan could have passed South Mountain and caught up with Lee around Boonsboro before all his troops were assembled there. But by the time he had reached the passes of South Mountain he found them already occupied by Confederate troops. General McClellan began to be known as "the Virginia Creeper."

He was kept at bay all day September 14, while Generals Jackson, McLaws and Walker began to assail the defenses of Harper's Ferry, and Generals Lee, Longstreet and Hill moved west before him, crossed Antietam Creek, which flows into the Potomac five miles away, and took up positions on gently rolling meadows near a village called Sharpsburg.

8   THE STREAM THAT CHANGED HISTORY

What, brother, dust thou fall?
Ay, and thou too, Calypha.
—George Peele, *The Old Wive's Tale.*

Lee's decision to fight a vastly superior army at Sharpsburg, with the Potomac at his back, has often been belabored. There were doubtless reasons for doing so, and obvious reasons against it. Here at any rate a Union Army of 70,000 met Lee's Army of 40,000, on September 17, 1862, and the most ruinous slaughter in all American history was consummated.

McClellan relied on faulty reconnaissance, and did so throughout his military career. He believed that instead of 40,000 men at Sharpsburg, Lee had "pretty close to 100,000," and these phantom divisions were, he thought, deployed to the right, left and behind him. McClellan, irresolute to the point of timidity, *always* thought the army he was facing to be two or three times larger than it actually was. Lee understood McClellan like a book and took some pains to encourage him in his delusions.

On the evening of the 16th, having at last made up his mind, McClellan moved his right flank over Antietam Creek, and at dawn next day the Union assault began. The battle at once became so furious that by nine o'clock it was already "the worst single day in all American history," before World War I.

The Battle of the Antietam (or Sharpsburg) raged for a single day over the fields and woodlots of members of the Dunkard sect—so called because of these people's devotion to entire submersion in the ceremony of baptism (three times). They were pacifists and that day their farms were submerged in blood.

It is unnecessary to follow the battle all that terrible day. Between nine o'clock and one o'clock the Union attack against Confederate units in a sunken road, ever since known as Bloody Lane, was followed by an assault against the south end of Lee's line which was thought to require the gaining of a small stone bridge, now known as Burnside's Bridge, after the General in command. The creek here was in fact shallow, and the General and his men could have waded across without the bridge for which so many died.

When darkness fell on the once peaceful Dunkard farmland, 22,719 men lay dead or dying. Brother fought brother, for many Maryland families were divided in their allegiance.

The Army of Northern Virginia held its position, and since Washington was no longer menaced, McClellan did nothing.

When dawn broke Lee held fire as he sought some weakness in the Union lines. He found none, and that night he and his army slipped away. The Army of Northern Virginia returned to Richmond to build defenses there. McClellan had again let victory slip through his fingers.

The Battle of the Antietam had one effect that drastically changed the character of the war. When the war began, its objective was solely to preserve the Union, but as time went on, bringing incredible loss of life, hatred mounted on both sides, and with the abolitionists relentlessly working their propaganda in the North, hatred of slavery mounted too.

Lincoln wanted slavery done away with by law in the various states, with government compensation for slave owners, but his attempt to induce the loyal slave states to adopt this policy was without success.

By the early summer of 1862, before the Battle of the Antietam, Lincoln became convinced that the Government should announce an antislavery policy, and had been working in secret on an Emancipation Proclamation. This document has been called "probably the most momentous state paper since the adoption of the Federal Constitution."[1]

Only two members of the Cabinet had any previous knowledge of what was going on in the President's mind when he called a Cabinet meeting on July 22, and read his Proclamation to the startled men. He explained that he had fully made up his mind and would issue the thing, and had called them together only as an act of courtesy.

The Proclamation declared that on the first day of January 1863, "all persons held as slaves within any state at that time in rebellion against the Federal Government, shall then, thence-forward and forever be free."

Once the war was won this Proclamation would set "forever free" only those slaves in states still in rebellion, but did not free those in the border states. The President had no constitutional power over property in states not at war with the Union. Even if he had wished to, he could not have freed the slaves in Delaware, Maryland, Kentucky, Missouri and western (now West) Virginia. And even if he could, such an act would not have strengthened loyalty in those places.

Though this Proclamation set no slaves free at the time, once the war was won

the Confederate slaves would be automatically free. The rebellious states were offered several alternatives which would compensate owners for their slaves. All were
rejected.

But there would be no use in issuing this Proclamation while the Union was
suffering humiliating defeats. It would be "like the Pope's bull against the comet,"
Lincoln said; and it would look like a sign of weakness, even though things were
improving in the border states. But now the Confederate forces in Missouri had
been defeated, anchoring that state to the Union; Grant had had his victories on
the Tennessee and Cumberland Rivers; and the reaction of the people of western
Maryland when Lee came to "liberate" them was disappointing.

The Battle of Sharpsburg had forced the withdrawal of the invincible Lee and
the moment to announce the Emancipation Proclamation was ripe. Lincoln had an
unerring sense of timing. Now the Proclamation could not be compared to the
Pope's bull against the comet. It was issued on September 23, 1862, five days after
the battle, and ended all thoughts of intervention.

This famous document was hailed with delight by liberals and radicals everywhere, but was roundly attacked both in America and Europe by the rest of the
population. "Monstrous, reckless, devilish" proclaimed the prestigious British mag-
azine, *Blackwood,* in its wisdom. The British aristocracy greeted it "with laughter
and jeers"[2] and said it would not free a single slave, and was a bid for sympathy.
General McClellan was outraged and considered marching on Washington and de-
posing the Government! Over dinner with three of his generals he was warned that
no more than a corporal's guard would follow him "if he sought to exalt the military
over the civil authority."

The Proclamation made it impossible for any western nation to embrace the
Southern cause. The jeering aristocrats had not thought of this.

In England as the weeks went by there was a noticeable change in the wind.
Pro-Union meetings were held in several English cities. Six thousand workmen at
a meeting in Manchester sent a message to President Lincoln, and these were the
ones who suffered most from the lack of American cotton for their looms.

"The erasure of that foul blot upon civilization and Christianity—chattel slavery—during your Presidency will cause the name of Abraham Lincoln to be honored
and revered by posterity. Accept our high admiration of your firmness in upholding
the proclamation of freedom."

The aristocracy jeered, but the millworkers of Manchester turned out to be
right.

(The Christian Gospels do not mention slavery.)

In January 1863, a huge mass meeting was held in London's Exeter Hall. So
great were the crowds that they spilled into the Strand, disrupting traffic "for hours."

Adams described it as one of the most extraordinary demonstrations ever seen in London. The *Times* tried to make it appear that it had been stimulated by money dispensed by the American Minister. Adams smiled grimly.

This great demonstration by the masses of the people did not mean any change in the attitude of the Upper Crust. But though the South was supposed to be where the aristocrats dwelt (if America could be supposed to have any—all those First Families)—in contrast to the money-grubbing North, the British Government, Lord Palmerston, Lord Russell and the rest were hamstrung by the Proclamation. Now that the war had taken on the character of a crusade and was being waged against slavery, and not merely to preserve the Union, which no one in England could care about, Britain (who had freed her West Indian slaves in 1833) could scarcely recognize a government that was fighting to preserve slavery. (Alexander II had freed the serfs in 1861. Freedom was in the air.)

Lincoln dismissed General McClellan from command of the Army of the Potomac permanently in October and replaced him with General Ambrose Burnside, he of Burnside's Bridge and of the magnificent whiskers now called "sideburns." But in spite of his celebrated whiskers General Burnside's military performance was abysmal.

9   THE DARKEST HOUR YET

Like a stairway to the sea
Where down the blind are driven.
—Edwin Arlington Robinson, *Eros Turannos*

General Burnside planned to cross the Rappahannock at Fredericksburg, Virginia, a town which stood halfway between the Federal capital and the Confederate capital. There was to be another try for Richmond with the North's most incompetent general in command.

Lee consolidated his army behind the town in impregnable positions, but Burnside, like a lemming to the sea, plunged ahead. The Army of the Potomac crossed the river on pontoon bridges and occupied the town.

Then, in wave after wave, the troops charged the Confederate defense line head on while Lee's artillery from nearby Mayre's Hill devastated them. The losses were terrible. This was on December 13, and the next day Burnside ordered the evacuation of Fredericksburg. It is said tears were streaming down his cheeks. He was replaced by General Joseph Hooker—"Fighting Jo," also known as "Big Brains."

It seems inconceivable that another fumbling general could be found to equal Ambrose Burnside, but Big Brains did his best. (Why were the worst generals Union men?)

While cavalry attacks and skirmishes were going on at various places in Virginia, Tennessee and elsewhere, withdrawals here, sieges there, advances in another place, Hooker was planning a major offensive. He had 125,000 well trained men.

In late April he retraced Burnside's calamitous steps and forded the Rappahannock. His army gathered at Chancellorsville, a town about ten miles west of Fredericksburg. Hooker had more than twice as many men as Lee, who sent out Stonewall Jackson's corps of 28,000 to meet them. The men struggled through rough and tangled country and took up their positions on the unsuspecting Union flank.

On May 2, at 6 P.M. the surprise came. The Union line crumbled, but darkness intervened. Next morning the fighting resumed, and kept on until the 5th, when Fighting Joe Hooker abandoned the field and led his army—what there was left of it—back across the Rappahannock—in good order.

The Confederates lost 12,000 men, the Union even more. Among the casualties was Stonewall Jackson, shot by mistake by one of his own men. Two bullets lodged in Jackson's arm near the shoulder, and the arm had to be amputated. Pneumonia developed, and while the entire army prayed, and Lee "wrestled in prayer" all night, the intrepid and beloved Stonewall Jackson, attended by an army surgeon and his wife, sank slowly into death. His last words were, "Let us cross over the river and rest under the shade of the trees."

The Battle of Chancellorsville was a Confederate victory, but the fearful loss of hard-to-replace men, and the loss of Stonewall Jackson, made it a pyrrhic one. The North's prestige sank to rock bottom.

The year 1863 was the dark hour all round. Discouragement and defeatism reigned in the North, and in the South too, in spite of Chancellorsville. Voluntary enlistments had fallen so low that Congress was obliged to pass the first conscription law on March 3. It was an absurdity. All men between 20 and 45 were required to register for military service. No attempt was made to levy first on younger men or bachelors, there were no exemptions—but one could buy a substitute for $300. In the Confederacy conscription had been adopted the year before, the levy resting on men between 18 and 35, with many exemptions and the privilege of buying a substitute for $300, as in the Union (later raised to $600).

Riots broke out in many cities in the North, the worst occuring in New York. There rioters wrecked the draft offices, looted, burned, began lynching blacks, and set fire to a black orphan asylum. Sailors from a ship in the harbor, West Point cadets and troops hastily summoned from Meade's army restored order after four days. The estimate of the dead ranged from 500 to 1200. Meade's army was so weakened that he could not resume the offensive after the Battle of Gettysburg.

The South had Chancellorsville, but had failed to win Maryland and had lost ground in the South (Kentucky and Tennessee). Her ports blockaded, she was deprived of the essentials of life and warfare—food, clothing, munitions. The printing of paper money made inflation soar as it had not since the Revolution. With the Emancipation Proclamation the Confederacy's hopes of recognition by the European powers faded, for the South was battling to preserve a way of life now an anachronism in all of western civilization.

Lee continued the war. He crossed the Potomac with 75,000 men and headed northwest, just as he had done when the Marylanders at Frederick had refused to be "liberated." This time, late in June 1863, he succeeded in reaching within ten miles of Harrisburg, capital of Pennsylvania, and 107 miles from Washington. It was the first time Confederate troops had invaded the North.

10   THE HIGHPOINT OF THE CONFEDERACY

He saith among the trumpets, Ha, ha!
—Job, 39:25

Momentous events sometimes begin in inconsequential ways, or over inanimate objects like the tea at the Boston Tea Party. This time it was shoes. As has been mentioned, the Army of Northern Virginia had long suffered from a scarcity of shoes, and many of the wretched men marched and fought barefoot. Hoping to find shoes in a town that lay southwest of Harrisburg, some Confederate troops went searching.

The place was called Gettysburg.

Here they unexpectedly encountered a Union cavalry unit that was stationed there, and a clash began. Reinforcements were summoned by both sides, and the Battle of Gettysburg, the greatest battle of the War of the Rebellion, and the beginning of the downfall of the Confederacy, was joined.

On the first of July the Confederates had the upper hand. The Union forces were driven through the town and rallied on a high spot of ground southward called Cemetery Ridge. The Confederates occupied a parallel ridge called Seminary Ridge.

On July 2, Lee decided to attack, and Culp's Hill, on the right end of Cemetery Ridge, was partially taken. A corps commanded by General Daniel Sickles occupied

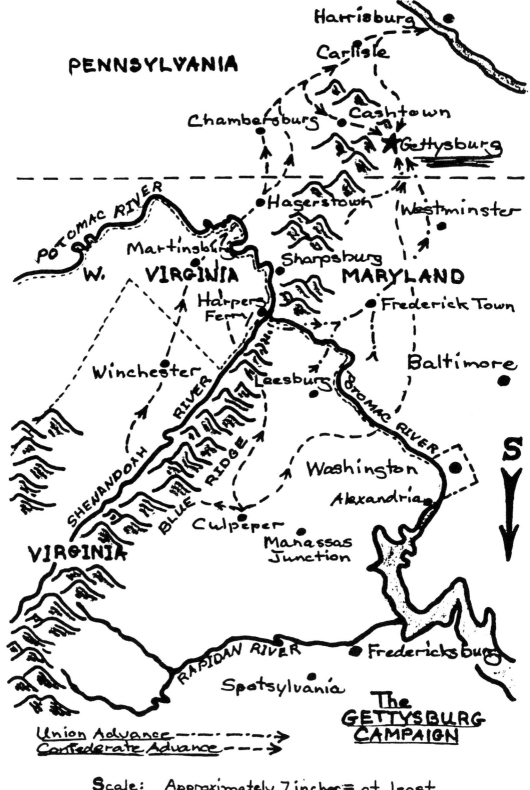

The Gettysburg Campaign

Little Round Top, at the other end of Cemetery Ridge which, if controlled by the Confederates, would have allowed their artillery to strafe the entire Union line.

July 3, saw a desperate attempt by Union forces to retake Culp's Hill, which was partially accomplished. Then silence descended! an ominous silence. But Meade guessed what was coming, and it did. At one o'clock a burst of artillery fire caused little damage on Cemetery Ridge, but the greatest moment of the battle followed.

Lee ordered a direct attack in an attempt to break the Union center, against the protests of General Longstreet. Three divisions, Pickett's, Trimble's and Pettigrew's, emerged from the wooded slopes of Seminary Ridge. This was the famous "Pickett's Charge," 15,000 men crossing the valley towards Cemetery Ridge. Halfway across the valley the Union artillery on Little Round Top opened fire. Amid the roar and the blast those who survived came bravely on. Between drifts of gun smoke they could be seen, bayonets flashing, colors flying. They started to climb the ridge; they approached close enough for faces to be recognized. The Union men let go a deadly barrage. Two of Pickett's brigadier generals were killed, Pickett wounded. Fifteen Regimental commanders died and five others were wounded. The ground was carpeted with the dead.

General Lewis Armistead, raising his cap on the point of his sword, leaped a stone wall into the Union lines, followed by a hundred of his men, and for one brief moment the Stars and Bars of the Confederacy "floated on the crest of Cemetery Ridge." All these gallant men were mowed down or taken prisoner. Armistead was mortally wounded; a monument marks the spot where the frenetic General fell. This fanatical rashness has scarcely been equaled until the Sheehite Muslims of the 1980's.

It was the high point of the Confederacy.

Lee lost the Battle of Gettysburg for various reasons, one of which was surely his order to advance across a field covered by rifles and artillery. It was a repetition of what happened at the Battle of New Orleans.

Next day, the Fourth of July, Lee retreated in a pouring rain towards the Potomac, with his Army, his prisoners, and his baggage. He could not cross the river, because it was flooded, until July 14. Lincoln urged Meade to seize this golden opportunity and not waste his time with councils of war and so forth, but that is just what Meade did. Lee and all his cohorts forded the river and disappeared towards Richmond. Though Meade had put the invincible Lee to rout, he failed to deliver the knockout blow that might have ended the war.

Gettysburg is a favorite battle among military men and is still studied and argued over. As a design it is thought beautiful, the movement of the troops like those in a classic ballet. Sir Winston Churchill greatly loved the Battle of Gettysburg.

The names associated with this battle live on: Culp's Hill, Cemetery Ridge, Seminary Ridge, the Peach Orchard, the Devil's Den, Round Top, Little Round

Top, Pickett's Charge—will be remembered as long as American history endures.

But the most famous thing of all connected with the Battle of Gettysburg is the immortal 263-word address Abraham Lincoln delivered there on November 19, 1863, three and a half months after the battle, at the dedication of the military cemetery.

> Four score and seven years ago our fathers brought forth on this continent a new nation, conceived in liberty, and dedicated to the proposition that all men are created equal. Now we are engaged in a great civil war, testing whether that nation, or any nation so conceived and so dedicated, can long endure. We are met on a great battle-field of that war. We have come to dedicate a portion of that field as a final resting place for those who here gave their lives that the nation might live. It is altogether fitting and proper that we should do this. But in a larger sense, we cannot dedicate—we cannot consecrate—we cannot hallow—this ground. The brave men, living and dead, who struggled here, have consecrated it far above our poor power to add or detract. The world will little note nor long remember what we say here, but it can never forget what they did here. It is for us, the living, rather, to be dedicated here to the unfinished work which they who fought here have thus far so nobly advanced. It is rather for us to be here dedicated to the great task remaining before us—that from these honored dead we take increased devotion; that we here highly resolve that these dead shall not have died in vain; that this nation, under God, shall have a new birth of freedom; and that government of the people, by the people, for the people, shall not perish from the earth.

11   THE FATHER OF WATERS

The Mississippi, as a map will show, is the natural boundary between the state of Mississippi on the left or east bank, and Louisiana on the other one, and is the most meandering of all the great rivers of the world. It has more twists in it than the most convoluted intestine—the Great American Bowel, 2350 miles long. Vicksburg, Mississippi, fortified on a high bluff in a practically impregnable position at one of the most acute bends in this intestinal waterway, was of tremendous strategical importance because in southern hands the trans-Mississippi region could send men and supplies to all the Confederacy. It was defended by 56,000 troops under General John C. Pemberton, and was Grant's objective for eight months. Grant started down stream, on the west bank, towards this Confederate citadel, struck west through the "treacherous and fever-laden" bayous for which Louisiana was famous, giving Vicksburg a wide berth, and ended up opposite a place called Grand Gulf on the other side of the river.

Admiral Porter and his seven ironclads, the amphibious arm of this campaign, had to run the gantlet of the Vicksburg batteries to get down stream and support Grant's army in crossing the river. Sneaking at night with engines stilled and lights out, the boats were nevertheless detected. There came a great barrage from the Vicksburg batteries high on the bluff, a torrent of shots and shells, all lighted up by roaring guns, flaming funnels and steam as the boats sped by the batteries. It was the most spectacular fireworks of the war.

Porter got through with the loss of one boat. Twelve steamers went through the same baptism a week later, all needed to get Grant's Army, 20,000 strong across the river.

Porter's gunboats destroyed the Confederate batteries at Grand Gulf in a five hour bombardment. Grant's army crossed the river below, at a place called Bruinsburg, and set out for Jackson, the capital of Mississippi. His motive was to cut the railroad that supplied Vicksburg; and he did. General Sherman's corps defeated General Joseph E. Johnston's men, and occupied Jackson.

Then Grant started back towards Vicksburg. General Pemberton's army was defeated in two brief engagements, and they were driven inside the fortifications of Vicksburg. Grant encircled the city, and waited.

The siege of Vicksburg began May 18, and Pemberton surrendered on the Fourth of July. The inhabitants had taken to eating rats, which is traditional in besieged cities. Pemberton's men were staggering from hunger.

The fall of Vicksburg opened the Mississippi to shipping its entire length. Lincoln said, in his noble prose, "The Father of Waters flows again unvexed to the sea."

On this same Independence Day, the Battle of Gettysburg was over, and Lee and his Army started back to Virginia in a pouring rain.

Texas and Arkansas, with the fall of Vicksburg, were isolated and as good as lost to the Confederacy. The bridge over which supplies were brought from Texas and Mexico was closed.

12   THE ALABAMA CASE

Charles Francis Adams was having more troubles and frustrations in London. After the Seven Days' Battle and McClellan's retreat from Richmond, a motion was introduced in Parliament calling for mediation for the purpose of ending hostilities in America. Though Palmerston, in a short speech, agreed that everyone wished for the end of the war, arguments in Parliament would merely serve to irritate and anger both sides. The South had not firmly established its independence, and it would be wiser to leave the Ministry to manage "the delicate and difficult questions" as they arose. The motion was withdrawn.

Adams was relieved, but not fooled into thinking the Government was anything but unfriendly to the Union.

This was made abundantly clear by the construction of a gunboat in Liverpool that was destined for the Confederacy. Adams had learned of this early in July from Thomas Dudley, the alert American consul in that city.

Adams instructed Dudley to send all available evidence of the ship's destination to the Collector of Customs at Liverpool, and consulted the Judge Advocate of the Fleet for legal advice. The Collector of Customs at Liverpool paid no attention to Mr. Dudley. The Judge Advocate gave it as his opinion that under the law the American Government would have serious grounds for complaint were the vessel allowed to go to sea, so Adams, armed with this opinion, renewed his demands to Lord Russell that the vessel be detained; because of delays, and one thing and another, the ship known to fame as the *Alabama*, slipped out of port just before Lord Russell's telegram to detain her reached Liverpool.

This ship caused widespread destruction to Union shipping in various parts of the world, even invading the Indian Ocean and preying on defenseless ships in the China trade. In all the *Alabama* destroyed 64 ships before she met a spectacular fate.

The ship, with Southern officers but a British crew, put into Cherbourg for repairs, supplies (and doubtless illegal ammunition) and was there caught by the *U.S.S. Kearsarge*, Captain John S. Winslow, who took station outside the port and waited for the *Alabama* to sortie. The news was telegraphed far and wide, and thousands converged on Cherbourg to see the fun—an international sports event. The *Alabama* came out and a battle took place, broadside to broadside. Though the ships were evenly matched in weight, Captain Winslow's superior gunnery sank the Confederate ship in an hour and a half, the *Kearsarge* sustaining only minor damage, due to the sheets of heavy steel mail hung at her sides.

Among the spectators at this exciting event was Edouard Manet, whose painting, *Alabama and Kearsarge*, is in the Philadelphia Museum of Art, John G. Johnson Collection.

There were other ships built in Liverpool that managed to slip between someone's fingers and put to sea as commerce destroyers, to prey on the Union's merchant shipping, notably the *Florida* and the *Shenandoah*. But whose were the slippery fingers? Palmerston's? Russells? A couple of "rams," as ironclads were then called, were in the works at Liverpool (Laird Shipyards) for an obvious destination, but after the fall of Vicksburg and the Battle of Gettysburg the British Government prudently prevented their departure. They were bought by the British Navy to solve the problem.

In all, the Confederate Navy destroyed 257 Union vessels, and caused another 100 to be transferred to neutral flags.

When Lord Palmerston died, shortly after the war, the Diplomatic Corps dutifully attended the obsequies. The American Minister was able to choke back his tears.

The "Alabama Claims," the name that designated all the claims, were finally settled in 1870 by an international tribunal of five arbitrators appointed by Her Britannic Majesty, the President of the United States, the Emperor of Brazil, the King of Italy and the President of the Swiss Confederation, meeting in Geneva. Mr. Adams represented the United States.

In the end, after long deliberations the International Tribunal awarded the United States $15,500,000.

Lord Chief Justice Cockburn, the British arbitrator, went home in a towering rage, saying good-bye to nobody. (This high placed Englishman was famous for his bad temper and his bad manners.) The *Times* of London, usually anti-American, was one of the papers that thought the award fair.

Gettysburg and Vicksburg should have ended the war; instead the Confederacy held out for nearly two more years—a ruined country now, without necessities. Even salt was scarce, clothes and shoes unobtainable, her ports blockaded, her railroads destroyed, half her states either conquered or isolated from the rest.

Confederate bonds, which had a brisk sale in England and France, sank from $95. to $37; a motion actually pending in Parliament for the recognition of the Confederacy was hastily withdrawn at the news of Gettysburg and Vicksburg.

Lincoln made Grant a Major General and put him in command of all Federal troops west of the Appalachians.

After the above successful battles the Federal Government adopted a new strategy, called the Anaconda Plan. The Union Armies were to encircle the South and slowly squeeze. Sherman's direction was to be eastward, while the Army of the Potomac was to move south, towards Richmond, under Grant.

Chattanooga and Chickamauga are names forever linked, like Tweedledee and Tweedledum, in the history books. The former is a large Tennessee town on the border of Georgia, and the latter a creek in the mountains of Georgia, a few miles over the line.

Braxton Bragg, the most fierce sounding and fierce looking of the Confederate

GEN. COLQUET. GEN. A. P. ARCHER. LT.-GEN. RICH. S. EWELL. MAJ.-GEN. J. E. B. STUART.

BRIG.-GEN. FITZHUGH LEE. B.-G. WADE HAMPTON. LT.-G. JAMES LONGSTREET. B.-GEN. ROGER HANSON.

A Muster of Confederate Generals.

generals, who had been driven out of Kentucky after winning it, by General Rosecrans, withdrew to a mountainous retreat in the northwest corner of Georgia, Rosecrans in pursuit. At Chickamauga Creek Bragg suddenly turned and Rosecrans' troops were routed. Bragg was the meanest and most hated general in either army. Perhaps this is why Fort Bragg, North Carolina, is named in his memory. Samuel Eliot Morison attributed the general's disposition to dyspepsia.

It would have been another Union defeat except for General George H. Thomas, who was a Virginian, loyal to the Union. He kept Bragg's superior forces

MAJ.-GEN. N. P. BANKS.   MAJ.-GEN. FRANZ SIGEL.   MAJ.-G. G B. McCLELLAN.   MAJ.-G. WM. S. ROSECRANS.

MAJ.-G. WM. T. SHERMAN.   MAJ. GEN. O. M. MITCHELL.   MAJ.-GEN. A. E. BURNSIDE.   MAJ.-G. ULYSSES S. GRANT.

A Muster of Union Generals.

at bay all one afternoon and earned the proud title, "The Rock of Chickamauga." Rosecrans was replaced by Thomas and reinforcements arrived from the victorious armies on the Mississippi.

Grant appeared at Chattanooga on November 23, and began a three day battle to dislodge Bragg's forces from the strong positions they occupied across the Tennessee River. Here comes into note another evocative name forever linked to this fratricidal war—Lookout Mountain. Bragg and his men were driven down the mountain and away.

13   GRANT AND LINCOLN IN COMMAND

Oh you are not one of those who linger on the brink.
—Dostoevsky, *The Possessed.*

On March 1, 1864, a grand soirée was held at the White House in honor of Ulysses S. Grant. Lincoln had summoned him to Washington to receive his commission as Lieutenant-General of all the armies of the United States. In some quarters dismay was expressed at this choice. Though an educated man and a graduate of West Point, Grant did not have a soldierly air. Instead of embodying the "chest up" military ideal, he slouched about, half the time his uniform was buttoned up wrong, and he *drank.* Lincoln's reply to this shocking intelligence is well known: "Find out what he drinks and give it to the other generals."

Grant gave Sherman command of the Armies of the West (Sherman was still at Chattanooga.) The Anaconda Plan went into action. Early in May the two Generals were at it.

Sherman started on his "Atlanta Campaign" from Rocky Face Ridge, Georgia, with 100,000 men. Grant with an equal number headed south of the Rappahannock to the area around Chancellorsville where Hooker met disastrous defeat a year before. This section of the country was known as The Wilderness.

The Battle of the Wilderness raged for two days, a time of great confusion in that tangled terrain, and the first time that the two generals, Lee and Grant, were pitted against each other. Lee had 60,000 troops.

At the end of the engagement the North had sustained 18,000 casualties, the Confederates far less. But unlike McClellan, Burnside and Hooker, Grant pushed on. He moved his army to the southeast, hoping to outflank Lee.

Lee rushed his divisions in the same direction, to Grant's right, and earthworks were quickly thrown up around Spottsylvania Court House, and the battle of that name went on for six days.

Twelve thousand Union men died, and the Confederate lines still held. Nothing could make Grant flinch. "I propose to fight it out on this line if it takes all summer," he wired Hooker and pressed on to Cold Harbor, only nine miles from Richmond. Once more Grant found the Confederate in strong positions. At dawn he attacked and was thrown back with heavy losses.

There had now been 60,000 casualties in less than a month, and in the North dismay was universal. Grant was called a butcher; there were demands that he be removed from his command, which Lincoln did not heed.

For a time it was more cheerful in the South. The movement of the war opponents in the North grew stronger. Their aim was to make peace with the Confederacy and shatter the Lincoln Goverment. Richmond was keenly appreciative of these endeavors. Agents of the Confederacy were busy in Canada, too, engaged in deft negotiations to influence Northern peace sentiments.

There were formidable peace movements both North and South. Those defeatists in the North were called Copperheads. A negotiated peace was desired by many, both North and South; people were surprisingly outspoken, and neither Lincoln nor Davis could do much about it. There were too many. In fact they were treasonous, particularly in Ohio, Indiana and Illinois. General Burnside, in a general order, declared that sympathy for the enemy would not be allowed in his jurisdiction.

The most prominent of the Ohio Copperheads, Clement L. Vallandigham, arrested for his inflammatory rhetoric during a campaign speech, was tried by a military tribunal and sentenced to confinement in the military prison, Fort Warren, for the duration of the war.

Here Lincoln saw the chance for a little fun—which no one could begrudge him! He altered the sentence to banishment to the Confederacy, whither Mr. Vallandigham was escorted in May 1863 and left securely inside the Confederate military lines.

After Cold Harbor Grant moved southeast still trying to outflank Lee, who had fought without a single reserve regiment, while Grant's army was larger than at the start of the offensive. Lee was suffering the attritions of this terrible war while Grant had huge numbers of men to draw from.

Grant struck south of the James River towards the city of Petersburg, an important railroad junction, and Lee had to rush his troops to that city. The Confederates dug in, and here began another siege. Long stretched-out trenches and breastworks almost surrounded the city and Grant gradually, inexorably, tightened his Anaconda squeeze. Trench warfare thus began.

Lee was caught in the squeeze. If he moved, he would be abandoning Richmond.

The siege of Petersburg began the first of July, 1864, and continued till the second of April, 1865, a good nine months. "The immobility of trench warfare!"[1] But during this time there was much activity in other places.

Sherman encountered opposition on his march from Chattanooga towards Atlanta, which he finally reached on the 28th of July, 1864. Here began another siege, interspersed with cavalry raids and skirmishes in various places with colorful names, with which the South is so plentifully supplied: North Anna, Totopotomoy Creek, Jerusalem Plank Road, Peach Tree Creek, Big Shanty, Altoona Pass, Gilgal Church and Dinwiddie Court House are a few of them.

Lincoln had been nominated for a second term at Baltimore on June 6. The Republican Party was renamed the Union Party to win the votes of the war Democrats. This was while Grant was stalemated at Petersburg and Sherman was encountering difficulties. By July 1, Washington itself was threatened. The Confederate

General Jubal A. Early raided Harper's Ferry and pressed on to the very District of Columbia, at Fort Stevens. By August, Lincoln thought it very probable that his Administration was doomed due to the many military defeats.

The Democrats, meeting in Chicago in August, nominated General McClellan on a platform demanding that immediate efforts be made for the cessation of hostilities after four years of failure to restore the Union by "the experiment of war."

McClellan himself repudiated a plank that called the war a failure, and though not one of great sensibility, he said, "I could not look my old soldiers in the face if I ran on such a platform."

Admiral Farragut, the victor of New Orleans, had stifled blockade-running in the Gulf of Mexico except at its chief source, the city of Mobile, Alabama. Mobile Bay was strongly defended by two forts, Gaines and Morgan, a double row of "torpedoes," as mines were then called, in the channel, and a flotilla commanded by Admiral Franklin Buchanan. When Farragut's ships approached the bay, the lookout on his flagship *Hartford* spotted the torpedoes, but the dauntless Admiral climbed high in the rigging on his 63 year old legs to get a better view and shouted, "Damn the torpedoes—full speed ahead!" and "Damn the torpedoes!" entered the lexicons of familiar quotations.

After a fierce battle between opposing gunboats and sloops of war, Admiral Buchanan's flagship, the iron-clad ram *Tennessee,* was put out of commission, Buchanan was taken prisoner with a broken leg, and Fort Morgan surrendered to a troop assault. The city of Mobile was in the hands of the Union, which now controlled the Gulf of Mexico. With the Confederates' last stronghold on the Gulf of Mexico gone, and the fall of Atlanta to Sherman ten days later, the carpet was pulled out from under the Democrats, their peace party, and the ambitious McClellan.

Lincoln won with an electoral vote of 212 to 21. He carried every state but New Jersey, Delaware and Kentucky, but his popular vote was only 400,000 more than McClellan's.

Though Lincoln appears to have wanted Hannibal Hamlin, his first Vice President, on the ticket again, Andrew Johnson was nominated for the position. A strong Unionist from Tennessee, Johnson was the only member of Congress from a seceding state who remained in his seat in Washington, and Lincoln had appointed him Military Governor of Tennessee.

Sherman, having taken Atlanta, set out for Savannah on October 17, on his unopposed "March to the Sea." This "March" is a sorry episode in the history of the Civil War. Sherman had 60,000 men, the distance to Savannah was 300 miles, and the March took two months.

The General believed in the scorched earth policy, the object being to destroy anything useful to the Confederate Army. His men, as they went along, helped themselves to everything, and an army of camp-followers, freed slaves and bummers of every description completed the havoc. Discipline was lax. A stretch of country sixty miles wide was devastated. Public buildings and factories were burned, railroads torn up, stores of cotton destroyed, 10,000 horses and mules seized, as well as all available food: beef cattle, chickens, ducks, turkeys, pigs, corn and sweet potatoes. A stretch of Georgia was laid waste that took years to recover.

Yet "outrages on persons were surprisingly few, and on women none."[2] The looting of private houses was forbidden, and it was mostly the work of the bummers. The soldiers were having a great time—no fighting, succulent food, and the weather was delightful.

A delegation from the Confederate Government, headed by the Vice President, Alexander H. Stephens, who had never approved of secession in the first place, secretly met Lincoln and his Secretary of War Seward, aboard the *River Queen*, at Hampton Roads on February 3. They had come to discuss peace terms. Lincoln had known Alexander Stephens since they served together in Congress. He watched the little man divest himself of his greatcoat and numerous scarfs and shawls, and later told Grant, using a thoroughly Lincolnian metaphor, that it was "the smallest nubbin for so much shucking that he had ever seen."

But the conference was a small nubbin too. Lincoln's two objectives—the restoration of the Union and the abolition of slavery—for which the war was being fought were rejected as "unconditional submission to the mercy of conquerors," and the commission went home.

14   THE PHANTOM PEERAGE

Many of the people of the South believed they were descended from Cavaliers, and perhaps some of them were. But Webster gives several definitions of this word. "A mounted soldier of rank; a knight," is the first; another is, "One of the court party in the time of Charles I as contrasted with a roundhead, or adherent of Parliament; a Royalist." Thus everyone was a royalist, a cavalier, and wore his hair long, or a wig, who wasn't a roundhead and wore his hair short. He could be a yeoman, a cobbler, a tinsmith. But how much nicer to be descended from a knight than a tinsmith!

Thus developed "that enormous peerage which largely populated the Confederacy,"[1]—due to the confusion in the meaning of the word "cavalier." The South developed a superiority complex. Northerners with their undistinguished lineage— mere yeomen—were looked upon with some disdain, and this attitude probably prolonged the conflict.

President Davis said he had no common country with the Yankees (Yankees meant all Northerners in the South), and General Lee was for continuing the war. But with what would Lee continue the war? The South was bankrupt, much of the country a wasteland. Nothing functioned, the railroads were demolished, the land uncultivated, torn up with bloody conflicts. The supply of fighting men was getting low. The industrial demands of the war could not be met without employing the slaves, but how? Purchase? Conscription? Temporary impressment? The plantation owners were not patriotic enough to like this idea.

A remarkable fact is that nowhere did the slaves attempt to revolt, though when Union troops appeared many of them laid down their tools and quietly slipped away.

The women of the Confederacy were heroic. Those accustomed to a life of ease were suddenly deprived of everything. To the poor this was less of a shock, for they had never had anything anyway. But husbands, sons, brothers, fathers— they were gone. To find food for their children and themselves was the concern of all women of all degrees, and this was coupled with anxiety, fear, and the heart-break of losing their men. The blockade destroyed communications. This failure, a ruined transportation system and the evils of speculators were among the factors that broke the Confederacy. The shortage of medicine was one of the severest features of southern life.

There were only two foundries in the entire South capable of casting the heavy ordnance needed to wage war. Powder mills and gun factories were few. Indeed, the South had been doomed from the start. In view of this, why did the powers hang on so long, bringing more and more misery to the people? Why did the high-minded Lee not see?

The Confederate press began battering away at President Davis and his conduct of the war. A movement, begun in an editorial in the Charleston *Mercury*, advocated that Lee take charge of the Government and "save the Confederacy." This did not daunt President Davis.

Three days after the abortive Peace Conference on board the *River Queen,* a great public meeting was held at Richmond, and Davis made an eloquent speech. He urged more drastic conscription laws, though most able-bodied men were already under arms, and cried, "Let us then unite our hands and our hearts, lock our shields together. . . . Before another summer solstice falls upon us it will be the enemy that will be asking us for conferences."

He had no grounds for such an assertion. Like other leaders of lost causes he was unrealistic, and blind to the enormous handwriting on the wall.

On the 10th of January, 1865, Sherman invaded the Carolinas as Cornwallis had done in 1780. On the 17th of February he seized Columbia, South Carolina, and the Confederates fled Charleston, where all the shooting started.

On the 4th of March Lincoln was inaugurated for his second term. It was a cloudy, gusty day. On the east steps of the Capitol Lincoln delivered his address, known as "the Second Inaugural." It was short, he explained, since the progress of arms "upon which all else depends" was as well known to the public as to himself. "With high hopes for the future," he said, "no prediction in regard to it is ventured." No one had expected the war would be of such magnitude and duration.

The final paragraph of this short address, voicing hope for a just and lasting peace, opens with a phrase that has become part of the language, so well is it known:

With malice towards none; with charity for all; with firmness in the right, as God gives us to see the right, let us strive on to finish the work we are in; to bind up the nation's wounds; to care for him who shall have borne the battle, and for his widow and his orphan—to do all which may achieve and cherish a just and lasting peace, among ourselves, and with all nations.

The radicals in Congress did not like this non-vindictive and noble address. They had plenty of malice towards a great many people.

Sherman, inexorably advancing from Savannah, reached the town of Goldsboro, North Carolina, on March 23, on a direct line for Richmond. The Confederate troops around Petersburg gave way to the vastly superior forces of Grant, and Lee desperately withdrew to the Richmond and Danville railroad. Lee sent word to President Davis that Richmond must be evacuated.

Davis, with a trainload of civil servants and Government papers (vast quantities had been hastily destroyed) boarded the train for Danville. At this place he issued a last Address to the People of the Confederate States. It revealed the fact that the man could no longer think clearly. Confident as ever, he declared that the Confederacy would prevail; even if the Army was obliged to withdraw further, it would be but temporarily. "Again and again we will return until the baffled and exhausted enemy shall abandon in despair the endless and impossible task of making slaves of a people resolved to be free!"

But he lacked the sinews of war—and who is talking about slaves?

15   LINCOLN IN RICHMOND

Grant's headquarters were now at City Point on the James River, below Richmond, and the General invited the President to visit him. The *River Queen* dropped anchor there on March 21. Accompanying the President were his wife and his 11 year old son Tad. Robert Lincoln, made a captain on his staff by Grant, arrived next morning before breakfast.

Abraham Lincoln, by George P. A. Healy, 1869. Reproduced by permission of the White House Collection.

There was much activity on the river, transports and gunboats unloading supplies and removing the wounded and the prisoners.

On arriving at City Point, Lincoln took time to endorse Stanton's order of exercises to be observed at Fort Sumter on the fourth anniversary of its surrender, and corrected Stanton out of the top of his head on the exact date, which was the 13th, not the 14th. Major (now Colonel) Anderson was to raise the Stars and Stripes over the fort on the fourth anniversary of the day he had been obliged to haul them down.

A grand party of important personages was to attend the exercises: an Admiral, the Adjutant General, and various others, including the preposterous Reverend Henry Ward Beecher (brother of Harriet Beecher Stowe), whose carryings-on with a parishioner caused a sensational scandal that rocked the nation in 1875. (The nation was easily rocked then.) The Reverend Henry Ward Beecher, Congregationalist, was the most prestigious man of God in Protestant North America, and his Plymouth Church in Brooklyn, the most prestigious church. A lengthy church trial (several months) ended in a miraculous verdict: the Reverend Henry was found not guilty but his fellow-sinner Elizabeth Tilton (wife of Theodore Tilton, editor of *The Independent*, a liberal Congregational weekly, and close friend of the Reverend Henry) was kicked out of the church. The Apple Theory, dating from Genesis, was still alive and kicking in 1875, though not as impartially. Adam was expelled from Eden along with Eve, but the Reverend Henry remained in his Eden unscathed. He had declared at his trial that he was innocent. At this, Susan B. Anthony, who was a close friend and confidant of Elizabeth Tilton, observed, "If God ever struck anyone dead for telling a lie, He would have struck then." So great was the man's prestige and renown that it was noised about that President Lincoln used to sneak over to Brooklyn to consult the great and holy man, though nobody ever saw him sneak.

Lincoln stayed at City Point until April 8, but Mrs. Lincoln returned to Washington in a week, leaving little Tad with his father. The President was in almost hourly communication with Grant on the progress of the war and forwarded the dispatches to Washington. The map on the table in Lincoln's tent, at Colonel Bower's headquarters, was covered with black and red pins. A war correspondent, Sylvanus Cadwallader came from Grant on April 1 with a number of captured Confederate flags as a gift from the General. "This means victory! This *is* victory!" exclaimed Lincoln.

On the same day Lee's resistance crumbled before the hundreds of guns of Grant's front, and he and his men abandoned Petersburg and Richmond after the battle of Five Forks when the Confederate line was broken. The next day Union troops occupied Richmond and by 9 A.M. Grant telegraphed the President inviting him to meet him there. The city had surrendered to General Weitzel.

Early in the morning of April 3, the *River Queen* moved up the James, preceded by a tug and followed by Admiral Porter's flagship and the transport *Columbus*, with a cavalry escort for the President. But as the channel was blocked further up the river, the President transferred to a barge "rowed by twelve husky sailors."

Lincoln entered Richmond, holding his little son Tad (Thomas) by the hand. He was accompanied by Admiral Porter and three other officers and an escort of ten seamen armed with carbines. They headed for General Weitzel's headquarters.

The city had been put to the torch by the fleeing Confederates and two sections of it were in ruins. Walls tottered, stark chimneys marked the spots where warehouses

"Abraham Lincoln Entering Richmond, April 3rd, 1865."
Engraved by J.C. Buttre after the drawing by L. Hollis.
Reproduced by permission of the National Portrait Gallery, Smithsonian Institution, Washington, D.C.

stood a few hours before. Broken glass covered the streets and the stench of smouldering bales of cotton filled the air.

A Yankee newspaper correspondent saw the almost unnoticed President and said to a group of blacks engaged in clearing the street, "Do you know that man?"

"Who is that man, master?"

"Call no man master," said the Yankee. "That man set you free. That is Abraham Lincoln."

The blacks rushed forward crying, "Savior! My Jesus! There is the great Messiah!" One old man fell on his knees, caught the President's hand and covered it with kisses. Abraham Lincoln took off his stovepipe hat.

As Lincoln walked through those ruined streets, gazing about him, the news spread and crowds were seen approaching, a throng of black people, slaves suddenly and at last made free! Bowing, laughing, weeping, they followed the President. Faces peered out of windows, men climbed telegraph poles for a better view. No one yelled, no one cheered. Only the blacks capered joyously.

Mr. Linthicum was a Maryland planter and an enlightened man. He freed his slaves before the war, giving each a cabin and a piece of land. Years later he saw an old black man in tatters walking along the road, and recognized him.

"Tom," he said, "you were better dressed when I was your master."

"Yes, Massa," the old ex-slave replied, "but freedom in rags is sweet."

Followed by the capering blacks, Lincoln walked on with a set face.

General Weitzel was occupying the house Jefferson Davis had so lately vacated. Lincoln looked about with interest, sat down and said, "I wonder if I could get a glass of water."

Later he was taken to see Libby Prison and Castle Thunder, where Federal prisoners of war had suffered and died. When an officer said Jefferson Davis should be hanged, Lincoln said, "Judge not, that ye be not judged." When General Weitzel asked him how the people of Richmond should be treated, he said, "If I were in your place I'd let 'em up easy."

He could scarcely pardon Jefferson Davis, he said, but few secessionists need fear punishment at his hands.

Lincoln returned to City Point and anxiously awaited news of Lee's activities.

Lee, short on rations, spent two days foraging, during which time Sheridan seized the Danville Railroad. Lee was blocked in that direction. Another engagement, at Saylor's Creek, caught a corps commanded by General Elwell. Lee had now lost half of his army and most of his wagons.

At this point Lincoln received word that his Secretary of State had suffered a carriage accident and was severely injured. The *River Queen* started for Washington, arriving early in the evening of April 9.

The President went to Seward's bedside. The injured man, in great pain with a broken jaw and a broken arm, his face encased in an iron frame, whispered, "You are back from Richmond."

"Yes," said Lincoln, "and I think we are near the end at last."

Lee's Army was making its way westward. Ragged and half starved, the men pushed on, heartened by the news that there were provisions on a train at Amelia Court House. But when they reached there they found the train had been sent on to Richmond, provisions and all. With half rations of "green corn and roots," they started on towards Lynchburg.

At Appomattox Court House, Lee, cut off on three sides from the rest of his army, and with even the green corn and roots now gone, received a message from Grant, appealing to him to realize his position was hopeless; and Lee faced the fact.

A nearby farmhouse was commandeered for the meeting of Grant and Lee to discuss surrender terms, and whose house should it be? Why, Mr. Wilmer McLean's—he who had moved from Manassas to escape the alarms of war! Thus the Civil War began and ended in houses owned by this gentleman, two hundred miles apart.

The scene of the surrender of Lee is part of American folklore. It has been depicted in the cinema, on stage, and in (bad) paintings: Lee wearing a full dress uniform with sash and carrying a jewel-studded sword; Grant in a soldier's blouse, buttoned up wrong, or unbuttoned, casual to the last. The picture is familiar to all.

It was the moment for both men to rise to a great occasion, and both of them did.

The meeting began with a little chit-chat, to put the Generals at ease. They spoke of the Mexican War of twenty years before, in which both had served. Then they sat down, and Grant, intent like Lincoln on peace and reconciliation, wrote out his terms of surrender.

Officers and men to be paroled, under obligation not to take up arms against the United States. Arms, artillery and public property to be returned to the proper Union officials, side arms of officers, and their swords and baggage to be retained. Likewise horses and mules. "They will be needed for the spring ploughing," Grant said, "to put in the crops to carry themselves and their families through the next winter."

Grant supplied Lee's starving army with food, but for the poor horses there was nothing.

Cheers and the firing of salutes started in some of the commands were quickly stopped by Grant. "The war is over," he said. "The rebels are our countrymen again."

The next day, as the Confederate troops marched out to stack their arms and furled battle-flags, the Union division lined up to receive them and on Grant's orders, snapped from "order arms" to the "carry" position, the marching salute. All through the negotiations Grant displayed a magnanimity and delicacy unexpected of victors.

"This was the greatest day in the career of General Grant," wrote Sir Winston Churchill, "and stands high in the story of the United States."

That night, when the President returned from his Secretary of State's bedside, a telegram from Grant was delivered to him: "General Lee surrendered the Army of Northern Virginia on terms proposed by myself." Grant included a full account. He had acted on Lincoln's instructions to be generous.

At dawn next day the people of Washington were roused from their beds by the booming of cannon. Bells pealed, flags broke out everywhere. All business was suspended and crowds converged on the White House.

Lincoln appeared briefly at a window. Little Tad wildly waved a captured Confederate flag. The President, happy but looking exhausted, promised a speech the following night.

"Emancipation." Reproduced from the Collections of the Library of Congress.

The Surrender of Lee. Reproduced from the Collections of the Library of Congress.

The President had a great fondness for the song "Dixie" "and now that the Union has rightly captured it," he asked the band to play it.

"I wish I was in de land ob cotton,
Old times dar am not forgotten!"

The band played it with a will. (This song was composed by a Northerner, Daniel Decatur Emmett of Ohio, for a minstrel show in 1859. When it was appropriated by the Confederacy during the war, the Union composer was dismayed.)

16   THE UNSPEAKABLE AT FORD'S

It is some dream that on the deck
You've fallen cold and dead.
—Walt Whitman, *O Captain! My Captain!*

The next night, as he had promised, the President gave a speech. He was greatly distressed at the spirit of vindictiveness all about him. The men of his own party seemed bent on revenge against the South, and he wanted, above all, to "restore the practical relations" between the "seceded states, so-called" and the Union. This was not the sort of speech his audience wanted to hear, now in the high tide of victory. The speech fell flat and Lincoln was upset.

On the morning of April 14, Lincoln paid his usual visit to the War Department. The Secret Service had been reporting to Stanton that there were rumors of plots to assassinate the President, the members of his Cabinet, and General Grant. Stanton protested to the President against his announced visit to the theatre that night to see Laura Keene, the English actress, and her company in a performance of the (perfectly dreadful) comedy *Our American Cousin.* Lincoln said that General Grant had backed out of his invitation and he must find someone else. Again Stanton urged the President to give up the whole thing, but if he wouldn't to have a competent guard. (Things were extraordinarily relaxed and informal in those days.)

But when the President asked Stanton if he might borrow Major Eckert, Chief of the War Department Telegraph Staff, for this purpose, "because I have seen him break five pokers over his arm," Stanton said he had important work to do and could not be spared. Lincoln replied, "Well, I will ask the Major myself."

"You can do Stanton's work tomorrow, and Mrs. Lincoln and I want you with us."

It is hard to believe, but this invitation from the President of the U.S., commander-in-chief of all the armed forces, including Major Eckert himself, was turned down by that military man, who gave the same excuse Stanton had given—important work to be done. The nature of this important work has never come to light.

Later that morning General Grant paid a visit to the President and his Cabinet. The men listened attentively to his account of the final drive against Lee, and the particulars of the surrender. Lincoln spoke kindly of Lee, his officers, and the men who had fought so bravely for a cause they held so dear. He hoped there would be no repercussions, no bloody work; enough blood had been shed.

After the meeting broke up Grant lingered behind to explain to the President why he and Mrs. Grant felt obliged to decline the President's invitation to the theater. They were anxious to see their children at Long Branch, New Jersey, and the train left in the afternoon. This seems like a great breach of protocol on Grant's part; it was the second refusal of Lincoln's invitation by a member of his Army.

Another reason may have been that Mrs. Lincoln, who at times appeared quite out of control, had accused Mrs. Grant publicly at City Point of scheming to supplant her in the White House. She had made a scene. She often made scenes. She flew into jealous tirades when the President was polite to women. This was a further great burden of Lincoln's. Ladies were anxious to avoid Mrs. Lincoln. Several other couples, invited to replace the Grants, had found themselves unable to accept too.

The Lincolns set out for the theater a little after 8 o'clock. They stopped at the residence of Senator Ira Harris, whose daughter Clara and stepson, Major H. R. Rathbone, had finally accepted the Lincolns' invitation.

The Lincolns' coachman, Charles Forbes, drew up to the entrance of Ford's Theatre at half past eight. The play was in progress. As the presidential party appeared in the upper right hand flag-draped double box—two boxes thrown into one by the removal of a partition for the occasion—the play stopped and the audience rose and cheered.

The President bowed, and the presidential party was seated. Miss Harris and Major Rathbone sat together on a small sofa on the right side of the box, Mrs. Lincoln took the chair at the center, and the President sat down on an upholstered rocking chair especially installed for him, further back at the left. The play proceeded.

A chair had been placed in the corridor outside the box for the accommodation of a White House guard, a rather shiftless member of the metropolitan police force, who for some reason had been selected by Mrs. Lincoln to accompany the party to the theater as a guard for the President. Since he couldn't follow the play from there, he moved off. No one noticed that a small peephole had been bored in the door of the box, nor that a two-inch strip of plaster had been chipped away from the opposite brick wall of the narrow corridor, as though for the purpose of holding a prop against the door.

Vice President Andrew Johnson was living at the Kirkwood House at the corner of 12th Street and Pennsylvania Avenue, two blocks from Ford's Theatre. That afternoon a flashy young actor entered the hotel lobby and asked for Mr. Johnson. Told he was not in his apartment, the disappointed visitor handed the clerk a card on which was written:

> *Don't wish to disturb you. Are you at home?*
> *J. Wilkes Booth*

At about 10 P.M. this flashy actor entered Ford's Theatre, with which he was familiar having often played there, mounted to the balcony, went down the narrow corridor to the door of the President's loge, which was unattended, entered, and shot the President in the back of the head with a derringer as he sat watching the play. Lincoln slumped forward. There was laughter at this moment and few heard the sound.

The other occupants of the box looked around and saw the intruder, who said in an ordinary voice, "Sic semper tyrannis!" He then strode to the front of the box between the President's chair and the one occupied by Mrs. Lincoln. Major Rathbone jumped up and tried to gapple with him. Booth dropped his derringer and pulled out a knife with which he slashed the major's left arm to the bone. Nobody knew what was happening. Mrs. Lincoln looked at her husband who seemed to be dozing.

Booth said loudly, "Revenge for the South!" and proceeded to climb over the edge of the box, turned his back to the audience, and began to let himself down over the side. As he turned to jump to the stage the spur on his right boot caught on a banner decorating the front of the box. He fell and broke his left foot just above the instep. He got up and began limping across the stage.

The actor who was alone on the stage, Harry Hawk by name, stood stupified. Laura Keene, waiting in the green room, came out to see why the noise on the stage had suddenly stopped. Booth brushed against her and she recognized him.

The audience was bewildered by what was going on when they began to realize that this was not part of the play. A piercing scream came from the State Box. It was Mrs. Lincoln. Clara Harris was now leaning over the box crying, "Water!" The audience at last was roused. Major Rathbone, pointing to the wings where Booth had vanished, shouted, "Stop that man!" Another terrible scream from Mrs. Lincoln.

A man stood up in the orchestra and cried, "For God's sake what has happened?"

Miss Harris continued to beg, somewhat hysterically, for water. A man's voice from the box—Major Rathbone's—cried, "He has shot the President!"

Then there was bedlam in the theatre. "It can't be true! Oh no!" The aisles were crowded now. A few women fainted. Those who got out of the theatre shouted the news. "The President has been shot! He is lying dead in the State Box!" People came running from every direction. Harry Hawk stood on the stage and wept.

Major Rathbone, after some difficulty with the door in the corridor which led to the box, and which Booth had barracaded, got it open. Many were crowded against it, but the Major demanded that only doctors be admitted. A bewhiskered young man said he was a doctor and the crowd pushed him forward into the corridor. Doctor Charles Leale, assistant surgeon of the United States Volunteers, was 23. The young doctor had long worshipped Abraham Lincoln, collected photographs of him, and had come to the theatre to catch a glimpse of him. He now took complete charge of his dying idol.

Mrs. Lincoln, pressing her head against her husband's chest, cried, "Oh Doctor! Is he dead? O my dear husband!" Dr. Leale assured the First Lady he would do what he could, and motioned to some men who had crowded into the box to remove her. She was led back to the sofa where Clara Harris sat and held her hand.

Leale thought the President had been stabbed. Seeing some soldiers peering in he told them to lift the President to the floor. They did so and stepped away.

Another medical man, Dr. Charles Taft, was lifted into the box from the stage. Though senior to Leale, he placed himself at Leale's disposal. Leale raised the President into a half-sitting position and Dr. Taft held him while Leale sought the wound. He found the President had been shot behind the left ear. "His wound is mortal," he said to Dr. Taft, and to a Dr. King who had joined them.

Laura Keene had come into the box and was sitting with Mrs. Lincoln and Miss Harris. Though Mrs. Lincoln seemed not to hear Dr. Leale's words, the two other ladies did. The President was lying flat on his back, there being no pillow, and Miss Keene came over and asked the doctor if she could hold the President's head. Laura Keene sat on the floor of the box and held Lincoln's head in her lap.

As it would be fatal to move the President as far as the White House—Leale feared he would die on the way—he was carried across the street to a house owned by a tailor, William Petersen, laid on a bed much too short for him in a small rear bedroom which was nine by fifteen feet in size; and here he died without regaining consciousness at 7:22 next morning.

Thus perished the only man who could have saved the prostrate South.

Prints of the death of Lincoln depict all the men who put in an appearance that terrible night at one time or another, surrounding the bed, and the tiny room has taken on the dimensions of a ballroom. The distraught Mrs. Lincoln, was attended by the Misses Keene and Harris. Robert Lincoln was summoned and sat with them and the Major, or stood at the head of the bed looking down at his father's face. Major Rathbone finally fainted from loss of blood and was carried away.

There are many stories about Lincoln's death. Stanton's classic epitaph, "Now he belongs to the Ages," supposed to have been uttered as Lincoln breathed his last, seemed not to have been heard by anyone present, though several people were busily recording everything that was said. Stanton himself saw to it that his beautiful words were taken down by Dr. Taft—who had assisted Dr. Leale in the theatre. Taft was an Army surgeon and was obeying his boss. The famous line may have been an afterthought, but it is a very good line.

Many farmers in the West testified that the moon that night emerged from the clouds blood red.

Booth's name as the assassin was first mentioned by someone on the crowded stage while Drs. Leale and Taft were attending the President in the State Box. He was too well known not to be recognized. Soon his name was being shouted in the street. "Booth did it! The actor Booth!"

Secretary Stanton, who had suddenly become a dictator, gave the orders, and everyone from Vice President Johnson to Cabinet ministers who had gathered in the Petersen house humbly obeyed. Stanton convened a special court of inquiry right there, and Chief Justice Cartter administered the oath to the witnesses, including Harry Hawk who had been alone on the stage when Booth limped hurriedly by. "I believe to the best of my knowledge it was John Wilkes Booth," he said. All said, "Booth."

A bright young fellow, Corporal James Tanner, who could take shorthand, was pressed into service to take testimony. "In fifteen minutes I had testimony enough to hang Wilkes Booth higher than Haman ever hung," he said. (The Corporal knew his Old Testament.)

Yet no orders went out from the Petersen house to apprehend Booth.

At 1:30 A.M. Stanton wrote his first report to Major General Dix in New York, and made no mention of Booth. At 3 A.M. he sent a second report to Dix, this time stating, "Investigation strongly indicates J. Wilkes Booth as the assassin of the President."

There are many mysteries about the murder of Lincoln that have never been solved in over a hundred years of research. Why the 4 or 5 hours' delay in making public the name of the assassin, when it was known within a few minutes of the crime? Why were all the telegraph lines leading out of Washington grounded fifteen minutes after the crime and remained so for two hours? Why, though the city buzzed with rumors of an assassination plot against the President, and Stanton had urged him not to go to the theatre that night, did he refuse point blank to let Major Thomas T. Eckert, his chief aide, accompany the President to the theatre with the excuse that he had important work to do? Seeing Lincoln was determined to go to the theatre anyway, why did Stanton, the Secretary of War, not order an adequate bodyguard to accompany him? Why did General Grant, the nation's hero, announced to appear at the theatre that night, suddenly change his mind and leave the city to see his children in New Jersey? Why was the irresponsible member of the Metropolitan police, and known to be so, John F. Parker, who left his post in front of the door to the box to which he was assigned, so that he could follow the play, never arrested, let alone questioned? There are a host of unanswered questions here.

Stanton believed the murder was part of a vast plot and that Washington was teeming with secret Confederate agents who would rise at a given signal and assassinate everybody; he was less interested in capturing Booth. He was wrong.

The murder was part of a conspiracy hatched in the boarding house of a Mrs. Surratt in H Street, not only to assassinate Lincoln, but all his Cabinet. Another of the conspirators, Lewis Paine, entered Secretary Seward's house that night under pretext of delivering medicine, wounded Seward's son, Frederick, and stabbed a male nurse through the lungs. He struck Seward twice in the face and throat, inflicting serious wounds, but the iron frame that encased his broken jaw saved his life. The assassin then escaped. Others marked for death that night were not attacked.

Andrew Johnson was sworn in as seventeenth President of the United States at the Kirkwood House next morning.

The aftermath of that tragic night is full of mysteries too.

Booth escaped on a little mare that was tethered in an alley behind the theatre and took the obvious road to Port Tobacco in southern Maryland, accompanied by David Herold, a member of the conspiratorial brotherhood. Herold was fresh from lending moral support to Lewis Paine by waiting outside in the street while Paine made his savage attacks on Secretary Seward and the others in Seward's house. The two were on their way to what they thought would be safety in the South, but Booth's broken foot caused such pain that they left the direct route and appeared at the house of a Dr. Mudd near Bryantown, who, roused from his sleep, attended the broken foot and applied splints. Later Booth and Herold were pursued by a huge, disorganized posse that combed every possible place all over the region, including swamps, except the place where Booth was most likely to be. He was discovered eleven days later hiding in the tobacco barn of a Mr. Garrett near Point Conway at the head of the Rappahanock River, having arrived there with the help of various people along the way. When Booth refused to come out of the barn, and since he was brandishing firearms, the barn was set afire and he was finally shot through a crack in the wall. Even the one who fired the shot that tradition claims was an "eccentric sergeant" named Boston Corbett is disputed. Here a question of rewards color the picture.

Some of those associated with the night of Lincoln's murder had bad luck thereafter. Finally Robert Lincoln was obliged to commit his mother to an asylum, and when released, spent the rest of her life swathed in black in a darkened room. Major Rathbone married Clara Harris, went insane, killed her, and spent his life in an asylum. Dr. Mudd was tried and convicted of "conspiracy" because Booth's boot, which the doctor had to cut away to apply the splints, was found in his house. He was sentenced to prison in the Dry Tortugas, off Key West, but was pardoned in 1869 after tending prisoners in a yellow fever epidemic when the prison doctor died. There was conflicting evidence of whether he knew Booth or not, but even if he did, it is not likely that Booth confided to everybody he knew that he had plans to assassinate the President. Laura Keene, the Englishwoman who rose nobly to the exigencies of that terrible night died at Montclair, New Jersey in 1874, age 47.

As for the remaining accused conspirators, eight were given a mock trial. Secretary Stanton, who had no authority to do so, ordered them sheathed in masks, bound, gagged and blindfolded. They could neither see nor speak. The Constitution was at this moment a dead document. What was Stanton afraid the prisoners would say? Of the accused, Mrs. Surratt, Lewis Paine, David Herold and George A. Atzerodt were hanged. (Atzerodt was certainly one of the conspirators and seems to have been assigned the task of dispatching Vice President Johnson, though he made no attempt to do so.) The most puzzling question is why Mrs. Surratt should be especially "singled out to bear the brunt of the prosecution." "Throughout the trial she was put foremost among the defendents." The guilt of Mrs. Surratt was never proved and she was the most unlikely of all the defendents to be guilty. But innumerable pleas for her release were ignored by the Judges and Stanton, and President Johnson said he had never seen the petition for mercy filed in her behalf by Judge Advocate General Holt. It was kept from him.[1]

The tremendous upsurge of grief throughout the North surprised the politicians of Washington, who did not realize the place Lincoln had earned in the hearts of the people. "Honest Abe," or "the Rail-splitter," was already a folk hero. He was "the Great Emancipator" and "the Savior of the Union." Simple people called him "Father Abraham."

As the black-draped funeral train wended its slow way to Springfield, Illinois, with stops in New York, Chicago, and other cities, also all draped in black, the huge outpouring of grieving people in the cities and along the railroad tracks wherever the train slowly passed proved that the populace knew better than the politicians.

In the light of later events Jefferson Davis said, "The greatest tragedy of the South was losing the war, and the next greatest, the assassination of Abraham Lincoln."

17   THE SWEET SONGS DIE AWAY

With the surrender of Lee and his 26,676 men on April 9, the war was nearly over. General Johnston surrendered his army of 37,000 to General Sherman at Durham, North Carolina on the 26th, and other Generals in the southwest followed his example.

Thus the great and tragic Civil War of which Winston Churchill said, "The number of battles fought and their desperate, bloody character, far surpassed any events in which Napoleon ever moved," fizzled out like the undeclared naval war with France in 1800. There was left a huge land that had come apart at the seams, with a large population, many of whom could be technically called traitors, and hundreds of thousands of manumitted, illiterate blacks with no place to go; and no government. But the only one who suffered was Jefferson Davis. He was confined in Fortress Monroe in chains in a damp cell, and released in 1867.

Robert E. Lee went home a hero and became president of what is now Washington and Lee University, one of the outstanding universities of the South. President Johnson never granted him the official amnesty for which he applied, but he didn't need it. Idolized in the South, he came to be highly admired in the North too. A few others were imprisoned, but soon released. As Grant said at Appomattox, "They are our countrymen again."

The war was over and the South was ruined. General H. V. N. Boynton reported that window glass had given way to boards, furniture was broken, dishes glued together. Few had enough dishes to set a table, a set of forks with whole tines was a curiosity. Clocks and watches had nearly all stopped. Hairbrushes and toothbrushes were worn out, combs broken. Pins, needles, and thread were almost nonexistent. No tea, coffee, sugar nor spices were available. Candles had been replaced by cups of grease with a shred of cloth for a wick.

Life was in shambles. A lady asked in bewilderment, "If I don't own my slaves, who does?" The fact that nobody owned them, that they were free human beings, like herself, was beyond her comprehension. Auction blocks and slave warehouses vanished.

Five years after the war, Robert Somers, an English traveler, described conditions in the Tennessee Valley: plantations in semi-ruin or total ruin and complete, burnt up gin-houses, ruined bridges, mills and factories, large tracts of land stripped of fencing, impassable roads.

In his excellent short book, *The American Civil War* (1926), David Knowles, an Englishman as well as a Benedictine monk, waxes nostalgic over the lovely life the South lost forever. Lolling under the magnolia blossoms (magnolias apparently bloomed all year 'round in the South in those days), while the work was done by others (free), sounds fine, if a little boring. The haunting and beautiful songs about the South, expressing so well that wistful longing the Portuguese call *saudades—Old Folks at Home, My Old Kentucky Home*, etc. (written by a Northerner, Stephen Foster of Pittsburgh for Bryant's Minstrels)—paint a beguiling picture. The birds make music all the day, the sun shines bright, the darkies are gay. But there was another side to life in the South which also disappeared: the side that struck Lincoln when he sailed down the Mississippi to New Orleans on a raft when he was 17—the slave girl trotting up and down, punched and prodded as if she were a horse, so that "bidders might satisfy themselves of the soundness of the merchandise." The sweet old songs never mention that. (The sweet old southern songs seem to have been written by Northerners.)

The Civil War accomplished three things: (1) It ended slavery. (2) It proved that the United States were one country united under one flag. (3) It proved that the Federal Government superseded the "rights" of the States. But the problems the end of the war brought were enormous and took longer to solve. The main problem was Reconstruction, and it was a quagmire of party politics and constitutional perplexities.

What was the political status of the conquered states? Were they still states of the Union they had done so much to break? Or had they lost their rights as states and become territories, to be admitted into the Union at the decision of Congress which, under the Constitution, had the sole right to admit states into the Union? Or was the South a conquered province? Or was it merely a rebellion of recalcitrant children, subject to presidential pardon? Lincoln held to the latter theory, and it certainly would have been the easiest way—a scratch of the pen.

In December 1863 Lincoln had declared that when 10 percent of the voters in any seceded state should form a government and accept the legislation of Congress on the subject of slavery, he would recognize that government as legal. This had happened in Louisiana, Tennessee and Arkansas during the war.

Congress did not like this—it was letting the South off too easy. The law Congress proposed was much stiffer. It would require 50 percent of the voters to take a loyalty oath, and Confederate leaders would be forever excluded from voting or holding office. Lincoln refused to sign this bill, and matters were left up in the air. The struggle with Congress was inherited by Lincoln's successor, Andrew Johnson.

Part Four

THE PAINS STILL GROW

1   ANDY JOHNSON PUTS HIS FOOT IN IT

Andy Johnson was a runaway tailor's apprentice from Raleigh, North Carolina, who settled in Greeneville, Tennessee, and opened "A. Johnson's Tailor Shop." A bright young man, he had been taught to read by his wife. (There were no public schools in Raleigh.) He taught himself to speak slowly and distinctly by practicing the rules laid down in *Enfield's Speaker*—this in snatches between plying his needle and his tailor's goose. (Many members of Congress and those who speak on television should follow Andy's example.)

His tailor shop was frequented by the young men of the town who used it as a meeting place and a debating club. As he worked with his goose or sat cross-legged sewing, Andy listened.

He became so popular with these young men that they got him elected to the Town Council—an alderman at 21. His next step up was that of Mayor of Raleigh, to the consternation of the elite of the town, but he performed his duties well. When he was 23 the county court made him a trustee of Rhea Academy; he had never gone to school in his life.

Andy was proud of his humble origins. Though both his parents were illiterate, they were highly regarded. His mother was Scotch; his father, admired and trusted by all who knew him, died after heroically rescuing two drowning men when Andy was three. He was a porter at Casso's Inn in Raleigh.

Andrew Johnson's one hatred was the aristocracy, the slave-owners, and his two passions were the Union and the Federal Constitution. He went from glory to glory, as congressman for ten years, a senator for five, and was appointed Military Governor of Tennessee by Lincoln. But when he fell heir to the Presidency his glory was over.

Andrew Johnson was congenitally unsuited for leadership. He was stubborn, and insensitive to public opinion. In May, 1865, while Congress was not in session, he stunned the North by issuing without warning a proclamation of amnesty to the millions of former rebels, and welcomed them back into the fold. He was forging ahead with Lincoln's reconciliation policy but without a shred of psychology nor even common sense. The Congress was furious when they got back from their vacations. Johnson was without a particle of discretion. After four years of fratricidal war the North was not quite ready to embrace its former foes.

Johnson appointed military governors in seven states. He ordered conventions to be held in those states and in them ordinances of recession were repealed and new constitutions framed. State officials were elected, legislatures chosen and the Thirteenth Amendment, abolishing slavery, was ratified by all except Mississippi.

He could have done no more to infuriate Congress. They hated him for being a Southerner. They rejected everything he had done.

Thaddeus Stevens was a representative from Pennsylvania, and the most radical Republican of them all. He was vindictive, nasty and 78 years old. Speaker of the House, he ruled it with a rod of iron. He hated the South. His espousal of the abolitionists' cause was fervid, but his actions now seem more for the purpose of aiding the radical Republican party than for anything altruistic.

The ire of the radical Republicans was not soothed by the men whom the Southern states had elected to Congress. One was Alexander H. Stephens, Vice President of the Confederacy and Lincoln's old acquaintance (the "nubbin" that took so much shucking). Men who had served in the Confederate Congress, four generals and other high officials of the defunct Confederacy appeared in Washington with feathers flying to assume their places in the House and the Senate, to begin to rule the Union they had so lately tried to destroy. It was too much for northern blood and bone to bear. So Stephens instructed the clerk of the House to omit the names of Southerners when reading the roll call, and Senator Charles Sumner, recovered from Preston Brooks' brutal attack, had the same thing done in the Senate. This questionable trick seems to have squelched southern ambitions to rule the nation. Congress feared that if southern senators were admitted into the Congress they would join with northern Democrats and the Republicans would be ousted from power.

The Johnson-encouraged governments of the Southern states had passed laws known as the "Black Codes" to handle the hundreds of thousands of ex-slaves, uprooted and homeless, who posed a prodigious problem. They were assigned "guardians" for whom they were obliged to work without pay. It seemed like slavery returned, but these hordes of manumitted slaves, penniless, illiterate, uneducated, who had never known responsibility, were totally incompetent to shift for themselves. They fell ready prey to hordes of Northern bounders who swarmed into the South posing as their helping hands to a rich free life, but in effect poisoning them against the only people who could help them. They were called "carpetbaggers" because "they brought all their belongings to the South in a cheap kind of valise made out of carpet material," as Professor Muzzey explains in his famous school textbook, "A History of Our Nation." (The word has travelled far afield: "A carpetbagger is an American term to describe someone who moves to another place, where he or she has no ties, to seek financial or political gain"—*The Egyptian Gazette*, Cairo, December 20, 1979. The *Gazette* failed to note that the word is derogatory.)

These unprincipled people encouraged the poor bewildered blacks to believe that the Year of Jubilee had come, and each was to receive "forty acres and a mule."

2   THOSE THINGS THAT PAVE THE ROAD TO HELL

A "Freedman's Bureau" was established, supposedly to take care of the blacks. The hearings resulted in its being expanded. It exerted considerable coercive influence in the South, and though it was designed to protect the black population, and had wide support in the North, it was under the War Department. Johnson vetoed the bill, saying it was an unconstitutional extension of military authority in peace time.

So Congress produced a Civil Rights Act which declared blacks were citizens and denied the states the power to restrict any of their rights, including their rights to testify in court and hold property. Johnson vetoed this one too, and for the first time a major piece of legislation was passed over the veto of a President (requiring a two-thirds vote in both Houses). From now on Congress called the tricks.

The next move was another amendment to the Constitution. This was the fourteenth and a very important one because it reduced the power of the states and marked the beginning of a more integrated social and economic structure for the nation. But it also stirred up a new hornets' nest. It defined citizenship: "all persons born or naturalized in the United States, and subject to the jurisdiction thereof are citizens of the United States and the State wherein they reside." This obviously included blacks. It struck down discriminatory legislation (the Black Codes); it tried to force the Southern states to permit black voting by reducing its proportional representation in Congress if any citizen were denied the ballot.

Women being "persons" it would seem that the Fourteenth Amendment to the Constitution, in its first paragraph, gave them the franchise along with the blacks without more ado. But the second paragraph of the Amendment was more particular about who could vote and for whom and what and included the restrictive word "male" three times. Men were giving political power to uneducated, illiterate men over their own wives, mothers and daughters, as well as their sisters, (female) cousins and their aunts, not to mention their grandmothers—so ingrained was "male chauvinist piggery," a phrase invented a hundred years later—by a female, one hazards the guess.

The Fourteenth Amendment did not outlaw segregation, nor did it prevent a state from disenfranchising its black citizens if it were willing to pay the price of reduced representation in the Congress. Only Tennessee ratified the Amendment, in 1868.

Andrew Johnson was against this Amendment, and in an effort to rally public support for his views he became the first President to go campaigning. This trip was called "the Swing around the Circle."

Johnson invited William Seward, Lincoln's Secretary of State who had re-covered from the assassination attempt, and was still Secretary of State, and Gideon

Wells, Secretary of the Navy, to come along. For greater glamor he invited the two heroes, General Grant and Admiral ("Damn the torpedoes!") Farragut. Grant hated the idea, but Johnson had lately signed promotions for a number of his favorite officers.

On August 28, 1866, the Swing began and it began well. In Baltimore Johnson was greeted by 100,000 cheering people, but Baltimore was a strong Confederate city in its allegiance and Johnson had pardoned those who had waged war against the Union. However, Philadelphia was welcoming, New York City enthusiastic, and so on throughout New York State as far as Buffalo. But in Ohio the trouble began. At a whistle stop he explained to the crowds that time did not permit him to make a speech there.

"Don't!" cried a voice.

In Cleveland he declared Congress was illegal since it denied representation to eleven states. People laughed when he said he had begun life as an alderman. (He had said this everywhere and the speeches had of course been printed in the papers. People were fed up with this alderman stuff.)

The crowds got uglier. They shouted they had come to see General Grant. The Governors of Ohio and Indiana stayed pointedly away when he appeared in their states. In Indianapolis he was told to "Shut up!" In Illinois someone cried, "Impeach him!"

Hooting and shouts of "Liar!" accompanied the poor tailor's apprentice every-where now, and he shouted and hooted back, and pounded his fists. Andy Johnson was never able to learn that shouting and pounding fists is no way to win friends and influence people. He shouted about the Constitution when he was asked why he didn't hang Jefferson Davis.

General Grant, the Nation's hero, spent his time hiding in the baggage car, horrified, smoking cigars. He told his aide he did not wish to accompany a man who was digging his own grave, and planned to leave the train at Cincinnati to visit his father (perhaps an invented excuse). He began fortifying himself. Dr. Barnes, the Surgeon General, also of the party, attempted to take Grant's pulse before he left the train, and toppled over on his patient. He had been fortifying himself too.

The Swing around the Circle turned out a disaster; it had driven at least two of Johnson's traveling companions to drink. The result of the Swing was that the radical strength of Congress increased; it won more than a two-thirds majority in both houses and Johnson was a President without a party.

3   A RASH OF AMENDMENTS

The rejection of the Fourteenth Amendment by all the southern states but Tennessee brought sterner methods of coercion upon them. There was continuing evidence of the persecution of blacks and in 1867 the First Reconstruction Act was passed, and the semi-freedom the South had enjoyed for a brief time was over. The former Confederacy was divided into five military districts, each ruled over by a Major General with almost dictatorial powers, to protect the civil rights of "all persons" and maintain justice and order. Tennessee alone was exempt, a reward for having voted for the Fourteenth Amendment. The others would have to adopt new constitutions guaranteeing blacks the right to vote and disenfranchising all Confederate big-wigs, and if they were good about this, and Congress approved, military rule would cease and they would be admitted to Congress.

But the states made no effort along these lines. They had no wish to enfranchise the blacks and preferred the status quo to disenfranchising their former leaders.

Congress was extraordinarily patient. It proposed new rules, changed old ones, enacted Acts, and finally ended up with a law decreeing that all state constitutions must be ratified by a majority of voters. This was first done in Arkansas, and that state was readmitted to the Union in 1868.

The Legislature of the Territory of Wyoming passed a bill the following year, 1869, granting women the vote and sent it to the Governor as an hilarious joke. The Governor signed the bill and congratulated the Legislature for giving the women of Wyoming justice and political equality. Picture the open mouthed astonishment of the lawmakers! (The Governor had heard Susan B. Anthony speak.) Wyoming achieved statehood in 1890, and was the first state to elect a woman Governor, Nellie Taylor Ross, in 1924. One hopes Elizabeth C. and Susan B. heard about this in the otherwhere.

These dedicated women had gone on the lecture circuit undeterred by the torturous difficulties of travel in those times: long waits in uncomfortable railroad stations at all hours of the day and night for connecting trains, sometimes being driven in wagons and sleighs for miles through rain and snow to keep their appointments. The valiant brigade gained a high reputation for reliability.

It was obvious that a Fifteenth Amendment to the Constitution would be necessary in order to win for the blacks unrestricted voting rights. A bill had been introduced in the House of Representatives in December 1868, by George W. Julian of Indiana which would enfranchise all citizens "without distinction or discrimination founded on race, color or sex," and Senator Pomeroy of Kansas put forth for the consideration of his peers an amendment making citizenship the basis of suffrage. But these two bills were not even debated.

The Fifteenth Amendment ended by declaring that the right of citizens of the United States to vote "shall not be denied or abridged by the United States or by any State on account of race, color or previous condition of servitude."

There was a "little word wanting,"—as English nannies used to tell their charges who failed to say "thanks"—and that word was "sex."

The Revolution was the name of an Equal Rights paper published in New York and edited by Elizabeth Cady Stanton and Parker Pillsbury. The name of this paper offended many in the movement. Protests poured in at the shocking name! "This *is* a revolution," said Mrs. Stanton, "and we are *not* going to call our paper *The Rosebud*." She proceeded to come out with a long article against the Fifteenth Amendment. The abolition forces were furious, and they included many women. "It is the Negro's Hour!" was their slogan. And the women said, "We are willing to wait."

Frederick Douglass, Mrs. Stanton's old ally from Seneca Falls days, was not with her now. The black man must have the vote *first,* he said, for "when women, because they are women, are dragged from their homes and hung on lamp posts, when their children are dragged from their arms, then will they have an urgency to obtain the ballot equal to the black man." Is Douglass saying that women must be hanged and their children dragged from their arms before they will have an "urgency" to obtain the ballot, but not before? The reasoning here seems a little vague.

When Frederick Douglass married, *en seconde noce,* a white woman, there was a "storm of disapproval" from blacks and whites alike. The abolitionists and "Equal Righters" proved to be less liberal than they supposed themselves to be, but Mrs. Stanton, ignoring their former strained relations over the Fifteenth Amendment, wrote Frederick Douglass a warm letter of congratulations and good wishes. Elizabeth Cady Stanton was a great lady.

Only a few women stood by Stanton and Anthony in their insistence on woman suffrage *now.* They were abandoned by most of their former friends over their stand on the Fifteenth Amendment. But the intrepid pair called a convention in Washington on January 19, 1869. It was the first Women's Rights convention held in the capital.

Senator Pomeroy, whose excellent amendment had not even been debated, presided, but soon yielded the chair to Lucretia Mott. One of the three pioneers in the suffrage movement, she was now 76.

Twenty states were represented at the convention; among the new converts was Clara Barton, the great Civil War nurse, who said, "I follow the cannon." (Miss Barton founded the American Red Cross in 1881.)

The Fifteenth Amendment had passed Congress and was waiting the President's signature before being submitted to the states for ratification when Mrs.

Stanton urged the introduction of a Sixteenth Amendment specifically to enfranchise women. Mr. Julian introduced such an amendment; needless to say it got nowhere.

A group of ladies with more piety than brains asked Miss Anthony if she had ever resorted to prayer to obtain rights for women? Susan B. was never at a loss for an answer: "Frederick Douglass told me that when he was a slave in Maryland he used to go to the farthest corner of the cornfield and pray to God to give him his freedom. 'But,' he said, 'God never answered my prayers until I prayed with my heels.' "

The amendment to enfranchise women, often called the Susan B. Anthony Amendment, though it should have been called the Elizabeth Cady Stanton Amendment, turned out to be not Amendment Sixteen but Nineteen and was ratified in 1920, 72 years after Seneca Falls, when all the old guard were dead.

4   A TAILOR'S APPRENTICE DEFIES THE SENATE

Tell me, have you read about Grishka Otrepyev, how he
was cursed in seven cathedrals?
—Dostoevsky, *The Possessed.*

Johnson retained most of Lincoln's cabinet, including the Secretary of War, though Stanton had become more and more at one with the radicals and was co-operating with them in his command of the military units in the South. To protect him from being dismissed by the President, Congress dreamed up the nastiest of acts: the Tenure of Office Act, which forbade the President to dismiss civil officials, including memebers of his own Cabinet, without the consent of the Senate. It was an out-rageous act, and drastically reduced the power of the President. Every President heretofore had the right to dismiss members of his Cabinet, just as he had a right to appoint them. How could the executive branch of the Government be run by men at loggerheads?

Johnson and Stanton had been at loggerheads for a year, the other members of his Cabinet always on Johson's side. Gideon Welles and others had urged the President to remove this thorn in his flesh, but for some curious reason he did not. And with the Tenure of Office Act, Stanton, feeling secure in his position, became openly defiant to the man who was his chief.

Finally Johnson suspended Stanton and appointed General Grant to fill his place. The imbroglio that followed has some of the elements of a French bedroom farce played by an all-male cast—if the War Department can be visualized as a French bedroom.

In mid-January Johnson sent a message to Congress relative to his suspension of Stanton and his appointment of Grant. The House, thrown into an uproar, resolved that the President had no right to do this and sent copies of the resolution to the President, to Stanton and to Grant. This was on January 13, 1868.

Ulysses S. Grant, the nation's hero, was nervous. What would the reaction of the Senate be to Johnson's defiance of the Tenure of Office Act? Where would it leave him? He had a long talk with the President. What about this $10,000 fine and a jail sentence awaiting anyone who violated that Act? Johnson said he was certain the Act would be overthrown by the Supreme Court, and if not he would pay the fine and take the jail term himself!

Two days after this conversation the Senate voted thirty-five to six to reject the President's discharge of Stanton. Grant was rather up a tree. He wrote out his resignation as Secretary of War and at 9 o'clock next morning he went over to the War Department, locked the door of the Secretary's office and put the key in his pocket. He told Assistant Adjutant General E. D. Townsend he would be at his office at Army headquarters.

An hour later when Stanton arrived at the War Office, all smiles, he found his office door locked and was told that General Grant had the key. He asked Townsend to get it, and in a short time the Assistant Adjutant General returned with it, and in a mock "present arms" delivered it to the triumphant Stanton.

Johnson was furious, for the agreement had been that if Congress interfered Grant would give the key back to him. There was a rather stormy Cabinet meeting at which Grant appeared and was bombarded with questions. Had Grant agreed to oppose Stanton's return to the War Office? Had he not promised to hold the fort? It was implied, though not actually spoken, that Grant had broken his word to the President. Had he been plotting with the Radicals?

Grant departed. Johnson was very angry, but as in any small town the story grew with the telling, until we have Johnson kicking over the chairs, cursing Grant, and the two nearly coming to blows.

It is warming to learn how faithful Johnson's Cabinet was, and how it backed his actions. The members assured him he could be removed from office only by impeachment, and until impeached he could not be suspended. Gideon Welles called the Senate a "debouched, debased and demoralized body without . . . a sense of right or moral courage."

Johnson offered the office of Secretary of War to General Sherman, but Sherman, seeing what sort of a mess he might get in, declined. Johnson then offered it to Lorenzo Thomas, titular Adjutant General, continuing to fly in the face of the Tenure of Office Act. "Damn it!" he said. "I am tired of talk of impeachment. Let them go on and impeach if they want to!"

Lorenzo Thomas was a rather merry and convivial gentleman of the old school, and somewhat a friend of the bottle. Tall and startlingly thin, Stanton had said of him, "Only fit for presiding over a crypt of Egyptian mummies." He had seen no action in the war. This emaciated gentleman entered Stanton's office, exhibited his authority, and demanded possession. Stanton asked time to consider. While Thomas went home, feeling his oats, Stanton furnished the House and the Senate with Johnson's order of removal.

That night General Thomas attended a great ball and was the hero of the hour. When the milling crowd around him asked him what he would do if Stanton resisted him, he said, "Break down the door!"

The next morning, while still feeling a bit under the weather from the previous night's festivities, he was roused from bed by the Sheriff with a warrant for his arrest, sworn out by Stanton. When he appeared before the judge he asked if the order of arrest forbade him "having it out with Secretary Stanton." The Judge said it did not. Thomas then conferred with the President, who said he was glad Stanton had taken the matter to court. "The Tenure of Office Act will now be tested. When you are taken into custody we will sue out *habeas corpus* and the courts will settle the matter."

Thomas, one assumes greatly enjoying himself, then stepped over to Stanton's office and again demanded that he surrender it. Stanton said *he* was Secretary of War and ordered General Thomas to remove himself. General Thomas refused. "Do you mean to use force?" Stanton asked. General Thomas said he did not wish to use force but his mind was made up as to his next move. According to Thomas' testimony at the impeachment trial that followed, the conversation took a more convivial turn.

Thomas said to Stanton, "The next time you have me arrested please don't do it before I have had something to eat." He said he had had nothing to eat or drink that day. The upshot of this was that Stanton sent out for a bottle of whisky—what he had handy being but a spoonful or two—he explained he kept it for dyspepsia. And the two rivals for the great office of Secretary of War had a drink together, dyspepsia or not.

"This at least is neutral ground," said Stanton.

When the President sent his appointment of Thomas to Congress he included his veto of the resolutions of Congress condemning Stanton's removal in the message, and added a warning to Senate and House: Whatever the consequences to himself, considerations could not prevail against a public duty "so clear to my mind, and so imperative." Were his own removal to follow his removal of Mr. Stanton, "defending the trust committed to my hands ... I could not have hesitated, actuated by public considerations of the highest character." This was Andrew Johnson's finest hour.

Congress was in an uproar again and resolutions for the impeachment of Andrew Johnson for "high crimes and misdemeanors" followed.

The trouble was that it proved difficult to discover any high crimes and misdemeanors to impeach him for. Nevertheless the radicals were not deterred. They dreamed up eleven articles of impeachment, ten of which were founded on the removal of Stanton, in various keys and stops, and one on inaccurate and garbled newspaper reports of his speeches.

The trial, after days of inevitable red tape, began on March 15, 1868, the Senate sitting as a High Court of Impeachment with Johnson's old friend Justice Salmon P. Chase presiding. Johnson, on the advice of his lawyers, did not appear. He stayed in the White House attending to business.

During the trial Stanton barricaded himself in the War Department, and he and his cohorts guarded the place in relays night and day against any overt move by "old General Thomas."

Washington was at fever heat; tickets for the trial were eagerly sought. "The most memorable attempt of an English-speaking people to dethrone their ruler" sounded sensational. Of course Charles I had been dethroned by the simple process of chopping off his head, but this was not contemplated now. Johnson could only be disgraced, removed, and in a jury trial fined $10,000 and imprisoned for five years.

The important thing about trials, as about battles, is the outcome. The Impeachment Trial of Andrew Johnson lasted till May 26, a period of 73 days, and ended with his acquittal—by a single vote. Thirty-five senators had voted for conviction, nineteen for acquittal. Thirty-six were needed to convict. Among those voting Not Guilty were seven Republicans. They put their integrity above their party, and only two were elected to public office again.

Andy Johnson was still President of the United States and the Johnsons did not have to move out of the White House yet.

Secretary Stanton at once resigned. William M. Evarts, one of the lawyers who had brilliantly defended Johnson at the trial, accepted the office of Secretary of War, and was confirmed. (General Thomas seems to have been lost in the shuffle.) The country breathed a sigh of relief, the stock market rose, the verdict was applauded in Europe.

The Radical Republicans might, with justice, be called Rabid Republicans, so blinded were they in their hatred of Johnson. Only the seven moderate Republicans had the courage to uphold the Constitution at the expense of their political careers. Had these senators not resisted intimidation to the end, the weapon of Impeachment could have been held over the head of every succeeding President, and the independence of the executive branch destroyed. The legislative branch would have become supreme, and the Founding Fathers' great scheme of checks and balances fatally overturned.

5   JOHNSON'S POLAR BEAR GARDEN

Shortly after the Tenure of Office Act was passed over Johnson's veto, and before the farce it begot had had time to get into high gear, there was a pleasant and unexpected interlude.

Secretary Seward was seated, of a fine spring evening, in his fine house on Lafayette Square, playing a game of whist with his family, when a caller was announced. It was Baron Edward de Stoeckl, the Czar's Minister in Washington. The Baron explained that he had just received authority from his government to "close with you for our colonies in America." "Our colonies in America" referred to Alaska.

"If agreeable I will call at your office tomorrow," said the Baron.

"Why not tonight?" asked Seward. The Baron protested that Mr. Seward's office must be closed at that hour and all his clerks and officials gone home.

"They'll be there," said the Secretary of State confidently, all thoughts of whist forgotten.

The clerks and officials had a busy night. By 4 A.M. next morning the treaty was drawn and executed. The United States had bought five hundred thousand square miles of territory with a coastline of four thousand miles, and the circumstances were somewhat like those at the time of the Louisiana Purchase in 1803 when Robert Livingston and James Monroe had had to act quickly.

The Treaty was presented to the Senate that day by Charles Sumner, chairman of the Committee on Foreign Affairs, and the Senate ratified it on April 9. The price set, after some very mild haggling, was $7,200,000. But the House refused to vote the money; it was against *anything* Johnson's administration did. The radical press jeered and was full of vicious cartoons. Alaska was "Johnson's Polar Bear Garden"; it contained nothing but polar bears and icebergs; it was "Seward's Folly."

Russia agreed to wait for her money. Sumner said a republican form of government there was worth more than "quintals of fish and sands of gold." The astonished British Minister cabled home asking what should be done about the matter.

Andy Johnson did not wait for the House to appropriate the funds. In October there was a ceremony at Sitka with Russian and United States troops parading before Government House. Artillery boomed and bands played as the Russian colors were lowered and the Stars and Stripes raised.

Congress went on raging, but pro-Russian sentiment grew in the country. Russia had been the only foreign power friendly to the United States during the Civil War, and the appropriation passed the House on July 14, 1868.

The day General Grant, the new People's Choice became President, March 4, 1869, Andy and his family left the White House spic and span for the Grants, and did not attend the Inauguration; they went home to Tennessee, doubtless as fast as they could.

Andrew Johnson returned to Washington, the newly elected Senator from Tennessee, on March 5, 1875, six years after he left the White House. His entrance into the Senate Chamber caused intense embarrassment to those remaining senators who had voted "guilty" at the Impeachment Trial. (Those who had voted "not guilty" had all been defeated at their bids for reelection, and Andy did not have a friend in the house.)

Senator Edwards of Vermont was addressing the Chair. He faltered in his speech and sat down to retrieve some papers that had providentially fallen to the floor. Other senators stared into space or looked away. As Johnson passed the desk of Senator Morton of Indiana he stopped, smiled and held out his hand. Senator Morton took it.

"There are not many men who would have done that," Morton said later.

Vice President Henry Wilson was presiding, one of a Vice President's duties. Now he descended from the podium, instead of remaining on it for the new senator to mount to him, and swore Johnson in on the floor of the Senate. At the end of the brief ceremony a roar of applause came from the galleries. Johnson turned away and made for his desk. A page handed him a bouquet. Andy found his desk heaped with flowers and his eyes filled with tears.

"Here in this room he had spoken for the Union, here he had made his vice presidential inauguration speech. Here he had been judged."[1]

Johnson made one speech in the Senate two days before its adjournment and returned to Tennessee. While talking to his granddaughter about her marriage plans he suffered a stroke and fell to the floor. He was conscious and forbade his family to send for a doctor. He spoke of his youth and early struggles and died the next day, July 31, 1875. His body was wrapped in the flag, and his copy of the Constitution in which he had made notes for forty years, was buried with him.

6   A CENTURY OF DISHONOR

Bury my heart at Wounded Knee
—William Rose Benet, *American Names*

A quarter of a million Indians inhabited the Rocky Mountain region and the Great Plains, and they were an obstacle to white settlement. There were the warlike Sioux, the Blackfoot, Cheyenne, Crow, Arapaho, and Nez Percé in the north, and the Comanche, Apache, Ute, Kiowa and southern Cheyenne and southern Arapaho further south. They all lived chiefly off the huge herds of buffalo, and they had splendid swift horses. All were determined to defend their hunting grounds, which were menaced from every direction. First came the great migration of the 1840s, followed by the miners—the '49ers and their followers. Ten years after the miners took over California the 100,000 Indians living there were reduced to 35,000.

The Congressional Committe on Indian Affairs was well aware of this. "Despoiled by irrestible forces of the land of their fathers; with no country on earth to which they can migrate, in the midst of a people whom they cannot assimilate," was how an official report painted the tragic picture. Miners, transcontinental railroads, cattlemen—the irrevocable march of Civilization and Progress doomed the Indians and their way of life.

The huge buffalo herds were wantonly destroyed by trigger-happy palefaces, just for the fun of it, and buffalo was the chief food of the redmen, as well as a necessity for their tepees, lariats, bowstrings, and even fuel. Driven to raid the white settlements in search of food, and to acts of desperation, their retribution swiftly followed.

Colorado was invaded in 1862 by hordes of prospectors, settlers followed the Mississippi and Missouri Rivers northward, and armed clashes resulted. The Sioux of the Dakotas went on the warpath and laid waste to the Minnesota frontier; 1,000 whites were captured and massacred.

There were 200 pitched battles between the U.S. Army soldiers and the Indians between 1869 and 1876, but these battles were not as unequal as one might think. The Indians, with their keen eyesight, had learned to be excellent shots. They had rifles and ammunition, and their horses were fully equal to army horses. Had all the tribes united against the palefaces, and if they had had another Tecumseh, the outcome might have been different. But there was no Tecumseh now.

In 1866 a command of eighty men was ambushed and killed by the Sioux chief Red Cloud and his braves at Fort Phil Kearny, Wyoming. Reports of a "horrible massacre" at Fort Bedford on the Missouri the following year roused the public, but no such massacre took place. The Commissioner of Indian Affairs accused "the rapacity and rascality" of frontier settlers for this false report: they hoped to bring on war and supply the Army with necessities at a huge profit.

Congress tried to do something. In 1867 an Indian Peace Commission was set up to stop the fighting. It included General Sherman, who had marched through Georgia, and General Terry, and for a year or so they succeeded.

Francis A. Walker, appointed commissioner by Grant in 1871, did what he could. He put defeated tribes on new reservations, set up schools, and issued rations to those who were without food. It wasn't enough.

The doom of the Sioux was sealed by the discovery of gold in the Black Hills

Custer's Last Stand. Reproduced from the Collections of the Library of Congress.

of Dakota in 1874. General Sherman succeeded in holding back the avaricious miners for one summer; the following spring they poured in.

It was then that two Indian chiefs, famous partly for their enchanting names, Sitting Bull and Crazy Horse, led the Sioux in an attempt to save their hills, the holy land promised by the Government to be kept forever inviolate.

There was a paleface who won equal fame at this juncture, Colonel George A. Custer. "Custer's Last Stand" is an integral part of American folklore.

Custer's career in the Civil War was distinguished. Since then he had been fighting the Indians for nearly a decade, and had come to admire them. He said he would prefer to cast his lot with the Indians than be confined to a reservation "and be the recipient of the blessed benefits of civilization with its vices thrown in."

Colonel Custer was glamorous. He wore his hair in long flowing locks, and a scarlet scarf of considerable length blowing behind in the wind set off these yellow locks nicely. The colonel was a brave if swashbuckling fellow, and belonged in Hollywood which, unfortunately, had not yet been invented.

The Sioux and northern Cheyenne tribes had left the Black Hills to the miners, and General Terry for some reason divided his regiment into thirds, Custer's cavalry being one, to pursue and disperse them.

The Little Big Horn is not a mountain but a river. The name is forever linked with that of the unfortunate Colonel, who with his men was surrounded there by Crazy Horse and Sitting Bull and their 2500 braves. Poor Custer and his 265 officers and men were massacred, and the Colonel, with flowing hair and scarlet scarf, galloped into the hearts of several generations of schoolboys as his reward.

The history of the American Indian is unmitigated tragedy. In Colorado the vast lands of the Utes were confiscated and opened to settlement. In Montana the Crow and Blackfoot Indians were ejected from their reservations. The Nez Percé, a peaceful tribe in Idaho, were doomed when gold was found along the Salmon River. They were driven out by the Government in 1877. In the Southwest the Apache tribe, after twenty years of intermittent warfare, were subjected by the surrender of their chief, Geronimo, in 1886.

Speculators in land, and the ever-advancing railroads, found it child's play to cheat the Indians of large areas of their granted lands. Cherokee country, to the amount of 800,000 acres in Kansas, was acquired by one railroad which the Governor of the state called "a cheat and a fraud in every particular." It was sold to settlers at a huge profit.

The Secretary of the Interior prevented another railroad from buying eight million acres from the Osage Indians for 20¢ per acre.

Congenitally the Indian lived a day at a time. He had no vision of tomorrow. Why the Government enacted no law which would prevent these wards of the nation from selling their granted land, or anyone from buying it, is unknown.

Reformers like Carl Schurz and spiritual and intellectual leaders were not silent about all this. Helen Hunt Jackson, author of the popular novel *Ramona,* published in 1881, *A Century of Dishonor*, an account of the Government's treatment of the Indians. It stirred the national conscience.

The Dawes Act of 1887 was well-meaning but demonstrated how little psychology the Government had to bring to bear on the Indian problem. The reservations were to be broken up into individual homesteads which would "civilize" the redskins and turn them into palefaces with the stroke of a pen. But the Indian cared not for Home, Mother and Apple Pie. He was a hunter, not a tiller of the soil; a nomad, not a homesteader. It is difficult to believe that others do not think as you do and can hold very different views.

After Sitting Bull's death another Sioux chief, with the glamorous name of Big Foot, led a band of his people to the badlands of South Dakota where they were captured by the 7th Cavalry near a creek called Wounded Knee. The members of this band were adherents of a prophet named Wovoka who had devised a Ghost Dance and bullet-proof ghost shirts. Unfortunately, as in the case of Tecumseh's brother Tenskawatawa, also a prophet, when push came to shove Wovoka's magic evaporated. In an attempt by the cavalry to disarm the Indians, a handful of dust—perhaps ghost dust—was thrown into the air by a medicine man, another Indian fired a gun, and 200 men, women, and children were slaughtered by the United States Army. The soldiers said, in excuse, that it was difficult to tell the men from the women. No mention was made of the children. The "Battle of", or more correctly the "Massacre at" Wounded Knee in 1890 is considered the landmark end of the Indian Wars.

But the bungling, if not the slaughter, went on and on. Allotments of land began in 1891. Congress, to make sure this would not work, passed a law allowing the allotees to lease their lands. They could not live on the meager proceeds, they were surrounded by white neighbors, they didn't know what to do with their land anyway, and soon they were paupers.

In later years indemnities were made to some of the tribes; others were located on new (and this time inviolate) reservations. In Oklahoma they became citizens, and could one day enjoy coping with the income tax.

7   THE ROBBER BARONS AND OTHER ROBBERS

And this was not the work of days
But had gone on for years and years.
—Richard Monckton Miles, Lord Hougton, *Shadows.*

The year 1868 was one of those distressful years that, in the United States, come one in every four—a "Presidential Year." Both the Republicans and the Democrats would have liked the Nation's Hero for their candidate, for there is something about military heroes that anesthetizes the electorate. Grant chose to go along with the Radical Republicans and was elected in November. His running mate was Schuyler Colfax, a dispensable congressman from Indiana.

Attempts to nominate Johnson for a second term failed and the Democratic candidate was Horatio Seymour, a former Governor of New York. Though he was a Sound Money man, and preferred a return to gold rather than the millions of paper dollars or "greenbacks" issued during the war, which many western Democrats wanted to keep for paying off the national debt, he got the nomination but carried only eight states.

Grant's popular majority was only 310,000 and this was attributed to the black vote in the reconstructed states. It would appear that radical Republican policies were not altogether approved of in the North.

Under Grant military rule continued in most of the South. He sent federal troops to bolster up sagging carpetbag governments in various states, and reports of goverment corruption and extravagances kept trickling into the North. Many became convinced there was a growing and dangerous militarism there.

This led to suspicions of corruption nearer home, in the Federal Government, suspicions that were all too well founded. The great Age of Grab had arrived: the inevitable reaction to the idealism of the Civil War.

Grant was independent, honest and naive. Astute in military matters, he was a child in politics. He appointed his cabinet without consulting politicians and surrounded himself with men who added no political clout to his administration. He did nothing to prevent the scandals that disgraced his administration, and even protected some of the worst malefactors out of a misplaced belief in the sanctity of friendship.

There was the Whisky Ring affair which implicated the President's private secretary, Orville E. Babcock, and cost the Government millions in lost revenues. The tax on whisky had risen to eight times the cost of the liquor, and certain distilleries in the Middle West bribed government officials in order to keep most of it.

The defalcations of the Secretary of War, William W. Belknap, in the management of Indian affairs, discovered in Grant's second term—for he had a second term in spite of all—did not boost the Republican image either.

All this inspired a reform group calling themselves the Liberal Republican Party, and they nominated Horace Greeley, the editor of the *New York Tribune*. This eccentric gentleman (whose famous advice to ambitious youth, "Go West, young man," is still quoted) was also nominated by the Democrats, though Greeley had spent years excoriating the Democrats in his influencial paper.

Due to this absurd caper, and the total unfitness of Mr. Greeley for the office of President, both the Democrats and Liberal Republicans lost, and Grant triumphed, this time with a popular plurality of 800,000. The country was not ready for reform after all.

But in Congress the reform movement did some good. In the 1874 elections the Democrats carried the House of Representatives, which presaged the end of military control in the South. By the next year only South Carolina, Florida and Louisiana were under Republican control.

The Whisky Ring and the Indian Affairs scandals were but two. One that passeth the understanding of the average citizen was the Crédit Mobilier (no doubt pronounced "Credit Mobileer") mazurka. The Crédit Mobilier was a construction company, and the way it went on constructing fortunes for its shareholders was a caution. It all came to light during the Grant-Greeley campaign.

This construction company helped build the Union Pacific Railroad. It was controlled by a few of the Union Pacific stockholders who handed out huge and fraudulent contracts to the company (themselves), thus in a most ingenious way milking their own company, in which they owned but a minor interest, of money that came mostly from Government subsidies. They were robbing Peter to pay Paul, they themselves being both Peter and Paul.

To avert a congressional inquiry the directors sold shares at a discount to key members of Congress and other key figures, including Schuyler Colfax, Vice President of the United States, and James A. Garfield, representative in Congress from Ohio, former lay preacher, a dependable, rabid (excuse it please), radical Republican. These gentlemen, it turned out, had paid nothing for their stock. Garfield later became President.

The scandal in the Navy Department, which was suspected of selling business contracts to contractors, and in the Treasury Department, where a special agent named John A. Sanborn, appointed to collect overdue taxes, collected $427,000 and retained 50 percent commission for his pains, seemed peanuts.

Next, the President's salary was raised from $25,000 to $50,000, the first pay boost since George Washington's time. Members of Congress upped their salaries from $5,000 to $7,500, and it was no doubt justified. But the public was outraged when it discovered that its representatives had, in addition, voted themselves two years' back pay. The next Congress repealed the "Salary Grab."

In 1862 Congress had passed, and Lincoln signed, the Homestead Act, which gave 160 acres of land to any settler who would farm the land for five years; and the same year the Pacific Railway Act was passed, which gave to companies subsidies in land and money for the construction of a continental railroad. Half the public land in a strip ten miles wide on both sides of the track was bestowed on these companies. Bonds bearing six per cent interest for each mile of track completed were the bonus for meritorious achievement—$16,000 a mile over the prairies, where the going was easy, $32,000 a mile across the arid plateau between the Rockies and the Sierras, and $48,000 a mile through the great mountains and over the great chasms. A hundred million shares were offered to the public at $1000 a share, but even with additional grants of land and lush subsidies, the public was reluctant to invest and could not believe this great feat possible in less than a hundred years.

The Union Pacific was to start westward from Omaha, Nebraska, the Central Pacific eastward from Sacramento, California, until their tracks met.

This event occurred at Promontory Point, near Ogden, Utah, May 10, 1869. The last rail was fastened to a tie made of California laurel by a golden spike. This spike was driven by a silverheaded hammer struck alternately by President Leland Stanford of the Central Pacific and Vice President Thomas Durant of the Union Pacific, the sound of the epoch-making strokes being carried by electric wires connected with every telegraph office in the land.

The first through train from California arrived at the Hudson River station in New Jersey on July 29, 1869, after a run of six and a half days.

The building of the Central Pacific and other Western railroads attracted Chinese workers, and added to the gallimaufry of races that inhabit North America.

The overland stage coaches, the Pony Express, all the romantic paraphernalia of the Old West, were at once a thing of the past, relegated to Wild West shows, and later to the movies.

The Atlantic and the Pacific coasts were now only a week apart. Business boomed. Trade with China and Japan increased 100 percent in three years, freight carried by the Central Pacific nearly doubled in ten months.

So began the Pacific fever. Other companies which had been granted lands and subsidies pushed for the completion of their tracks in order to be able to dip into this rich pie—the Kansas-Pacific, the Southern Pacific, the Atlantic and Pacific, the St. Paul and Pacific, and the Northern Pacific. All this being a 100 percent American phenomenon, it followed the usual American pattern: the financial panic of 1873 abruptly ended most of these companies.

Though the public had been shy about buying railroad stock, the grants of land and money by the prodigiously generous Congress attracted top class malefactors, who were not shy. They knew a good thing when they saw it, and knew what to do with it.

Jay Gould became a speculator when he was 21, buying into small railroads with an original investment of $5,000 earned as a clerk in a country store and as a surveyor's assistant. At length he became a director of the Erie Railroad. Other directors were Jim Fisk and Daniel Drew. By their sleight-of-hand manipulation of stock they ousted Cornelius Vanderbilt from his directorship, but as Vanderbilt (called "Commodore" for owning a fleet of tugboats in New York harbor) also owned the New York Central, a very profitable road, one need shed no tears for him.

William Marcy Tweed, known as Boss Tweed, was "elected" to the board of the Erie as a reward for rendering aid to these questionable characters. They had a jolly time manipulating the stock, gained millions for themselves, and wrecked the Erie.

But Tweed, the greatest grabber of the lot, made a fortune out of the city of

New York. A power in Tammany, the Democratic machine, he controlled party nominations and city expenditures. The Mayor, A. Oakley Hall, was a member of the Tweed Ring himself.

Tweed padded expenses, bought votes, corrupted corruptible judges, and gathered in some $30,000,000 in thirty months ending July 31, 1871. He had become a state senator, and this enlarged his sphere of influence to the breaking point.

Gould and Fisk were busy too. They hatched a scheme to corner gold.

Gold opened at 100. Fisk started buying, and bought all he could get. The price rose to 165. Then he sold out at the crest of the wave. The Government released gold and the price dropped. Thousands were ruined, a financial panic hit the land. Banks closed their doors from coast to coast. September 24, 1869, is known as Black Friday.

Forced out of the Erie by "public outcry," Gould bought into the Union Pacific and other Western roads, ending up with control of four.

The downfall of Boss Tweed came about from the publication of some of his letters, and the powerful cartoons of Thomas Nast in *Harper's Weekly*. Audits of the Tweed Ring kept revising the value upward until it reached close to $200,000,000. One wonders how there was any New York left.

Tweed died in prison in 1878.

8   FROM BLACK FRIDAY TO EASTER EGGS

In 1873, four years after Black Friday, the country was visited by another panic which, predicted for some time, was given its final boost by the failure of two banking houses in New York, Jay Cooke and Company and George Opdyke and Company, which had advanced huge sums for the building of more railroads. Railroad building had become a mania in America. On September 19, the blow fell, and stocks tumbled so precipitously that the Stock Exchange was closed for the rest of the month. Station houses were nightly crammed with men, women and children who had nowhere to go. Bankruptcies increased monthly, reaching their peak in 1878 when 10,478 businesses failed. Crooked banking and the wild speculation spree that followed the Civil War had done their uttermost.

But the year 1873 had its bright side too. Along with railroad building, mining had become a favorite get-rich-quick pursuit. Since the discovery of silver and gold in the Rockies, those mountains were thick with prospectors all the way from British Columbia to Tucson, Arizona. Towns of 4,000 grew up overnight. Claims were staked along every stream, gully and ravine. Gold and silver were everywhere, if not always in commercial quantities. It was the great companies who could afford heavy machinery that eventually made the money, but being very American and without restraint, it was boom or bust.

It was good while it lasted, however. Virginia City, Nevada was the gold-mining capital. The Comstock Lode produced $12,000,000 a year of the precious stuff, and 25 saloons helped assuage the thirst of 4,000 inhabitants. The Big Bonanza, a rich stream of silver 150 feet thick, promised Virginia City a long life and a merry one.

Gold was discovered in the Black Hills of South Dakota in 1875 by an expedition led by George Custer. This meant the Indians had to leave, but the discovery had enriched America in another way. We have to thank it for the colorful characters who have contributed so much to Western folklore: Deadwood Dick, Wild Bill Hickok and the ever treasured Calamity Jane. Poker Alice was another tasty morsel, stemming from the town of Deadwood.

In March of that year Alexander Graham Bell transmitted the first intelligible sentence over his invention, the telephone. There are divergent opinions about this invention, but the decade was a rich one in many ways.

In 1876 Grant rather fancied running for a third term, but the Republicans decided twice was enough. What they needed was a man unsullied by scandals. The Democrats had too much ammunition. Though Grant himself was honest, he was surrounded with men of questionable ethics as well as men who were outright crooks, about whom he never did anything but get them out of hot water.

To find an unsullied politician seemed a difficult task, but it proved not impossible. His name was Rutherford B. Hayes. This gentleman, though a radical Republican, was untouched by scandal. He was (of course) originally a lawyer, and so, after a distinguished military career in the Civil War, he served in Congress and then became Governor of Ohio for three terms.

The Democrats put up Samuel J. Tilden, a Free Soil Democrat and Governor of New York. He did much to break the Tweed Ring and to uncover graft in another notorious ring (swindles were as thick as flies in August in those days). The Canal Ring was a group of malefactors who made illegal profits from contracts for the repair and extension of the New York canal system. In short, Tilden was a respectable man.

The election resulted in more disputed votes than had hitherto been known. Tilden carried all the Southern states from which the carpetbag regimes had been evicted, and New York, New Jersey, Connecticut and Indiana. In Florida, Louisiana and South Carolina the majority seemed to be for Tilden too, and be it noted that these were the only Southern states still under a carpetbag (Republican) regime. It looked like 203 electoral votes for Tilden against 165 for Hayes. Something had to be done!

The Republican Party leaders bestirred themselves. They ordered their henchmen in these states to get busy and throw out enough Democratic votes to swing the election their way. The electoral votes in these states amounted to nineteen, just enough needed to elect Hayes. The board of canvassers went at it with a hearty will, invalidated Democratic ballots right and left, and filed returns which showed conclusively that Hayes was the winner!

The cheated Democrats raised such an uproar that Congress was forced to create an Electoral Commission to decide the case. It ended by consisting of eight Republicans and seven Democrats, and it will occasion no surprise to learn that the disputed ballots were all assigned to Hayes, making the final tally 184 to 185.

The historian John A. Garraty has said, "To such a level had the republic of Jefferson and John Adams descended!"

The popular vote gave Tilden a plurality of 250,000. Such is the result of the unjust and outmoded Electoral College, which still flourishes today.

In spite of the mendacious manner in which he was handed the office of Chief Executive, Hayes proved a good President. He ended the carpetbaggery in the three states that had wanted to give Tilden their votes, followed a conciliatory policy, and worked for Civil Service reform.

Rutherford B. Hayes was a lover of Sound Money (who isn't?), and resumed specie payments on the public debt. Presumably people had gold coins to jingle around in their pockets again. But he was opposed to the free and unlimited coinage of silver. Naturally he annoyed both his own party and the Democrats, and wisely refused to run for a second term.

During the Hayes Administration an invitation to a State Dinner at the White House caused qualms to diplomats and other invited guests. Mrs. Hayes refused to serve liquor in her house, a quirk that earned her the mellifluous sobriquet of "Lemonade Lucy." The guests arrived well fortified, no doubt, but it was not quite the same thing.

Yet in the middle of the banquet, when the icy water-ice was served, a custom of the period supposed to shrink the over-extended stomach and rehabilitate it for the next onslaught of rich viands, first-time guests were startled to find it liberally laced with rum. A gentleman privately asked the President how he managed to introduce this grateful interlude into the bill-of-fare under the very nose of the hostess. Rutherford B. did not reply, but his smile was—presidential.

The Hayes administration had one lasting effect on the White House. It was Lemonade Lucy who inaugurated the annual Egg Roll for children on the White House lawn on Easter Monday. She approved of innocent pleasures.

The nation's choice for next Chief Executive was James A. Garfield, though believe it or not, there was a strong movement to reelect Grant for a third term.

The Republican Party was thus split in twain. One faction was called the Stalwarts, led in Congress by Senator Roscoe Conklin of New York. They were the ones who wanted Grant for a third term and a return to those good old days. The other faction was called the Half Breeds. They didn't want Grant back, and their leader was Senator James G. Blaine of Maine.

This diversion of opinion caused friction, which was accelerated when Senator Blaine described his colleague, Senator Conklin, as "a majestic, supereminent, overpowering turkey-gobbler strut."

Blaine was immortalized later in a catchy couplet still occasionally quoted:
"Blaine, Blaine, James G. Blaine,
Continental liar from the State of Maine."

In spite of all this the campaign was said to be dull. Even the mud-slinging "was done in an unimaginitive way."

Garfield had a good record. When the Crédit Mobilier scandal was brought up and he was accused of receiving a dividend of $329 he said this was a borrowed sum from one of the Crédit Mobilier men, to help finance a trip to Europe, and had been repaid. Another bit, about receiving a sum for helping to put through a contract for a wooden sidewalk was a little more difficult to explain, but when he was said to have an unpaid tailor's bill at Troy, New York, it all sounded pretty small potatoes to a public used to the swindling of millions.

Garfield began his career guiding mules along a towpath of the Ohio and Erie Canal, had been president of a small college where he taught Latin, Greek, Mathematics and other things, had fought at Shiloh and Chickamauga, and been returned eight times to the House of Representatives. He was about to take his seat in the Senate when he had to change it for a seat in the White House.

It would be wearisome to write or even read about the Republican convention in Chicago. Garfield was nominated on the 36th ballot.

Garfield's running mate was Chester A. Arthur, the Convention allowing New York to make the selection. Arthur was born in Vermont, the son of a Baptist Minister. He studied law, and helped the anti-slavery cause. Then he was Quartermaster General in New York, which experience of course "fitted him for a career in politics." President Grant appointed him Collector for the Port of New York and he is said to have run the Custom House honestly.

Collector of the Port of New York was a most coveted plum, and Garfield had problems about bestowing it. Roscoe Conklin was the undisputed czar of the Republican machine in New York and was mightily annoyed when President Hayes removed Chester A. Arthur from the Custom House at the report of an investigating committee that said there was too much boondoggling there. He now called upon the President to discuss Federal appointments. He said they must all be his men. Garfield, in spite of this, appointed a man of his own choice for the Collector job, a man named William Robertson, without consulting the senator from New York.

Conklin was fit to be tied! Patronage in New York was slipping from his grasp.

The President seemed to be building a political machine of his own! Conklin demanded "senatorial courtesy" as he called it, but Garfield stood firm.

"This will settle the question whether the President is registering clerk of the Senate or the Executive of the United States," said Garfield. It reminds one of Andrew Johnson's stand against the Senate in 1868.

But Garfield's administration was destined to be the second shortest in the history of the American Presidency. On July 2, while in the Washington Railroad Station, he was shot by a disappointed office seeker, Charles J. Guiteau. Today the shot would not have been fatal, but before the days of the X-ray the doctors could not locate the bullet. Their probing, no doubt with unsterile instruments, brought on an infection. Removed to Elberon, New Jersey, on the seacoast, to escape the stifling heat of Washington, Garfield died there on September 19, 1881, less than four months after taking office.

In spite of his stand against patronage, and the promise of an honest administration this gave, poor Garfield's name is familiar today solely because he was the second president to be assassinated.

Thus Chester A. Arthur was sworn in as 21st President of the United States at half past one in the morning in the parlor of his house on Lexington Avenue, New York City. The nation had been without a Chief Executive for several hours, but had got on about as well as usual during the interregnum.

Chester A. Arthur was not entirely unbesmirched with machine politics and there was shock in respectable circles when he was fortuitously raised to the presidency.

But when his former boon companions hurried to Washington, their lips smacking, and called on dear old "Chet," Arthur said, "I'm not 'Chet' any more, I am President of the United States," and the disappointed spoilsmen left for home.

The assassination of Garfield has roused the public to the disgraceful state of the Civil Service, which had been a patronage pie. Chester A. Arthur, himself at one time a recipient of political favors, is the President responsible for the modern Civil Service system. He drew attention to the need for reform in his message to Congress in December 1882, and Senator George H. Pendleton of Ohio introduced a bill providing for a commission to classify the grades of the Civil Service and to provide competitive examinations for the selection of candidates. The bill was passed by large majorities in both houses of Congress and signed by Arthur the following month. It is called "the Magna Carta of Civil Service reform." Arthur put 15,000 government employees into the classified service before he left office. It was also made illegal to solicit or otherwise force civil servants to make contributions to political parties. As could be expected, the Pendleton bill infuriated politicians; they would now have far fewer sweets to hand out.

Arthur's list of achievements and good acts is impressive, from laying the foundation of a modern Navy of ironclads, to his veto of bills appropriating huge sums of money for unnavigable rivers and small, useless harbors. (These raids on the Treasury were called "Pork Barrel Bills.")

At the Republican Convention in June 1884 James G. Blaine was early the favorite, with Arthur the runner-up. But Arthur had been too independent to please the party bosses. This Convention should have been held in a Roman arena, perhaps the Coliseum, instead of an exhibition hall in Chicago. There were sixteen nominating speeches and rhetoric rose to unprecedented heights.

"Nominate Blaine!" cried a frenzied judge named West, "and the campfires and beacon lights will illuminate the continent from the Golden Gate to Cleopatra's Needle" (the one in Central Park, New York—presumably) and so forth. It was intoxicating. Flags and bunting were stripped off the walls, delegates stripped off their coats, they almost stripped off their pants.

Then they went home to snatch a few hours' sleep and came back, sobered, for the balloting. Blaine won on the fifth ballot.

The reform Republicans were disgusted with "corrupt men and corrupt methods in politics." They told leading Democrats that if an honest and progressive candidate were nominated at the Democratic convention scheduled for July, they would vote for him. The great iconoclast Robert Ingersoll had called Blaine "the Plumed Knight," but if Edwin Godkin, editor of *The Nation,* was correct, the plumes were bedraggled. He wrote of Blaine that he "wallowed in spoils like a rhinoceros in an African pool." There was no mincing of words in those days.

9   FROM GROVER CLEVELAND TO THE PSALM-SINGING POLITICIAN

> *In glowing health with boundless wealth,*
> *But sickening of a vague disease.*
> —Tennyson, *Lady Clara Vere de Vere*

The Democrats had a man they thought filled the bill. He was Grover Cleveland, Governor of New York. He, too, was the son of a minister, this one Presbyterian, and had at one time held a teaching position in an asylum for the blind, and clerked in a lawyer's office. When he was 45 he was elected Mayor of Buffalo.

Cleveland did such an honest, able and courageous job that the next year he received the Democratic nomination for governor of the state; and he won by a huge plurality. He was a fearless fighter against corruption and machine politics. He did not make decisions with an eye to his own political advancement, and this novel policy ended by advancing him to the presidency.

The campaign of 1884 was the most disgraceful ever held in the United States. The press barred no holds. There were allegations that Blaine accepted bribes from railroad promoters and sold worthless bonds to his friends; Cleveland was a drunken libertine from "the back parlor of a Buffalo saloon!" The papers outdid themselves in scurrilous libels, the cartoonists dipped their pens in vitriol, though Celveland's excellent record as Mayor of Buffalo and Governor of New York was there for all to see.

A few days before the election a group of clergymen gave Blaine a reception at the elegant Fifth Avenue Hotel. Blaine should have stayed away! The Reverend S. D. Burchard of the Murray Hill Presbyterian Church opened his mouth to give a flowery address, and put his foot in it. He described the Democrats as "the party of Rum, Romanism and Rebellion." That did it. Blaine lost the Roman Catholic vote. Cleveland won the election, though by a narrow margin.

Cleveland was the first Democratic President since the Civil War, and the Republicans announced that dire calamity was now facing the nation. Congress would fill up with Southern "Brigadier Generals"; pensions to Union veterans would be stopped; the Confederate debt might be honored. Worst of all, the many offices at the disposal of the President would be filled with men hostile to the great machine the Republicans had been building up for 26 years, nurtured by a favorable tariff, grants of public land to the railroads, and the favors a generous Congress was in the habit of bestowing on private corporations.

Though Cleveland had a majority in the House, the Senate was Republican and hampered him in everything he tried to do, including exercising his constitutional right to dismiss Federal employees. He wanted to keep taxes down and to weed out frauds in the huge pensions the country was paying to veterans of the late war, which kept rising and rising.

Labor grew very restive in the mid-eighties. The International Working People's Association was founded in 1883. Declining prices embittered the farmers, and farmers' organizations sprang up. The trade unions which had been functioning in the '70s, lost their grip after the panic of '73, and the railroad strike that year had panicked the nation.

There were now so many labor organizations that it is difficult to keep them apart—should one care to do so. The Federation of Organized Trade and Labor Unions of the United States and Canada, whose president was Samuel Gompers, was the most powerful. They wanted an eight-hour day, imagine that! and a general strike was called on May 5, 1886. The McCormick Harvester Company workers were on strike, the police harassed the strikers, and a meeting at Haymarket Square, Chicago, was called in protest of this too. The police appeared and ordered those present to disperse. A bomb was thrown—it was never known by whom—and seven policemen were killed and sixty-seven people injured. The police fired into the crowd, and four were killed.

Hysteria gripped the respectable middle classes, and justice was demanded. The police came up with eight "anarchists," and they probably were anarchists. At a mock trial all eight were found guilty of murdering the policemen by inciting the person, whoever it was, who had thrown the bomb. All were found guilty without a shred of evidence that could have held up in court, if Blind Justice were not so blind. Seven were sentenced to death and one to life imprisonment. Four were executed, one committed suicide in jail, and the last two had their sentences commuted to life imprisonment.

That was the Haymarket Affair, a dismal milestone in the thorny Capital-Labor road.

Cleveland's big headache was the Tariff, of all subjects the dullest. This was the time of a High Protective Tariff, and as foreign trade was flourishing, the Treasury was getting richer at the rate of about one hundred million dollars a year. It was a real problem to know what to do with all that money. (Subsequent presidents have not had to face this particular problem.)

Cleveland was opposed to spending this surplus on appropriations for coastal defense, the Navy, or the like. To repurchase the national bonds would encourage speculation in the bonds and likewise undermine the basis for the banknotes required for the expanding business of the country. President Cleveland figured that the surplus must be reduced, not by paying it out, but by taking in less. The high tariff protected only about fifteen percent of the workers; eighty-five percent were burdened with taxes on all the necessities of life and had no protection by advanced salaries.

Cleveland got a bill (the Mills Bill) through the House reducing the tariff six or seven percent, but the Senate ignored it. James G. Blaine called Cleveland's attempted reform a "free trade policy" which were fighting words, and suggested to the Republican convention that it nominate Benjamin Harrison.

So it did.

General Harrison was a senator, and the grandson of the wordy William Henry Harrison who had *not* been born in a log cabin.

Though Cleveland was nominated by acclamation at the Democratic Convention, Harrison won the electoral vote but not the popular vote, which showed a plurality of more than 100,000 for Cleveland. This was done by the deft handling of the two "doubtful" states which had gone for Cleveland the last time—Indiana and New York. It is wonderful what campaign funds will do. The campaign was run almost entirely on the high-low tariff issue and there was none of the mud-slinging of the previous campaign. A dull time was had by all.

Harrison thought his job was purely executive and left the framing of legislative programs to the party leaders in Congress. Like Cleveland, he was for Civil Service reform, but the reform moved slowly. Harrison appointed the young Theodore Roosevelt to the Civil Service Commission, and then undercut him systematically. Teddy Roosevelt was full of his usual beans and he was finally inspired to characterize the President in vivid language: "A cold blooded, narrow minded, prejudiced, obstinate, timid old psalm-singing Indianapolis politician."

At the ceremonies marking the centenary of Washington's inauguration as president, which took place on the steps of the Sub-Treasury Building in New York, April 30, 1789, President Harrison, suitably attired in his black suit and tall black silk hat, was rowed up the bay in a barge by thirteen symbolic rowers, who were not dressed in the picturesque sailors' uniforms of 1789, but wore black suits and tall black hats too, a novel outfit for oarsmen. But perhaps their attire was symbolic of Harrison's administration. They landed at the Battery and proceded up Broadway to Wall Street amid wild applause.

All of Cleveland's policies were reversed. They *liked* the surplus in the Treasury and could think of plenty of ways to spend it. The Dependent Pension Bill, which Cleveland had vetoed, was revived, and the expenditures for pensions rose from $81,000,000 to $181,000,000 during Harrison's administration. The Democrats made loud noises about the "Billion Dollar Congress," to which the Speaker of the House, Thomas B. Reed of Maine, replied blandly that this was a billion dollar country.

Business was growing bigger every day. Small businesses became fewer and fewer as one by one they were gobbled up by huge corporations. Between 1880 and 1890 plants making agricultural machinery decreased from 1,943 to 910, though the capital invested in them more than doubled. It was the same with textile mills, refineries, distilleries and meat-packing houses. Protests against these growing monopolies began to be heard. Henry George's *Progress and Poverty*, which advocated a single tax based on land alone—a new concept which might have solved all of America's problems—appeared in 1879, and the methods of the Standard Oil Company were exposed in *The Story of the Great Monopolies*. All the big industries came in for scrutiny.

The free-swinging Republicans did not like this scrutiny, but were obliged to *do something*. The Sherman Anti-Trust Act was passed in 1890, making "restraint of trade" illegal, but in vague terms. It was a dead letter from the start. Not only the Republicans, but the courts were in favor of restraint of trade. The corporations won seven of the first eight cases brought before the courts.

10   SUSAN B. ANTHONY AND BUFFALO BILL

In May 1893, the World's Congress of Representative Women convened in Chicago, with delegates from the United States, Canada, South America, Europe, Asia, Africa, Australia, and New Zealand. Susan B. Anthony was there, of course and it was revealed that she was the most famous woman in Chicago, and an international celebrity. There were cheers and shouts at the mention of her name. When she was advertised to speak, a squad of police was required to keep the corridors of the Art Palace from becoming a dangerous jam.

The Columbian Exposition of 1892 was still in progress and controversy raged as usual over whether the Fair should be open on Sunday. Miss Anthony was questioned. She said she would like the Fair to be open all day Sunday. "If I had charge of a young man in Chicago at this time, I would far rather have him securely locked up in the fair grounds on Sunday than let him roam the streets."

A horrified clergyman exlcaimed, "You would let him go to the Wild West Show on *Sunday!*"

"Of course I would," said Susan placidly. "In my opinion he would learn more from Buffalo Bill than listening to an intolerant sermon."

On learning this the delighted Colonel Cody sent Miss Anthony a box for one of his performances, inviting her to "bring some of your suffrage friends."

Buffalo Bill made his famous entrance under a spotlight with a flourish of trumpets and roll of drums, galloped to Susan's box, reined his horse to its haunches, and swept his hat to the saddle in a magnificent salute.

Miss Anthony rose and bowed low, and for a moment these two immortals faced each other "to the wild applause of thousands."[1]

11   A PRESENT DEITY

The listening crowd admire the lofty sound!
A present deity! they shout around.
—Dryden, *Alexander's Feast*

In the next election there was a landslide for Cleveland, but hardly had he settled back in the White House when another depression hit the land; it had been brewing for years. Farmers had been banding together in various alliances since the '70s, and now they grew more articulate. In the Dakotas, Kansas and Nebraska a series of drought years had wiped out the crops, and the bitter winter of 1886–87 wiped

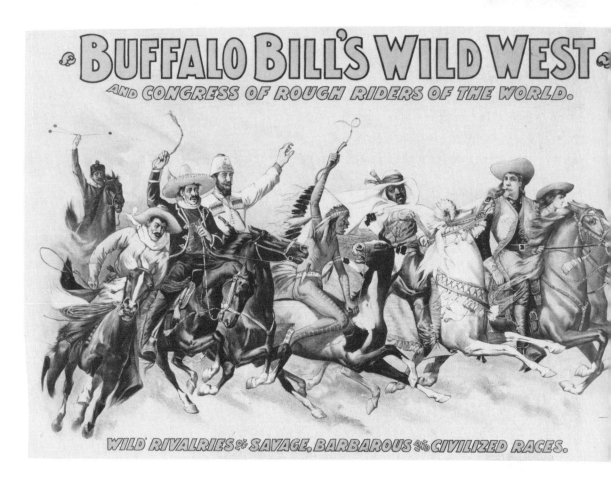

"Buffalo Bill's Wild West." Reproduced from the Collections of the Library of Congress.

out much of the cattle. Farmers' alliances from the West, Middle West and South all agreed on three things: prices were too low, transportation was too high, and there was something radically wrong with the financial system of the country. They were dead right on all three counts. As neither the Republicans nor the Democrats paid them any attention, they formed a new party, the Populist Party.

The other problem was silver versus gold. The country had always been "bi-metallic," meaning both metals could be coined, the value ratio between them being regulated by Congress, and this had been going on since 1792, when the ratio was established: 371.25 grains of silver and 24.75 grains of gold were each worth one dollar at the Mint. This ratio changed slightly from time to time, but when silver was worth more on the open market than it was worth when coined, nobody brought silver to the Mint any more.

When the Big Bonanza and other great silver strikes in Colorado and Nevada reduced the market value of silver it became profitable to coin it again. But when

"Miss Anthony Making an Unanswerable Argument."
Susan B. Anthony Memorial, Rochester, NY, 1908.

it was brought in for this purpose, the owners of the metal discovered that the Coinage Act of 1873 had "demonitized" silver, none having been seen at the Mint for so long. There was an uproar. The Sherman Silver Purchase Act of 1890 was aimed to help. It authorized the Government to purchase a certain amount of silver each month, but this and other measures were not of much use. President Cleveland

346

346 DID MOLLY PITCHER SAY THAT?

brought pressure to bear on Congress, and the abortive Sherman Silver Purchase Act was repealed. It split the Democratic Party.

In 1894–95 the Depression was at its nadir. In 1894 a small army of the unemployed led by an Ohio businessman named Jacob S. Coxey marched on Washington to demand relief. They were called "Coxey's Army," and they wanted the Government to undertake public works. They had a reasonable plan for financing these works through non-interest-bearing bonds issued by local communities to be exchanged for $500,000,000 in greenbacks. These funds would supply work for the jobless, improve transportation through the building of roads, and bolster the economy. This sounds more like the 20th Century than the 19th.

When the men reached the Capitol grounds Coxey and his leaders were arrested for "walking on the grass," and the others dispersed by club-wielding cops. End of Coxey's Army.

On top of this there was a strike at the Pullman Palace Car Company's plant outside Chicago when the company reduced salaries by 25 percent. The workers lived in a model town called Pullman, owned by the company, which refused to reduce rents. A committee tried to meet the management. The leaders were discharged.

The upshot was that switchmen refused to handle Pullman cars. They were dismissed too. The Railway Union instructed its members to quit work when this happened, and they did. In no time all the other workers were on strike, and transportation was paralyzed all the way to the Pacific Coast.

The railroad companies bypassed the Governor of Illinois, John P. Altgeld, because he was known to be liberal—he had pardoned the Haymarket "anarchists" still in prison—and appealed to President Cleveland. The President, against the loud protests of Altgeld, who said the Illinois Militia was capable of handling the situation, ordered 2,000 Federal troops to the scene. Ostensibly this move was to "keep the United States mails moving." Eugene V. Debs, organizer of the American Railway Union (and who was doubtless burnt in effigy nightly by Mr. Pullman and his cohorts) was served an injunction to "cease from interfering with the interstate transportation of the mails." He refused to do so, and he and the other leaders were jailed for six months for contempt of court. Federal troops protected newly hired workers, the leaders of the strike were in jail, and the strike simmered down and died.

Capital still had it all its own way.

The greatest agitator of them all in the American Labor Movement was a little woman scarcely five feet tall, born (so she claimed) in Cork. After a life of tragedy she became absorbed in the organization of the Knights of Labor. Having the defect of belonging to the wrong half of the human race she was not allowed to join the Knights but her career was nevertheless launched. Wherever there was a strike, there was Mother Jones. She was recognized as the greatest speaker in the labor movement. A little blue-eyed lady in a bonnet and lace who spoke educated English (she had attended a normal school in Toronto), she could swear splendidly when necessary with many god-damns and hells, and could put on a rich authentic brogue when it was useful.

In 1897 she became interested in the coal miners of West Virginia and Pennsylvania and was hired as a field organizer. At a textile workers' strike in Pennsylvania in 1903 she found that of the 75,000 strikers, 10,000 were children, many under ten. Children of six worked in the factories ten and sometimes eleven hours a day, and their wages ran from three dollars to six dollars a week. They frequently were mauled by the machinery, fingers and even hands severed. Some of them were bowed like people of eighty.

Mother Jones' single most publicized exploit was the March of the Mill Children from Kensington, Pennsylvania, to Oyster Bay, New York, where Theodore Roosevelt was vacationing on his estate. At Princeton, New Jersey, Grover Cleveland lent them a barn on his property, but when they got to Oyster Bay, Theodore Roosevelt refused to see them. The march received enormous coverage, front page news. Child labor laws began to appear on the books, though at first sketchily enforced. When Mother Jones was a hundred years old a great birthday celebration was held in her honor at Silver Spring, Maryland, where she was living, attended by most of the important characters in the labor movement, and even John D. Rockefeller sent a telegram.

Mother Jones said, "The militant, not the meek, shall inherit the earth."

As another presidential year approached, the Republicans were confident. Cleveland's second term would soon be over, and there was a depression for which he could be blamed, though it was not of his making. He displeased the industrialist by attacking their dearly loved protective tariff; he was displeasing to the Populists for his insistence on the gold standard; organized labor detested him for his handling of the Pullman strike. And he had been elected four years before in a landslide.

Among the Democratic congressmen who lost their seats in the landslide was William Jennings Bryan, a 36-year-old lawyer from Lincoln, Nebraska. He had a strong antipathy to Wall Street, which he blamed for all the economic evils of the day. Wall Street had control of the gold supply and kept its hoarded gold the only standard of value. Free silver coinage was the answer.

Bryan campaigned for "free silver" up and down the land. He called upon the Democratic Party to steer a new course to represent the struggling masses and to support legislation for a better life.

Bryan had little training in economics and didn't understand much about that arcane subject, but he was the last of the Great Ranting Orators. At the Democratic convention in July he delivered a speech that brought down the roof—the last Great

Oration in American history. (Great Orations have gone out of style.) Bryan spoke for the farmers of the West and against the industrial East. "Burn down your cities," he cried, "and leave our farms, and your cities will spring up again as if by magic. But destroy our farms and grass will grow in the streets of every city in the country!"

He ended, "You shall not press down upon the brow of labor this crown of thorns. You shall not crucify man upon a Cross of Gold!" And he flung wide his arms and made like the Cross.

It was terrific.

12   McKINLEY AND THE PEARL OF THE ANTILLES

In spite of the crown of thorns and the cross of gold, Bryan did not win the election of 1896. It was won by the Republican candidate, William McKinley. William Jennings Bryan was not to achieve the spotlight again until 1925 at the Stokes Trial, celebrated in the history of American jurisprudence as the "Monkey Trial," in Dayton, Tennessee. Professor Stokes had broken a Tennessee law that forbade the teaching of Evolution. Mr. Bryan was all for Adam and Eve, the Serpent, and the whale that swallowed Jonah. Clarence Darrow, Stokes' lawyer, made short shrift of Bryan, but when Bryan loudly proclaimed that man was not a mammal, even some of his fundamentalist brethren were a little taken aback. (Queen Victoria suffered doubts about Jonah and that gluttonous whale, but Bryan swallowed them both.)

McKinley won the election largely through the extraordinary efforts of Mark Hanna, a rich Ohio businessman and king-maker. McKinley had long served in the Congress and when he lost his seat in the Democratic landslide of 1890, Hanna got him the governorship of Ohio. McKinley was honest, highly moral and had good judgement, but he was not glamorous and he lacked the golden (pardon—silver) tongue of William Jennings Bryan. Mark Hanna doted on McKinley.

Bryan stumped the country as had no other presidential candidate before. He traveled nearly 20,000 miles and made full use of his oratorical powers in over 600 speeches before huge crowds.

McKinley stayed home in his unpretentious frame house in Canton, Ohio. His was what came to be known as a "front-porch" campaign. The country came to *him*—on special trains with reduced fares from distant points, all arranged by Mr. Hanna and the McKinley campaign staff with the cooperation of the railroads. It was very informal and corny, and all carefully stage-managed: agéd mother (made of granite), and invalid wife Ida (neurotic, psychotic and epileptic, and likely to have a seizure at State Dinners)—listening in rapt attention to their wonderful William on the front porch. His speeches never mentioned crosses and thorns.

Afterward, handshakes on the front lawn, perhaps even milkshakes.

Behind all this Mark Hanna was pulling the strings. He had gathered a huge campaign fund by browbeating banks, insurance companies, corporations and businessmen. He circulated millions of pieces of campaign "literature" in innumerable languages, and sent out more than a thousand speakers in every direction.

The East, the Middle West, and most of the Northwest went for McKinley, while Bryan had the South, the Plain States and of course the Rocky Mountains, where all that silver was. But in addition to the business and financial intersts which voted Republican, many farmers voted for McKinley, and more than half of the labor vote went to him. Thus, though the victory of the financial interests over the agricultural was assured, it was not a complete division of the people into two camps. Perhaps the election of McKinley at this point served to prevent such a thing; perhaps the United States was growing up.

McKinley's troubles began soon after his election, and were centered in the sunny Caribbean. For the past year guerilla warfare has been going on in Cuba against the Spanish regime, and the guerillas had resorted to their usual ruthless measures. Spain sent General Valeriano Weyler to her strife-torn island as the new Governor, and he soon became known as "Butcher Weyler." To deprive the rebels of food he herded much of the rural population into concentration camps where conditions were such that many died. This hardened the resistance of the Cubans, and also roused the sympathy of the Americans.

Another matter that roused American sympathy was the fact that there were huge American investments in the sugar plantations and tobacco fields of the island.

President McKinley, at earlier reports of atrocities in Cuba, thought that they were probably not all committed by the Spaniards, and remained unmoved when Congress, in excitement, passed a resolution to recognize Cuban belligerency. He offered America's good offices to mediate the conflict, which Spain, it would seem foolishly, declined.

McKinley renewed the American mediation offer, and Spain again refused. In sterner tones, he protested against Spain's "uncivilized and inhuman" conduct, and then Spain got the message. Fearing the danger of American intervention, Butcher Weyler was recalled, conditions in the concentration camps were somewhat ameliorated, and the island granted a qualified autonomy. It looked as if the war scare was over.

But there were two men who thought this would never do: Joseph Pulitzer, who owned the New York *World,* and William Randolph Hearst who owned the New York *Journal.* They were engaged in a war of their own—a circulation war— and a war in Cuba was exactly what the doctor ordered. As with rabble-rousers of every age, "truth" took an inferior position to "yellow journalism," an invention of these ingenious gentlemen. Lurid descriptions of atrocities filled those yellow pages and the American public—bless it!—believed every word Mr. Hearst and Mr. Pulitzer said.

One piece of sensational news was sober fact. The American battleship *Maine* had been sent to Havana on a "friendly" visit, to protect American lives and property if attacked by one side or the other. On February 15, 1898, the *Maine* blew up in Havana harbor with the loss of more than 266 lives. A naval board of inquiry came to the conclusion that an external explosion by a submarine mine was the cause.

Considering the already whipped-up emotions of the American people, nothing could restrain them now.

"Remember the *Maine*! To hell with Spain!" almost became the national anthem. It seemed to occur to nobody that Spain had nothing to gain and everything to lose by blowing up the *Maine,* whereas the insurgents had nothing to lose and everything to gain. War hysteria gripped the country and Teddy Roosevelt fanned the flames by crying, "An act of dirty treachery!"

In March, President McKinley asked Spain to agree to an armistice. On April 9, Spain accepted the agreement. On April 11, McKinley asked Congress for authority to use military force to end hostilities in Cuba, and only mentioned casually at the end of his message that Spain had already capitulated to his request for an armistice. He didn't emphasize this point; nobody wanted to hear it. The American people were not going to be cheated out of their little war, and neither were Messrs. Pulitzer and Hearst.

Thus the U.S. plunged into a war that began with "the complete irrelevance of a boiler explosion" and was conducted (though on the highest moral plane) "like an absent-minded comic opera."[1]

The cause of the explosion of the *Maine,* after two boards of inquiry had long sat upon the matter, was never definitely explained, and remains to this day a mystery.

On April 19, both the House and the Senate passed resolutions recognizing the independence of Cuba and authorizing the President to use the military and naval forces of the country to carry the resolutions out. To these was added the Teller Resolution, which declared that the United States had no intention of annexing Cuba, but would leave the government and control of the island to its own people as soon as the Spaniards were driven out. And this was done, to the astonishment of all of cynical Europe.

Hostilities began, not in the Caribbean after all, but in the South China Sea.

The American Asiatic Fleet, which consisted of seven vessels commanded by Commodore George Dewey on his flagship *Olympia,* was in the British port of Hong Kong when the war broke out. Now, being belligerents, the fleet would be interned in a neutral port, and Dewey and his fleet went to sea in a hurry. A cable ordered him to proceed to the ancient Spanish colony of the Philippines and engage the enemy. Manila is 628 miles from Hong Kong, and Dewey's fleet entered Manila Bay before dawn on May first.

The Spanish squadron was lined up at the naval base in a little bay at Cavite, four miles from Manila. They had their steam up, and the battle began. But the Spanish ships, in spite of their fine names—the *Reina Cristina,* the *Don Juan de Austria,* and the *Castilla,* the latter all made of wood and perhaps left over from the Armada— were no match for the American ships. By noon every one was sunk or in flames, the batteries at the navy yard at Cavite silenced, and Manila lay at the mercy of Dewey's guns.

The Commodore waited for American troops to come and occupy the island, which they did in three months. Meanwhile Filipino insurgents were making life unpleasant, and the Americans and their conquered foes, the Spanish officers and men, struck up a friendship and a mutual admiration society developed. The Spaniards said the Americans were *muy caballeros,* and the Americans compared the Filipinos most unfavorably to the Spaniards.

While Dewey was approaching Manila to annihilate the Spanish Pacific Fleet, the Spanish Atlantic Fleet left the Cape Verde Islands, Admiral Cervera in command, destination unknown. Immediately the dreadful thought arose that this fleet's destination was the Atlantic coast of North America, there to bombard the unprotected cities all the way from Boston to Miami. People moved inland, others doubted the wisdom of spending the summer in their seaside cottages.

The news of Dewey's victory at Manila caused wild rejoicing in spite of the worries, though many had to get out their atlases to find out where the Philippines were.

Cervera's fleet showed up in the harbor of Santiago, on the southern coast of Cuba, before anyone knew it. Cervera had stopped at Martinique to coal, and the French wouldn't let him have much; only enough to get to Santiago, the nearest Cuban port. Santiago Bay is connected with the ocean by a long, narrow channel, with ancient Morro Castle guarding it on one side and Scapa Battery on the other. The city stretches along the east side of the inner bay, and before it Cervera and his ships dropped anchor. Admiral William Sampson easily bottled them up, and there Cervera and his men sat out the month of June. The poor man knew he and his ships were doomed.

The Spanish-American War was the most inefficient, blundering war the U.S. had engaged in, surpassing in the intricacies of its blunders the War of 1812. Since the Army had no general staff, there was no organization.

Tampa was selected as the embarkation point for the regular Army after it was discovered that there was no water at Key West. There was little at Tampa either. It was also a very hot place, and soldiers arrived from mountainous regions with woolen clothes and woolen underwear. One regiment came without shoes and stockings, another without arms; some had no uniforms. ("Red flannel underwear for the tropics! Trousers made of paper! Embalmed beef! It's great to be a volunteer soldier in a big, free, inefficient democracy!"[2]) Teddy Roosevelt and his First Volunteer Cavalry, known to fame as "The Rough Riders," arrived on June 3, late enough to escape the hurricane that nearly blew the place away on May 7. The confusion was such that it took them twelve hours to get themselves and their luggage into camp.

To send these men to fight in the tropical summer of Cuba, the malaria and yellow fever season, was another of the awful blunders of the war. These two diseases were supposed to result from "the miasma of marshes." The mosquitoes in the miasma were unsuspected. Major-General Nelson A. Miles was the only one who knew about the "miasma" but his repeated warnings to the War Department, run by Russell A. Alger, Secretary of War, went blithely unheeded. Secretary Alger was ineptitude personified, his ineptitude climaxing in his placing in command of the Army, Major General William Rufus Shafter who had seen service in the Civil War, was now 63 and weighed over 300 pounds, if reports can be believed. He had to be lifted onto his mule—"a small white mule with a stout heart"—by two muscular orderlies—the perfect man for a tropical assignment.

Eighteen miles east of Santiago there was a village consisting of a few huts and a steel pier built by an American mining company for loading its boats. This insignificant place was called Daiquiri though the name generally refers to an excellent rum drink. Here the American troops began landing on June 23, 1898. It is a wonder they ever got out of Tampa; it is a wonder that they ever got to Cuba. Thirty-two small chartered transports carried 17,000 men and were thus loaded with twice the number they could be expected to carry. Above decks and below there was scarcely room to sit down.

The rations supplied were inedible and many were thrown overboard; it is unknown whether the fishes could stomach them either. There were no facilities for cooking, no ice, and no potable water. "It smelled like a frog pond" a report declared. Examined by the doctors at Tampa it was pronounced safe "in spite of the bad smell and taste." But the doctors didn't have to drink it.

Tents were on one ship, tent poles on another; shoes on one ship, socks on another. The only reason the American expeditionary forces were not a total failure is that they were fighting a government even more inefficient than their own.

Thus "the happy-go-lucky expedition plowed along over the hot, tropical sea," as Gregory Mason envisioned it, and, as a reporter observed, "under the care of the God Who takes care of drunks, sailors, and the United States."

The ill-equipped and badly prepared men were accompanied by war correspondents, some of them romantics like Richard Harding Davis, who described the war as if it were a tennis match or a regatta; and artists from realists to romantics whose drawings immortalized things that never happened.

It took five days to land the army at Daiquiri. The beach was sandy but there was a high surf running, the Navy launches were overcrowded, and someone had forgotten to provide the transports with boats for this purpose. A few men fell overboard and were drowned because of their heavy equipment or their inability to swim. Instead of opening fire and annhilating the Americans, the few hundred Spanish soldiers lurking in the bushes took to the hills, most fortunately.

Major General Lawton of the Regular Army had been given charge of the advance to Santiago, but there was present a member of the Volunteer Army, Major General "fighting Joe" Wheeler, a Confederate hero. Both generals had a burning desire to get there first and snatch the glory from the other. But Fighting Joe was stricken down by fever (as was General Young). Commands had to be shifted. The confusion was too great to be described in a short book.

But the jealousy existing between the Regular Army and the Volunteer Army came close to causing a disaster. The Regular Army is given credit for saving the day, but the Volunteer Army was more glamorous and the public loved it better.

Engagements occurred on the road to Santiago, all jungle and uphill, and there were contrary orders and mixups and small murderous engagments, and death. A brook gained the name of Bloody Brook. The injured were unlucky; medical supplies had been left on the transports.

El Caney was a village consisting of six blockhouses, a stone fort and a stone church. General Lawton thought that it could be taken in two hours: it took ten and a half and cost the lives of 235 Spaniards and 77 Americans.

Next came San Juan Hill to be breached, a few miles east of Santiago. This place, crowned with a blockhouse and enmeshed in barbed wire is famed for one of the things that never happened—Teddy Roosevelt and his Rough Riders dashing gloriously up it. Romantic artist-reporters are the source of this soul-stirring non-incident. (It must have delighted Mr. Pulitzer and Mr. Hearst.)

There are four claimants to be the first to reach the summit of the hill—the Rough Riders, the Sixteenth Infantry and two cavalry units, the Ninth and the Tenth, who were blacks. The irrepressible Teddy was the star of any occasion in which he took part—he saw to it—and later being questioned about San Juan Hill, answered after some thought, that he was mounted though his men were on foot, and Walter Millis in his history of the war said that "the Colonel could not recall the presence of any commander in the neighborhood save himself." This is easy to believe. The humorist Finley Peter Dunn, who disguised himself under the well known pseudonym of "Mr. Dooley," naughtily observed that Roosevelt's book on the war should be titled *Alone in Cuba*.

The Hill was gained after bloody fighting. The Spaniards were brave fighters and some were deadly accurate marksmen. But when Shafter was before the city he found that his Army was so weakened by malaria and dysentery that he feared he would have to abandon his position. He sent imploring messages to Admiral Sampson to come to his aid. The Admiral replied that the harbor was mined and it would be too dangerous to bring in his heavy ships. The Army and Navy were deadly rivals.

It looked as if the Americans would have to retreat, but unknown to General Shafter, the Spanish government had decided that Santiago was lost, and Madrid ordered Admiral Cervera to attempt to escape with his ships out of Santiago harbor.

Cervera cabled Madrid that his officers agreed with him that "the absolute certain result of a sortie from Santiago Bay will be the ruin of all the ships and the death of the greater part of their crews."

Here is where that Spanish concept called *pundonor* came fatally into play. Pundonor is a rich mixture of honor, dignity, self respect, with a soupçon of self-esteem, and is a potent force in Spanish thinking. The effect of surrendering meekly without any show of prowess would be disasterous to pundonor; the people of Spain would be humiliated beyond belief.

Admiral Cervera's answer to this was noble:

"I, who am a man without ambitions, without mad passions . . . state most emphatically that I shall never be the one to decree the horrible and useless hecatomb which will be the only possible result of the sortie from here by main force, for I should consider myself responsible before God and history for lives sacrificed on the altar of vanity and not in the true defense of the country."

Madrid was adamant, and so the Spanish ships broke out of Santiago Bay to their doom. There had been one ray of hope for the Spaniards—their ships were faster and lighter than the American ships, and possibly some of them could escape. But it was just as Cervera said. The awful battle began.

One American sailor was killed and one injured but the entire Spanish fleet was destroyed and some 500 men killed or drowned. The toll would have been much higher except that the American sailors rescued hundreds of men from the burning ships and wreck-strewn waters, including brave Admiral Cervera himself. The Admiral wrote a beautiful letter to the American authorities thanking them for saving so many of his men. Rear Admiral Pasquale Cervera y Topete was a great gentleman.

One presumes that pundonor was amply appeased, if not satiated.

A few days later the Spanish Army commander surrendered Santiago after General Shafter had consented to generous terms including transportation to Spain for his troops. After all, they had no ships.

An American Army under General Nelson A. Miles landed in Puerto Rico and took it with scarcely a show of opposition. Through the French Ambassador in Washington, Spain asked for peace and the fighting was over August 12, 1898. The tragic farce had lasted fifty days.

It is said that Europe was surprised at the outcome of the Spanish-American War; Spain was expected to win with her cleverness and old-world subtleties over the powerful but bungling American pups. But the old world subtleties and cleverness never materialized, and the Americans *bungled* better.

Britain was the only power that had fought the Americans in two wars, and the pundits of Whitehall had history books they could dust off and read; they were less surprised at the outcome of the squabble in the Caribbean. They let it be known that Britain would look with disfavor on any overt action in Europe with a view to interference with events in the Pearl of the Antilles. Germany among other nations was casting covetous glances in that direction, but Britain was a formidable power. Britain for the first time in history was on the American side, and had her reasons.

Commissioners from Spain and the United States met in Paris in October, 1898. Spain recognized Cuba's independence, consented to assume Cuba's debts, and cede Puerto Rico and a small island in the Pacific, needed for a coaling station, to the victor. (This island is Guam.) But when, by McKinley's instructions, the United States commissioners astounded the Spaniards by demanding the Philippines, it was not such smooth sailing.

However, what could the commissioners do? To keep the Philippines meant continued war for the Spaniards, and for one thing they no longer had a Navy. They yielded to the inevitable when the United States offered $20,000,000 for the Philippines, and the Treaty of Paris was signed December 10, 1898.

The United States had become an empire without meaning to. There were bitter reactions in America and a voluble anti-imperialistic movement grew. The acquisition of the Philippines was a repudiation of the American high moral position in the war, it was a violation of the Declaration of Independence to govern a foreign territory without the consent of the governed.

Senator Hoar of Massachusetts denounced this appropriation of "vasal states in barbarous archipeligoes" ("barbarous archipeligoes" is good, Polonius would say). America was trampling on "our great Charter which recognizes alike the liberty and dignity of individual manhood." He had something there, though the good Senator had forgotten the Indians and the Mexicans, but McKinley was not insensitive to his argument. Yet what would be the alternative? Public opinion would not sanction handing the Philippines back to Spain, or letting some other power have them, such as Japan. It was pretty certain the Filipinos were not sufficiently advanced socially or politically to form a stable government. McKinley faced a hard direction, but eventually made it.

The Peace Treaty had not yet been ratified by the Senate when a great battle

The Night After San Juan. The way it was. William Glackens.
From the author's collection.

was fought between partisan politicians and anti-imperialists. William Jennings Bryan, titular head of the Democratic party, thought the whole problem should be submitted to the people in a national referendum. However, the Treaty was ratified in February. The U.S. had become an empire without wanting to, and against bitter opposition.

Cuba became an independent nation in 1902, to the wonderment of Europe. When before in history had a conquering nation on its own volition handed away its conquest? "Erratum Number One" as old Ben Franklin would say today, in the light of later events.

In the Philippines this could not be. The leader of the Philippine insurgents against the Spaniards, Emilio Aguinaldo, was furious because the Americans did not remove themselves from the barbarous archipelago and leave it to him. Guerilla warfare broke out between various factions and the civil population, and neither side had any regard for the rules of war. Reports of unheard of atrocities began again, and the American troops had to remain to try to restore order.

Teddy Roosevelt and his Rough Riders at San Juan Hill. The way it wasn't. W.G. Read. Reproduced from the Collections of the Library of Congress.

Aguinaldo was seized in 1901, but hostilities did not cease for another year. It was not till 1935 that the last American governor (Leonard Wood) left the Philippines and a commonwealth was formally established with the inauguration of its first president, Manuel Quezón. Once again the United States gave away its conquest as it had promised to do.

Puerto Rico was a peculiar case. In 1900 Congress established a civil government for Puerto Rico which left the people neither citizens of the United States nor with full self-government. They were mostly illiterate, and desperately poor. But things improved under the Americans. A sewage system, clean water, hospitals, schools, and increasing industries, turned Puerto Rico into a modern community, and in 1917 President Woodrow Wilson signed the bill giving Puerto Rico full territorial status.

The year 1900 was another presidential one. It was inevitable that McKinley would be renominated and equally so that Theodore Roosevelt would be his running mate. The irrepressible Teddy did not fancy taking such a back seat as that of Vice President, but for party loyalty he was obliged to.

William Jennings Bryan was again McKinley's opponent. No referendum on the Philippines had materialized, but Bryan's fixation on free silver, which was included in the Democratic platform, assured more conservative votes than ever for McKinley.

McKinley's second term began on March 4, 1901, in rosy circumstances. His Administration had been endorsed by a large plurality, the war was over, and though problems resulting from it were thickening, time would surely solve them.

There were other reasons for rejoicing. National problems were largely resolved, causes of discontent between East and West were greatly lessened, and gold had been discovered in 1897 on the Klondike River in Alaska—plenty of it. The value of gold thus fell, making farmers richer; they got higher prices for their products and could pay off their mortgages and spruce up their buildings.

President McKinley set off in late April on a grand tour to the Pacific coast, accompanied by Mrs. McKinley and 43 others, including several members of his Cabinet. He was received with gratifying tokens of affection by large crowds at every stopping place.

Then, in September, the Pan-American Exposition opened in Buffalo and the President was obliged to attend. He made a fine and suitable speech. "Commercial wars are unprofitable," said the President. "A policy of good will and friendly trade relations will prevent reprisals. Reciprocity treaties are in harmony with the spirit of the times; measures of retaliation are not. Let us ever remember that our real eminence rests in the victories of peace and not those of war."

This was McKinley's last public utterance. The next day, as he was holding a reception in the Temple of Music, and was shaking hands with all comers in the reception line, there were two sharp cracks of a pistol. The President stared fixedly at the man who had shot him, who stood for a moment with vacant eyes before he was knocked down and pinioned under a heap of assailants. As the President was assisted to a chair he said, "Don't let them hurt him."

The man was a young Pole, Leon Czolgosz, who had been reading lurid anti-McKinley papers that called the President "Czar McKinley."

William McKinley lingered until September 13, when he died. Church bells tolled from coast to coast. For the first time the entire nation, East, West, North and South, was united in appropriate grief. There were five days of mourning, and the newspapers were bordered with black—for they knew how to do things in those days. When the President was buried in Canton there were five minutes of silence throughout the nation, and traffic and business were suspended.

Theodore Roosevelt, when he took the oath of office as the 26th President of the U.S., surpressing his intense delight at the turn of events, said suitable words:

"I will show the people at once that the administration of the government will not falter in spite of the terrible blow. I wish to say that it will be my aim to continue, absolutely unbroken, the policy of President McKinley for the peace, the prosperity, and the honor of our beloved country."

These were reassuring words for Wall Street.

Then Teddy came rough-riding into the White House, with or without a horse, and turned into a trust-buster.

The trouble with history is that it never stops. But here is the place for this history to stop. Two hundred and ninety-four years had passed since those wretched men had landed in Virginia. A nation had been born, and had survived after copious shedding of blood. Now a new century was beginning. Much was hoped for it. . . .

THE PRESIDENTS ALL IN A ROW

Washington, Adams, Jefferson, then
Madison, Monroe, and an Adams again.
Jackson, Van Buren—Harrison died;
The Whigs hated Tyler and cast him aside.
Polk kept his promises; Taylor arrived—
His lease on the White House was rather short-lived.
Fillmore and Pierce were both duds and came next;
Buchanan, old fellow, was sorely perplexed.
Abraham Lincoln through dark bore a light;
Johnson stood firm when he knew he was right.
Grant was a soldier who smoked quite a lot;

Hayes loved Sound Money and Garfied was shot.
Arthur and Cleveland and Harrison run;
Then Cleveland comes back when we thought he was done.
McKinley was shot in a Prince Albert coat;
Roosevelt came with a grin and a gloat.
Taft was the cheerful one, pleasant and stout;
Wilson had dreams that would never pan out.
Harding had friends you had better not know;
Coolidge was cool and Hoover was slow,
And Roosevelt had it four times in a row.
Truman was cocky which some do not like;
Dwight Eisenhower was best known as Ike.
Kennedy slain in his prime and his flower,
Lyndon B. Johnson succeeded to power.
Nixon's career had an end unexpected;
Ford became chief without being elected.
Carter came beaming on foe and on friend,
Reagan foretold a conservative trend—
Bush was a twig not easy to bend,
Presidents, Presidents, never end.

WORKS CITED

All sources are suspect.
—A.J.P. Taylor

Note: References are cited by chapter/page number.

PART ONE

8/3   [1]Edgar Wilson Nye, *Bill Nye's History of the United States* (Chicago, 1894).

15/35   [1]Morison.

17/43   [1]John A. Garraty, *A Short History of the American Nation* (New York, 1974).

17/45   [2]Henry Adams, *The Education of Henry Adams* (New York, 1918).

21/54   [1]*Encyclopedia Britannica*, 11th edition.

23/58   [1]Franklin's "armonica" consisted of tumblers of various sizes, arranged on a kind of spindle, the sounds produced by rubbing wet fingers over the rims. The instrument enjoyed great popularity in Europe. Among composers who wrote music for it were Mozart and Beethoven, and Donizetti employed it in the famous "Mad Scene" in *Lucia di Lammermoor*.

28/69   [1]F. J. Huddleston, *Gentle Johnny Burgoyne* (Indianapolis, 1927).

32/80   [1]Bruce Lancaster and J.H. Plumb, *The American Heritage Book of the Revolution* (New York, 1958).

32/80   [2]Lancaster and Plumb.

33/82   [1]E.S. Creasey, *The Fifteen Decisive Battles of the World* (London, 1851).

37/94   [1]The frigate *Serapis* (pronounced Se-ray-pis) was named after the Egyptian deity Serapis. Connected with Osiris, he had a bull's head and wore a solar disc between his horns. His chief center of worship was Alexandria during Ptolemaic times, a very powerful god.

PART TWO

1/121   [1]Howard B. Lee, *The Story of the Constitution* (Charlottesville, VA, 1932).

7/143   [1]Morison.

        [2]Morison.

9/149   [1]Morison.

13/161   [1]For details of this historic episode, the author is greatly indebted to Walter Lord's account in *Dawn's Early Light* (New York, 1972).

17/169   [1]Robin Reilly, *The British at the Gates* (New York, 1974).

19/176   [1]Kate Caffrey, *The Twilight's Last Gleaming: Britain vs. America 1812-1815* (New York, 1977).

29/206   [1]For his account of the death of John Quincy Adams, the author is indebted to Leonard Falker, *The President Who Wouldn't Retire* (New York, 1967).

33/214   [1]J. Patrick McHenry, *A Short History of Mexico* (New York, 1962).

PART THREE

6/265   [1]Burton J. Hendrick, *Lincoln's War Cabinet* (Boston, 1946).

8/277   [1]Hendrick.

8/278   [2]Martin Duberman, *Charles Francis Adams*, Chapter 21.

13/291   [1]Luigi Barzini, *The Europeans* (New York, 1983).

13/293   [2]Morison.

14/293   [1]F. Scott Fitzgerald, "The Curious Case of Benjamin Button," in *Tales of the Jazz Age*.

16/309   [1]Otto Eisenschimel. *Why Was Lincoln Murdered?* (Boston, 1937).

PART FOUR

5/326   [1]Gene Smith, *High Crimes and Misdemeanors: The Impeachment and Trial of Andrew Johnson* (New York, 1977).

10/343   [1]Rita Childe Dorr, *Susan B. Anthony* (New York, 1925).

12/350   [1]Walter Millis, *The Martial Spirit* (New York, 1931).

12/352   [2]Gregory Mason, *Remember the Maine* (New York, 1939).

BIBLIOGRAPHY

Acton, Sir John. *Acton in America: The American Journal of Lord Acton*. 1853. Shepherdstown, West Virginia: The Patmos Press, 1979.

Adams, Henry. *The Education of Henry Adams*. New York, 1918.

Alsop, Susan Mary. *Yankees at the Court: The First Americans in Paris*. New York, 1982.

Anthony, Katherine. *Susan B. Anthony: Her Personal History and Her Era*. New York, 1954.

Asbury, Herbert. *The French Quarter*. New York, 1936.

Bacon, Margaret Hope. *Valiant Friend: The Life of Lucrezia Mott*. New York, 1946.

Barzini, Luigi. *The Europeans*. New York, 1983.

Bates, David Homer. *Lincoln in the Telegraph Office*. New York, 1917.

Bishop, Jim. *The Day Lincoln Was Shot*. New York, 1955.

Bradford, William. *Of Plimouth Plantation*. New York, 1946.

Brodie, Fawn. *No Man Knows My History: A Life of Joseph Smith*. New York, 1946.

Caffrey, Kate. *The Twilight's Last Gleaming: Britain vs. America 1812-1815*. New York, 1977.

Catton, Bruce. *The Centennial History of the Civil War*. Garden City, New York, 1961.

Charnwood, Lord. *Abraham Lincoln*. London, 1917.

Chidsey, Donald Barr. *Victory at Yorktown*. New York, 1962.

Churchill, Sir Winston. *A History of the English-Speaking People*. New York, 1959.

Creasy. E. S. *The Fifteen Decisive Battles of the World*. London, 1851.

Cummings, William P. and Hugh Rankin. *The Fate of a Nation*. London, 1975.

Curtis, James J. *The Fox at Bay*. Lexington, Kentucky, 1970.

Davis, Burke. *The Campaign that Won America*. New York, 1970.

Denn, John C., ed. *The Revolution Remembered*. Chicago, 1980.

Dorr, Rita Childe. *Susan B. Anthony*. New York, 1925.

Douglass, Frederick. *My Bondage and My Freedom*. New York, 1855.

Duberman, Martin. *Charles Francis Adams*. Stanford, California, 1960

Eaton, Clement. *Jefferson Davis*. New York, 1977.

Eisenschimel, Otto. *Why Was Lincoln Murdered?* Boston, 1937.

Falkner, Leonard. *The President Who Wouldn't Retire*. New York, 1967.

Fitzgerald, F. Scott. "The Curious Case of Benjamin Button," in *Tales of the Jazz Age*. New York, 1922.

Fleming, Walter Lynwood. *The Sequel to Appomattox*. New Haven, 1919.

Flexner, James Thomas. *The Traitor and the Spy*. Boston, 1953.

————. *George Washington: The Forge of Experience*. Boston, 1965.

————. *George Washington in the American Revolution*. Boston, 1968.

Fortenbaugh, Robert. *The Nine Capitols of the United States*. York, Pennsylvania, 1975.

Forneaux, Robert. *The Battle of Saratoga*. New York, 1971.

Garraty, John A. *A Short History of the American Nation*. New York, 1974.

————. ed. *Historical Viewpoints*. 2 vols. New York, 1979.

Grafton, John. *The American Revolution*. New York, 1975.

Griffith, Elizabeth. *In Her Own Right: The Life of Elizabeth Cady Stanton*. Oxford and New York, 1984.

Hendrick, Burton J. *Lincoln's War Cabinet*. Boston, 1946.

Henry, Robert Selph. *The Story of the Confederacy*. Indianapolis, Indiana, 1927.

Howson, Gerald. *Burgoyne of Saratoga*. New York, 1980.

Huddleston, F.J. *Gentleman Johnny Burgoyne*. Indianapolis, Indiana, 1927.

Josephson, Matthew. *The Robber Barons*. New York, 1934.

Knowles, David. *The American Civil War*. Oxford, 1917.

Lader, Lawrence. *The Bold Brahmins*. New York, 1961.

Lancaster, Bruce and J.H. Plumb. *The American Heritage Book of the Revolution*. New York, 1958.

Lane-Poole, Stanley. *The Barbary Corsairs*. New York, 1891.

Langer, William Leonard. *An Encyclopedia of World History*. New York, 1948.

Lee, Howard B. *The Story of the Constitution*. Charlottesville, Virginia, 1932.

Leech, Margaret. *The Days of McKinley*. New York, 1959.

Lord, Walter. *The Dawn's Early Light*. New York, 1972.

Lutnick, Solomon. *The American Revolution and the British Press*. Columbia, Missouri, 1967.

Lutz, Alma. *Created Equal: A Biography of Elizabeth Cady Stanton*. New York, 1942.

Lynch, Denis Tilden. *The Wild Seventies*. New York, 1941.

Madison, Dolley. *Memoirs and Letters*. Port Washington, New York, 1971.

Martin, Joseph Plumb. *A Narrative of the Adventures, Dangers and Sufferings of a Revolutionary Soldier, Interspersed with Anecdotes of Incidents that Occured within his Observation, Written by Himself*. Hallowell, Maine, 1830. Reprinted under the title *Private Yankee Doodle: A Narrative of Some of the Adventures, Dangers and Sufferings of a Revolutionary Soldier*. ed. by George F. Scheer. Boston, 1962.

Mason, Gregory. *Remember the Maine*. New York, 1939.

McHenry, J. Patrick. *A Short History of Mexico*. New York, 1962.

Millis, Walter. *The Martial Spirit: A Study of Our War with Spain*. New York, 1931.

Morison, Samuel Eliot. *John Paul Jones*. Boston, 1959.

————. *The Oxford History of the American People*. New York, 1965.

Murfin, James V. *The Gleam of Bayonets: Battle of Antietam*. New York, 1965.

Muzzey, D. S. *A History of Our Country*. New York, 1936.

National Park Service History Series, *John Brown's Raid*.   n.d.

Nelson, Truman. *The Old Man: John Brown at Harper's Ferry*. New York, 1973.

Nies, Judith. *Seven Women: Portraits from the American Radical Tradition*. New York, 1977.

Ogg, Frederick Austin. *The Reign of Andrew Jackson*. New Haven, 1919.

Reilly, Robin. *The British at the Gates*. New York, 1974.

Rossiter, Clinton. *The Grand Convention*. New York, 1966.

Schultz, Harold S. *James Madison*. New York, 1970.

Shepard, Jack. *Cannibals of the Heart: A Personal Biography of Louisa Catherine and John Quincy Adams*. New York, 1980.

Smelser, Marshall. *The Democratic Republic 1801-1815*. New York, 1968.

Smith, Gene. *High Crimes and Misdemeanors: The Impeachment and Trial of Andrew Johnson*. New York, 1977.

Stampp, Kenneth. *The Era of Reconstruction*. New York, 1965.

Stanton, Elizabeth Cady. *Eighty Years and More*. London and New York, 1896.

Starkey, Marion L. *The Devil in Massachusetts*. New York, 1949.

Stephenson, Nathaniel W. *The Day of the Confederacy*. New Haven, 1919.

Taylor, E. R., ed. *Jackson vs. Biddle's Bank*. Boston, 1949.

Thomas, Benjamin P. *Abraham Lincoln*. New York, 1952.

Thomas, Emory M. *The Confederate Nation*. New York, 1979.

Tocqueville, Alexis de. *Democracy in America*. New York, 1945.

Trollope, Anthony. *North America*. 2 vols. New York, 1951.

Tuchman, Barbara W. *The March of Folly*. New York, 1984.

von Closen, Baron Ludwig. *The Revolutionary Journal of Baron Ludwig von Closen*. Chapel Hill, North Carolina, 1959.

Werner, W.R. *Brigham Young*. New York, 1925.

Wesley, Charles H. *The Collapse of the Confederacy*. New York, 1968.

Winston, Robert. *Andrew Johnson, Plebeian and Patriot*. New York, 1928.

INDEX

Note: Numbers in bold refer to illustrations.

Other books by Ira Glackens:

Yankee Diva: Lillian Nordica and the Golden Days of Opera
Pope Joan: The English Girl Who Made It—An Unorthodox Interlude
A Measure of Sliding Sand, a novel
Poor Mad Valery and other poems
William Glackens and the Eight